More praise for
Rilke and Andreas-Salomé

"Rilke's letter are long and full of rich language. . . . The letters reveal much about European intellectual life in the early 20th century. Highly recommended." —*Library Journal*

"An invaluable collection. . . . The letters reveal in both tender and insightful prose Rilke's creative and mental insecurities, along with his enormous poetic talent and innovative thinking." —*Booklist*

"This collection of some two hundred letters, written over nearly three decades, enriches our picture of Rilke and Salomé with curious details: Rilke makes arrangements for Salomé's beloved dog, in advance of a visit; Salomé, practicing in mid-life as a psychoanalyst, claims success treating patients with Rilke's poems: 'They heard *your* tone as that of Life.'" —*The New Yorker*

"How fascinating it is to eavesdrop, as it were, on the conversations between a creative genius and his muse." —*History Wire*

"Mr. Snow continues his triumphant forced march through the overgrown territories of Rilke, ecstatic letters this time, actually revved a notch higher by the great Frau Lou. No prisoners are taken, the notes are ruthless, and for the first time truth prevails over truthiness, all is made clear."—Richard Howard

"For lovers of Rilke, whether as dedicated readers or professional critics or biographers, the name Lou Andreas-Salomé casts a magic spell. Available for many decades in Ernst Pfeiffer's famous editions of 1952 and 1975, this monumental collection has finally appeared in a brilliant English translation by two important translators and scholars, Edward Snow and Michael Winkler. It is their second valuable work presenting Rilke in English, following their fine translation of Rilke's *Diaries of a Young Poet.* The gracious language, along with its clarity and rich documentation, will go far towards making this painstaking work a must in every library dealing with Rilke and modern poetry." —Ralph Freedman, Princeton University

"This superb translation gives us both the long arc and the intense, edgy radiance of one of the most relentlessly searching correspondences in the history of poetry. At times almost a psychic collaboration, Rilke's and Salome's letters carry us and their authors into ever deeper realms of inwardness and astonishment, of terrifying isolation and ecstatic recoveries. Any reader of Rilke will want to keep this book as a radiant companion—itself a work of companionship—close beside (perhaps inside) the enduring freshness of the poems, seen here in the quick of genesis and of amazed reception."

—Peter Sacks

Rainer Maria Rilke

TRANSLATED BY EDWARD SNOW AND MICHAEL WINKLER

Diaries of a Young Poet

IN TRANSLATIONS BY M. D. HERTER NORTON

Letters to a Young Poet

Sonnets to Orpheus

Wartime Letters of Rainer Maria Rilke

Translations from the Poetry of Rainer Maria Rilke

The Lay of the Love and Death of Cornet Christopher Rilke

The Notebooks of Malte Laurids Brigge

Stories of God

Letters of Rainer Maria Rilke. Volume One, 1892–1910,
Letters of Rainer Maria Rilke. Volume Two, 1910–1926,
translated by Jane Bannard Greene and M. D. Herter Norton

Duino Elegies, translated by David Young

IN VARIOUS TRANSLATIONS

Rilke on Love and Other Difficulties. Translations and Considerations of Rainer Maria Rilke, compiled by John J. L. Mood

Lou Andreas-Salomé

You Alone Are Real to Me: Remembering Rainer Maria Rilke, translated by Angela von der Lippe

Nietzsche, translated and edited by Siegfried Mandel

Looking Back, translated by Breon Mitchell

The Freud Journal, translated by Stanley A. Leavy

RILKE *and* ANDREAS-SALOMÉ

A LOVE STORY IN LETTERS

TRANSLATED BY

Edward Snow

AND

Michael Winkler

W · W · Norton & Company New York London

Originally published in German as: *Rainer Maria Rilke/Lou Andreas-Salomé/Briefwechsel.*
Herausgegeben von Ernst Pfeiffer, who also contributed "Erläuterungen" on pp. 489–624.
The Notes in the present edition were prepared by Edward Snow and Michael Winkler.
They are in part a translation of Ernst Pfeiffer's annotations.

Originally published in hardcover as *Rainer Maria Rilke and Lou Andreas-Salomé: The Correspondence.*

Printed in the United States of America
First published as a Norton paperback 2008

Manufacturing by RR Donnelley, Bloomsburg
Book design by Margaret M. Wagner
Production manager: Julia Druskin

Library of Congress Cataloging-in-Publication Data

Rilke, Rainer Maria, 1875–1926.
[Correspondence. English. Selections]
Rilke and Andreas-Salomé : a love story in letters / Rilke, Andreas-Salomé ; translated by Edward Snow and Michael Winkler. — [Norton paperback]
p. cm.
Originally published as: Rainer Maria Rilke and Lou Andreas-Salomé : the correspondence, 2006
Originally published in German as: Rainer Maria Rilke, Lou Andreas-Salomé : Briefwechsel / herausgegeben von Ernst Pfeiffer.
Includes bibliographical references and index.
ISBN 978-0-393-33190-5 (pbk.)
1. Rilke, Rainer Maria, 1875–1926—Correspondence. 2. Andreas-Salomé, Lou, 1861–1937—Correspondence. 3. Authors, German—20th century—Correspondence. I. Andreas-Salomé, Lou, 1861–1937. II. Pfeiffer, Ernst. III. Snow, Edward A. IV. Winkler, Michael, 1937– V. Title.
PT2635.I65Z52213 2008
831'.912—dc22
[B] 2008012133

W. W. Norton & Company, Inc., 500 Fifth Avenue, New York, N.Y. 10110
www.wwnorton.com

W. W. Norton & Company Ltd., Castle House, 75/76 Wells Street, London W1T 3QT

1 2 3 4 5 6 7 8 9 0

Contents

Introduction

RILKE'S CORRESPONDENCE with Lou Andreas-Salomé is the record of his most intense and enduring friendship. The letters they exchanged over some twenty-five years, half his lifetime, chart his tormented maturation as a poet under the guidance of a shrewdly observing confidante who had been his lover before she became his counselor in all matters of his aggrieved soul. It is to her that he addressed his most trenchantly self-revealing "confessions," some of them plaintive with no small admixture of self-pity, many of them unrelenting in their exploration of his psyche's innermost complexities and their search for whatever resources his frail constitution and precarious hold on sanity might provide. And Lou responded with an unusually clear-eyed intelligence and compassion. Without the support of her analytical skills and her honest objectivity Rilke might well have succumbed to the confusions and self-destructive anxieties he traced back to the psychological devastations he had carried inside himself since childhood. Instead, her insights into his personality, without ever evading unpleasant truths or deflecting them into professional jargon, elicited from him a style of writing in which, as he presents his experiences to her for understanding, the eloquence of epistolary conversation becomes difficult to distinguish from the art of narrative prose.

Louise von Salomé was born in St. Petersburg on February 12, 1861, the youngest of six children and the only daughter of a German-Baltic family with Huguenot ancestors. Her father, Gustav von Salomé (1804–1879), was a general in the czar's service. Her family felt Russian even though its social contacts did not extend much beyond the immigrant community. They lived in apartments across from the Winter Palace reserved for high-ranking generals and kept a country house near Peterhof, the imperial summer residence. She was brought up in the reformed Protestant Church but left it at the age of seventeen in protest against its restrictive rules. Her search for a God who could fulfill her personal needs led her toward Hendrik Gillot, the charismatic pastor of the Dutch Legation and a tutor of the czar's children. Without her parents' knowledge he became her private instructor and spiritual-intellectual guide, a kind of Father-God persona with whom she read Spinoza, Leibniz, Kant, Kierkegaard, and books on comparative theology. Her daydreams and fantasies, in other words, while never fully dispelled, were being attenuated by enthusiastic yet disciplined studies of systematic philosophy—until Gillot, age forty-two and a husband with two children, proposed marriage to her. She let him confirm her at his hometown of Santpoort but then quickly departed for Zürich to study theology and art history until the recurrence of pulmonary bleeding forced her to abandon her scholarly pursuits. When her condition did not improve during a cure in Scheveningen (on the North Sea near The Hague), her mother, early in 1882, took her south, eventually to Rome.

There she joined a circle of young intellectuals, avid readers of Schopenhauer and passionate Wagnerians, who gathered at the house of the expatriate writer Malwida von Meysenbug. Through her she met Paul Rée, a philosophical historian of morals whose ideas failed, however, to gain academic approval, which meant the end of his quest for the stability of a university position. He was twelve years her senior, and during that spring introduced her to his former teacher Friedrich Nietzsche, then thirty-seven years old and still virtually unknown as a thinker. Both men were quickly captivated by her and each eventually proposed marriage—which she declined. Rée soon moved into an apartment in Berlin with her and remained a close friend (and unrequited lover) for over three years, her partner in philosophical studies with a small group of like-minded young thinkers and her companion during frequent travels. Nietzsche was for over half a year her rigorous teacher and briefly even thought that she might become his intellectual heir. But by the end of 1882, in no small measure duped by the jealous intrigues of his sister Elisabeth, he felt betrayed by his independent-minded and at times incautious disciple and denounced her with bitter intensity.

In 1886 Lou became engaged to Friedrich Carl Andreas (1846–1930), a man with an extraordinary background. Andreas was born in Batavia (now Jakarta), the son of a German-Malay mother and an Armenian father, a Prince Bagratuni from Isfahan in Persia. At the age of six he attended a private school in Hamburg and in 1860 enrolled in a *Gymnasium* in Geneva in preparation for studies of classical and oriental philology at various German universities. In 1868 he obtained a Ph.D. and went to Denmark to study Persian manuscripts in the Copenhagen Library and to learn Scandinavian languages and literatures. Following his military service in the Franco-Prussian War, he studied in Kiel. In July 1875 he was to join a scientific expedition to Persia as an expert in Sassanide inscriptions. But he arrived half a year late, having contracted cholera in Bombay. He stayed in Persia for six years as a language teacher and, for a time, as the supervisor of the country's postal system. In January 1882 he returned to Germany in the company of a Prince Ihtisam-ed-daule, physically exhausted and destitute. It took him the rest of the year to recover. In 1885 he met Lou, who was living in the boarding house where he gave private lessons in Turkish and Persian to Prussian diplomats, officers, and businessmen.[1]

Andreas was a dark-bearded and passionately forceful man, fifteen years older than Lou. He was determined to overcome her resistance to marriage, and in the end accepted her condition that they abstain forever from having sex together. His courtship must have been tumultuous. Even on the day before they were to announce their betrothal he plunged a knife into his chest during an argument with her, barely missing an artery but collapsing unconscious. They were married a year later in June 1887, in a civil ceremony in Berlin-Tempelhof followed by a wedding in the church where she had been confirmed, the Reverend Hendrik Gillot officiating. The couple returned to live in Berlin, where Andreas had been appointed a professor of Persian (and later a professor of Turkish) at the newly established Institute of Oriental Languages, a position he had to relinquish two years later when colleagues questioned his academic credentials. After his dismissal he returned to working as a private language teacher. Lou, for her part, began to establish a career as a writer. The first years of their marriage were never free of tensions, in part because she felt guilty of having betrayed Paul Rée, in part because she and Andreas sought to hide their basic incompatibility behind the illusion that they were joined in a bond of high ideals. It was not long before their life together turned into a connubial father-daughter relationship rather than a mature companionship.

This arrangement appears to have remained placid enough until 1892, when Lou met Georg Ledebour (1850–1947), the editor of a socialist newspaper, *Berliner Volkszeitung*, and a highly-principled politician. Their love was mutual and serious. But Andreas forced her to renounce it some two years later after he had resolutely refused her requests for a divorce. Her immediate response was to immerse herself in long trips, to Petersburg, Paris, Switzerland, and Vienna, and to cultivate her friends among the emerging cultural elite. She gave the impression of a happily independent woman who lived a life of her own choosing. But it took her years to overcome her deep estrangement from her husband, a circumstance—as with so many other personal woes—she never mentioned in any of her letters. Later in life they settled for a polite co-existence, and Andreas acquired the dignified composure of a reclusive scholar.[2]

René Maria Rilke first met Lou Andreas-Salomé on May 12, 1897, at the Munich apartment of a mutual acquaintance, the novelist Jakob Wassermann. Rilke was twenty-one years old, a student of art history, prolific though nearly unknown as a poet but busily expanding the purview of his contacts. Lou was thirty-six and an established author.[3] Soon after her arrival at the end of April to meet an old friend, Frieda von Bülow, he began to send her, anonymously, handwritten copies of his poems, along with effusive letters, which she shrugged off as an annoyance. He persisted, and soon she was enamored of him. They became lovers during a stay of three months (until September 8, 1897) in the farming village of Wolfratshausen in the foothills of the Alps. (It was during this period that "René" became "Rainer," adopting the "plain fine, German name" by which Lou chose to call him.) For three and a half years, and with only three extended interruptions, they spent almost every day in one another's company, at times under strained circumstances and more than once precariously close to an irreconcilable break. But to help them through such periods of stress there was the discipline of shared studies, most doggedly of Russian literature and culture, the routine of daily chores and the enjoyment of nature, and, not least, their need for complementary emotional support.

It is easy to dismiss the prolix weave of exalted adorations in Rilke's earliest letters to Lou as so much ludicrous flattery. Their recipient, at any rate, distanced herself from them as soberly as she vetoed his plan to publish the nearly one hundred poems he had written for her and to call the volume *Dir zur Feier* (To celebrate you). She may well have done so with an intuitive awareness of what they foretold of Rilke: a still juvenile propensity for expressing erotic emotions in sacral language, and for imagining new experiences with an excess of grandiosely "inspired" subjectivity. Such foibles Rilke would learn to outgrow before long. But these early poems also suggest the outline of a poet-imago and a psychic disposition which he was to describe incessantly and respecify with ever new details throughout his life.

This self-image entails three aspects: (1) the presence of an exemplary artist (Pushkin, Tolstoy, Jens Peter Jacobsen, Rodin, Cézanne, Valéry, and others), existing in the imagination and implicit in all his epistolary monologues as a powerful, often overwhelming challenge; (2) his inner Enemy-Doppelgänger—what he and Lou called the "Other" in him—that is, the unknown, stubbornly defiant side of his personality, including his frequent physical ailments and his susceptibility to psychosomatic illnesses; and (3) an "understander," preeminently, but not exclusively, Lou, as the embodiment of a superior mode of being, who will explain to him the anxieties and phobias that block his creativity, and whose empathic affirmations encourage him in his struggle to break through to new aesthetic beginnings. It was therefore inevitable that he should keep returning to her, even after their seemingly final break toward the end of February 1901.

The immediate cause of this separation was Lou's angered reproval of Rilke's decision to marry Clara Westhoff, whom he had met in September 1900 during his stay at the artists' colony of Worpswede, near Bremen. But her remonstrations had a number of precedents, most notably her less-than-satisfactory reception of the diary he had written for her in April–May 1896 in Tuscany,[4] and her frustration with the extreme mood swings he suffered on their long journey through Russia and the Ukraine in the spring and summer of 1900. Her own diary of this trip, to be sure, gives an exuberant account of their many profound experiences and revelations and only once points to her "not always good mood."[5] But her autobiography speaks of recurrent outbursts of "anxiety, almost states of terror" on Rilke's part, of irrational behavior escalating into panic attacks and of "an explosive dissolution into feelings which tumbled over into a monstrous immensity—as if he felt a compulsion to let them overwhelm him."[6] She attributes these problems to his inability to reconcile "the conflict between hymnic experience and its expression in creative form," calling it, in a paraphrase of his own words, a kind of pseudo-productivity "that has been led astray by fear, like some desperate substitute for the command"[7] to give tangible, tensile shape to diffusely subjective impulses. This discrepancy between grand emotional transports and completely inadequate aesthetic means to structure them into poems made Rilke the spiritual pilgrim feel like a blaspheming outcast. In her words: he was far short of that "immanent harmony" and spacious resplendence with which "the great soul" makes productive use of "everything that falls into it."[8] And she, her nerves badly frayed by his morbidly monopolizing fixation on her, craved "quiet,—more being by myself, the way it was until four years ago."[9]

Hence Lou's abdication of her role as mother-protector in the reckoning of her "Last Appeal" (February 26, 1901), a letter that Francine Prose calls a "document remarkable for the imperious, heartless self-absorption disguised (from Lou herself, one senses) as compassion and concern."[10] And Lou's advice that Rilke should abandon any expectation of "normal" happiness—as a husband with perhaps a supportive wife, among fellow artists, in the company of congenial friends—and only follow the "dark God" of his art can indeed be read as a retaliatory (and devastating) assault on an apprehensive bridegroom's state of mind. But her assessments of his character and of his prospects are also, in large measure, accurate. And that could have well meant the end of their correspondence. Rilke, though, did not read her letter as his final castigation. After his monograph on Rodin had reassured him that in some new and deepest sense he *could* write, he probed in the summer of 1903 for an opening to revive the relationship, and when she acceded, reluctantly, to epistolary contacts, he responded with an outpouring of finely honed prose—as if now at last he had gained the confidence to express in artful *letters* his encounters with facets of a harsh reality that his Diaries had evaded.

Rilke's life during the first decade of the new century, though never as unabatedly precarious as many of his letters suggest, continued to lack a sense of steadiness and assurance. His ambition as an artist, however, had found a clear purpose and direction: to accomplish the breakthrough to an absolutely modern aesthetic. He began to write a new type of short lyric, which he sometimes called a "Kunst-Ding": a poem in which the obtrusive interferences of an authorial self and all subjective, accidental occasions have been replaced by an inwardly tensile, self-contained sculptural presence, delimited by strong contours but filled with an utmost of interacting visual and visible reality.

This fundamentally new way of creating art Rilke found exemplified in Rodin, and, with the fervor of a proselytizing convert, he sought to articulate it in ever expanding aesthetic reflections. His nearly immaculate Rodin, of course, is an "art-figure" in whom Rilke adored, again in consonance with cultural trends prevalent not only in Germany, a liberating Messiah of Art.[11] In view of this it is surprising that none of his lyrics collected as *New Poems* (1907–1908) figure even tangentially in his correspondence with Lou. They are, after all, the evidence, most copiously written in August 1907 and during the following summer, that vindicated his sustained commitment to all that Rodin's ethos of "*rien que travailler*" demanded.

It is true that Lou's understanding of art remained conventional even as she may have recognized in Rilke the emergence of a supremely modern artist; and it is more than likely that she was put off by the gestures of haughty self-sufficiency in the *New Poems*, by their sometimes "hard" indifference to cruel impulses that generate aesthetically pleasing effects. Her attention, therefore, whenever it was being solicited, focused on Rilke the highly problematical individual. And so she did not become truly important to him again as a correspondent until the end of the decade.

The time after Rilke's departure had been difficult for Lou as well. Her recovery from an anguished exhaustion and its lingering psychological causes was slow, even though, in October 1903, she had bought a spacious house in the country outside of Göttingen that was to be her permanent home for the rest of her life, and even though she had found, in the Viennese neurologist Dr. Friedrich Pineles, a devoted lover and a companion with whom she took frequent and often extended trips. But the state of her health remained worrisome. By early 1905 she was diagnosed as suffering from a heart condition that would continue to afflict her.

The crisis that caused Rilke to write Lou with renewed urgency was brought on by the poet's acute disorientation after the completion in 1910 of his novel *The Notebooks of Malte Laurids Brigge.* He had hoped that he could rid himself of his destructive "Other" and unravel a spiritually suffocating web of traumatic memories by creating a fictional character through whom he might, so to speak, observe himself in the refraction of mirror images of his psyche. But instead of the expected therapeutic catharsis, he encountered feelings of blockage, emptiness, and irrevocable self-damage, and when after two years they persisted he turned again to Lou. "Can you understand," he wrote to her from Duino on December 28, 1911,

> that in the wake of this book I have been left behind like a survivor, stranded high and dry in my inmost being, doing nothing, never to be occupied again? The nearer I approached its end, the more strongly I felt it would mark an indescribable division, a high watershed, as I always told myself; but now it turns out that all the water has run off toward the old side and I am walking down into an arid world that stretches on unchanging.

Lou wrote back, and over the next three months they entered into an intense exchange (ten letters from him, eight or nine letters and a telegram from her, everything on her side now tragically lost), with Rilke this time forcing the question that in their earlier days had been the one Lou put to him: "What to do?"

One option was an extended psychoanalysis, and when on January 20 Rilke presented this to Lou as something for which he had already laid the groundwork, despite his distrust of its exploratory technique and his fears of its efficacy ("something like a disinfected soul results from it, a non-thing, a freakish form of life corrected in red ink like a page in a schoolboy's notebook"), she responded swiftly on January 22 by urging *against* this course of action. The exchange marked a key moment for both of them,[12] and especially for Rilke. *Immediately* upon writing Lou he received the "task" of the Elegies in a moment of epiphany on the cliffs of Duino, and by the time her January 22 reply reached him the whole of the First Elegy had already been written. He could thus receive her advice as corroboration not just of his own first impulse but of their profound rapport: "*Kind heart,* you *speak* to me while you write, I am so at home in the reading of your letters . . . ; my own feeling, that initial, ever anew strongest feeling to which you lend credence, has so prepared me for what you say that I find myself already persuaded" (January 24, 1912). And she does in some strange sense "come back" to him through her counsel. With Rilke once more on the verge of trying "normal" life, Lou repeats the gesture of her "Last Appeal," yet in the process its black magic is undone. It would be during the following two or three years before the outbreak of the First World War, as the Elegies began to dominate Rilke's poetic quest, that he could accept Lou's insights into the psychology of his creative compulsions with the most consistently grateful consent. And this would be in no small part because her solicitude toward him and his importance for her seemed closer, more clearly genuine. Their exchanges, despite her at times almost impenetrable style, show a remarkable degree of interanimation: her insights are reflected in his images, and his metaphors follow the guidance of her observations, so that he feels relieved to exclaim: "You *know* and *understand*" (June 26, 1914).

Lou's counsel against psychoanalysis was all the more remarkable considering her commitment to it. As early as 1910 she had taken up the systematic study of Freudian psychoanalysis—some say specifically for Rilke's sake.[13] After attending the Weimar Conference in the autumn of 1911, she wrote in April to Freud himself, asking permission to attend his 1912 Vienna lectures and even to participate in his private Wednesday evening sessions. Both requests were granted, and between October 1912 and April 1913 she became a student of Freud and a member of his inner circle, interacting with Adler, Jung, Tausk, Ferenczi, Eitingon, Abraham, and above all Freud himself, with whom she formed a lifelong friendship. (Over two decades they exchanged some 200 letters.) She also became a theorist in her own right, publishing on narcissism and infantile sexuality. When she returned to Göttingen she set up a lay practice in her home (Freud, among others, sent her patients), and after 1914 her work as an analyst would be her chief passion.

Rilke and his closest confidante spent much time together during her frequent stays in Munich between 1914 and 1919, without, however, meeting again in person thereafter. Their correspondence, for this reason, takes on a new intensity only during and soon after the final completion of the *Duino Elegies* on February 11, 1922. At that moment, as if in some Rilkean dream of reparation, Lou becomes almost deliriously *his reader*, while he assumes in her reflections a significance for her comparable to that which Rodin once held for him. The feelings of rapproachment and full arrival in these letters (especially in Lou's) make the infrequency of their epistolary contact after 1924 all the more lamentable. Their one crucial exchange of 1925 is especially disconcerting, not least because it leaves a number of questions, specifically about Rilke's and Lou's awareness of his fatal illness, and about his confusion over its symptoms and her perhaps over-analytical responses, in the realm of pure speculation. It also causes the whole correspondence to end on a note of failed understanding, as two intimately caring people seem to miss each other in differently impenetrable languages.

On November 30, 1926, Rilke returned to the Clinique Valmont sur Territet, near Montreux, which he had first entered three years earlier, hoping for an accurate diagnosis of his lingering illness. Since he was no longer capable of writing more than a few letters, he had his devoted friend Nanny Wunderly-Volkart send out well over a hundred printed cards informing his friends of his grave condition. On December 13 she also forwarded his last letter to Lou, together with her own message on his behalf: "You know everything about him, from the beginning until this day. You are aware of his unlimited belief in you—he said: Lou must know everything—perhaps she knows a consolation . . ." His physician also wrote her, informing her of his diagnosis that Rilke had entered the final, excruciatingly painful stage of leukemia, and advising her, as was customary at that time, against disclosing the full diagnostic report to his patient, who was "anticipating a long, long time of suffering."[14]

Lou wrote Rilke five days in a row, and he reportedly read three of her letters.[15] He did not, however, allow any visitors to see him, not even his wife Clara, who had traveled to Muzot, nor his lover Baladine Klossowski, who was nearby and desperate to be with him. The only exception was Nanny Wunderly, who tended to all his medical needs and read to him in French, sometimes for up to six hours into the evening. At Christmas he declined to have her send further messages.

Rilke died on December 29, 1926, at Valmont. Friends received the news of his death by telegraph. They buried him four days later in the little mountain cemetery of Raron, near Sierre. He had designated his daughter, Ruth, as the heir to his literary estate, and she and her husband, the lawyer Dr. Carl Sieber (1897–1945), agreed to establish a family-owned archive. On the evening before the funeral, Rilke's publisher, Anton Kippenberg, took possession of the poet's notebooks and all other written material at Château Muzot. Rilke had kept all his correspondence in meticulous order, sorted into bundles by sender and year. He had also authorized their publication.

Lou Andreas-Salomé survived Rilke by a little over ten years. She had lived through a mastectomy in 1935 but was nearly blind from diabetes and close to destitute. She died in her house at the Hainberg, in Göttingen, on February 5, 1937.

THE CORRESPONDENCE between Rilke and Lou Andreas-Salomé was first edited in 1952 by the executor of her literary estate, Ernst Pfeiffer (1893–1986), who also supervised a second, expanded printing (1975) which adds one new letter from Lou, that of February 16, 1914. This edition served as the text for the present translation, which contains all 199 pieces of their extant correspondence—134 from Rilke, 65 from Lou—unabbreviated.

Lacunae exist for all years, beginning with the time from 1897 through the end of February 1901 when Lou, in breaking with Rilke, proposed that they burn each other's letters (he complied; she kept a good many of his). For the years after June 1903 it can be ascertained from internal evidence that at least thirteen communications from Rilke and over thirty-five from Lou have been lost. It is possible that Kippenberg withheld a number of these letters, or that Lou herself destroyed some of them after receiving them back through Frau Wunderly.

We have followed Pfeiffer in utilizing excerpts from Rilke's Diaries and Lou's journals and other autobiographical writings to help bridge informational lacunae and supplement the emotional context of certain exchanges. This has proved chiefly useful for the early years of the correspondence, since so much material from that period is missing, and since Lou and Rilke, still together, assume each other's knowledge of the lived experience out of which they are writing. Once the correspondents separate, and the letters themselves take on the task of filling in, we have resorted less frequently to non-epistolary material. We would like to thank Dorothee Pfeiffer (Göttingen) for allowing us to adapt her father's annotations to the needs of English-speaking readers. Our thanks also to Ulrich von Bülow, of the Deutsches Literaturarchiv in Marbach (which has acquired Rilke's letters to Lou Andreas-Salomé), who was kind enough to verify that what in a few instances appear to be questionable transcriptions are indeed accurate renderings. Last but not least, we would like to thank Jill Bialosky, our editor, for her infinite patience with this project.

NOTES

1. These and further details of Andreas's early life can be found in H. F. Peters, *My Sister, My Spouse: A Biography of Lou Andreas-Salomé* (New York: Norton, 1962), pp. 168–179.
2. His tenured appointment in the newly created department of Oriental Languages at the University of Göttingen in the fall of 1903 allowed him to teach small seminars in his private library during late evening hours. He was highly respected among fellow Iranists but hapless in his academic career.

   On the questionable paternity of their housekeeper's child, Maria, born in 1904, see the note to p. 157. Lou had no doubt that Andreas was the father and forbade him to enter her area of their three-story house.
3. Lou had published, in 1892, an interpretive monograph on the female characters in the dramas of Ibsen, then the most widely discussed playwright in Europe, followed by a study of Nietzsche's personality as revealed in his works (1894) and three books of (largely autobiographical) fiction, including the short novel *Ruth* (1895), of which Rilke was particularly fond. In addition to a number of poems, she had written essays and reviews on philosophical and literary subjects.
4. See *Diaries of a Young Poet,* translated by Edward Snow and Michael Winkler (New York: Norton, 1997), pp. 1–78.
5. "*Russland mit Rainer,*" edited by Stéphane Michaud in cooperation with Dorothee Pfeiffer, Marbach: Deutsche Schillergesellschaft, 2000, p. 90. It should be noted, however, that Lou tore out all the pages that mention Rilke when she reread this journal in preparation for her autobiography, *Lebensrückblick* (published 1951; translated by Breon Mitchell as *Looking Back: Memoirs* [New York: Paragon House, 1991]). He appears in just one marginal notation (p. 73), as "R."
6. See *Looking Back,* p. 89, which tones down her perfervid descriptions considerably.
7. "*Russland,*" p. 131.
8. Ibid.
9. According to an entry in Lou's diary: see below, p. 38.
10. "Lou Andreas-Salomé," in *The Lives of the Muses: Nine Women & the Artists They Inspired* (New York: HarperCollins, 2002), pp. 137–186.

11. How extensive Rilke's preoccupation with Rodin was becomes apparent from a compilation of all his literary descriptions of the "*grand et chère maître,*" including the more than one hundred often long and effusive letters he wrote to him (in French). See *Rainer Maria Rilke/Auguste Rodin: Der Briefwechsel und andere Dokumente zu Rilkes Begegnung mit Rodin,* edited by Rätus Luck (Frankfurt am Main/Leipzig: Insel, 2001). This documentation is no less revealing for all the pragmatic issues that Rilke was careful to overlook, among them the fact that Rodin by then no longer worked with a chisel but administered a workshop of some fifty employees who turned out copies of his sculptures.

12. Lou would later describe the decision as one of the most difficult of her life. Rudolph Binion (*Frau Lou: Nietzsche's Wayward Disciple* [Princeton, New Jersey: Princeton University Press, 1968]) remarks with characteristic shrewdness and cynicism that Lou actually had no objection to Rilke being analyzed as long as *she* was the one doing the analyzing, and that she advised *no* in 1911 because she didn't want the psychoanalyst in question (Gebsattel, whom she knew well) "messing around in *her* past" (p. 450). There are undoubtedly part-truths here, but interpreting dreams together on the train is obviously different from undertaking an extended analysis, and the issues underlying Lou's decision not only genuinely concerned her but (in her mind) bound her and Rilke together as a couple: "That key point of ours: *why* and *by what means* analysis is disastrous for all creative production" (September 12, 1914).

13. This also is partly true, as confirmed by one of Lou's own remarks. But psychoanalytic thinking also attracted her in and of itself. For a succinct summary of Lou's affinities with psychoanalysis, see Angela Livingstone, *Salomé: Her Life and Work* (Mt. Kisco, New York: Moyer Bell Limited, 1984), pp. 144–147.

14. The two direct quotes from Frau Wunderly's letter of December 13, 1926, and the physician's summary are included in Ernst Pfeiffer's note (*Rainer Maria Rilke/Lou Andreas-Salomé: Briefwechsel* [Frankfurt am Main/Leipzig: Insel, 1975], p. 622) on RMR's last letter to LAS. For details see J[ean] R[obert] von Salis, *Rainer Maria Rilkes Schweizer Jahre: Ein Beitrag zur Biographie von Rilkes Spätzeit.* Third, newly revised edition (Frauenfeld [Switzerland]: Huber, 1952), p. 229.

15. None of these letters from Lou survive, and we cannot be *absolutely* sure she wrote them. For further details of this last exchange, see the final notes to the present translation.

Rilke *and* Andreas-Salomé

A LOVE STORY IN LETTERS

[RMR to LAS in Munich, sent by messenger]

[*Letterhead:*] *Wegwarten*

René Maria Rilke
Munich, Blütenstrasse 8/I
May 13, 1897

Most gracious lady,

Yesterday was not the first twilight hour I have spent with you. There is another in my memory, one that made me want to look into your eyes. It was winter, and all the thoughts and aspirations that the spring wind scatters into a thousand faraway places were crowded into my narrow study and my quiet work. Then suddenly a gift arrived from Dr. Conrad: the April 1896 issue of *Neue Deutsche Rundschau*. A letter from Conrad referred me to an essay in it titled "Jesus the Jew." Why? Dr. Conrad had recently read a few sections of my *Visions of Christ* (five will soon appear in his journal *Gesellschaft*), and he thought I might find this sage treatise interesting. He was wrong. It was not interest that drew me deeper and deeper into this revelation; a devout fellow-feeling walked ahead of me along this solemn path—and then at last it was like a great rejoicing in me to find expressed in such supremely clear words, with the tremendous force of a religious conviction, what my *Visions* present in dreamlike epics. That was the mysterious twilight hour I could not but be reminded of yesterday.

You see, gracious lady, through this unsparing severity, through the uncompromising strength of your words, I felt that my own work was receiving a blessing, a sanction. I was like someone for whom great dreams, with all their good and evil, were coming true; for your essay was to my poems as reality is to dream, as fulfillment is to a desire.

Can you imagine, then, the feelings with which I looked forward to yesterday afternoon? And I could have told you all this yesterday as we talked—over a cup of tea, casually, with a few well-chosen, heartfelt words of admiration. But nothing could have been farther from my thoughts. In that twilight hour I was alone with you and alone I had to be with you—now, as my heart was overflowing with thanks for such a blessing.

I always feel: when one person is indebted to another for something very special, that indebtedness should remain a secret between just the two of them.

Perhaps someday I'll be granted the privilege of reading to you one or another of my own *Visions of Christ*, from the ones I have kept copies of here. I can think of no deeper joy.

Should I arrange tomorrow, Friday, to come to the Gärtner Theater, I hope I will find you there, gracious lady.

But these are the words of an old, long-harbored gratitude; to be allowed to express them now feels like

an honor awarded

to your:

René Maria Rilke

[RMR to LAS in Munich, inscribed in a copy of *Traumgekrönt, Neue Gedichte von Réne Maria Rilke* (Leipzig, 1897)]

This is an old medieval lie: that the nuns
Who cocooned themselves in hollow cells
In the hottest frenzy of their hidden raptures
Seared Christ's stigmata on their bodies,
In which Love lay sick, like that waiting well
From which no weary one drank heart and coolness.
This is an old medieval lie. But those *others*,
Unshielded from the everyday, stride through all times
And everything they do is like a preparation—
Those strangers who blaze the paths of what is new,
Who lead the way through struggles into peace
And out of death into eternities—
Those strangers *truly* bear unbeknownst
Jesus' burning wounds on their bodies:

Feet walked raw, hands blistered by travail
And that wild bleeding in their breast . . .

For Frau Lou Andreas-Salomé
In gratitude for being allowed to meet her!

René Maria Rilke

Munich, in May 1897

[RMR to LAS in Munich]

[Munich, May 31, 1897]
Monday Morning

Songs of Longing

V.

Longing sings:
I am a way of preparing you
And I smile gently when you stray;
I know that out of loneliness
you will emerge into that greatest happiness
And will take my hands.

I walk with you through all prose
And obliquely teach you
the deep lesson in every fate.
Which is: to see in each small rose
The great Spring's unfolding.

Yesterday at noon there was sun so lavish that one could have gilded a kingdom—even if it had not been a small and very poor one. But gold alone is not enough. I was very sad. I had been wandering about the city near the entrance to the Englische Garten with a small bouquet of roses in my hand, intending to present them to you. Yes, instead of going directly to the door with the golden key, I carried them around with me, trembling with sheer determination to meet up with you somewhere. In that I was not unlike someone who casts a letter into the ocean so that the waves will carry it to the shore of the friend for whom it is meant. The letter, of course, will merely float out into the boundless sea and finally sink. Thus also my roses. When after all my rushing about I finally stopped at noon and looked down at the sad faces of the faded flowers, a melancholy, fear-filled loneliness came over me:

Found on far-off pathways:
Sprigs of roses. With stems in hand,
Unsure of how to hold them,
I want to meet you.

As with pale orphaned
children I look for you,—
And to my poor roses
You would be a mother.

In the afternoon I found Frau Rütling in the Englische Garten. She had been looking for you at Fräulein Goudstikker's and was also disappointed at not being able to find you. So I could at least talk to someone about you. — She sympathized at once when she heard that I had been called up to register for military service. She even wanted to go see an ambassador about it. How kind she is!

The induction notice, however, even when I think of all the possible consequences, frightens me less at this moment than the prospect of having to leave here.

About that I am full of dread.—

I'll probably have to leave Wednesday evening or early Thursday, and until then I stretch out both my hands for every second you will give

Your

René Maria

About plans for this afternoon you will let me know?

———

May 31/June 1: RMR and LAS make a two-day excursion to the village of Wolfratshausen, south of Munich near Lake Starnberg, in search of a retreat near the mountains for a longer sojourn. During this trip they almost certainly become lovers.

[RMR to LAS in Munich]

[Munich, June 3, 1897]

*Tomorrow morning, as soon as the verdict regarding the military business has been reached, you shall receive a telegram that will tell you how it all came out and whether I can get back immediately and many another thing that will not be put in words but that you will nevertheless be able to read there.

Songs of longing!

And they will resound in my letters, just as they always have, sometimes loudly and sometimes secretly so that you alone can hear them . . . But they will also be different—different from how they used to be, these songs. For I have turned and found longing at my side, and I have looked into her eyes, and now she leads me with a sure hand.

I can become quieter in every phrase.

For I believe that in our conversation yesterday evening you hinted to me of what it means to have this word at one's core, preserved in all its greatness and depth: "simplicity." This utterance of yours shall be the key to my secret writing. Touch my every sentence with the pure gold of its power, and as from a Gothic reliquary there will flow toward you: the sparkling stream of my thousand coinages of tenderness.

And every fleeting thought, every wish, every dream will be veiled in my words. You will recognize them all.

Last night I entered my room smiling. I know: always, except for this, there would have

[*approximately seven lines missing*]

*The first quarter of this page has been removed—resulting also in the missing text in the middle of the letter.

so much, that if it were spread smoothly and evenly throughout my quotidian days, there would be enough for a very long life. —At last I have a *home.*—

Are you fond of roses? It feels to me: as if all the roses in the world bloom for you and by means of you, —and that only through an act of royal condescension do you maintain the pretense that they aren't really yours and allow the Spring to keep them.

Now I am closing my manuscript folder: the *Visions* are in it, the 12 novellas, many of which I will some day read to you, letters, pages filled with notes, and *Ruth.*

Did not I myself write these lines once in some dream filled with presentiments?

"... until the whole world dropped away from me
And nothing of all that life remained
Except a boundless gratitude
And a love stretching on forever! ...."

If they had not existed, I would have written them now. How wonderful that they do exist. For hence this strange exchange: I can express my happiness in your words. —And thus you in turn will understand my happiness. Is it not so?

Goodbye for now,
René.

Here is the Prague address: Wenzelsplatz 66. Rear Building. III. Floor. — But I am confident that I'll be back before a letter can reach me.

[RMR to LAS in Munich, telegram]

Prague, June 4, 1897, 11:10 A.M.

Free and soon also full of joy

R.

[RMR to LAS in Munich]

[Munich, June 6, 1897]
Whitsunday

Whitsun Greetings!

With bells pealing everywhere
And life on holiday in town and farm,
Today I greet the Feast of Roses
With open heart, and greet also the One
Who handed me this Spring
That shall determine all my days;
She received the poor, tired, homeless wanderer
And relieved him of his staff.

*

Kindest One,
In your great splendor
Humble
All my soul for you.

Deliver it
From its dark spell
And chain it
To your compassion.

And imagine:
It blooms in your May,
And you grant it
Your sweet slavery.

*

In no other May have I felt
How richly the world can fill with sound;
Spring touches all the hours
And all the hours send forth chords.
They sing far out into the twilight gleam

Their loudest joy, their softest joy,
And like desire lured, in dance-like waves
The echo backbeats through the night.

*

It's so good to know you aren't in Syrgenstein. Throughout that whole oppressive trip I kept dreading the possibility that after so late a return home yesterday, there would be a stretch of days when you lived so far away from me in a lonely mountain chateau that I would not be able to reach you without watching the sun die several times. —But now you are here and I only have to wait until six o'clock to see you.

Then let us be together again.

It is good of you to give the little novellas a hearing. But what I feel when I read them is, strangely: none of this is part of me any longer. It all seems so remote, as if from an earlier existence.

In the old garden that I have abandoned.

There is my old unhappiness
Like an abandoned garden
Where I had once sown wishes;

I couldn't linger
until they came to bloom;
perhaps now they flower too late.

What a great revolutionary you are. —You didn't overthrow thrones inside me. But the one throne that waited there: you strode past it gently smiling.

Ever upward.

And my desires, which before had crowded and become tangled around the vacant throne like wild roses, now rise as white columns around the space from whose temple friezes you smile down into my soul and bless my longing.

René

[RMR to LAS in Munich]

[Munich, June 8, 1897]
Tuesday

The wildflowers I brought home from that fairy-tale morning a week ago have been nestled ever since between two wide sheets of soft blotting paper; but today as I gaze at them, they smile back at me a blissful memory and all try to look as happy as they were back then. —

—

That was one of those rare hours. Such hours are like an island with flowers blooming thickly all around it: the waves breathe very quietly on the other side of the spring walls and no barge approaches out of the past and none waits to move on into the future.

—

The inevitable return to the everyday means nothing to these island hours. They remain detached from all the rest, as if lived in a second, higher existence.

—

A heightened island existence such as this, it seems to me, is the privileged future of the very few. —

A bliss peals out, blooms from far away
And wraps round my solitude
And attempts like a golden bracelet
to ring my dreams.

And though my poor small life
is hoarfrost frightened and snowdrift sad
A holy season will present to it
The blesséd Spring . . .

I wish I were in Dorfen already. The city is full of noises of every kind and completely foreign to me. And during the most important periods of inner development nothing that is foreign should disturb the widening circles. —

One day many years from now you will fully grasp what you are to me.

What the mountain spring is to someone dying of thirst.

And if the person whose life it saves is thankful enough and just, he won't simply drink in its clarity to become cool and strong again and then move on

into the new sun. No: he will build a hut in its shelter, build so close that he can hear its singing, and will remain in the flowery meadow until his eyes are suntired and his heart overflows with riches and clarity. I will build huts and—remain.

My clear fountain! What thankfulness I want to feel toward you. I want to see no flower, no sky, no sun—except in you. How much more beautiful and like a fairy tale is everything gazed at through your eyes: the flower at your edge, which (as I know from before, when I had to look at things without you) shivers alone and lifeless in the gray moss, then brightens in the mirror of your kindness, stirs lightly and with its little head almost touches the sky that reflects back out of your depths. And the sunbeam that arrives dusty and unfaceted at your borders grows clear and multiplies itself a thousandfold to become radiant splendor in the waves of your luminous soul. My clear fountain. I want to see the world through you; for then I will see not the world but always and only you, you, you!

You are my saint's day. And when I walk toward you in a dream, I shall always wear flowers in my hair.

—

I want to put flowers in your hair. But what flowers? There are none with touching enough simplicity. And from what May would I fetch them? But I'm convinced now that you always have a wreath in your hair . . . or a crown. . . . I've never seen you any other way.

I've never seen you without wanting to pray to you. I've never heard you without wanting to place my faith in you. I've never longed for you without wanting to suffer for your sake. I've never desired you without wanting to be able to kneel before you.

I am yours as the staff is the pilgrim's—only I don't support you. I am yours as the scepter is the queen's—only I don't enrich you. I am yours as the last little star is the night's, even though the night may be scarcely aware of it and have no knowledge of its glimmer.

René

[RMR to LAS in Munich]

[Munich, June 9, 1897]
Wednesday evening

Leaving you, through rain-dark streets
I steal quickly and feel
That everyone whose eyes meet mine
Can see blazing in them
My blissful, resurrected soul.

And on this road I try furtively
To hide my joy from the horde.
I bear it home with me in hurried steps;
Not till deep in night do I
Unlock it quietly, like a golden chest.

Then I lift its golden treasures
Out of deepest darkness, slowly, piece by piece,
And don't know what to gaze on first;
For all the places in my room
Are overflowing, are overflowing.

It is a richness beyond compare—
Such as the night has never gazed on,
Such as the night has never dewed;
More precious even than any royal dowry
Bestowed on a young king's bride.

Among it are rich crown-imperials,
And all the jewels set in them are stars.
And no one suspects. My dearest:
I am among my treasures like an emperor
Who knows he has an empress.

And after the recent wild thunderstorm the sun now pours in so richly that a solid-gold happiness really does seem to have covered all the places in my room. I am rich and free and re-dream each second of the afternoon in deep breaths of contentment. I don't want to go out again today. I want to dream gentle dreams and with their splendor deck my room as with vines of flowers to receive you. I want to enter my night with your hands' blessing on my hands and in my hair. I don't want to talk to anyone, lest I squander your words' echo, which ripples like a sheen over mine and lends their sound a richness. And after the evening sun I don't want to gaze into any more light, so that I may kindle a thousand gentle sacrifices at the fire of your eyes. . . . I want to rise in you, like a child's prayer in a loud, jubilant morning, like a rocket among the solitary stars. I want to be you. I want to have no dreams that don't know you, and no desires that you will not or cannot fulfill. I want to perform no deed that does not praise you and tend no flower that does not adorn you. I want to greet no bird that does not know the way to your window and drink from no brook that has not once tasted your image. I want to go to no country in which your dreams have not roamed like strange miracle-workers and dwell in no huts in which you have never taken refuge. I want to know nothing of the days that preceded you in my life or of the people who dwell in those days. As I pass by them I want to place a rare faded wreath of remembering on the grave of these people, if they deserve it, since I am too happy not to be thankful. But the language in which they speak to me now is the language of tombstones, and when they say a word I grope about and touch only cold, rigid letters. I want to praise these deceased with a happy heart; for they disappointed me and misunderstood me and mistreated me and down this long road of woes led me to you. —Now I want to be you. And my heart flames before your grace like the eternal lamp before the image of the Virgin Mary. You.

Thursday morning.—

I'd like to spread out purple blankets,
Then fill the myriad flower-lamps
With oil of balsam from golden cruses
Until they're brimming everywhere.

So should they burn and burn
Till we, blinded by the red days,
In the pale night come to know each other
And our souls—are stars

How rich you are. You give dreams to my night, songs to my morning, aims to my day, and sun-wishes to my red dusk. You give without end. And I kneel and hold my arms up to receive your grace. How rich you are! I am everything you want. And I shall be slave or king as you grow angry or smile. But what makes me exist—is you.

I shall tell you this often, very often. My confessing shall ripen into something humbler and humbler, simpler and simpler. And when at last I tell it to you with perfect simplicity, you will understand it simply and our Summer shall have arrived. And it will extend out over all the days of your

René.—

You *will* come today!?

[RMR to LAS in Munich]

[Munich, June 1897]

. . . I ask myself so many things these days, as is always the case in times of great upheaval. I am in the first dawn of a new epoch. — I have left the garden in which I paced wearily for so long. . . .*

June 14: LAS and F. von Bülow move to Wolfratshausen, where they rent a small house (Lutzhäuschen); RMR first lives in nearby Dorfen, a village about twenty miles south of Munich, before he joins them. Toward the end of July they move to a different house they call Loufried, probably alluding ironically to Wagner's house Wahnfried in Bayreuth. During this "bohemian" period of rustic simplicity RMR, at LAS's urging, changes his name from René to Rainer. When LAS's husband visits them (July 23–August 29), RMR leaves for Munich but returns after a week's absence on August 1.

---

*Part of a letter quoted in LAS's *Rainer Maria Rilke* (Leipzig: Insel, 1928), p. 17.

[RMR to LAS in Kufstein]

[Wolfratshausen, July 17, 1897]
Saturday morning

I am alone and before me on the table
Stands, soft and pale, your little childhood picture;
And what I now know as dream and longing
I recognize in it: the gentle wistful
Far-off smile, and, in the vaulted niche
beneath the brow, the eye watching tenderly,
And even then seeking far out into life
And even then with a hundred graces to bestow!

I love this little picture. There is so much more of you in it than in the most recent one from *Elvira.* This pure simplicity in the features, this dark seeking of the eye, which at every moment is being soothed and countered by the sense of calm discovery in your smiling lips—this isn't in the new one. And yet it is one of your greatest miracles: your eyes find an enigma and pause above it for a few moments, shading it as if with outspread wings. And then suddenly, without your thoughtful eyes yet suspecting it, a smile awakens and blooms about your mouth, spreads its tendrils over your cheeks and finally reaches up to your dark eyes, so that they blaze in hot redemption. And then the glow of this smile exceeds you and surrounds your body like a transfiguration. And this isn't in the new picture. There you appear the way Puck sees you. You: if there existed a picture of you that was exactly like you, all the children who pass by it would fall on their knees before it. And I would mingle with those children and kneel down in their midst.

You, my love.

Come back, oh come back. It was so sad when to my "good night" no answer came. As I was falling asleep I said it aloud a few more times—and waited . . . waited . . .

Today it is raining. No doubt also on Kufstein and Pushkin.

[RMR to LAS in Kufstein]

[Wolfratshausen, July 1897]

Then your letter brought me its gentle benediction
And I knew: there are no distant places:
From all that's beautiful you come toward me,
You, my spring breeze, my summer rain,
My June night with its many thousand paths
None before me was blessed to tread:
I am alive in you!

September 3: LAS leaves for a trip to Hallein, south of Salzburg; RMR returns to Munich six days later to await her there on September 15.

[RMR to LAS in Hallein]

Wolfratshausen near Munich
Sunday, September 5, 1897

Today is only the second day of my solitude—and I must confess to you: when I take inventory of that small store of courage I call my own, I scarcely know how I shall survive on it for eight days more. Yesterday was long, and I accomplished just about what I had hoped. First I wrote my father, without mentioning as yet that I will scarcely have any time to spend in Prague. Between now and then I will write him a few more letters so that he will gradually understand and not be taken unawares. Next I wrote to the publisher of *Le rire*, ordered a subscription, wrote a few words to Paul Bornstein, at the editorial office of *Moderní Revue*, concerning that article about avant-garde Czech literature, and finally sent a few words to the "illustrated women's journal." That took me until noon; after lunch I sank more and more sleepily into my weariness, read through bits of Rembrandt and Velasquez, and around six o'clock, even though there was a steady rain, went for a walk along the edge of the village, past the Kasten mill, on the road to

Dorfen. Lost in thought I walked on beyond the little church with its brooding cemetery toward the studio of the woods-and-rhythms people, which is now ramshackle and desolate, and suddenly found myself on the meadow path we took that first evening when we entered golden Dorfen. Today it was autumnal and unoutlined and the pearl-gray rain lay thickly over it. I thought about how many bright lovely flowers we had found here and how long ago that was and how plowed and empty the meadows are. And I said goodbye to this land as to someone dying. And behind the last dark bushes there awakened a pale monotonous red—and it flowed softly and evenly across the western edge of the sky. It blended with the vague gray of the autumn sky in a high half-circle, and out beyond its edges delicate white clouds emerged from the glow and drifted toward night like birds with soundless silver wings. It only lasted a moment: then the landscape was extinguished and grew even more melancholy and desolate and furrowed than before; and I said goodbye as to someone dying. And I will say goodbye to something each impending day. To Lutzhäuschen and that spot above it from which we greeted for the first time the pale, nocturnal valley with its veil of light; to those gentle rolling meadows with the islands of beech trees in them; to the path to Ammerland. I have come to cherish all this like a homeland . . . and after I have said goodbye to it all (and that will be in three or four days), I will return to Munich. Why should I remain here? Once in the city I will visit diligently the two Pinacothecas, the Collection of Prints, and the Schack Gallery and peruse many beautiful things. And there will be more happiness and hope in this because it will be the setting for what during these ten days has been and will continue to be my longing and my faith—"the joyous moment of your return." I feel more strongly now that I am preparing something for you, —and will thus be calmer. I will also be better informed when we go through the museums together; perhaps I can even add a bit of warmth and festiveness to your rooms. To that end I am writing the Brümmers today to see if I can rent a suitable room with board near your apartment for the three weeks from the ninth of September through the thirtieth. The ninth is Thursday and after that there will be only two more days to survive—until Sunday. No Sunday in my life can have been as festive as the one to which I am now looking forward!

I think of you every moment of the day and my thoughts and cares are with you wherever you go. Every breath of wind you feel on your brow kisses you with my lips and every dream speaks to you with my voice. My love surrounds you like a cloak, warming and protecting you!

September 5, 1897

My day also wishes me to tell you: it is poor because you are not near it; it is rich because your goodness spreads light over all its things. I talk to you often and speak of you with all that is mine. Live, sad to say, among people who interrupt my dreams with their loudness, and know, of course, not a single one of them. They are people who talk about trips, rainy days, and raising children, who bow deeply to each other, smiling and rubbing their hands, and greet each other with "Good Morning" ten times a day in loud, disagreeable voices. And so I associate only with Stauffer-Bern, who, though unpleasant in many respects, still seems an interesting and remarkable man. I look forward to telling you about this strange Bernburger, who is a mixture of daring and cowardice, of quiet, pellucid feeling and brutal, callous assertion, and who seems to express these inner contradictions (always magnifying them awkwardly) whenever he is in the presence of a woman. But the real tragedy of Stauffer's life lies not in the self-doubt that again and again subjects his hope to bitterness and leads him away from one branch of art off toward some other, before he can ever really flourish in any one: but rather in the fact that neither he nor Frau Escher recognized early enough (or wished to recognize?) what really attracted them to each other; and that then, when such recognition did belatedly arrive, in the sacred day of their having at last found each other, such violent storms erupted that all the young sprouting seeds could not but be destroyed. It is not enough for two people to find each other, it is also very important that they find each other at the right moment and hold deep, quiet festivals in which their desires merge so that they can fight as one against storms. How many people have parted ways because they did not find the time slowly to grow close to each other? Before two people can experience unhappiness together, they have to have been blissful together and possess a sacred memory of that time, which evokes a kindred smile on their lips and a kindred longing in their souls. They become like children who have lived through the festivities of a Christmas night together; when they find a few minutes to catch their breath during the pale, drawn-out days, they will sit down together and tell each other with glowing cheeks about that pine-tree-scented nighttime full of sparkling lights . . .

Such people will weather all storms together.

I am convinced of it!

Rainer.

[RMR to LAS in Wolfratshausen]

Put my eyes out: I can see you
Slam my ears shut: I can hear you
And without feet I can still walk to you
And without a mouth I can still beseech you.
Break off my arms: I will grasp you
With my heart as with a hand
Tear out my heart: and my brain will beat
And if you throw a torch in my brain
I will bear you on my blood

[RMR to LAS in Hallein]

[Wolfratshausen]
Eight at night on September 8 [1897]

Love, I am drunk from so much gazing. As you know, I went to say goodbye. First to Frau Wildenauer. Kathi met me on the way and showed me into their living room. We exchanged regards and wished each other well and I went on up the path to see old lady Reissler. That's when it all began. The whole day had been cold and gray, but when I stepped out of the last stand of spruces, I beheld a clear, warm twilight casting golden tenderness on the bright house and its garden full of red. A serene happiness lay over it, and my thankful memory made me a confidant of this bliss of flowers. And her large, solemn living room struck me as all the more dark, all the more mystery-filled, with a soft, deep-red little fire flickering at the center of its hearth and everything empty and silent, as in a fairy tale. I found the old woman surrounded by cool meadow-scents, turning hay. She seemed so happy to see me, was touched that I had come to find her, enthused like a child over the group picture and spoke of you full of awkward, helpless love, spoke of the winter and of our returning and of the weather and of a carpet I had forgotten to take with me. And all this almost in a single breath, so that I was deeply moved. I managed to break away from this tireless old lady with a few polite, sincere words, and later found myself thinking: if only I had had a mother who was so simple and direct, as alive deep down in her heart with cheerfulness and piety as this old lady . . . but I took the path toward Ammerland and forgot everything I had been thinking; for the deeper I penetrated into the beech trees' secrecy, and the farther the flowers and tall gray thistles in the pale meadows beckoned me with their waving, the clearer it became to me: all this is a festival. There was nothing of the everyday up here; only the few times we had walked alone, up above, our souls silent and oh so close, had it been like this. I followed the quiet path and it led me to a place where squirrels darted through moss and morass and everything around had its own serene, intimate stillness and stirring. And today there was no sudden flight in this sanctum, even though the brittle leaves cracked and shattered under my timid steps. A woodpecker tapped contentedly at his spruce tree like a prudent doctor, and seemed to find it in good health. Large birds stood unfrightened on mossy tree stumps and tolerated my stare; the squirrels slipped unconcerned through the thick branches with their customary cheerful haste. They had all decided: "It's all right; he's not an intruder, he won't betray us, and besides: he's come to say goodbye." No, I won't betray you, nor your holy secrecies, because my soul is in love with you. I stood as if praying in this blessed solitude which began far back behind rows and rows of tree trunks, and I felt—there are a hundred walls between me and all that is loud. Only *your soul* was with me in this quiet hour, for it is only through you that I can take this deep a pleasure, only through your grace that I am this rich, only through your love that I am this happy. —I felt: this has been a beautiful goodbye—and greeted the larger world once more. It was festive and suffused in a thousand colors. And as I walked home through this splendor, I myself must have been as if in Sunday clothes, and with the sun like jewelry on my shoulders. And I must have become brighter and better, for children who encountered me greeted me almost reverently with bright little voices and one of them even allowed me to place my hand on her blond hair. And had I been able to bless at that moment? What do you think?

Munich, September 9, 1897 [Thursday]. Afternoon. —So now I am in Munich, have already eaten in my room and after a cup of coffee will go visit the Schack Gallery. Your rooms are also ready now; if only they didn't have to wait for your arrival! Spend not one second longer there than those weightiest reasons (whatever they are) require. —I know, I must go on being patient for days, for days . . . The sun was shining when I left Wolfratshausen and now it is beginning to rain again in that dear old way it has of falling lightly, almost inadvertently. And with the sun scarcely vanished, it is already cool. Take good care of yourself and come back sound and—soon—to

Your

Rainer.

October 1: LAS returns to Berlin, accompanied by RMR, who takes up residence there (Berlin-Wilmersdorf, Im Rheingau 8). He enrolls in art history courses at the university, studies Italian, and makes the acquaintance of various poets and writers, among them Stefan George, Carl Hauptmann, and Richard Dehmel. He continues to write poems, novellas, and short plays.

February–March 1898: RMR and LAS decide he should visit Florence to study Renaissance art firsthand. LAS will join him there later after she sees to family affairs. (Some biographers speculate that LAS arranged this separation in order to terminate a pregnancy secretly.) They plan the trip elaborately together, and LAS instructs RMR to keep a diary, which she will read on their reunion.

April–May: Traveling via Arco, RMR arrives in Florence during the first weeek of April. There the Swiss art collector Gustav Scheeli introduces him to Heinrich Vogeler, a Jugendstil artist who will later illustrate RMR's Stories of God. *He also meets the poets Stefan George and Rudolf Borchardt. In the middle of May RMR departs abruptly for Viareggio, a seaside resort town directly west of Florence, where he stays until the first of June.*

June: RMR travels via Vienna and Prague (where he visits his parents) to Wilmersdorf (June 8) and almost immediately on to Zoppot (Baltic Sea), where LAS joins him after visiting Johanna Niemann in Danzig. Their stay together in Zoppot, fraught with tension and frequently interrupted by LAS's trips to friends as far away as St. Petersburg, lasts until the end of July.

[RMR, *The Florence Diary,* concerning LAS]

FLORENCE, APRIL 19, 1898 [FIRST ENTRY]. Whether I have come far enough yet and possess the calm to begin this diary I want to bring home to you—I cannot say. But I know that my joy will feel far-off and unfestive as long as you—at least through some honest and deep-felt inscription of it into a book meant for you—do not share in it. And so I begin; and I take it as a good omen that I commence this testament of my longing in these days that by a year's length follow those when, with kindred longing, I walked toward something vague and uncertain and didn't know yet that you are the fulfillment for which I was preparing myself in songs of intense listening.

VIAREGGIO, MAY 17. How I have admired that in you, love: this unworried trust in all things, this kindness impervious to fear. Now it is approaching me also, on a different path. I am like a child who was hanging from a precipice. It is reassured when its mother grasps it in dear, quiet strength, even if the chasm is still below it and thorns splay between its cheek and her breast. It feels itself held, lifted—and is reassured. . . .

This day a mother writes me, a mother who was deep in many a fear before she experienced the miracle. She writes: "Now spring has come to us also, albeit amid storms and tears; but I feel now as though I had never seen a spring before. . . . Today I sat all afternoon in the garden with Rolf, and out in the air I felt him opening like a rose; he has become so much more beautiful since you last saw him, his hair is thicker and he still has those big eyes."

I read this like a hymn, Lou. And I long for the moment when I shall read it before YOU; then it will become melody.

All I need is strength. Everything else that would make me a prophet I feel within me. I don't want to journey through all countries and try to spread my teaching. Above all I don't want to let it petrify into a doctrine. I want to live it. And only into your soul, love, do I want to pilgrimage, deep, deep inside, where it opens up into a temple. And there I want to raise my longing like a monstrance in YOUR splendor. *That* is my desire.

You have seen me suffer and have consoled me. Upon your consolation I want to build my church—in which joy has bright altars.

[VIAREGGIO] It was a strange Sunday, this May 22. A deep day. I was even able to record in these pages what I have long felt burning in me, a confession and a clarity and a courage. On a long walk in the festive pinetum the three *Mädchenlieder* . . . came to me along with YOUR high hymn that concluded the new notebook. Everything seemed so ripe for celebration: yet there can be no festival without YOU. And so I moved my high armchair close, dreamed YOU into it, sat down across from you and, as evening deepened outside, read one song after the other and sang the first and wept the second and was pure blissfulness and woe: a toy in the hands of these delicate pale songs that now did to me as I had done with them. All the longing and tenderness I had locked inside them came over me and surrounded me like a wild springtime and lifted me up as if with white, gentle, unseen hands—into what realm, I don't know. But so high that the days were like little villages with red roofs and tiny church steeples and memories were like people standing small and silently in their doorways, waiting for something . . . .

[VIAREGGIO] After a day of prayer, a day of penance—as is so often the case. I found your letter after dinner and was dismayed and then afraid. Now I am still full of sadness. I have been anticipating the summer with such joy and felt it like a dear bright promise over everything. And now doubts arrive and worries, and all the paths grow tangled . . . and lead where?—

Suddenly it is so dark around me. I don't know where I am. I only feel that I must sit among strangers and travel one day and then another and then a third in order to be with you at last—in order perhaps: to say goodbye to you.

And yet I feel something else in me saying: Wait. There is so much newness crowded before me, I cannot name it nor sort it out. But gaze for a while into forest and ocean, into the great beneficence of this splendor, and wait: clarity will come.

And clarity arrived.

Today there is no more fear in me, only bright joy: to have you again in six to seven days, love.

Why should a dreary beach in East Prussia concern me! For two whole months I have been scooping beauty with blissful hands; I have enough of it to tower up treasures before the both of us so that we will disappear from sight, no matter what others happen to be there.

[VIAREGGIO] . . . with a flickering candle at my side I thought: Lou, how magnificent you are, how much space you have opened up inside me. For if these Italian days showered me with treasures, it was you who created room for them in my soul—where the dreams once crowded, and the many timidities. It was you who made me festive. To return to you so clear, my love: it's the best of what I'll bring you.

[ZOPPOT, JULY 6, 1898 (FINAL ENTRY).] Here at the edge of a cooler sea I bring to an end this book, which I have denied more than three times; for much fear and poverty lie between back then and right now: days like flat country roads with poor leafless chestnut trees on either side, thoughts like endless villages passing by with dull lifeless doorways and windows ruined by rain. And yet all this had to come, and I am like this not because it came but because it happened now, at a moment when I wished nothing more than to bring you so much festiveness, unspoiled and holy, and surround you with it as with a dark niche that is receiving its statue. But I was like the child who for love of his desperately ill little sister runs to the city from the dark farmstead through night and need to fetch her medicine, and in the light of morning, enticed by childish games, forgets the very purpose of the trip and cheerfully returns without the longed-for cure. . . . This cheerfulness will become a weeping, and a despair stands behind it: I know too well.

And furthermore: the circumstances under which we first saw each other again were such that I perceived in you only various things from the world of yesterday; something past, something overcome, something narrow that had been hurtful for both of us crowded in on me and blocked the memory of our solitary happiness that is timeless and not tied to any "once." I know only that you patiently listened to my innumerable small complaints, and suddenly I noticed that I was complaining again and you were listening again, just as before. That made me so ashamed, it almost embittered me. It was much like the people of Prague, who for their entire lives live their own past. They are like corpses who cannot find peace and therefore in the dark of night live their dying again and again and pass one another by across the hard graves. They have nothing left: the smile has wilted on their lips, and their eyes have drifted off with their last crying as if they were floating on twilight rivers. All progress in them amounts only to this: their coffin rots and their clothes disintegrate and they themselves crumble and grow wearier and lose their fingers like old recollections. And they tell each other the story of this in their long-dead voices: that's how the people of Prague are.

Now I came to you full of future. And from habit we began to live our past. How could I observe that you became free and festive through the confidence in this book, since I did not see YOU, but only your forbearance and gentleness and the endeavor to give me courage and raise my spirits. Nothing at this moment could more incense me than this. I hated you like something *too big. I* wanted this time to be the rich one, the giver, the host, the master, and you were supposed to come and be guided by my care and love and stroll about in my hospitality. And now in your presence I was again only the smallest beggar at the outermost threshold of your being—which rests on such broad and certain columns. What help was it that I put on my accustomed holiday words? I felt myself becoming more and more ridiculous in my masquerade, and the dark wish awakened in me a desire to creep away into a deep Nowhere. Shame, shame was all there was in me. Every reunion with you made me ashamed. Can you understand that? Invariably I said to myself: "I can give you nothing, nothing at all; my gold turns to coal when I hand it to you, and I become poor in the process." Once I came to you in such poverty. Almost as a child I came to the rich woman. And you took my soul in your arms and rocked it. That was good. Back then you kissed my forehead and had to bend far down to do so. Do you understand that at your side I grew up until it was only a short distance from your eyes to my eyes? But that I wanted finally, strong of stem, to bend down toward your lips exactly as your soul once bent down to my forehead? I didn't want to be embraced by you, I wanted you to be able to lean against me when you are tired. I didn't want to feel your consolation, I wanted to feel the power inside me to console you, should you ever need consoling. I didn't want to find the memory of our Berlin winter days still inside you, I wanted you to be more than ever my future, since I had the faith for happiness and the confidence for fulfillment. And meanwhile this book told you what happened to me down below, and you lived through it like a deep dream and became the future. But then I no longer believed in it. I was blind and bitter, full of helpless and hateful thoughts and day in, day out tormented by the fear: that now you, with the riches that I had brought you and that you had so quickly raised and made your own possession, could begin presenting me with gifts, and already I felt in the best hours how I was beginning to accept as alms of your untiring goodness what I had fetched in blessed victories. I had brought golden bowls to you, bright vessels of festiveness, and then I had compelled you with my neediness to mint from this noble treasure small coins for everyday use, and thus slowly pay me back the gift. I felt myself becoming so pitiful and wretched as this happened that I threw away or lost the last of my own wealth and in my desperation felt only the vague imperative to flee the environs of this goodness that was humiliating me.

But during that time, in the very midst of this convulsion, I realized that were I to shake off my paralysis and gather myself in a resolve: each of my deeds, all movement in me, would strive toward you; then, when for the first time after this dull sadness I was forced to think about tomorrow, when behind your figure Fate stood and through your estranged voice put to me the iron question: "What to do?" —then everything inside me was as if freed from the ice; the wave sprang from the floe and cast itself with all its might toward the shore—without delaying and without doubt. When you asked me about the future and I lay helplessly and remained awake that whole night wracked by this worry, then I knew, when in the morning I found you again, that you are the ever new, the ever young, the eternal goal, and that for me there is one fulfillment that includes everything: to move toward YOU. . . .

Your strings are rich; and however far I may go—You are always there before me. My struggles have in your case long become victories, and therefore I am sometimes so very small in your presence; but my new victories are yours also, and I may present them to you. I have traveled across Italy on the long path toward the summit, which this book represents. You flew to it in swift hours and stood, before I was all the way up, on its clearest peak. I was far up, but still surrounded by clouds; you waited above them in the eternal light. Receive me, love.

Be always there before me, you dear, peerless, sacred one. Let us go upward together, you and I—as if up to the great star, each leaning on the other, each resting in the other. And if sometimes I have to let my arm drop from your shoulders for a while, I will fear nothing: on the next height you will smilingly greet the tired one. You are not a goal for me; you are a thousand goals. You are everything, and I know you in everything, and I am everything and direct everything your way in my moving toward you.

I needn't say: Forgive! For I ask that from you in every silence. I needn't ask: Forget! For we want to remember these hours also, in which I tried to flee from you in shame; and on my blind flight I was always running toward you. Nor do I want to say: Trust! For I know that this is the language with which we recognized and greeted each other in these new sanctified mornings after a long distantness and an estranged closeness that was our last separation and my last peril. . . .

As for ourselves: we are the ancestors of a god and with our deepest solitudes reach forward through the centuries to his very beginning. I feel this with all my heart!

July 31: RMR and LAS return from Zoppot to LAS's and her husband's residence in Schmargendorf, on the outskirts of Berlin. RMR moves into a rented room nearby (in the villa Waldfrieden, in Hundekehlstrasse 11). He is a frequent visitor, at times almost a member of the Andreas household, sharing their barefoot walks, adopting their peasant dress and vegetarian diet, helping with daily chores.

December 19: Heinrich Vogeler invites RMR to visit him in Worpswede, a small artists' colony near Bremen. After stops in Hamburg and in Bremen (to celebrate Christmas Eve with Vogeler's parents), they proceed to Worpswede on December 25. RMR stays there briefly before returning to Schmargendorf.

March 18, 1899: Returning from a visit with his mother at Arco, RMR stops in Vienna, where, accompanied by Arthur Schnitzler, he attends premières of two verse plays by Hugo von Hofmannsthal, both of which leave a strong impression on him.

[Postcard from RMR to LAS from Vienna, March 18, 1899]

Greetings from the Vienna of Schnitzler and Loris! *Rainer.*

RMR travels on to see his father in Prague, where an attack of flu keeps him in bed for approximately two weeks. He arrives back in Schmargendorf on April 17.

April 24: RMR, LAS, and F. C. Andreas leave for their long-planned trip to Russia. They arrive in Moscow on Thursday, April 27. On Good Friday (at RMR's insistence) they visit Leo Tolstoy at the Tolstoys' winter residence in Moscow. On Easter at midnight they experience the bells and the jostling crowds of the Kremlin. After a week they move to St. Petersburg, where RMR more or less has to fend for himself. LAS and RMR spend a last weekend together in Moscow (they take the night train both ways) before returning to Schmargendorf on June 28.

July 29: RMR and LAS join Frieda von Bülow in a small country house she has rented on the Bibersberg (Thuringia). There they spend six weeks happily immersed in Russian studies, already preparing for an eventual second Russian trip. News that Lotte, LAS's pet dog, is gravely ill prompts her abrupt return to Schmargendorf on September 12. RMR follows a day later. Lotte dies two days later and is buried ceremoniously with RMR in attendance.

[RMR to LAS in Schmargendorf]

[Schmargendorf, September 13, 1899]

How glad I am that Lottchen is recovering. Let her know that I've returned too. I rummaged about and was in the city despite the bad weather. Until the fifteenth nothing can be done in my rooms. I long to read something Russian; but I don't have Власть Т[ь]мы with me here; so if you are able to send me something tomorrow, include a Russian book—the first volume of Lermontov, perhaps, or anything in prose, no matter what. Kindest regards.

Rainer

Wednesday evening at 6:30

[RMR to LAS in Schmargendorf; postcard: Prague, Altstädter Ring, 1780]

Prague, December 23 [1899]
[*Imprint:*] *Greetings from Prague*

For Christmas Eve 1899!

from *Rainer*

May 7 through August 24, 1900: LAS's and RMR's second Russia journey, this time alone. They travel from Berlin via Warsaw to Moscow; from Moscow south to Tula to visit Tolstoy at Yasnaya Polyana (June 1); then to Kiev and Kremenchug on the lower Dnieper, through the Poltava region by train to Kharkov, Vorenezh, and Saratov; by steamship up the Volga to Kazan, Nizhni Novgorod (now Gorki), and Yaroslavl. From Moscow to the village of Nisovka to meet the peasant poet Spiridon Droshin, and to nearby Novinki to meet the poet Nikolai Tolstoy. Via Novgorod Velikiye to St. Petersburg, where after one day together (July 26) LAS departs for Rongas (Finland) to visit her family. She remains there for almost a month, leaving RMR behind in their St. Petersburg rooming house, without his knowing when she plans to come back. LAS returns August 21; they leave only days later, arrive back in Berlin August 26; on August 27 RMR accepts Vogeler's invitation to stay with him and leaves for Worpswede, where he will remain until October 5.

[RMR, "from a letter. St. Petersburg, July 31," entry in the Schmargendorf Diary]

On the Volga, on this restfully rolling ocean, to be days and nights, many days and many nights: a broad, broad stream, tall, tall woods along one shore, along the other a deep moorland in which even big cities only stand like shacks and tents. One sees: land is big, water is something big, and above all the sky is big. What I have seen until now was no more than an image of land and river and world. Here, however, everything is itself. — I feel as if I had been witness to the Creation; a few words for all existences, *things* in the measure of God the Father. . . .

[RMR in St. Petersburg to LAS in Rongas, first week of August 1900]*

[LAS in Rongas to RMR in St. Petersburg, end of first week of August 1900]

[LAS, *Looking Back*, "With Rainer, Epilogue [1934]," addressing RMR posthumously]

We were already discussing to what extent the world and people needed to absorb you now into their midst, in place of that symbolic realm in which you had thought to grasp and celebrate the dream of the ineffable alone and directly. But only toward the end of our second stay in Russia did it become

*Letters no longer extant but identifiable from subsequent letters or reliable external sources will henceforth be indicated in brackets.

fully clear to me what an urgent necessity that was. I had gone—very briefly—to visit my family on their [current] summer estate in Finland, when I received your letter that characterized you as almost depraved on account of the presumption and arrogance of your Prayers. Granted, a second followed very quickly in a different key: yet it in turn was in that excessive, egregious mode you had long since smilingly called "pre-Wolfratshausen," and seemed to me like an incomprehensible reversion.

[RMR to LAS in Rongas]

Ст-Петербургъ, уголь Невскаго и Фонтанки, Мебл, Комн. "Централь."
[St. Petersburg, August 11, 1900]
Saturday, late morning

I have your letter, your precious letter that comforts me with every word, that caresses me as with a strong, surging wave, that surrounds me as with gardens and builds up heavens over me, that makes me happy and able to say to you what in my previous, burdensome letter struggled so vainly: that I long for you, and that unutterable fears took hold of me as I lived these last few days without any news whatsoever, following that unexpected and swift farewell, alone among the almost hostile impressions of this difficult city, where there was not any one *thing* through which you might speak to me from far off. And this is what brought about that ugly letter of a few days ago, which could scarcely find its way out of my inner isolation, out of the unaccustomed and terrible aloneness of my experiences, and was only a clamoring, a confusion and a bafflement, jagged things that must be incomprehensible to you in the rich, rounded beauty to which your life has so quickly returned amid the new circumstances.

Now I cringe to think that in the great chorus that surrounds you, and in which you are again finding small children's voices, *my* voice should have been the alien one, the single banal one, the voice of the world amid these holy words and silences from which the days around you are woven. Was it not so? I fear it must have been. What shall I do? Can I silence with this letter the other one? In this one your words resound, the other one was predicated on your faraway life, of which I could find out nothing at all, and now that I do have news, its right to exist has ended. . . . but it *does* still exist, doesn't it?

Will you tell me one thing? That in spite of that letter everything is as you write in yours; that no squirrel has died on account of it, and that nothing, nothing has darkened under it or even remained in shadow behind it.

Remember the squirrels I told you about that I raised in Italy when I was a child—how I bought long, long chains so that their freedom might come to an end only high up in the trees? Doubtless it was very wrong to intrude upon their light lives at all, especially as an authority (when they had already grown up, that is, and no longer needed me), but in some small measure they themselves strove to preserve their link with me, for they often came running after me, so that at the time it seemed to me as if they were actually wishing for chains.

How they will miss you, the little ones. And will they be grown-up enough to go without you into wood and world? High up in the firs of Rongas their childhood will sometimes come back to them, and on a bough that is still swaying from the weight of their leap, you will be remembered. And though they are only three little squirrels in whose small eyes you don't have room, somewhere inside them it is so immense that you can exist there in their lives. Dearest!

Come back soon, come back as soon as you can leave them. Lead them out into the forest, tell them in your voice how lovely it is, and they will be the happiest squirrels in the most beautiful wood.

Yes, please, be here by Sunday. You can't imagine how long the days in St. Petersburg can be. Nor in spite of that, how little goes into them. Life here is a continuous being on one's way, and, due to this, all destinations suffer. One walks, walks, rides, rides, and regardless of where one arrives, the first impression is of one's own weariness. One almost always, moreover, takes the longest trips in vain. Nevertheless: I know now that we still have many beautiful things to see when you come. It must be that every sentence I have thought for the past two weeks has ended with those same words: when you come.—

I also cherish the moonlit night between last Wednesday and Thursday's dawn. I walked along the Neva quite late, out to my favorite spot, across from St. Isaac's Cathedral, where the city is at its simplest and greatest. There I also (and quite unexpectedly) felt peaceful and happy and solemn—as I do now, having received your letter. I am hurrying to send off these lines so that what you send me Monday (and you will surely send me a few words by way of your brother? Only a few words, I shall understand them all!) will already be an answer to *this*. An answer to the one question: are you happy? I am, behind all that torments me, so fundamentally, so very confidently, so invincibly happy. And I have you to thank for it. Come soon!

Your
Rainer.

[*In the margin:*] Vogeler has written very warmly, and is expecting me. And I am already needed for my beautiful book. The first proofsheets are waiting. So it will be out in October!

[RMR to LAS in Schmargendorf, written on the cover of a special issue of the Catalan periodical *Juventut* devoted to Heinrich Vogeler]

[Worpswede, probably September 1900]

Warmest greetings and thanks for card and printed material!

[RMR to LAS, entry in the Schmargendorf Diary]

Worpswede, September 1, 1900

Moscow, Stshukin Museum: across from the Japanese painting in the room with the translucent ceiling (inserted from May 1900):

Goddess of Grace

She stands in deep-blue ocean depths
into which many rivers pour
from distances on high.
A gray fish carries her along,
delighted by her weight's lissomness,
which trickles over his fins.

Out of his gills spews excited
spraying—bubbling rush of breath.

But into her beauty rises,
coolly, ushered along in waves,
his forever level feeling.

When I read this to you in the Amerika house, do you remember my saying: Yes, everything that has truly been seen *must* become a poem! Oh, I felt such happiness saying that. And I still can't really believe I was wrong then—although . . .

Both possibilities are equally disheartening: either I have not seen anything since then, have not truly, with my entire being seen, or else my seeing is not so intimately bound up with my creating as I once thought.

For back then there was only pure sound in me: once in Poltava, at evening, when the huts were so pale and solitary in the coming on of night, once in Saratov among the Cossack houses of the eastern districts, later in the midst of the Volga waters, then again when through a long night we felt ourselves journeying farther and farther into the light . . . but I can extract no word from the fabric of these sounds, indeed I don't even know if words accompanied them.

Nonetheless, just outside Kazan, late at evening, a song did come forth, it began, I think:

. . . From all others I will absent myself,
I will build my life stone by stone,
not from the rubbleheap of rich housefronts,
from ashlars that still bathe in rivers,
from mountains that still stand in meadows . . .

But it seemed wrong to express my inner happiness, which was independent of everything external, in these words, which had just lost their meaning in the face of mundane reality. So I was glad when my sound died out, and its sense only flared up in me again much later in Moscow, as landscape . . . evening:

The horses saunter over with their red yokes
as if passing under many gateways,
the evening glows, called to by bell-chimes,
and all huts stand as by the sea . . .

This may have been an echo of Yaroslavl-Kresta. — Then came Droshin, then Novgorod, where on that one morning I felt the potential for something in me . . .

I made nothing of it, as was the case with so many potentialities on this trip. Countless poems I failed to hear. I passed over a spring; what wonder now that there is no true summer. Everything that arrived found me locked up. And now, when I open the doors, the roads are long and empty . . .

But this is not the journey's sum. The tremendous *is* still in me somewhere. I *did* experience it all, I was surely not just dreaming. If only it would somehow come back to me. I have such longing for what has passed. I don't want to hold onto it and think about it. But I wish I could feel its presence half-intuitively in the things that are around me now. I will never cease to mourn these losses. Why did I forget that not dying is not the same as being alive, and that not sleeping is still a long way from being awake. To be awake and to be alive are deeds, not states. And I did not *do* them!

[RMR to LAS, around September 15, entry in the Schmargendorf Diary]

You have written me just now: "Tolstoy has fallen seriously ill in Yasnaya Polyana." Perhaps we did bid him farewell. How clearly I see every moment of that day before me! What elation I felt as we drove through the wavy meadow with its trembling bells, journeying through the Russian landscape for the first time, the same way that Gogol and Pushkin journeyed, loudly with jangling harnesses and galloping steeds. And thus into the startled hamlet with eyes peering from all its weather-beaten doors. And thus out of the hamlet and down the road and up to the two white gate-towers that mark the entrance to the tall park. Our passage into its shadows is silent; we're anxious, we feel the weight of what's to come, and wish we could have this park and this day to ourselves without the old man toward whom all this is heading. And then we stand for a while in front of the white house inside of which everything remains silent, go around past the green oval bench and at last find someone in the courtyard next to the well. He takes our cards. We wait again. A dog, trusting and friendly, comes right up to us as we stand there in front of the small glass door. I bend down to the white dog and as I straighten up again I see behind the glass, vague and distorted by the flaws in the pane, a pair of searching eyes in a small grizzled face. The door opens, lets you in and slams sharply against me, so that I, only after the Count has already greeted you, come in and now also stand before him, feeling clumsily big beside his slim bright figure.

He leaves us alone with Lev Levovich and withdraws again into his study after this reception. Then I climb the wooden stairs behind you and step into the light-filled room where only the old oil paintings are dark. The table is long, narrow, covered in white, and a large silver-white samovar stands at its upper end. We sit down. There is very little in this large hall whose three windows receive shimmering reflections from the rich green of mighty trees. We inquire about the ancestral paintings. The oldest one is especially interesting. A nun from the time of Alexei Mikhailovich. Apparently painted by an icon maker, she all but replicates the character of St. Sophia in posture, integument, and the strongly conventional expression of her face. Only with her hands did the painter, the observer, come to life in the craftsman, and he painted these exactly, with realistic attention to his subject; in doing so he lost sight of the overall proportions, painted the hands accordingly bigger, and now this saintly woman bears the heavy weight of her earthly hands, with which she must be able to raise a very big prayer indeed. And yes, I remember, there was one of those fine "portraits" there. A powdered nobleman from the end of the eighteenth century, his clothes and the area around his face—with its black eyebrows and the witty mouth of that talkative era—turned completely dark. The frame made of old, grayed, silver-coated wood, oval and unornamented. This painting was oddly beautiful on the bright, cheerful wall of the long hall. Modern works were there as well: a sculpture by Ginsburg and the "Tolstoy" of Prince Trubetskoy. We spoke occasionally, drank coffee, and gazed out often into the sun-drenched day, where strangely nearby a bird snarled and called out *knarr-knarr* with a fierce *r*. We chatted about this bird for a while and finally followed it out into the park. So much was in bloom there. The avenue of old birch trees was shadowy and beautiful, and at the end of it there was a balcony that shook strongly under our steps. We gazed out fondly onto the landscape, which with its meadows of forget-me-nots was rippling calmly and ripely as if with waves. Far off the train went past, much too distant for the ear, and for the eye no more than a toy. Then we came back slowly along the path, carrying flowers and asking the names of many trees that were old and stately. From the back we walked up to the house again. In the entrance hall the Countess was busily putting books back into a window case, and we had to endure her annoyed welcome and all the displeasure she expressed out loud to someone invisible. What a harrowing half-hour that was in the small room with the walnut furniture! We examined books that lay behind glass and on top of cases, tried to concentrate on various portraits, but were really only listening for the footsteps of the Count, who walked into the entrance-hall. Something had happened: voices grew agitated, a girl wept, the Count consoled, in the midst of it all with complete indifference the Countess's voice going on . . . the sound of footsteps on the stairs, all doors in motion, and the Count walks in. Coldly and courteously he asks you something, his gaze is not really there with us, but its glance comes toward me and I hear the question: "What do you do?" I'm no longer sure, I seem to recall answering "I've written some things . . ."

August 27 until October 5: RMR in Worpswede, where he lives in Vogeler's Barkenhoff, a farmhouse with garden V. purchased and remodeled to his own art-nouveau designs. RMR quickly falls under the spell of the life there, and grows increasingly enamored of two artists his own age, Paula Becker (painter) and Clara Westhoff (sculptor), whom he elaborately "poetizes" (to use LAS's later word of warning) in his diaries. September 27: RMR, writing in his diary of a previous night's culminating moment: "It was then that I decided to stay in Worpswede." October 5: RMR abruptly departs from Worpswede in early dawn, without explanation or goodbyes, leaving behind for Paula Becker an evasive note and one of his pocket notebooks. He will not return until 1901, after his marriage to Clara. Back in Schmargendorf RMR moves into a new flat (Misdroyerstrasse 1) and renews his bond with LAS under strained circumstances.

November 12: Paula Becker informs RMR of her engagement to the much older Otto Modersohn, one of the original group of Worpswede painters.

December 19: RMR and LAS attend alone the dress rehearsal of Gerhart Hauptmann's Michael Kramer.

January 13: Paula Becker arrives in Berlin to take (at her father's insistence) a cooking class. She seeks RMR out and they begin to see each other regularly, especially on Sundays, which they reserve for one another.

February 3: Clara Westhoff arrives in Schmargendorf. The three play at being reunited, while RMR continues to see LAS, who increasingly feels him as an impediment to her own creative work.

February 16: RMR and Clara declare their engagement to Paula.

Late February: RMR informs LAS of his decision to marry Clara. LAS insists on a complete break, proposes that they destroy all letters they have exchanged. RMR fully complies.

[RMR, December 1, 1900, Entry in the Worpswede Diary]

Today I saw Gerhart Hauptmann for the first time. He and Vogeler were invited to Lou's. Grete M[arschalk] was with Hauptmann. It was a beautiful evening. . . . There was a conversation about the deaths of animals, about the ailing of some small defenseless rabbit or bird that one doesn't know how to help. I remarked that I always thought it unfair to accustom an animal to oneself, to persuade it, as it were, to enter into exchanges and friendship. It gradually gives in to trust, and the very moment it lacks the smallest something, we cannot but betray this trust, since we have no way of knowing the reason for the animal's distress or the meaning of its desires. What can we give it? We can train it to be close to us, coddle it with our own habits, i.e., play with it. The truly serious things that happen to it are beyond our help and involvement—has anyone really managed to share in the fate of his favorite pet like its friend and brother? We incur a guilt, a host of unredeemed pledges, and a perpetual failure: that is our portion in this exchange. And with people: there both parties bear equally this incapacity, and that makes their relationships more serious and deeper perhaps than a complete understanding of each other would allow.

[LAS, Diary, passages concerning RMR]

NEW YEAR'S EVE, 1900. Almost the only thing I want from the coming year, the thing I need, is quiet, —more being by myself, the way it was until four years ago. That will, that *must*, come back. For the rest, I look back today only on the *one* experience of 1900 for me, on Russia.

JANUARY 3, 1901. In the afternoon Rainer came and after lunch we walked out to the "Volga" on our forest path, which was already in moonlight on the way back. The evening hours upstairs in the blue garret, beside the lighted Christmas tree, the Songs of the Monk and the other Songs. After dinner downstairs, amidst table talk, the Nikolai Tolstoy material surged up irresistibly in me, —for the first time as a compelling whole: he had been slumbering there since the days of Novinki. Now it was as if after the last dying sounds of Christmas . . . Nikolai Tolstoy had appeared for a New Year's visit, with hat in hand, in order to fill me with pure New Year's happiness through the dawning of this material.

JANUARY 5. And today I waited for Rainer in the afternoon beside the lighted Christmas tree downstairs, next to which the red carnations are blooming today in their Christmas basket, almost as red as the early morning sun when it shines through the icy window panes.

JANUARY 9. Very early, after just the most pressing necessities had been taken care of, I began, proceeded as if I had neither the novella nor Michael Kramer around my neck, wrote grandly and freely and indulgently both title and beginning, pages long. Rainer came by in the light of morning, just as I was starting; outdoors an incredibly soft frost full of sun was everywhere, I ran into the woods, then in the dark of evening ran once again down the street. Now I shall sleep—with a bad conscience and a still completely unquenched desire for that wicked band [of characters in her novel *Rodinka*] on the other side of the wall. . . .

JANUARY 10. Yesterday morning late, Rainer and I out walking in the Grunewald amid soft, wondrous sun-frost; we encountered Gerhart Hauptmann and Grete, strolled on with them a long way. Day after tomorrow we'll be at Gerhart's. And this evening I'll begin the Michael Kramer piece.

But in the struggles with my work these days I've certainly been horrid sometimes at home. Afterwards I always feel terrible about it. I'd like to have oceans of love with which to extinguish it all. I'm a monster. (I was mean to Rainer too, but that never bothers me.)

JANUARY 17. Yesterday afternoon the door quietly opened again on my new year's gift: full of happiness the first episode written, am proceeding today from that. In the afternoon Rainer and I walked for over two hours in the woods; in the evening looked at "Russian Monuments."

JANUARY 20. Yesterday and today celebrated gloriously. Today toward evening everything for the most part blocked out and accomplished in large rapid strokes. Just as with a few dabs a painter marks the colors that have come to him. Later it all must run back together into the original nuances and thousand shadings, —if it does not die: when that happens one dabs paint on paint and it becomes a dead mosaic. But woe unto him who now would kill it for me. Outside rainy weather. To make Rainer go away, *go completely away,* I would be capable of brutality. *(He must go!)*

JANUARY 21. All day until evening still relished the breakthrough; then in the evening began to write the second chapter. Lied to R. when I had him told I wasn't home . . .

JANUARY 23. Yesterday, when Rainer was with us, read a section from Dostoevsky's "Poor Folk."

JANUARY 24. Yesterday Rainer said quite rightly of the great unconsummated work that defines Ivanov's life as an artist, the painting for which he created so many vivid, vigorous sketches: "this painting was like an epidemic; whoever happened to enter it died, no matter how radiantly he may have lived in the sketches." Ivanov was, like Gogol, one of those extraordinary beings about whom R. today came up with a wonderful phrase to explain why this kind of true Russian moves us so deeply: they must hold their ground "without weapons and without mimicry."

JANUARY 26. Yesterday finished the second chapter. Rainer and I took a long walk in the woods, two and a half hours long. . . . As we walked on, barefoot, quietly, we found deep in the overgrown forest an open place whose tangles of light-brown shriveled fern lay all about, like embers that had wafted down between the tree trunks, sun-embers. —About painters and Paula Becker's Worpswede diary: painters and sculptors must experience the same creative rushes of poetic, inspiriting emotions: but then, in order to create, they must fix rigorously and coldly and precisely on the "guilty object" that produced the rapture,—they must become like judges, like physicians, like craftsmen (this is what Rainer criticizes in women who paint and sculpt). . . .Toward evening further in our discussion of Benua: Victor Vasnetsov. His love (for Russian legend and religion) didn't help him, the way it helped Polyenova: "just as one can ruin a child by apishly dressing it up out of pure love for it." (R.) In the religious paintings I feel this so strongly that his paintings, which so want to be like icons, don't seem to have the icon at their roots at all, —rather on their surface as a kind of weak embellishment. R. said aptly: "he was a man already well along in years and with an old manner of loving, which he now simply clothed with new material." Thus he expressed this new material not in a new way, but in whatever way came to hand; had he attempted to wait, in order to give it just expression, then he would probably never have been able to give it to us at all. . . . Thus it is probably a mistake to follow Benua in considering Vasnetsov a highly complex intellect, when in reality his naiveté and a lack of critical discrimination have made him weak in confronting the dominant influences of his time.

[*There is a gap in the diary here: LAS at some later date destroyed the pages that cover the period from January 26 to March 21, 1901. The next existing page begins with the concluding fragment of an observation about Tolstoy, followed by: "21.3. A few black days because even the 'holidays' didn't bring back the rapture for work. Now the thing to do is at least get the last few hundred pages down on paper, in order to be able to come back to them later."*]

[LAS to RMR in Berlin]

[Schmargendorf, Tuesday, February 26, 1901]

Last Appeal.

Now that everything around me stands in pure sun and stillness and the fruit of life has grown perfectly round and full, a last responsibility devolves on me from that memory, which surely both of us must still cherish, of how in Wolfratshausen I entered your life like a mother. Let me then discharge as a mother the responsibility I incurred several years ago as the result of a long conversation with Zemek. As long as you are roaming about unattached in the realm of the uncertain, you are answerable to no one but yourself; but if you intend to commit yourself to another, then you must hear *why* I so tirelessly kept pointing you toward so precisely delineated a path to health: it was Zemek's fear of a fate that would be like Garshin's. What you and I called "the other one" in you—this now depressed, now overexcited, first much too fearful, then utterly carried-away You—to Zemek this was an all too familiar, sinister fellow who can take an ailing soul and prolong its sickness until it infects the spine's marrow or becomes insanity. *But this need not happen!* In your "Songs of the Monk," at certain earlier times, the past winter, this winter, you stood before me sound! Do you understand now my fear and my intense distress when you slipped back and I could see forming again the old clinical picture? Again the sluggish resolve alongside the sudden, nervous eruptions of will that tore through your organic being, gave in to every suggestion, and did not descend into the fullness of the past in order to assimilate things healthily, to digest them, to build up from the ground! Again the wavering uncertainty alongside the loud accents and strong words and protestations, manic compulsions without the compensating drive for truth! Gradually I myself became contorted, tortured, overstrained, only continued to walk by your side automatically, mechanically, could not put forth any vital warmth, expended only my own nervous energy! More and more often I would finally push you away—only to let you draw me back to your side again and again. For I kept remembering Zemek's dire words. I felt: you *would* recover, if only you could stand firm! But then another element entered—entered almost like a tragic culpability toward you: namely, the way that I, despite the difference in our ages, since Wolfratshausen have had to continue growing, —growing on and on, into what I told you about so joyously at our parting, —yes, strange as it sounds: *into my youth!* For only now am I young, only now may I be what others become at their eighteenth birthday: completely myself. And thus your figure—in Wolfratshausen still so cherished and close and clearly before me, —kept fading and fading from me like a small separate piece in an overall landscape, —in a vast Volga landscape, as it were, and the one tiny hut in it was not yours. I was obeying without realizing it the great plan of life, which was smiling and already holding in readiness for me a gift beyond all understanding and expectation. With deep humility I accept it: and know now with a seer's clarity, and call to you: take the same path toward your dark god! He can provide what I can no longer provide for you, —and for so long have not been able to provide with full dedication: the grace to reach sun and ripeness. Across the farthest distances I send this appeal to you, I can do no more than this to protect you from that "worst hour" of which Zemek spoke. That is why I was so moved when as we parted I wrote down the last words on a scrap of your paper, *because I couldn't make myself say them to you out loud: I meant every one of those words.**

May 1901: LAS renews her relationship with the Viennese neurologist Friedrich Pineles ("Zemek" in her "Last Appeal"), who watches over her slow recovery from an almost traumatic exhaustion and its lingering psychological consequences. They openly become lovers, and for nearly a decade he remains devoted to her, as her "therapist" and her companion on frequent, often extended trips—their last and

*"If one day much later you feel yourself in dire straits, there is a home here with us for the worst hour." [Words written hastily on the reverse side of Rilke's bill for milk deliveries.]

longest one in August 1908 through the Balkans to Turkey. For the next half-decade LAS also travels widely on her own, including trips to St. Petersburg to see her aging mother.

October 1903: Andreas is appointed to an "extraordinary" professorship for West Asian languages at the University of Göttingen. He and LAS move into a large house on the Hainberg overlooking the city. She christens it Loufried; it will remain her permanent home for the rest of her life.

April 18, 1901: RMR and Clara Westhoff marry in Bremen. They spend their honeymoon in the Weisser Hirsch, an exclusive sanitarium near Dresden (RMR was still recovering from an illness, either influenza or scarlet fever), then (end of May 1901) move into a farmhouse in Westerwede, near Worpswede, where they will live, with only brief trips elsewhere, through the summer of 1902.

December 12, 1901: Their daughter Ruth is born.

June 1902: Unable to make ends meet in Westerwede, RMR secures a commission to write a monograph on Rodin and departs for Paris. After a five-week stopover in Haseldorf Castle, he arrives in Paris on August 28, 1902. Clara remains behind to dissolve their Westerwede estate, then leaves Ruth with her parents in Oberneuland near Bremen and joins RMR in Paris in early October.

End of March 1903: RMR leaves Paris for a brief stay in Viareggio, where he had previously gone to "recuperate" from Florence; Clara remains in Paris, at work on a commission. RMR returns toward the end of April; he and Clara remain in Paris until the end of June 1903, when they accept an invitation from Heinrich Vogeler to visit him and his wife in Westerwede.

July 1, 1903: Clara and RMR leave Paris; their residence alternates between the Vogelers at Westerwede and Clara's parents at Oberneuland until the end of August, when they depart for Italy.

September 1903 through the first half of June 1904: Clara and RMR together in Rome.

[RMR to LAS in Berlin-Westend]

Paris
3, rue de l'Abbé de l'Epée
June 23, 1903

For weeks I have wanted to write these words and dared not for fear that it might still be much too soon; but who knows if in the worst hour I will be *able* to come.

This summer I will be in Germany during July and August (most likely in Worpswede).

If sometime during this period I might once, just for a single day, seek refuge with you two! I don't know if this is possible.

But if it cannot be, then may I ask this favor: will you have delivered to me (perhaps by Johanna Niemann) the address of Dr. Pineles? I will be in Paris until July 1, and will receive either news with equal gratitude.

Rainer.

[LAS to RMR in Paris]

Westend near Berlin
Rüsternallee 36
June 27, 1903

Dear Rainer,

You may stay with us any time, in difficult as in good hours. And yet I propose: let us in this case first reunite in writing. For two old scribblers like us there would be nothing artificial in proceeding this way; and whatever you want to talk to me about, it will come to me exactly as it came once before to

Lou.

[RMR to LAS in Berlin-Westend]

Paris, 3 rue de l'Abbé de l'Epée
last day of June, 1903

I thank you, Lou, for this little letter that I can read for hours as I would a very long one. A soothing power issues from it, and I take it in with all my senses. There is also in it that kindness by which I would recognize you among thousands.

I thank you.

So I may write to you now, and there is so much I would like to tell you: for so much has happened. When I look back, my life seems to me to have lengthened by so many more years than have actually passed. And yet I have not become older, not more adept at daily life and certainly not more proficient. I am still in the kindergarten of life and find it difficult.

I won't complain, and it's really no great effort not to. Many things have had me in their grip, and their instruction has at least simplified me a bit and made me more patient.

And that a young person who has allied her life with mine matures next to me and along with me in her work—this also is part of my learning. And that Ruth lives, our little child—amidst separation and foreignness this gives me a sense of home, brings me closer to all that happens with spontaneous directness, closer to the trees and the things and the animals about which I know so much more now.

Once upon a time the three of us lived in a very solitary house in the moors, and the winds circled around its walls and the night came like a world. Then we had to leave all that and go to the big city where Rodin lived: for we wanted to learn from him how to work. We wanted to have nothing but work, and wanted to be two people who stood by their work and felt peaceful and didn't fret about their life in common.

About that time I wrote a book on Rodin, a good book. And then I resolved to be hard on myself, resolved to immerse myself in work for long, silent stretches; and I felt such exasperation each time I failed in that.

The city was against me, in revolt against my life and like a test I didn't pass. Its unrelenting scream broke into my silence, its fearsomeness followed me all the way into my sad room, and my eyes lay pressed beneath the images of its days. And then came illness: three attacks of influenza with long feverish nights and great dread: and my strength and my courage had dwindled to practically nothing and I went away with the last vestige of them, went through many heavy mountains, went for the length of a lifetime and arrived one evening in Viareggio.

And it was quiet there. And the girls in those songs I call "Mädchenlieder" walked through the narrow streets, singing and silent, and were as they had always been. And the sea was vast and the forest was solitary and the people recognized me and said to me with friendly smiles: "*Signorino*, young gentleman."

But I recovered slowly. And when I did feel better and even began to chime a little, various painful conditions came which I attributed to my imagination, to a perverse ingenuity flitting about my body like a will-o'-the-wisp, and I fought against them with all my will. And I partially overcame them. But then something so fearful came, came once and came back and never completely left again, and I am at a loss to say what it was.

Long ago in my childhood, during the great fevers of my illnesses, huge indescribable fears arose, fears as of something too big, too hard, too close, deep unspeakable fears that I can still remember, and now these same fears were suddenly there again, but they didn't need night and fever as a pretext, they gripped me in the midst of day when I thought I was healthy and full of courage, and took my heart and held it over nothingness. Can you understand what that is like? Everything changes, melts away from my senses and I feel thrust out of a world where everything is familiar and close and meaningful into another vague, inexpressibly fearful world. Where am I? Then it was as if I wouldn't recognize anyone who might enter my room and as if I in turn would be a stranger to everyone who might see me, like someone who had died in foreign lands, alone, superfluous, a fragment of different connections.

And my apprehension was very great.

And the fear arose in me that my worst hour might lie in that other world from which I can come to no one.

In the days just after I had come back from Italy, this strange condition returned frequently and I had no resistance against it. Then there was a longer interval, a new attack of influenza from which I recovered only very slowly, a brief happier period of convalescence, all kinds of fresh starts with my work, —until it came back again the other night. (When it comes, I would like to cling to some one, most real thing; but nothing is real enough, everything withdraws, gives me up, goes away . . .)

The next morning I wrote you that letter by way of Johanna Niemann. Forgive me for coming into your clear days with my worries. But I can't ask anyone for advice but you; you alone know who I am. Only you can help me, and I feel already from your first letter what power your calm words have over me. You can make me understand what baffles me, you can tell me what I need to do; you know what I *should* be afraid of and what I shouldn't—: *Should* I be afraid?—

Perhaps I am exaggerating: perhaps the occasion is too slight and I shouldn't have bothered you with my distress. Perhaps it is only a consequence of this fearsome and difficult city for which I was too weak and self-pitying: perhaps it is a reflection of those fears that arose from our poverty: there were so many of them, during our stay in Westerwede and here, where poverty and perishing are so much alike . . . You will be able to judge. Perhaps not from this letter, which is confused and hurried (my hand is shaking from the joy of being able to write you—), but from other letters that I want to write you out of a greater quietness, when I am away from Paris and have green in front of my windows and a bird's voice that gathers up the distances outside.

I am writing as I pack, and that itself is an arduous task, since I have lived here almost a year. But in three or four days we'll be in Worpswede, as guests of Heinrich Vogeler, who has prepared a few rooms for us and with whom we plan to stay for two months. We would have preferred to go elsewhere, into an entirely unfamiliar quietness that evokes no memories; but we had no choice and had to accept what offered itself. And this offered itself in a friendly, heartfelt manner.

And there, where a quiet garden exists and gentle, unvarying days, I will write you occasionally and tell you of many things and ask you whenever I don't understand something. And then, when you gaze into my life again, tell me if it is good.

Don't be afraid that I'll come too often with unimportant matters. And at any rate you must tell me if you think I am writing too much. And every word from you will mean much to me and echo and live with me for a long time.

And now I send many greetings to you both and much, much gratitude.

Is it quiet out there in the new avenues of Westend? I remember them. I saw them once in the spring—many things were blooming, and the green was bright and clear and let the sun through. It will be that way again now. Here, though, all the trees are old and black already, and even though they drink water all day from long tubular roots their leaves are sick and rotten as if hanging there from a previous year. And all of that inspires fear if one does not actively refuse it.

And refusing is hard.

Goodbye, Lou. Thank you. I know that everything will be better now that I can talk to you and you will hear me. Thank you.

Rainer.

(Does Schimmel recognize this letter's smell? —My next address will be the German one; simply: Worpswede near Bremen.)

[LAS to RMR in Paris]

Westend, Rüsternallee 36
July 5, 1903

Dear Rainer,

No need to fear. The recurrence of influenza may be entirely to blame for these latest attacks: children as well as adults have been known to suffer afterwards the most severe depressions and the strangest mental states.

Here's my suggestion: every time it happens, write about how you feel and what's tormenting you—write it out of your system, as it were; this in itself may generate some curative strength. And perhaps also the thought: that your letters come to a person who is at home in happiness. For even I, Rainer, never possessed any strength other than the one that resides in all happiness.

In your letter I could see much of your old self.

My husband sends you his greetings and wants you to know: I alone will read and keep whatever you write me.

Schimmelchen got to sniff the inside of your envelope, but it was impossible to judge from his reaction, since at the same time he was preoccupied with a bluebottle. He and the two of us live in a house with garden, both quite small; our avenue, the last one here, connects us with the rest of the village and its avenues but then leads straight into the forest that surrounds us on three sides and is much wilder than the woods in Schmargendorf.

One request, one piece of advice: break off your relation with Johanna Niemann. It's a mistake.

I have only just returned from Russia!

Lou

[RMR to LAS in Berlin-Westend]

Worpswede near Bremen
July 13, 1903
Monday

You, dear Lou, say that I need not fear and therefore I will try not to fear. We have been in Worpswede for a week; but I have not had a chance yet to thank you for your good letter that was such a joy; for it was an evil week.

I have been constantly beset by pain and dwell always in adversity. My physical afflictions may have the same cause as my fears. Both are probably due to irregularities in the circulation of my blood, which can cause abnormal mental states or send pain toward one or another part of the body. Most recently the torment was in my head: first it was an unbearable toothache that lasted for days, then it turned into a stabbing pain in my eyes, and finally settled in as pharyngitis with dull feverish feeling (much like the attacks of influenza last spring); and my time was spent in a continual struggle to resist. I tried steam baths, took up walking barefoot again, which I had missed so much in Paris, and in this way dragged myself from one day into the next. And they were long rainy days, and at first I had a damp, cold room behind tall trees and I hated staying in it and when I went out and saw things and people, that proved difficult too and everything was cause for melancholy. Today I feel a little better; and if I can remain like this I shall be content, especially since Heinrich Vogeler has now given me the little red room too, the one with a bright window facing south. In all these years I've scarcely ever had a quiet room, and I feel this room that no one enters as what I've been looking for: solitude. But Barkenhoff is no longer as quiet as it once was. Vogeler's blond wife is due to give birth to their second child and pale little Marie-Luise Vogeler twitters about in the garden. She is the same age as Ruth but much frailer and more prone to sickness.

We will also be seeing Ruth again. She lives two hours from here on a country estate with my wife's parents. As soon as I am a little better we are going to visit Oberneuland for a week—with great trepidation, for the circumstances there are such that all sorts of tension and agitation are bound to arise, and that is precisely what I am afraid of right now. But I am convinced that only there is a good reunion with our child possible. Seeing her there will allow us to blend in (even if only for a few days) with the quiet good life she has there without the risk of frightening her or otherwise displeasing her. If she has any recollection of us, she will recognize us and feel affection for us most quickly if she finds us, like something lost, among her everyday and familiar things. I don't want to leave again without this reunion, even if it is virtually simultaneous with a new farewell. I need a happiness and I want to experience and hold onto this as happiness; and where else should I seek a happiness that is *mine.*

But perhaps above all I need quiet. I will sit here for long stretches in my room and walk barefoot up and down in the garden in my blue Russian shirt. And try my hand at some work. A translation of *Слово о полку Игоря* was begun back in Paris; perhaps it will grow here. Right now writing is hard for me, as you can see from this letter, which wished to bring you much and is unable to bear anything. And I want so much to write you about many things and ask you about many things. Well, I must wait patiently for an hour when words will be easier to write. Then I'll try to give you a better account of myself, if you'll allow it. And thank you, dear Lou, for writing me and telling me about the little house and about the little garden and about Russia; and in all of that about you.

Rainer.

[RMR to LAS in Berlin-Westend]

Worpswede near Bremen
July 18, 1903

I must tell you, dear Lou, that Paris was an experience for me not unlike that of the military school: for just as then a great fearful astonishment had seized me, so now I was gripped by terror at everything that, as if in some unspeakable confusion, is called life. Back then, as a boy among boys, I was alone among them; and now how alone I was among these people, how perpetually denied by all I encountered; the carriages drove straight through me, and those in a rush made no detour around me and ran over me full of disdain, as over a bad place in which stale water has collected. And often before going to sleep I read the thirtieth chapter of the Book of Job, and it was all true of me, word for word. And at night I got up and looked for my favorite volume of Baudelaire, the *petits poèmes en prose*, and read aloud the most beautiful poem, the one titled *À une heure du matin.* Do you know it? It begins: *Enfin! seul! On n'entend plus que le roulement de quelques fiacres attardés et éreintés. Pendant quelques heures, nous posséderons le silence, sinon le repos. Enfin! la tyrannie de la face humaine a disparu, et je ne souffrirai plus que par moi-même. . . .* And it ends magnificently: rises, stands, and strides off like a prayer. A prayer of Baudelaire's; a real, unpolished prayer, shaped by the hands, artless and beautiful like the prayer of a Russian. —He had to go a long way to reach that poem, did Baudelaire, and he went there on his knees and crawling. How far away from me he was in everything: of all my forebears perhaps the most alien; often I can barely understand him and yet sometimes deep at night, when I said his words after him like a child, he was the person closest to me and lived next to me and stood palely on the other side of the thin wall and listened to my voice falling. What a strange unity existed between us then, a sharing of everything, the same poverty and perhaps the same fear.

Oh a thousand hands have been building at my fear and it has grown from a remote village into a city a huge sprawling city in which unutterable things happen. It has been growing the entire time and has taken the quiet green out of my feeling, which no longer bears anything. Even in Westerwede it was growing and whole houses and streets arose from the fearful circumstances and hours that passed there. And when Paris came, it quickly took on huge proportions. In August of last year I arrived there. It was the time when the trees in the city are withered without autumn, when the burning streets, stretched by the heat, go on and on and one walks through smells as through many melancholy rooms. Then I walked past the long hospitals whose gates stood wide open with a gesture of impatient and greedy compassion. The first time I passed by the Hotel Dieu an open carriage was just entering, with a person dangling limply inside it, jostled by every movement, askew like a broken marionette, and with a terrible abscess on his long, gray, dangling neck. And what people I have encountered since then, almost daily! Ruins of caryatids upon which an entire suffering still rested, an entire edifice of suffering, beneath which they lived slowly like tortoises. And they were passers-by among passers-by, ignored and undisturbed in their fate. At most one caught them as momentary impressions and observed them with calm, detached curiosity like some new species of animal in which abjectness had developed special organs, organs for starving and dying. And they wore the comfortless, discolored mimicry of cities grown too large, and they endured under the foot of each day that stepped on them, like tough beetles—endured as if there was still something to wait for, twitched like pieces of a large chopped-up fish that is already rotting but still alive. They lived, lived on nothing, on dust, on soot and on the filth smeared on their surfaces, on what falls from the teeth of dogs, on any senselessly broken thing for which some buyer might still have some inexplicable use. O what kind of world is this! Pieces, pieces of people, parts of animals, remnants of things that once functioned, and all of it still astir, as though they were being driven about in an uncanny wind, carried and carrying, falling and overtaking one another in their fall.

There were old women who set a heavy basket down on some ledge in a wall (short little women whose eyes were drying up like puddles), and when they were ready to pick it back up, there slid slowly and ceremoniously out of their sleeve a long rusty hook, not a hand, and it reached inexorably for the handle of the basket. And there were other old women who walked about with a drawer from some old night-table in their hands and showed everyone that rolling around inside it were twenty rusty pins they had to sell. And once late in autumn a little old woman stood beside me one evening in the light of a shop window. She stood very still, and I thought that like me she was busy looking at the things displayed for sale, and so I scarcely paid her any mind. Finally, though, her presence began to make me uneasy, and, I don't know why, I suddenly looked down at her oddly clasped, worn-away hands. Very, very slowly an old, long, thin pencil emerged from those hands, it grew taller and taller and took a very long time to become completely visible, visible in all its wretchedness. I can't say exactly what it was that made this scene so terrible, but it seemed to me as if a whole destiny were being played out before me, a long destiny, a catastrophe that was building up fearfully to the moment when the pencil would cease growing and, trembling ever so slightly, topple out of the loneliness of those empty hands. Finally I understood that I was supposed to buy it . . .

And then those women who hurry past one in long velvet cloaks from the eighties, with paper roses on obsolescent hats beneath which their hair hangs down as if melted together into a single mass. And all those people, men and women, who are undergoing some transition, perhaps from madness toward healing, but perhaps also toward complete insanity; all of them with something infinitely sensitive in their faces, with a love, a knowledge, a joy, as with a light that burns only the slightest bit dimly and restlessly and could so easily be restored to full clarity if only someone would notice and help. . . . But there is no one to help. No one to help those who as yet are only the tiniest bit perplexed, frightened, intimidated; those who are only just beginning to read things differently from the way they are meant; those who are still dwelling in the very same world as always, except that they walk a bit crookedly and thus sometimes think that things are hanging over them; those who aren't at home in cities and get lost in them as in an evil forest that goes on forever—; all those whom affliction visits every day, all those who cannot hear their wills working in the noise, all those over whom fear has grown, —why does no one help them in the big cities?

Where are they going when they come so quickly through the streets? Where do they sleep, and when they cannot sleep, what transpires before their melancholy eyes? What do they think about when they sit all day long in the open gardens with their heads sunk over their clasped hands which have come together as if from far away in order to hide in each other? And what kind of words do they say to themselves when their lips summon up the strength to work? Do they still weave real words? . . . Are they still speaking sentences, or is everything crowding and shoving out of them now in total confusion as out of a burning theater, everything in them that was spectator and player, hero and audience? Do none of them realize that inside them a childhood is getting lost, a strength is beginning to sicken, a love is falling?

Oh, Lou, I have tormented myself like this day after day. For I understood all those people, and though I detoured around them in a wide arc, they had no secret from me. I was wrenched out of myself into their lives, right through all their lives, through all their heavy laden lives. I often had to say to myself out loud, "I am not one of them, eventually I am going to leave this horrible city where they will die"; I said it to myself and felt that there was no deception in it. And yet when I noticed how my clothes were becoming dirtier and heavier from week to week and saw how they had become frayed in many places, I grew frightened and felt that I would belong irretrievably to the lost if some passerby were merely to look at me and half unconsciously count me among their number. The slightest disapproving glance could sentence me to life down among them. And wasn't I really one of them, since I was poor like them and full of protest against everything that occupied and uplifted and deceived and deluded the other people? Didn't I deny everything around me that was valued, —and wasn't I actually homeless, despite the semblance of a room in which I was as much a stranger as if I had been sharing it with someone totally unknown? Didn't I go hungry, just like them, at tables laden with food that I couldn't bring myself to touch, because it wasn't pure and simple like the food I preferred? And wasn't I set apart, just like them, from the majority around me by the simple fact that I didn't have any wine in me or any other deluding drink? Wasn't I clear just like those solitary ones who are dimmed only on the outside by the haze and the heaviness of the city and the laughter that comes like thick smoke from the evil fires that it keeps stoking? Nothing was so little like laughter as the laughter of those estranged creatures: when they laughed, it sounded as though something were falling inside them, falling and smashing to bits and filling them up with shattered fragments. They were not funny but deep; and their depth reached out for me like the force of gravity and drew me down toward the center of their misery.

What good was it that some mornings I got up happier and went out in higher spirits and felt capable of a quiet productive day? . . . Once (it was quite early in the morning) I came down the Boulevard St. Michel feeling this way, my destination the Bibliothèque Nationale, where I used to spend a great deal of time. I walked along delighting in all the freshness, clarity, and courage that the morning and the beginning of a new day scatter about even in a city. The red on the carriage wheels was as moist and cool as it is on flower petals, and somewhere at the end of the street someone was carrying something—I didn't ask myself what—that was a wonderful bright green. The water wagons drove slowly uphill and the water leapt out of their pipes young and clear and made the street dark so that it didn't blind one anymore. Horses came by in shimmering harnesses, and their hooves clattered like a hundred hammers. The cries of the vendors had a different ring: they rose more lightly and echoed high above. And the vegetables on their handcarts were stirring like a little field and had a free morning all their own above them and within them darkness, greenness, and dew. And when it was quiet for a moment, one heard overhead the sound of windows being pushed open . . .

Then I was suddenly struck by the odd behavior of the people coming toward me: most of them walked for a while with their heads turned backward, so that I had to be careful not to collide with them; there were also some who had stopped, and by following their gazes I came upon a slender man in black among the people walking ahead of me. As he strode along he kept grabbing his overcoat collar—which apparently, to his great annoyance, insisted on standing up—and folding it back down with both hands. Absorbed in this effort, which was causing him visible strain, he repeatedly forgot to watch where he was walking and stumbled or hopped hastily over some small obstacle. When this had happened a few times in quick succession he turned his attention back to walking, but it was strange when after two or three steps he tripped again and hopped over something. I had quickened my pace without realizing it and now found myself close enough behind the man to see that the movements of his feet had nothing at all to do with the sidewalk, which was smooth and even, and that he was only trying to deceive those coming toward him when he turned around after each stumble as if to cast blame on some guilty object. In reality there was nothing to be seen. Meanwhile, the clumsiness in his gait slowly abated, and he hurried on quite quickly now and for a time went unnoticed. But suddenly the disquiet began again in his shoulders, it drew them up twice and then dropped them so that they hung down from him crooked and awry as he walked on. Then I could scarcely believe what my eyes had seen: his left hand shot up to his collar with indescribable speed, seized it almost imperceptibly and flipped it up, after which he expended much visible effort trying with both hands to get the collar to lie down again—a task he accomplished, as before, only with great difficulty. All the while he kept nodding to the front and to the left, stretching his neck and nodding, nodding, nodding behind his busy upraised hands, as if now his shirt collar were also starting to cause him trouble and there were work to be done up there for a long time yet. Finally everything seemed to be in order again. He walked some ten steps completely unobserved when all of a sudden his shoulders began twitching up and down again; at the same moment a waiter who was cleaning up in front of a café stopped and gazed curiously at this passer-by, who unexpectedly shook himself, halted, and then resumed his walking in little hops. The waiter laughed and shouted something into the shop, so that several more faces became visible behind the windowpanes. But in the meantime the strange man had hooked his cane onto his shirt collar from behind, and now, as he walked on, he kept it that way, so that it hung straight down, directly over his spine; it was relatively inconspicuous, and seemed to support him. The new position calmed him considerably, and for a moment he walked on relieved. No one paid any attention to him except for me—and I couldn't take my eyes off him for a second. I knew how the disquiet was returning bit by bit, how it was growing stronger and stronger, how it was trying first in one place, then in another to find expression, how it shook at his shoulders, how it grasped at his head in order to jerk it out of kilter, and how it suddenly descended without warning on his stride and destroyed it. As yet this was scarcely noticeable; it took place in short intervals, silently and almost secretly, but it was there already, and it was growing. I felt this whole man filling up with disquiet, felt this pent-up disquiet increasing, felt it mounting, and I saw his will, his fear, and the desperate expression of his convulsive hands pressing the cane against his spine as though trying to make it a part of his helpless body, in which lay the incitement to a thousand dances. And I witnessed how this cane grew into something crucial, something upon which a great deal depended: all the strength of this man and his entire will entered it and made it into a Power, into a Being which could perhaps come to his aid and to which the sick man clung with wild belief. A god came into being here and his world rose up against him. But while this war was being waged, the man who had to bear it was trying to walk casually on, and for a few moments he succeeded in looking harmless and ordinary. Now he was crossing the Place St. Michel, and though weaving through the rush of carriages and pedestrians would have been ample excuse for the most contorted movements, he remained utterly composed, and there was even a strangely rigid calm throughout his body when he stepped onto the sidewalk of the bridge beyond. By now I was close behind him, without a will of my own, drawn along by his fear that was no longer distinguishable from my own. Suddenly the cane gave way, right in the middle of the bridge. The man stood: stood there extraordinarily still and rigid and didn't move. Now he was waiting; but it was as if the enemy inside him didn't yet trust this surrender. He hesitated—but only for a moment. Then he erupted like a fire, out of all the windows at once. And a dance began. . . . A dense circle of people that had quickly formed started pushing me gradually back, until I could no longer see him. My knees shook, and I was emptied of everything. I stood for a while leaning against the railing of the bridge, and then finally went back to my room; there was no longer any reason to go to the Bibliothèque. What book could have been strong enough to help me get past what was inside me? I was as if consumed, utterly used up; as if another person's fear had fed on me and exhausted me—that's how I felt.

And there were many mornings like that—and many evenings too. Had I been able to *make* these fears I underwent, had I been able to shape things out of them, real, steadfast things that are bliss and freedom to create and that, once created, stand there quietly and exude reassurance, then nothing would have befallen me. But these fears that were my daily portion stirred a hundred other fears, and they arose in me and against me and banded together and I could not get beyond them. In striving to form them I became creative *for* them; instead of making them into things of my will I gave them a life of their own, and they turned that life against me and used it to pursue me far into the night. Had it been better with me, been quieter and friendlier, had my room stood by me, and if I had remained in better health, then I might have succeeded even so: succeeded in making things out of fear.

Once I did succeed, if only for a short time. When I was in Viareggio—yes, the fears broke loose there too, even more so than before, overwhelm-ingly so. And the sea that was never silent was too much for me and buried me under the crashing of its spring waves. And yet it came. Prayers came into being there, Lou, a Book of Prayers. I have to tell *you* this, because my first Prayers rest in your hands—those Prayers I have so often thought of and clung to from afar. Because they resound so deeply and because they are so much at peace with you [*in the margin*: and because only you and I know of them]—that is why I could cling to them. And perhaps one day I might be allowed to come and place the new ones, the Prayers that have since come into being, with the others, with you, in your hands, in your quiet house.

For I am a stranger and a pauper. And I shall pass. But your hands shall hold everything that once might have been my home, had I only been stronger.

Rainer.

Lou, have you seen my two books yet, the one about Worpswede and the one on Rodin's work? Would you like to leaf through them? And is there a new book by you? May I read it?

[LAS to RMR in Worpswede]

[Westend near Berlin,] Rüsternallee 36
July 22, 1903

Dear Rainer,

As I read your last letter there were moments when what you described made such an impact on me, came alive through the smallest physical detail and yet grew beyond it into the tremendously human, that I forgot about *you* completely. And I felt that odd process of "ensouling" that can emanate even from impressions of misery when they come not just straight from life but channeled through the life of that person creating them, transmuting them. For you are wrong when you say that you merely suffered through all these things as a helpless accessory without repeating them in some higher process. They are all *there*: no longer only in you, now also in me, and external to both of us as living things with a voice all their own, —no different from any Song that ever came to you.

Those "who labor and are heavy laden": now they have you as their poet. How I wish I could express adequately the twofold impression this reunion with you makes on me! On the one hand it reminds me of those impressions of you from the farthest past—those from the days even before Wolfratshausen, for instance, and from those first years when you were still suffering so much physical pain; I can well understand that you yourself, in the context of Paris, found yourself thinking all the way back to your time in the military school: to those most faraway moods. On the other hand it feels to me just the opposite: as though you were now standing already where even in the best subsequent times you have only occasionally stood: undivided from yourself. That something could so continually oppose you without eventually breaking you down is testimony to the heightened resistance of a united, concentrated sensibility. In previous times of recuperation, of transition and inner strengthening, you were repeatedly at risk of being carried away by your own sense of power, and squandering yourself on more trivial enthusiasms, on things of pure chance. As your strength grew, it lost track, so to speak, of its deepest object, —rather than bending down, like an adult to a child, toward the impressions arising from the earlier, more helpless world of experience, in order to lead them all upward into the light, clothed in its most difficult memories as in genius for everything that has ever suffered.

It was at heart only this one feeling I was expressing—simplistically and awkwardly, to be sure—when I sometimes told you: out of those terrible times in the military school one day *your work* shall come. Now it *has* come: the poet in you creates poetry out of man's fears. Don't imagine that this might just as easily have been possible at some other place or time! It takes so much courage and humility; you would have let more superficial things distract you, and you would have seen misery in a falsified way. To take an example: the man in Paris, the one walking about struggling against St. Vitus's dance—you would have taken on something of him, poetically and psychologically speaking, by being in his company, and you would have observed things in the manner of a St. Vitus's dancer: *now you describe him*. But only in your doing so does the martyrdom of his condition open up in you, seize you with the clarity of insight, —and what then truly distinguishes you from him is the very *power* with which you experience it along with him, a power that is without any of the mitigating self-deceptions of the primary sufferer. In this respect one may speak of a "justificatory suffering" of the artist, while all the other sufferers around him, whom he helps to resurrection, "know not what they do."

That one "most real thing" which in your recent letter you said you wished you could cling to when inner fears drive everything away from you and seem to leave you abandoned to an alien world, —you already have it inside you, that one real thing, planted there like a hidden seed and thus not yet present to you. You possess it now in this sense: you have become like a little plot of earth into which all that falls—and be it even things mangled and broken, things thrown away in disgust—must enter an alchemy and become food to nourish the buried seed. No matter if at first it looks like a pile of sweepings thrown out over the soul: it all turns to loam, becomes *you*. You have never been closer to the health you wish for than now!

Here it is very quiet and peaceful: a little squirrel that has strayed out of the forest is sitting on an old tall linden tree in our garden, and beneath him sits Schimmel, staring up perfectly still, as if hypnotized. Yes, do send me the "Worpswedians" and Rodin!

Lou.

[RMR to LAS in Berlin-Westend]

currently Oberneuland near Bremen
July 25, 1903.

Your letter, Lou, has followed me here from Worpswede. I received it yesterday morning, and little Ruth was with me when I first read it. I have read it often since, walking up and down in the garden, and each time I received it again, absorbed it like something new, unhoped-for, like a thing good beyond all measure. To those who were in the desert, this is how the birds came and brought bread; perhaps they found food in themselves, in the depths of their own anguish and solitude, but they didn't know it until the strange bird arrived with the little loaf of bread, as with the outward sign of the inner sustenance on which they had been living . . . In the same way your voice comes to me with its great approbation, which I may not deserve; for, Lou, all that experience from the time before Wolfratshausen, as you also sense, is strong in me, and I fear I am not master over it yet. The great daily encounter with so much suffering, the revelation of downfall and ruin that I received in Paris, was perhaps still too much for me and swept over my will like a wave. I could write about it to *you*, because I have so strong a desire to spread myself out before you, that you might survey me and better know me. But it was only a letter. And as yet nothing has taken shape from it, as yet no one thing stands there and testifies on my behalf; will it ever come? It is as if whatever I truly receive falls too deeply into me, falls, falls for years, and in the end I lack the strength to lift it out of me and I walk about fearfully with my heavily laden depths and never reach them. Yes, I know that impatience warps all those processes and transformations that take their course in darkness as in heart-chambers; and I know that in patience lies everything: humility, strength, measure. But life moves on and is like a day, and whoever wished to be patient would need a thousand such days, though perhaps not even one is given him. Life moves on, and it strides past many in the distance, and around those waiting it makes a detour. And thus my wish to be someone working rather than waiting, someone standing at the center of his work's workshop far into every day's dawn. And yet I cannot be, because almost nothing in me has reached fruition, or else I am not aware of it and let my far-away harvests grow old and outlive their time. There is still nothing but confusion in me; what I experience is like pain and what I truly perceive hurts. I don't seize the image: it presses into my hand with its pointed tips and sharp edges, presses deep into my hand and almost against my will: and whatever else I would grasp slides off me, is like water and flows elsewhere once it has mirrored me absent-mindedly. What should he do, Lou, who grasps so little about life, who must let it happen to him and comes to realize that his own willing is always slighter than another great will into whose current he oftentimes chances like a thing drifting downstream? What should he do, Lou, for whom the books in which he wants to read only draw open like heavy doors which the next wind will slam shut again? What should he do for whom people are just as difficult as books, just as superfluous and strange, because he cannot derive from them what he needs, because he cannot select from them and thus takes from them what is crucial and incidental and burdens himself with both? What should such a person do, Lou? Should he remain utterly alone and accustom himself to a life lived among *things*, which are more like him and place no burden on him?

Yes, Lou, I too believe that the experiences of the past few years have been good for me, that whatever came to me pressed me more firmly into myself and no longer scattered me as so often before; I am now more tightly knit, and there are fewer pores in me, fewer interstices that fill up and swell when things not my own penetrate.

And yet no one can depend on me: my little child must live with strangers, my young wife, who also has her work, needs others to provide for her instruction, and I myself am of no use anywhere and acquire nothing. And even though those closest to me, who are directly affected, never reproach me for this, the reproach is there nonetheless and the house in which I am just now staying is filled with it everywhere. And thus resistance becomes necessary again and self-control and fending-off, and strength dissipates and fear issues from all things.

And then I often feel as if this were true in every sense—as if, being as I am, I can neither provide for nor protect the two people (the little child and the adult) who are joined with me in this life. For I know so little and have learned badly how to care and scarcely at all how to help. And as far as I myself am concerned, I have so much work day and night that I am sometimes almost hostile toward those close to me when they intrude on me, even though they have a perfect right to me. And from one person to another everything is so difficult and untested and without precedent and example, and one would have to live in every relationship with full attention, poised to be creative at any instant that requires a new response and imposes tasks and questions and demands . . .

At least now we have seen our little girl again. She lives here in Oberneuland with my wife's parents, who for many years have rented a large old farmstead. A tall white house with a thatched roof stands there in a garden, or more precisely in a section of the park with very tall trees, stretches of meadow, and paths that curve slowly into the dark. And the wind enters from the broad meadows and brings distance and scent and makes the garden larger than it is. Ruth is growing up there. And is outside almost all the time and without clothes and, like a child from some savage tribe, secure in her uninhibited nakedness. And when she does put clothes on they are very simple ones, like those the children in Millet's paintings wear, work clothes, appropriate for the things she does, the continuous small labor of going about and grasping that fills her days from one end to the other.

When we arrived here, we at first tried to be very quiet and like inanimate things, and Ruth would sit and gaze at us for long spells. Her serious, dark-blue eyes would not let go of us and we waited for an hour almost without moving, the way one waits for a small bird to come closer when the slightest movement might frighten it away. And finally she did come closer, all on her own, and tried out single words to see if we would understand them; later, when she had come all the way up to us, she recognized in our eyes her own small, shining image. And spoke her own name and smiled. That was her first intimacy.

And then she allowed with almost aloof forbearance our shy attempts to get close to her and share everything with her. And all at once it seemed natural to her to say "mother," and not long after that she spread her arms, as if from remembering, and came up to us as to someone she loved. Now she is being consciously polite to us; and she calls me "man" and "good man," and seems pleased that I am still here.

We will stay for another three or four days. Then we will return to the Vogelers in Worpswede and from there I will send you the books at once; the one about Worpswede and the one on Rodin; read them then as you read these letters; for there is much in them that I wrote to you and with rich awareness of your existence.

Rainer.

[RMR to LAS in Berlin-Westend]

Worpswede near Bremen
the first of August 1903

You see, dear Lou, it is *not* getting any calmer around me. I keep waiting in vain for the quiet hour when I can write you a substantial letter again: but it doesn't come. The light of day is like a flickering lamp, like a candle in the wind, and the nights usher in a great unrest from things past or yet to be. And there is never any hospitable room around me and I find no window through which I can gaze on something calm. The house in Oberneuland is surrounded, it's true, by tall, old, branched-out trees that have an equipoise in them even when they toss and sway; but I have no undisturbed place of my own from which I might observe their rich, commotion-filled lives. There is a heavy and fearful mood in this house on account of its master, who with the unpredictable confused impulses of a man who has aged badly holds everyone in a state of anxious suspense. Earlier it was his irrational anger with its sudden outbursts that everyone had to fear; now it is a feeble plaintive melancholy with which he torments those around him, as with a new stage in a nervous disorder that increasingly possesses him and his still far from exhausted strength. In a way that frightens me the drama of this old man has intertwined with the impressions I received from our little girl, so that the memory of the one almost invariably evokes thoughts of the other. What havoc life plays with human beings if they must age this way with disfigured faces, with restlessly grabbing hands, with eyes that no longer hold onto anything and no longer find anything new. The laughter of old people like this has become worn out and bad and brittle, and their gestures fall away from them like old leaves in the wind and it doesn't matter where they land. And the house gradually dies out around them and shuns them and everything they do is dead. It was hard then to keep one's spirits up in this house and listen to the little child's voice, which is so eerily unsuspecting and so infinitely alone among all the noises.

And so after eight days in Oberneuland, which passed agreeably, thanks to the circumspection with which we lived them, I returned here and was looking forward to a few quiet weeks in Vogeler's house, in the red room that I had already furnished for peaceful retreats with a few of my things and books. But now it turns out that I can't stay here either, because the fast approaching confinement of the young Frau Vogeler is going to fill, configure, and constrict the entire house, more so than they themselves had originally thought, so that nothing superfluous can remain in it; and since it is impossible for us to stay at the inn and too expensive and complicated to arrange to live in Worpswede, we will have to go back to Oberneuland as soon as the delivery here takes place.

I do not anticipate much peace of mind during this new stay at the house of my wife's parents, and I am a little afraid of continuing any longer an experiment that has run its course as expected; but since my plans for winter demand frugality, I can't even think of leaving for somewhere else and must be patient and see how all this will turn out. But now that our summer has gone so badly and borne so little fruit, we want to try to leave before the end of August. First a reunion with my father is to take place in Leipzig, and then we will journey via Munich, Venice, and Florence to Rome, where my wife (at Rodin's wish) is to work during the next year. I myself will stay on a month or two in Rome, for I am very anxious to see antiquity and its works, about which I still know nothing at all, especially its small objects that achieve such a mature beauty. I have become drawn to them and to Gothic sculpture through Rodin's work, which I delved into at such length and so patiently, and I feel that an Italian sojourn now would be the natural continuation of the best that Paris taught me. But I don't want to stay in Rome too long and after a while I will go on alone to some remote place that has a good winter. Where I shall live then, I don't yet know. The Tuscan countryside is dear to me and I would love to be where St. Francis opened up his radiant poverty like a cloak into which all the animals came: in Subiaco, or in Assisi; but it is a mountainous country and perhaps too wild in winter. I may have

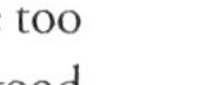

to go southward from Rome, perhaps to the little town of Ravello that lies near Amalfi, high above the blue gulfs of that happy coast. Perhaps there solitude will descend on me along with the great stillness that everything in me longs for; then I will live quietly among things and be grateful for all that keeps the clamor of daily life away from me. And I will write you occasionally and put into words for you much that now shrinks from all this disquiet. There are still many Parisian things I want to relate to you; and you must hear about Mont St. Michel, the archangel's gothic church-fortress that towers up on the north coast of Normandy, almost entirely surrounded by the ocean; and you must have at least some small token of so many other things that gripped me.

The little book on Rodin's work that I am sending you today will also tell you much; it is pure personal experience, all of it, a testament to that first time in Paris when in the shelter of an overwhelming impression I felt somewhat protected from the thousandfold fear that came later.

I am also sending you the Worpswede book,* which was written in Westerwede in the spring of 1902. You must show it lenience; for me it remains, much more than the Rodin book, a "commission," just as it felt while I was writing it. In the material itself there was too much that was unpleasant and restricting; the painters with whom it had to deal are one-dimensional as artists and as human beings small and drawn to unimportant things. To criticize them seemed to me a betrayal, and when I tried to appreciate them they ran through my hands like water; all that remained was the countryside and whatever greatness emanates from it. Back then I was able to see it greatly, and that helped me. (Today, on the occasion of this return, I found it small, German, and full of settlements.) It also helped that the given subject compelled me to be the sounding board for many different things, and material that had been forced back by confused days into the oblivion of the unformed approached again and entered easily into the lines I wrote.

I am glad that now, at a time when my writing is so inconstant and piecemeal, I may at least give you these two books, from which you will recognize what about me has grown. And don't, Lou, let yourself grow weary as these trivial letters keep arriving; it means so infinitely much to me that I may tell you about my everyday life as well, which is so full of confusion since I have no overview of it; before you it assumes a shape and order and becomes an entirely different thing. And knowing this helps me more than I can say.

Rainer.

(My address is still the same: Worpswede near Bremen, since I don't know yet precisely what day we will have to travel back to Oberneuland; when we are gone, everything will be forwarded to me from here to there.)

*I am sending you my own copy of the Worpswede book (since it is the only one I have at hand), but the Rodin book is meant to remain with you.

[LAS to RMR in Worpswede]

[Westend near Berlin,] Rüsternallee 36
August 7, 1903

Dear Rainer,

When your *Rodin* arrived and I gradually realized what was in it, I felt: it will be a long time now before I can write you! I wanted to retreat into long, uninterrupted stretches of calm and take my fill of this little book, which has the greatness of many thousand pages. It is unbelievably valuable to me, perhaps—no, beyond doubt—the most valuable of all your published books.

But now it turns out that I must write you, and do so without delay, on the old graph paper that happens to lie at hand. As the Paris letter nearly caused me to forget you yourself, as though I were reading an independent work, so now this book forces its way into my most immediate feelings, into the most intimate weave of my being, as though it were one of your letters.

After you had tried to dissuade me from believing that the Paris letter was more than just that, I had vainly pursued the question of why it spoke to you only of impotence, of things that had been stronger than you, but spoke to me of the positive, of the new resources of strength that had gone into their depiction. Or, what amounts to the same thing: how to explain the dual impression you make in that letter, namely: of being *at the same time* dejected and newly resilient. And now I understand, understand everything. Through your *Rodin*.

During the Rodin period you felt "somewhat protected in the shelter of an overwhelming impression" to which you sacrificed yourself *creatively* in order to give further, reflective form to what someone else had shaped. When you then emerged from that shelter, you were still under the influence of the sensibility you had taken in and transposed and in so doing made part of yourself. Everything you looked at you saw with incredible Rodin-eyes, saw with a view toward the corporeal-psychic detail, became a sounding board for whatever spoke of bodily existence, even though in your tools, the tools of the poet, the bodily does not find adequate means for its expression. And so the sheer optical aspect, all these unaccustomed experiences of the eyes, could have produced a state of overexcitement. Had you been a sculptor, this would have coursed through you with a powerful creative jolt, but instead it transported you into the uncanny dimensions of a foreign world, and drove a wedge between your mind and your senses. If you had been a mere copier or commentator, you would have experienced the calm satisfaction and pleasant exhaustion that follow a successful task; but as it was, your work stood on the borderline between what was yours and what was someone else's, held something passionately suppressed and also something of your own under infinite arousal, something that could not completely ring out in you and now kept echoing into an emptiness, as it were, because it was external to your work and yet under its spell. It is understandable that the symptoms of anxiety—surely the result of this—only increased in Viareggio, even though there you "began to chime." For the two different realms of art must have locked together there indistinguishably for a time, before they could separate out again and achieve equilibrium, and during that time the sculptural urges, i.e., those stamped by the corporeal, unable to find satisfaction through the poet's means, had to turn their energy against your own self, had, as it were, to hold in thrall *your own body* like a vampire.

You have undergone such severe after-shocks, and yet only because so much that is completely new has been born in you. Therefore you suffer, and I rejoice: for how should I not rejoice when you reveal even in the expression of your suffering who you have become. This happiness that lies over your letters has not yet filtered down to you yourself: but it is indeed yours, and in its shade you will yet find sanctuary from everything that would cause you harm.

Lou.

[LAS to RMR in Worpswede]

[Westend near Berlin,] Rüsternallee 36
August 8, 1903

Continuing what I couldn't finish yesterday:

The artistic and objective value the Rodin book received through your creative commitment is indeed great and worth the cost no matter what; yet that is not its only nor perhaps even its greatest strength: its most mysterious value and charm may lie in the fact that the commitment itself is not only to an objective and artistic achievement but to pure human intimacy. That you gave yourself to your opposite, your complement, to a longed-for exemplar, —gave yourself the way one gives oneself in marriage—. I don't know how else to express it, —there is for me a feeling of betrothal in this book, —of a sacred dialogue, of being admitted into what one was not but now, in a mystery, has become. Herein lies the centeredness and strength, fully confident, of which the second epigraph speaks, and it is a book made of words such as have deeds waiting behind them, —as if it wished, in order to be sufficiently close to its material, to make the first epigraph apply equally to itself. The suggestibility that is contained in your mixture of powers and frustrations is here like a strength that has grown beyond itself by committing you for long, deep, patient stretches to what was hard for you and contrary to your nature. Everything assailing you during that work, along with all the after-effects attendant on it, seem as nothing compared to the psychic reorientation it entailed. For as far as the work was concerned, this book lay here finished and uncontested, —something was behind you, something you could hold in your hands and reach for; but with regard to your state of mind, there were only expectations and intensifications pointing into a future—everything lay *before* you, and the awakened longing was no more able to envision its realization than after a wedding night the child-to-be can visibly approach its parents. I believe that in such experiences one touches the very limits of human possibility, one provides oneself evidence *of who one is*—. Perhaps only after many years will some of the most sublime truths about yourself arise in you as if in memory of these very hours, and reveal to you the deep logic that holds the man and the artist, life and dream together. I for my part am certain now of what you are: and this is the most personal thing about this book for me, that I believe us to be allies in the difficult mysteries of living and dying, two people united in that sense of the eternal which binds human beings together. From this moment on you can count on me.

Lou.

[RMR to LAS in Berlin-Westend]

Oberneuland near Bremen
August 8, 1903

At the Vogelers now there is another tiny little child, a girl; and she is to have a pale old-fashioned name, Helene Bettina, and if she does not struggle against it she will grow up into a life that seems to have ended long ago. And things are becoming smaller and smaller around Heinrich Vogeler, his house is contracting around him and filling up with everyday life, with contentedness, with roteness and with lethargy, so that no longer can anything unexpected happen. The petite woman who was so delicate and fairytale-quiet is taking on with each birth the strength and thickness of a peasant woman, and soon she will be the very image of her mother, who for years has given birth to dull, pale children in damp, shadowy rooms. And Heinrich Vogeler's art is becoming vague, is losing more and more of its brightness and confidence and is entirely at the whims of a frivolous invention that has lost connection with the world of things. In houses like these even the children no longer represent growth; they aren't birthed out into the world and no new possibilities arrive with them. Over and over again the past commences, and life and death repeat themselves and nothing about them is new. And no art can come of this, for art cannot repeat itself. And I, who have returned here from a foreign place, am filled with unease amid this life's casual unthinkingness and recall the stanzas I wrote in Viareggio this April:

Like one who has voyaged over foreign oceans
am I among those forever fixed at home;
The full days stand dumbly about their tables,
But to me the far-off is full of dream.

Deep inside my face a world reaches,
which perhaps is uninhabited like a moon, —

but they leave no star to itself,
and all their words have long been lived in.

And all the things I took with me
appear bizarre—compared to theirs—:
in their vast homeland they are wild animals,
now they hold their breaths for shame . . .

Heinrich Vogeler required a firm, steady house; but now that he actually has one, full and finished, it keeps on extending into the workaday world; and he fails to sense that it is growing heavy. Kramskoy felt it when the children arrived and with them the immediate present and the concern with the near future instead of the most distant one. When that happens all priorities reverse: the remote ceases to be important, only yesterday counts; and Tomorrow looms larger than Eternity.

When I first came to Rodin and had breakfast at his house out in Meudon with people to whom one was never introduced, with strangers seated at the same table, I knew that his house was nothing to him, a small wretched necessity perhaps, a roof for times of rain and sleep; and that it was no source of worry for him and no burden on his solitude and concentration. Deep in himself he bore the darkness and refuge and quietness of a house, and he himself had become the sky above it and the forest around it and the distance and the great river that always flowed past. Oh what a solitary this old man is: sunk in himself, he stands full of sap like an ancient tree in autumn. He has grown deep; he has dug out a deep place for his heart and its beating comes from far away as if from the core of a mountain range. His thoughts course through him and fill him with weight and sweetness and don't get lost on the surface. He has become blunt and hard toward the unimportant and stands among people as though closed in by a sheath of old bark. But he bares his heart to what *is* important, and is all openness when he is among things or where animals and people touch him quietly, the way things do. Here he is student and apprentice and observer and imitator of beauties that otherwise have always merely passed on among those who sleep, among the distracted and the indifferent. Here he is the watchful one who misses nothing, the loving one who constantly welcomes, the patient one who keeps no track of time and would never think to desire even what is next at hand. What he gazes at and surrounds with gazing is always for him the *only* thing, the *present* thing, the one world in which everything happens. When he sculpts a hand it is alone in space and there is nothing but a hand; and in six days God made just a single hand and poured the waters around it and arched the heavens over it; and he rested when all was finished, and there was something glorious and *a hand.*

And this way of looking and of living is ingrained so firmly in him because he attained it as a craftsman; as he was achieving in his art that element of infinite simplicity, of total indifference to subject matter, he was achieving in himself that great justice, that equilibrium in the face of the world that no name can shake. Since he had been granted the gift of *seeing things* in everything, he had also acquired the ability to construct things; and therein lies the greatness of his art. No longer now can any movement confound him, for he knows that there is movement even in the contours of a placid surface, and he sees only surfaces and systems of surfaces that define forms clearly and exactly. Nothing he chooses to sculpt has for him even the slightest hint of vagueness: it is a region where thousands of tiny surface elements have been fitted into space, and his task, when he creates an artwork after it, is to fit the thing even more tightly, even more passionately, a thousand times more adroitly than before, into the breadth of space around it—so that it wouldn't move even if one shook it. The thing is definite; the art-thing must be even more definite; removed from all accident, torn away from every uncertainty, lifted out of time and given to space, it has become enduring, capable of eternity. The model *seems*, the art-thing *is*. Thus the latter is that inexpressible advance over the former, the calm and mounting realization of the desire *to be* that emanates from everything in nature. By this is banished that error which would view art as the vainest and most capricious of vocations; art is the humblest service and founded absolutely on law. But all artists and all the arts are infected by this error, and so a very powerful man had to rise up against it; and he had to be someone whose pronouncements are deeds, someone who doesn't talk and incessantly creates *things*. From the beginning art for Rodin was realization (and as such the very opposite of music, which transforms the *seeming* realities of the everyday world, and de-realizes them even further by absorbing them into the easy glissando of appearances. Which is why this opposite of the art-work, this vague act of non-condensing, this temptation toward diffuseness, has so many friends and advocates and addicts, so many who are unfree, who are chained to pleasure, who have no inner powers of intensification and must be enraptured from without. . . .). Rodin, born in poverty and with no social standing, saw better than anyone that all beauty in human beings and animals and things is menaced by time and circumstance, that it is but a moment, a youthfulness that comes and goes in all ages but does not endure. What troubled him was precisely the *appearance* of that which he considered indispensable, necessary, and good: the appearance of beauty. He wanted it to *be*, and he saw his task as fitting things (for things endured) into the less threatened, more peaceful, more eternal world of space, and he instinctively applied to his work all the laws of adaptation, so that it might evolve organically and grow capable of life. From early on he had tried to make nothing by reference to "how it would look": there was no stepping back for him, only a perpetual leaning over and remaining close to what was about to come into being. And today this characteristic has become so strong in him that one could almost say that the way his things look is a matter of indifference to him: so intensely does he experience their *being*, their reality, their release on all sides from the vague and uncertain, their completedness and goodness, their independence; they do not stand on the earth, they orbit it.

And since his great work arose from handcraft, from the humble and almost unmotivated will to make perpetually better things, he stands today, still free and unspoiled by theme and abstract conception, as one of the simplest creatures among his fully evolved things. The great thoughts, the sublime meanings came to them like laws that find fulfillment in things of goodness and perfection; he did not summon them. He did not desire them; bowed deep, he went his way like a servant and made an earth, a hundred earths. Yet each of these living earths radiates its own heaven and casts star-filled nights into eternity.

He simply set to work: that is what gives his work this ravishing directness and purity; the groups of figures, the larger combinations of forms, he did not constellate beforehand, while they were still ideas (for the idea is one thing—and almost nothing, while the realization is something else and everything). Before anything else he made *things*, many things, and from these alone did he create the new unity or let it grow of its own accord; and thus his relationships became both intense and according to law, since it was not ideas but things that formed bonds. And this work could only come from a workman, and he who constructed it can calmly deny inspiration; it doesn't come upon him, because it is *in* him, day and night, provoked by each act of gazing, a warmth produced by every gesture of his hand. And as the things around him grew more numerous, the disturbances that reached him became less frequent; for all noises broke off when they came in contact with the realities that surrounded him. His very work has sheltered him: he has lived in it as in a wood, and his life must have lasted for a long time already, since what he himself planted has become a tall forest. And when one strolls among the things with which he dwells and shares space, which he sees again each day and each day completes, then his house with all its constant noises seems something trivial and irrelevant, and one sees it only as in a dream, strangely distorted and filled with an assortment of pale memories. His daily life and the people who are part of it lie there like an empty riverbed through which he no longer flows; but there is nothing sad in that: for nearby one hears the great roar and the powerful flow of the stream that would not divide into two arms . . .

And I believe, Lou, that it must be so; this is *one* life and the other is a different one, and we are not made to have two lives; back when I was always pining for a reality, for a house, for people who visibly belonged to me, for the everyday world—: how wrong I was then. For now that it *is* mine it keeps falling away from me, piece by piece. What was my house other than a stranger for whom I was expected to work, and what are those close to me other than a guest who doesn't want to leave? How I lose myself every time I try to be something for them; I depart so far from myself and yet I cannot arrive at them and remain in transit between them and myself and so lost in journeying that I don't know where I am nor how much of mine is with me and reachable. For whom can I be something, when the truth is that I have no talent for people and no claim on them? What sort of life would a man actually have to live in order to call his child his? Would he not have to work night and day trying to earn that right? Tasks arise out of every relationship, every connection issues demands and laws, and one can channel life's goodness and greatness into them and grow through them toward oneself. There are people who can do this. But others are fundamentally solitaries, it is not in them to be continually sociable; they see lurking in every relationship a danger and an enmity; the house they build rests on such feelings, since they have no sense of home to provide its foundation; and along with the very people they are fond of, the people who are close, things all *too* close crowd into them and what is wide and free stays out.

O Lou, in one poem of mine that succeeds there is much more reality than in every relationship and affection I feel; where I create I am true, and I would like to find the strength to base my life entirely on this truth, on this infinite simplicity and joy that is sometimes granted me. Even when I went to Rodin I was seeking that; for years already I had somehow sensed the infinite example and model his work afforded. Now, having come from him, I know that I too should seek and ask for no other realizations than those of my work; there my house is, there the figures are who are truly close to me, there the women are whom I need, there the children are who will grow up and live long lives. But how am I to start out on this road—where is the handcraft of *my* art, its least and deepest place where I might begin to acquire true mastery? I want to take every road back, all the way back to that beginning, and everything that I have made shall have been as nothing, less than the sweeping of a threshold to which the next visitor will again bring the dust of the road. I have patience for centuries in me and want to live as though my time were very great. I want to gather myself up out of all distractions, and from everything too quickly applied fetch back what is mine and invest it. But I hear voices that mean well, and steps that are coming closer, and my doors open . . . And when I seek people out they have no advice and don't understand what I mean. And with books I am just the same (just as clumsy and inarticulate) and they do not help me either, as though even they were still too human . . . Only *things* speak to me. Rodin's things, the things on the Gothic cathedrals, the things of antiquity, —all those perfect, absolute things. They showed me the way to the great prototypes; to the animate, living world, seen simply and without interpretation as the occasion for things. And I am beginning to see differently and anew: flowers sometimes now take on infinite value for me, and from animals come stirrings and strange intimations. And even people I occasionally experience this way: hands somewhere come alive, mouths speak, and I gaze on everything more calmly and with greater justice.

But I still lack discipline, the capacity and *compulsion* to work for which I have yearned so long. Do I lack the strength? Is there something wrong with my will? Does the dream in me hamper all action? Days pass and I sometimes hear life going by. And still nothing has happened, still nothing real surrounds me; and I keep dividing and flowing off in all directions, —and would like so much to course through one riverbed and become great. For that's how it's meant to be, isn't it, Lou: we should be like a river and not enter canals and guide water to the pastures. Aren't we to hold ourselves together and surge on? Perhaps, if we grow to a very old age, perhaps, at the very end, there comes a moment when we can let go, allow ourselves to spread, and empty into a wide delta. . . . *dear* Lou!

Rainer.

(On July 25 a letter left for you; another on August 1; and two books on that same day. This only to check if they arrived safely, since nothing was sent by registered mail. Our address now may be: Oberneuland near Bremen (c/o Herr Fr. Th. Westhoff); for we will probably stay here until our departure and only fleetingly return to Worpswede for one last short visit. [*In the margin*: Because we feel so estranged from everything there.]

[LAS to RMR in Oberneuland]

[Westend near Berlin,] Rüsternallee 36
August 10, 1903

Your letter arrived like a postscript to the Rodin book; but I feel somewhat differently about it than I do about the book. Perhaps because I'm convinced that art and life don't make their farthest advances when they remain two different things, but when they find, not just some compromise (which, by the way, they can never avoid, since artists are human beings), but that point of fusion where one serves as spur to the other's productivity. Rodin, especially, by your account, has found that point, but the sculptor's art is such that he came to locate it entirely within the area of his work: the purely practical style of one's hands in action, the hard quiet devotion to one's material, this stance of "leaning over it" instead of stepping back to check effects, —and finally to give over from one's hands a thing, and to have its reality be fully visible and fully contained in itself, —all this is like something done in the service of real life or that for which Life prepares its people. But the moment one considers a different art—that of the poet, for instance—none of this applies. With him the "artistic" dimension does not coincide with the sculptor's handcraft; the point where art and life become one has moved out far beyond that, into the soul, where he obtains *his* material. For words surely don't build like stones, literally and concretely; they are rather signs for indirectly conveyed suggestions, and in and of themselves are far poorer, of far less material substance than a stone. One can even conceive of art continuing along this path all the way past music, that art of the wordless which nevertheless provides just as strict a reality, in that it allows the rhythmic laws of material things to ring out immaterially (—you are doing it an injustice now, just as earlier you overburdened it with metaphysical raptures). And finally one could imagine the existence of an art in which life absorbs handcraft to the same degree that in sculpture handcraft grasps life. These, then, would be the two opposites between which we all fluctuate, and we must all seek our own combination, our own personal balance point between art's life and life's art. I believe as deeply as you that this requires much standing apart, much solitude, —and indeed I could say of myself that I (although no artist) have denied myself motherhood in response to the demands of both. For the more artistically one views life, the more urgently does each thing's perfection cry out for release, and of each thing one feels: it is worth an entire lifetime's creative strength. But each of us must also experience how little possible it is to maintain complete apartness, and once one has wrenched things of life into one's own destiny, one *can* no longer disregard them: because now they have become braided into the whole texture of our being, we are lodged in them, they in us. If they remain in us unassimilated, they will murder as nothing else all the quietness of the soul, and prevent the artist from descending into the depths and mineshafts of his being like a treasure-hunter, will drive him instead to the surface, toward forgetting and stupefaction. He has no choice then but to persist here, in the midst of life—where, for better or worse, he has documented himself as a human being—concentrated on that point over which he now leans in order to begin to work. This is a labor performed not merely as a human being but in the purest sense as an artist: exactly in the way that Rodin had to keep struggling with difficulties whenever his material was recalcitrant. As strange as it sounds: the technical aspect, understood as that creative command of things, depends for the poet most of all on the state of his inner being, which is to say the state of his soul's workshop and the tools of its trade. If he really and truly gives his life to art, —then he worked to imbue many figures with life for the sake of those figures of his art. Then he worked day and night on that space within him, so that nothing would pace around in it any longer like a phantom, restless and demanding, and it would become a stillness and quietness for the existence of his things. Perhaps when he succeeds in that he will then create just the one hand of which you speak in your words about Rodin, but *"around it [will be] pure splendor"*; for only then will it be *the* hand, the hand that exists as if it were all there is.

Lou.

[RMR to LAS in Berlin-Westend]

Oberneuland near Bremen
August 10, 1903 (Monday)

To learn that my little Rodin book had such an effect on you, Lou, was an inexpressible joy to me. Nothing could so fill me with self-confidence and hope as your enthusiasm for this the most fully matured of my works. Only now do I feel that it *stands*, only now is it completed, acknowledged by reality, upright and good.

And all those other insights your letter contained have been a beacon of quiet light to me, infinitely bright and helpful. My letter of Saturday (which you must have received by now) tried to find similar ways to explain the event Rodin was for me. He is one of the great ones who truly matter, a sign towering high over our times, an extraordinary example, a marvel visible from far away—and yet nothing but an inexpressibly solitary, old man, alone in a vast old age. And look: he has lost nothing, he has amassed and gathered things around him his whole incredible life long: he has left nothing in vagueness and has given everything reality: from the flight of a frightened feeling, from a dream's debris, from the stirrings of a presentiment, he has made *things*, and has arranged them around himself, thing upon thing: so that there grew up around him a reality, a wide, calm kinship of things that united him with other and older things, until he himself seemed to stem from a dynasty of great things: that is the source of his quietness and his patience, his fearless, ongoing old age, his superiority to those who move about so much, who vacillate, who keep shifting the balances in which, almost unconsciously, he rests. You are so wonderfully right, dear Lou; I was suffering from the huge example which my own art gave me no means of following directly: the impossibility of creating *physically* turned to pain in my own body, and even my fears (whose material content was the perpetual crowding in on me of something too hard, too stone-like, too big) arose from the irreconcilability of the two worlds of art: how keenly you feel it and illumine it with your great insight into human nature: you soothsayer. . . .

But precisely in the light of your explanation, your immensely helpful, receptive understanding, it becomes clear to me that I must follow him, Rodin: not by a "sculptural" alteration of my work, but by an inward ordering of the creative process; it is not shaping things that I must learn from him, but a deep collectedness for shaping's sake. I must learn to work, Lou, to work, that is where I fall so short! *Il faut toujours travailler—toujours*—he said to me one day when I spoke to him of the frightening abysses that open up between my good days; he could scarcely understand what I was talking about; he, who by now has become all work (so much so that even his gestures are simple movements that derive from his handcraft!) —Perhaps it is only a kind of ineptness that prevents me from working, that is, from choosing amongst everything that happens; for I am equally baffled when it comes to culling what pertains to me from books or from encounters; I barely recognize the important thing: external circumstances distort it and conceal it from me until I no longer know how to distinguish it from what is superfluous and become confused and intimidated by the sheer volume of everything. For weeks I sat in Paris in the Bibliothèque Nationale and read books I had long wished for; but the notes I made then are of no use at all; for while I read, everything seemed to me extraordinarily new and important, and I was tempted to copy out the whole book since I could not take it with me; inexperienced in books I roam about in them in perpetual dumb peasant-wonderment and emerge perplexed and burdened with things that are completely irrelevant. And I am similarly clumsy with events that come and go—without the talent for selection, without the composure for reception, a constantly shifting mirror out of which all images fall.

And how much it costs me to hold on to what *is* important! The perpetual interruption by all the trifles the day brings, the worries about money, the chance occurrences and useless complaints, the doors, the smells, the hours that toll over and over and forever summon one to something, —all of that has a voice and talks loudly without regard for me in the incessant gossipy prattle of the everyday world. Granted, it was like that in the past as well; but it has become much worse in these more anxious, unsheltered years: everything races straight through me, what is vital along with what is least significant, and no core can form in me, no firm, unassailable place: I am merely the scene for a series of inner encounters, a passageway instead of a house! And I would like somehow to withdraw more deeply into myself, into the monastery inside me that is replete with the great bells. I would like to forget everyone, forget my wife and my child, forget all, all those names and relations and interests and hopes that are bound up with others. But what good would it do to journey far from everything, since voices are everywhere and nowhere a refuge watched over by some quiet beneficence that might receive me. Nowhere the place where pettiness grows less insistent and less harsh. If I were to go into the desert, I would perish from sun and hunger; for the birds have ceased coming to the hermit: they toss their bread into the crowd and the crowd scuffles for it. . . .

But for this reason it is so frightfully necessary for me to find the tool of my art, the hammer, my hammer, so that it might become master and grow beyond all noise. There must be a handcraft in this art also: a faithful, daily labor that utilizes everything—surely it must be possible even here! If only I had days of work, Lou, if only the most secret chamber of my heart were a workshop and cell and refuge for me; if only all this monkishness in me might channel itself into monastery-building for the sake of my work and worship. If only I might lose nothing more and establish everything around me according to kinship and importance. If only I might rise again, Lou! For I am scattered like some dead man in an old grave . . .

Somehow I too must find some way to make things; written, not sculpted things, —realities that stem from handcraft.

Somehow I too must discover that smallest basic element, the cell of *my* art, the tangible immaterial means of representation for everything. Then the clear strong consciousness of the enormous task that lay before me would drive me and bend me toward it; then I would have so infinitely much to do that one workday would resemble another, and the work I had would always succeed because it would start out with things attainable and small and yet all along be involved in things great. Then everything would suddenly be far away, voices and vexations, and even what was set against me would weave its way into this work as loud sounds enter a dream and gently guide it toward the unexpected. My subject-matter would lose even more of its importance and weight and become nothing but pretext; but just this apparent indifference to it would enable me to *shape* it, to form and to find pretexts for everything with more exact, unprejudiced means.

Might this handcraft lie in language itself, in a better acquaintance with its inner life and will, its evolution and its distant past? (The big Grimms' Dictionary, which I once saw in Paris, led me to consider this. . . .) Might it lie in some specific study, in the more exact knowledge of *one* area? (For many this is certainly the case without their knowing it, and this area of expertise is for them their daily labor, their handcraft.) Or might it lie in a certain well-inherited and well-augmented culture? (Hofmannsthal would be an argument for this; a short essay in the *Neue Freie Presse* that I happened upon recently and that I am enclosing with this letter would also be an argument for it; it is beautiful, a beautiful piece of handcraft that belongs to its own beautiful art.) But with me it is different; everything I've inherited I must

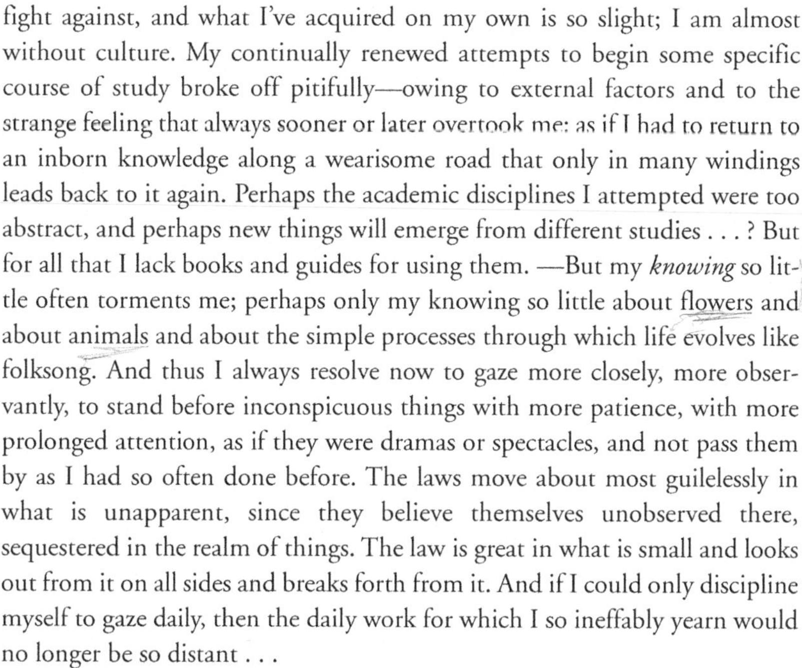

fight against, and what I've acquired on my own is so slight; I am almost without culture. My continually renewed attempts to begin some specific course of study broke off pitifully—owing to external factors and to the strange feeling that always sooner or later overtook me: as if I had to return to an inborn knowledge along a wearisome road that only in many windings leads back to it again. Perhaps the academic disciplines I attempted were too abstract, and perhaps new things will emerge from different studies . . . ? But for all that I lack books and guides for using them. —But my *knowing* so little often torments me; perhaps only my knowing so little about flowers and about animals and about the simple processes through which life evolves like folksong. And thus I always resolve now to gaze more closely, more observantly, to stand before inconspicuous things with more patience, with more prolonged attention, as if they were dramas or spectacles, and not pass them by as I had so often done before. The laws move about most guilelessly in what is unapparent, since they believe themselves unobserved there, sequestered in the realm of things. The law is great in what is small and looks out from it on all sides and breaks forth from it. And if I could only discipline myself to gaze daily, then the daily work for which I so ineffably yearn would no longer be so distant . . .

Have patience, Lou, have patience with me. It must seem to you that I am much too old to be indulging so youthfully in searching; but I am, after all, a child in your presence, and I don't try to hide that fact and I talk to you as children talk in the night: my face pressed up against you and my eyes closed, feeling your nearness, your safety, your presence:

Rainer.

[RMR to LAS in Berlin-Westend]

Oberneuland near Bremen
August 11, 1903
(Tuesday)

Dear Lou,

During a long walk barefoot through the cool early morning grass I read your two letters and now, before I begin the day, I want to thank you for them. Your letter of August 8 that continues with the Rodin book fills me with a great happiness, and a calmness and confidence comes to me from my faith in all your words. How impatient (despite my assurances to the contrary) I must seem to you in my letters, in Saturday's and then again in yesterday's. But don't be misled by either them or me. I *am* where you found me and *am* as you see me. Even if I don't know it yet; perhaps the joys I've invoked are already on their way here, and your letters precede them as harbingers.

And try to understand: I don't want to sunder art and life; I know that sometime, somewhere, they must agree. But I am all thumbs at life, and that is why, when it knits together around me, it so often turns out to be a stopover for me, a delay that causes me to lose so much; as when sometimes in a dream one can't finish getting dressed and because of two obstinate shoe-buttons misses something vital that will never come again. And in truth life does go by and leaves no second chances for things missed and the many losses; especially in the case of someone who wants to have an art. For art is something much too big and too difficult and too long for one life, and those who have entered a great old age are only beginners at it. *"C'est à l'âge de soixante-treize ans que j'ai compris à peu près la forme et la nature vraie des oiseaux, des poissons et des plantes"*—wrote Hokusai, and Rodin feels the same way, and Leonardo, who lived to a very old age, also comes to mind. And they have always lived in their art and have, concentrated on that one thing, let everything else grow untended. But how should one *not* be afraid, Lou, when one only rarely enters art's sanctum because outside in recalcitrant life one gets caught in all traps and bumps stupidly into all obstacles. Therefore I want so desperately and so impatiently to find the realm of work, the workday, because life, once it has become work, can become art. I know that I can't cut my life free of the destinies with which it is intertwined; but I must find the strength to lift it up, just as it is, all of it, into a peacefulness, into a solitude, into the quiet of deep days of labor: only there will everything that you have prophesied for me find me; and you as well, Lou, will seek me there. Be patient with me, if I keep you waiting; you have gone ahead like a sage, but I move the way the animals move when the hunting season is upon them.

Rainer.

[RMR to LAS in Berlin-Westend]

Oberneuland near Bremen
August 15, 1903

Dear Lou,

Behind the park that surrounds this house the express trains from Hamburg pass by, and their clatter drowns out all the wind in the trees; and each day that noise assumes more meaning, for already the little bit of quiet that enclosed us is losing its leaves, and one can see through it the impending journey and can feel, along with all the approaching difficulty, the promise of distant cities and the spirit of new things and faraway places. Next Friday perhaps or Saturday we embark on our journey; our first stop is Marienbad (where a meeting with my father has been arranged), and then we will make a brief pause in Munich to see a marvelous painting by a friend we made in Paris. It is the *Bullfighter's Family* by Ignacio Zuloaga, who made such an impression on us with his presence and simple modesty that we look forward to viewing this picture into which he has put so much of himself. It will be as if we had the pleasure of seeing him again in person. In Venice also (which is our next stop) we shall see paintings of his; perhaps they will be the only reality in that dreamlike city whose existence is like an image suspended in a mirror. Then after a short stay we travel on to Florence, to that bright, beautiful country that has inspired so much joy, reverence, and praise. Even there we will be granted only a few days' respite, for: Rome is imminent, that great summoning Rome which for us is still only a name but will soon be a thing made of a hundred things, a great shattered vessel out of which so much past seeped into the ground. Rome the ruin, which we want to build up again. Not the way it once may have been, but as seekers of the inner future in this past, the trove of eternity locked up inside it. We want to feel ourselves intimate descendants of these isolated, time-lost things, which scholarship misconceives when it burdens them with names and periods, and admiration misjudges when it perceives in them a specific and determinate beauty. For they held their faces into the earth and shed all name and meaning; and when they were found they rose, lightly, above the earth, and almost passed on among the birds, so very much creatures of space and standing like stars above inconstant time. Herein, I think, rests the incomparable value of these rediscovered things: one can respond to them so entirely as *unknown*. One doesn't know what purpose they were meant to serve and nothing in the way of content or subject matter (at least for the non-scholarly) attaches to them, no irrelevant voice breaks the stillness of their concentrated existence, and their enduring is without looking-back and fear. The masters from whom they derive are nonexistent, no misunderstood fame colors their forms, which are pure, and no history casts shadows on their unveiled clarity—: they exist. And that is everything. That is how I imagine the art of antiquity. The little tiger in Rodin's studio is like that, and the many fragments and shattered remains in the museums (which one inattentively passes by for a long time, until one day one of them reveals itself, becomes visible, shines like a first star beside which suddenly, when one notices it, hundreds arrive, breathless, from out of the depths of the sky—) have the same quality, as does the magnificent *Nike*, standing on its driving ship's fragment in the Louvre like a sail filled with propitious winds, —and much else that seems worthless to those who still misguidedly seek the sculptural in subject matter, in motif, lives in this same sublime perfection among humans, piecemeal and crudely formed as the latter are. Equally great are those Gothic sculptures which, though they stand much closer to us in time, are just as remote, just as anonymous, just as self-contained in their solitude: without origin like the things in nature. These, and what issued from the hands of Rodin, led us to the most distant art-objects, to pre-Grecian art, whose very nature seems to harbor a sculptural ruthlessness, an insistent thingness, heavy as lead, mountain-like and hard. Kinships were disclosed such as no one had ever felt before, connections formed and joined the currents that flow through the ages, and the history of endless generations of *things* could be sensed beneath the history of mankind, like a stratum of slower, quieter developments that take their course more deeply, more intensely, more unswervingly than ours. In *this* history, Lou, the people of Russia may someday find themselves a place; for they inhabit time the way Rodin does when he creates; avatars of patience and endurance, they trace their descent from things and are kin to them, kin by blood. That biding quality in the Russian character (which the German, with his busy, self-important zeal for trifles, calls indolence—) would thus appear in a new, more revealing light: perhaps the Russian was meant to let the history of human beings pass him by, so that he might later enter with his singing heart into the harmony of things. He has only to endure, to persevere and, like the violinist to whom no signal has yet been given, to sit in the orchestra, holding his instrument carefully so that nothing may befall it before its time. . . . More and more, and filled with an ever increasing feeling of assent, I bear within me my love for this vast, holy land: as a new ground for solitude, and as a high barrier against the masses.

August 15, 1903

Did I tell you that in Paris (especially during my early days there) I was often with Eugène M. de Vogüé? But how disillusioned I became with him and Louis Léger and all those whose names, in connection with Russia, had taken on such an aura for me. Vogüé is nothing like his books, is a little nobleman who has become vain and easily offended in his old age, reminding me a little of Professor Parlandt yet suffering even in this comparison, since in some comical way he has remained a bachelor, even though he has a portly, infinitely trivial lady as wife and four conceited young gentlemen as progeny. Good Lord, the consternation I felt before this person from whom I had hoped and expected to learn so much about Russia, the inability to gain anything from him at all, even though for a time he was more than willing to help. And thus it is always the same story: I have too few facts and practical information, too few dates regarding the object of my enthusiasm, to tread water in a casual conversation and, making slow diving ventures with my interlocutor, gradually descend into the deeper regions—: I always plunge straight down with the full weight of my passion to the bottom of any sort of water and frighten people, as with a too sudden (almost illicit) confiding, when I begin at once to tell of what is deepest and most secret; toward people that is a mistake, a rudeness almost, which leaves them gaping; and in me it is a lack, a mania, that makes real (that is, fruitful and useful) interaction with people impossible; it is hard for me—almost impossibly so—to conceive that a conversation that begins casually amid insignificant things can end in the realm of the important; some accident or distraction is sure to interrupt, or else a misunderstanding trivial in itself will end all wish to continue on: thus everything in me constantly plunges toward the final, the ultimate, the most important, and whoever happens to be my interlocutor no longer even tries to keep pace; tacitly marking my incivility, he remains behind, and when I reach the end of my course and look back breathless, I see him far away, very small but with a friendly smile and wholly occupied with acting as if nothing untoward had happened. . . .

But it is not from any wisdom in me that this economy of the important springs. It is a defect of my nature to forget all paths taken, yes, even all arrivals, right up to whatever happens to be the very last and most recent arrival, —of which alone then I am able to speak. Is this perhaps because I fly straight to so many destinations (or reach them walking blindfolded), so that I am given the end but not the way that led there? Or is it simply a negligence of my memory, which retains only the results and lets slip the complex path of reckonings that led to them? This defect is the source of my continual poverty, the paucity (in proportion to the daily intake) of my possessions, the emptiness and inactivity of many days: for since I carry nothing in me but some last-acquired product, while the reckoning itself, of which this product is merely an element, takes place illegibly inside me, —waiting period after waiting period appears to intervene between one result and another. Then too: that I seem so often to open excessively to people I barely know is not just a weakness of my soul's sphincter, as I long believed; there is always only *one thing* in me, and I must remain locked up (that is, keep silent or prattle) or else open myself and make visible the single thing that inhabits me. This inner disposition of mine is an affliction, and actually excludes me from all legitimate exchange, since it leads only to disjunctions and misunderstandings and pushes me into unwanted relationships amid which I suffer and from which many dangerous reversals can occur. It is typical that I have acquired all my "friends" by such illicit means and for this reason possess them badly and in poor conscience. Only thus is it possible (as for example in the Worpswede period three years ago) that I should have acquired a whole crowd of friends who could give nothing in return for my continual expenditure, and that at any rate no one *can* reciprocate me, since I give ruthlessly and brutally, without regard to others, unloading everything now at one place, now at another, instead of offering, of showing and bestowing things chosen considerately from an ordered store. During these past years I have gained increasing insight into my afflictions, including this one; and now I reach out to people with greater caution and make it a point to be the one to wait, whenever possible the one to respond and not the one to initiate. On this new basis a few relationships have been formed in which I can more honestly take pleasure than before: a correspondence with Ellen Key (who wants to help me in some practical way), a warm exchange with Gerhart Hauptmann which has brought me beautiful letters from the heart of his creative life, the contact with Zuloaga, and the great attainment of Rodin; in the two latter cases it was a great good fortune that no impetuous and blind opening-up on my part was able to create misunderstandings; language prevented that. With both only laborious communication in French was possible, yes, even my books (to which I would have gladly entrusted this task) were deprived the chance to speak for me and about me; —and that in spite of all resistances, which are inevitable in such circumstances, quiet relationships with these solitary people nevertheless did evolve, relationships that could perhaps forego preliminaries since they rested on an already secured knowledge of a few great shared experiences, makes me a bit more confident in my dealings with people. But a tendency like mine is a perpetual danger, especially when one is inept in the pragmatics of human affairs and always intimidated by the feeling of being amid people who are by contrast experts at life; such tendencies are impossible to defeat; the best one can achieve is to turn them to a higher purpose and use them more modestly, to grow more mature in them and *apply* them with greater experience. All my creative work, even that which issues from the very core of my being, bears traces of this tendency, which shows in the extremely unscientific developments any material or cause for work undergoes in me—since without fail the synthesis, the last and most distant thing appears as the point of origin, from which, proceeding backward, I must invent paths and chains of preceding events, utterly unsure of their course and initiated only into the goal, into the final concluding summation and apotheosis.

And this ignorance of the path, this certainty only of the last and most distant thing, of the point at the end of it all, makes all proceeding difficult for me and scatters over me all the sadness characteristic of those who have become lost, even if I *am* on the way to finding myself. That Russia is my homeland is one of the great and mysterious certainties in which I live, —but my attempts to *proceed* there, through journeys, through books, through people, are as nothing, are more a turning away than a coming closer. My exertions are like the crawling of a snail and yet there are moments when the inexpressibly distant goal is repeated in me as in a nearby mirror. I live and learn amid so much distraction that often I cannot imagine to what purpose it will all some day have been. In Paris I didn't really come any closer to Russia, and yet somehow I think that even now in Rome, in the presence of these ancient things, I am preparing for things Russian and for returning to them. If I did not know that all developments trace circular paths I should grow fearful, knowing myself again sent out into the temptation of a foreign country that speaks to me of what is native to it in an alluring and intoxicating language. More than once already Italian life has enthralled me and lured me into steep ascents from which I fell painfully; perhaps then it is good that this young artist will be beside me now, this woman who neither as creator nor for the sake of life has ever longed for this southern land, because her northern temperament mistrusted the overly open quality of its radiant splendor, and her powers of reception, already determined by the taciturn accent of the solemn moors, had no need of more voluble persuasion. Now, at a mature point in her art, she is undertaking this journey on Rodin's advice, after contact with antique remains in Paris has instilled in her a certain need to see Italy, not the Italy that crowds around an idle pleasure-seeker, nor around an art student indiscriminately given over to all impressions, but Italy as it exists around a woman quietly attempting to pursue her work there, so that during the periods of free time she might raise her eyes to the new world that surrounds her. During these periods we will see many things together; but for my own part, I will devote myself entirely to observing and to taking in as many things as possible; for I plan to hold out in Rome (where Clara Rilke will work the entire winter) only a short time and then, before I feel the press of the city, find a secluded little place (perhaps by the sea) which has both a mild winter and an early spring. If only the days would come there, Lou, in which I might learn to work deeply and collectedly; if only I might find a high room, a terrace, an avenue in which no one walks, and nights without a neighbor, and if the worry about everyday needs would grant me only briefly this life for which I cry out, —if that happens I will never again let a complaint issue from me, no matter what may come later.

Out of this stillness, if it is given to me, I will sometimes lift myself to you, as to the saint of that far-off homeland that I cannot attain, moved that you, bright star, stand exactly over the place where I am darkest and most afraid.

Rainer.

[RMR to LAS in Berlin-Westend]

currently: Oberneuland near Bremen
August 21, 1903

In a few hours we leave on our trip, Lou. I will be far from you again, much farther than during these strange summer days in which your letters took so little time to reach me. How often I have longed to take that path myself.

But now as I set out again for a distant land, I ask you, Lou, this one favor: take the new book with Prayers and keep it with you, put it with the first one and read it and feel the same fondness for it.

I am taking with me separate copies of the poems it contains, since I feel sure the desire to read them will come to me in the days and nights that lie ahead: but I will read these fragments differently if I know that all of it rests in your hands, in your equilibrium, —protected, looked over, unified by you.

I am sending you the book along with this letter (as manuscript, registered mail) and if you wish to acknowledge its receipt with a note, my address from today until the 25th will be: *general delivery Marienbad*, and after that: *poste restante Florence Central.*

Goodbye, dear Lou: my thoughts find rest by imagining, on the other side of this journey, a return when I might come to you and read to you from my Prayers, which by then will have long been in your possession:

Rainer.

[LAS to RMR in Oberneuland]

Bohemian Riesengebirge
August 22, 1903

Dear Rainer,

At Zemek's request, I've left for a few weeks of mountain hiking; and since I didn't want to make a long journey he came here to meet me. Your three letters have been forwarded to me but I reply to them only in my thoughts: I carry these thoughts across the mountains undisturbed, but they can be written down only when I am back home in quiet concentration. Cordial greetings to you until then

Lou.

[LAS to RMR in Florence]

Bohemian Riesengebirge
[August 25, 1903]

Dear Rainer,

am out hiking, and writing this against a tree trunk. My husband forwarded your letter of August 21 with the news that a manuscript of yours has arrived. It will be waiting for me in my room and will greet me there as the most secret part of your self.

Zemek wants to have me under his supervision for a few weeks more; I have been a bit ill. Postal address unchanged: Westend.

Lou.

[RMR to LAS in Berlin-Westend]

Rome, Via del Campidoglio 5
November 3, 1903

Do you still have memories of Rome, dear Lou? What are they? Mine will be only of its waters, these clear, exquisite, vivacious waters that enliven its squares; its steps, built on the pattern of falling water, each stair flowing so wondrously from the other, like wave issuing from wave; of the festiveness of its gardens and the splendor of its great terraces; of its nights that last so long, quiet and filled to overflowing with great constellations.

About its past, which so laboriously struggles to hold itself erect, I may well remember nothing at all; nothing of its museums full of meaningless statues, and little of its paintings; the bronze statue of Marcus Aurelius on the Capitoline Square I will remember, one beautiful marble piece in the Ludovisi Museum (the Throne of Aphrodite), a column in some small, forgotten church, a few utterly obscure pieces, a view out over the sparse Campagna, a lonely road leading into evening, and all the melancholy in which I lived.

In which I live.

For I am unhappy with myself, because I am without regular daily work, exhausted though not ill, but deep in anxiety. When, Lou, when will this pitiable life reverse itself and become productive, when will it grow beyond incompetence, lethargy, and cheerlessness into the simple reverent joy for which it longs? Is it growing at all? I scarcely dare question the steps in my "progress," for fear of discovering (like that man in Tolstoy) that they trace a circle, that they keep returning to that one notorious disconsolate place from which I have already started out so often.

From which even now I am planning to start out again, amid unspeakable difficulty and with so little courage.

So begins my Roman winter. I shall try to see many things, shall go to the libraries and read; and then, when things begin to grow a little lighter inside me, I shall be at home as much as possible and gather myself around the best that I have not yet lost. For my time and my strength, as things stand with me, can have but *one* task, *this* task: to find the road that will lead me to quiet, daily work, in which I can live with more certainty and support than in this vague sickly world that is collapsing behind me and does not exist before me. The question of whether I will find such a road is not new—but the years are passing and it has become urgent now and I must be able to answer . . . But you know from my Oberneuland letters how things stand. They are not good.

After the middle of November I will have a very quiet place to live: the last house deep in an old spacious garden before Porta del Popolo, next to the Villa Borghese; built as a summerhouse, it contains only a single simple high-windowed room, and from its flat roof one gazes out over the garden toward landscape and mountains. There I will try to arrange my life on the pattern of my Waldfrieden days; to be as quiet, as patient, as turned away from everything external, as I was in that good, joyous, always expectant time: so that they may become days of garden-peace. . . .

But now I'm utterly without books and, owing to my ineptness in dealing with libraries, it isn't easy to get on; so could I ask of you one favor: do you recall once mentioning a modern, scholarly German translation of the Bible, and if you do, can you give me the names of the translator and publisher, so that I can try to find the book here? And if I am not asking too much: perhaps give me the name of some other new book you've read: it might help me very much right now.

But above all I need a letter from you, Lou.

I have thought about you so often during the trip and since we have been here, and I have wished many times and with all my will that you return from the mountains in good health. Because, of all my thoughts, that one of you is the single one in which I find repose, and sometimes I lie down in it and sleep in it and rise from it . . .

Now where you are it is autumn, and you walk in the forest, in the great forest into which one can already see so far, in the wind that is transforming the world. I think of that little pond—the one on the left of the road to Dahlem—which always grew so large and solitary around this time. I think of the evenings which precede the stormy night that strips everything withered from the trees, and think of the storm itself, of the night which flies past the stars into morning. Into the empty, fresh, transparent, storm-cleared morning . . . Here, though, nothing alters; only a few trees are changing, as if they were sprouting yellow blossoms. And the laurel is always green.

Rainer.

[LAS to RMR in Rome]

Loufried on the Hainberg near Göttingen
November 9, 1903

Dear Rainer,

How do I remember Rome, you ask: as a backdrop indistinctly painted with all sorts of old ruins and in the foreground an experiencing of nothing but future and youthful things, the true onset of my youth, after my early years, though dear to me, had become almost tragically difficult. Rome was window-dressing, and as window-dressing, almost the opposite of what Russia was later when it soaked up everything that happened to me so completely that even now I don't know: where do I begin, where does it leave off—. The thing I remember most distinctly about Rome is its sun.

What will Rome be for you at winter's end? Might it be the place where something like your Prayers becomes possible?

Write me from there, I'll read it in a Loufried, as you can see; much of yours too that resides with me has only now come home. Ever since the Loufried of Wolfratshausen, I have been wandering step by step toward the new one here; each successive year has had to play its part in the building of it, perhaps beginning with the most inessential chambers, with a few festive chambers suspended in midair, and only then working down deep into its foundation. According to laws of construction that are beyond all comprehension.

And now it stands here. In a spacious landscape with beech tree forests and long stretches of hills somewhere behind which the Harz Mountains rise. At our feet, in the valley below, the city. And around us orchards, gardens full of old trees, and vegetable fields. We even have a chicken yard!

Here I have become a peasant woman and my husband a professor.

That this letter provides nothing now but an elaborate address, attribute to the following: yours arrived here by a series of detours, and mine rushes to catch you before you have changed lodgings. Write if it succeeded.

The two books are entitled:

Die Heilige Schrift des Alten Testaments. translated and edited by E. Kautzsch. (Freiburg i/B. and Leipzig: Mohr.)

Das Neue Testament. (transl. by Carl Weizsäcker; same publ.)

Books you want me to mention, some that I have read recently—, give me more time, Rainer; I am ashamed to say: *I haven't been reading.*

Lou.

[RMR to LAS in Göttingen]

Rome, Via del Campidoglio 5
[November 13, 1903]

Dear Lou,

It touches me wondrously that now a *home* surrounds you—a house filled with your being, a garden that has its life from you, a wide space that belongs to you; and yes, I understand that all of this has and *had* to come about slowly; for the world that has its life from you wants reality and has the strength to will it. That first, faraway *Loufried*: wasn't it almost like a dream, fragile and full of anticipated things; yet it drew substance from you, and whenever you arrived, the house was big and the garden endless. I felt it back then, and now, so much later, I know: that the infinite *reality* surrounding you was the deepest event for me out of all that inexpressibly good, expansive, generous time; the life-changing force that would seize me in a hundred places at once—it came from you, you who were real beyond words. Never had I, in my groping timidity, felt existence, believed in presence, and recognized the imminent with such intensity; you were the opposite of all doubt and irrefutable proof for me of the existence of everything that you touched, reached, and perceived. The world lost its cloudiness for me, that fluidity of self-shaping and self-dissolving that was the pose and poverty of my first verses; *things* came to be, one could distinguish between animals, flowers existed; I learned simplicity, learned slowly and with difficulty how unassuming everything is, and became mature enough to put simplicity into words.

And this all happened because I was able to meet you, back then when for the first time I was in danger of surrendering myself to formlessness. And if this danger always finds a way to return and always returns larger and stronger, it is also true that the memory of you grows in me, the awareness of you, and it too keeps strengthening. In Paris, in those most difficult days when all things were withdrawing from me as from someone going blind, when I trembled with the fear of no longer being able to recognize the face of the person closest to me, I held on tightly to the assurance that I still recognized *you* inside me, that your image had not become alien to me, that it had not deserted me like everything else, but had alone remained with me in that foreign emptiness where I was forced to live.

And even here, when, feeling torn so many ways, I made yet a new start, you were the calm place on which I fixed my gaze.

How well I understand: that the things come to you as birds do to their nests—from far away, as evening darkens. Thousands of great and thousands of small laws fulfilled themselves as this house took shape around you. And I am so glad that it is standing now, and I feel as though its goodness extends from there even here to me.

My struggle, Lou, and my danger lie in the fact that I cannot become real, that there are always things that deny me, events that go straight through me, more real than I am and as if I didn't exist. Earlier I believed this condition would improve once I had a house, a wife, and a child, had something real and undeniable; believed that this would make me more visible, more tangible, more factual. But lo, Westerwede existed, *it* was real: for I built the house myself and made everything in it. And yet it was a reality *outside* me, I was not part of it and was not taken up with it. And now, when the little house and its quiet beautiful rooms exist no longer: that I know there is still a person who belongs to me and somewhere a little child in whose life nothing is so close as she and I—this gives me a certain security and the experience of many simple and deep things, —but it doesn't help me achieve that feeling of reality, of being equal to it, for which I yearn so strongly:

To be a real person among real things.

Only in the (ever so rare) days of work do I become real, exist, take up space like a thing, have weight, lie in place, fall—and, when I do, a hand comes and lifts me up. Fitted into the edifice of a great reality, I experience myself then as a support on a deep foundation, touched right and left by other supports. But always, after such hours of existing as a close-fitting part of it, I am again the discarded stone which lies there so pointlessly that the grass of idleness has time to grow tall over it. And that these hours of being discarded don't grow less frequent but now last almost forever—, should that not make me afraid? If I keep lying there like that and become overgrown, who will find me beneath everything that flourishes on top of me? And have I perhaps not been crumbled up already long ago, spread almost even with the land, almost mixed in with it, so that any one of the sad paths that go back and forth across it might lead over me?

And so this perpetually is the *one* task before me, which I forever fail to begin and which nevertheless must be begun: the task of finding the road, the possibility of daily reality . . .

I write this, dear Lou, as in a diary, all of this, because I am not able to write a letter now and yet wanted to talk to you. I have almost grown unused to writing and so forgive me if this letter is crude and chaotic. Perhaps one cannot even see that it is full of joy for your house and enters it bringing many wishes. Many. Each and all.

Rainer.

Please, extend my warmest greetings to your husband; may my good wishes include him also and his new more public life!

Enclosure: This is a picture from Westerwedian days—in it one can see a portion of the room I built for myself back then. All the pieces of furniture were old, being Rilkean family property. I am sending it to you because it was at least a portion of house, not more than the broken shell of a snail, but a shell nonetheless. And because I want so much to give you something, in spite of the fact that this letter brings nothing at all.

[RMR to LAS in Göttingen]

(November 9, 1903)
Rome, Villa Strohl-Fern, January 15, 1904

Lou, dear Lou,

I am writing the date of your last letter above that of mine, —only because I want to make sure that nothing you wrote has been lost; the Italian postal service inspires such mistrust continually and in all possible ways.

Now, dear Lou, I am in my little garden-house, and after much disturbance this is the first quiet hour in it; now everything has its place in this simple room, dwells and lives and lets day and night come and go as they please; and outside, where so much rain has fallen, there is a spring afternoon, the hours of some spring which may be gone by tomorrow but which now seems to exist from eternity: so perfectly balanced is the light slender wind which is stirring the leaves, the laurel's shining leaves and the more retiring clusters on the bushes of evergreen oak, so confident are the small reddish buds on the newly barren trees, so intense is the fragrance that rises from the light gray-green narcissus field in my quiet garden valley which the arch of an old bridge spans deep in thought. I have swept the heavy pools of rain from my flat rooftop and raked withered oak leaves off to the side and that has made me warm and now, after this little burst of real work, my blood is singing as in a tree. And for the first time in so long I feel the tiniest bit free and festive and as if you might walk into my life . . .

This moment of bliss too will pass, and who knows if behind the distant mountains there is not already brewing a rainy night that will drench my roof again and a tearing wind that will fill my paths again with wilted things—

But I feel this hour mustn't go by without my having written you; for I can't afford to lose those few moments when I am able to write you, when I am calm, clear, and solitary enough to draw near you, —especially since I have so much to tell you. Once last spring in Paris there was an exhibition of paintings from antiquity at Durand-Ruel's, murals from a villa near Boscoreale which were being shown one last time in their ruined, fragmented unity before the hazards of auction dispersed them forever; they were the first antique paintings I had seen and I have seen none more beautiful here and they say that even the museum in Naples has no better paintings from that almost completely vanished time which must have had such great painters. Among these fragments one had survived whole and undisturbed, even though it was the largest and perhaps the most fragile; on it was portrayed a woman who sat quietly and with her grave, regal countenance listened to a man speaking softly and lost in thought, speaking to himself and to her with that dark voice in which past destinies are mirrored like shores at dusk; this man, if I remember correctly, had placed his hands on a staff, folded them together on the staff with which he had traveled for so long through distant lands; they were resting while he spoke (the way dogs lie down to sleep when their master begins to tell his story and they can hear in his voice that it will go on a long time—); yet even though this man was a good way into his story and probably still had a great stretch of memory before him (level memory in which, however, the path often veered unexpectedly), one knew, even at first glance, that he was the one who had come, the traveler to this quiet, stately woman, the prodigal to this majestic woman whose very essence radiates home: so infused he was with coming, the way waves on the beach are, always, even when they are already withdrawing in flat, glass-like sheets; he had not yet completely shed the haste which clings to even a more seasoned wanderer; his feelings were still attuned to unexpectedness and change, and his blood was still on the move in his feet—which, less relaxed than his hands, were unable to sleep. And so repose and movement were placed side by side in this painting, not as contrasts, more as complements, as a final unity that was slowly closing now like a healing wound; for even movement was already repose, it was settling as the snow settles when it quietly falls, was becoming landscape as snow does when it spreads over the shapes in the distance, and the past, having returned, took on the aspect of the eternal, and resembled those events that were the substance and magic of the woman's life.

I will always remember how this great, simple painting seized me, how absolutely it was painting because it showed only two figures, and how pregnant it was with meaning because these two figures were filled with themselves, heavy with themselves, and held together by some ultimate necessity. Just as the content of native legends can be intuited in good paintings, so I understood at first glance the meaning of this painting. In that so thoroughly confused Paris time, when every hurtful and heavy impression fell into my soul as from a great height, the encounter with this beautiful painting acquired its decisive note; as if, beyond all that was yet to happen, I had been permitted to view something achieved, final—that is how the sight of it moved me and upheld me. Just after that was when I had the courage to write you, dear Lou; for it seemed to me as if every path, even the most confused, could gain meaning through a final return to such a woman, to the one woman dwelling in ripeness and restfulness, who is great and, like a summer night, knows how to hear everything: the little noises frightened of themselves and loud calls and bells. . . .

But I, Lou, somehow your prodigal son, cannot for a long, long time yet be a storyteller, a soothsayer of my path, a describer of my past fortune; what you hear is only the sound of my step, still going forward, still on uncertain paths retreating, I know not from what; and whether it is approaching someone—I know not. Only that my mouth, when it has become a great river, may one day flow into you, into your listening and the great stillness of your opened depths—that is the prayer I recite to every hour that is mighty, to every apprehension or longing or joy that can guard and grant anything. Even if my life is insignificant now and often seems to me like an untilled field on which the weeds are master and on which birds of chance pick through its untended seed, —it will *be* only when I can tell it to you, and will be as you hear it!

Rainer.

[LAS to RMR in Rome]

[Göttingen,] Loufried, January 18, 1904.

Dear Rainer,

The white carnations with their hint of color came in the very last mail on New Year's Eve, and for ten days into the new year, into my first one here, they opened into bloom one bud after another! On New Year's they stood in the living room, which is about the same as the one you remember, but after that they stayed upstairs with me, where the two rooms in which I sleep and work are located, both of them done in gray-blue and with a wide balcony connecting them. I wanted to return your greetings on the very last night of the old year and thank you, but water had soaked through your address on the box of carnations, and it wasn't on your last letter, so that I couldn't even write you when your picture came: this picture very closely resembles you at certain hours, —but not you as a whole; I would say: shortly before bad hours, then you can look this way. I imagine that you have already changed since then. Would you like to have a little picture of me?

The few spring-like days your letter mentions have turned into the first real snowstorm here for us, it looks wonderful, up in the mountain forest one's whole heart opens. Until winter there were two views: above (to the east and north), this steep mountain forest against which we border (so closely that from the road one enters directly into our second floor), and into the distance, across hills and valleys; now it is almost the reverse: the winter days often cover the distant view with curtains of fog and snow flurries, while the mountain forest suddenly opens on trails in the leafless woods leading up and down and far away! And from far off one can see farmers' wives with wicker baskets on their backs as they come trudging over from the small village that lies in its little hollow somewhere on the other side. A peasant woman there makes my dresses and aprons and brings them in her panier along with kale and potatoes.

On New Year's Eve we hiked up to the top in order to hear the bells when they rang out in Göttingen. An indescribable peace over everything, a bit of moon, and Schimmel nibbled at the snow and sneezed. But the wind, coming from the east, blew the sound of the bells away from us and brought us instead, as if it were quite near, the pealing of the village bell. It made a very deep impression: below us the flickering festive city, which labored with all its churches and people and remained mute, —and rising up over and over again out of the dark the one loud festive bell—. It was my Иванъ Великій for 1904.

Since Christmas we have been putting up eggs for hatching; before then the chickens were still molting; in the spring we will add a goat, and from then on the garden will provide all our diet. Are you still a vegetarian? We both are, strictly now. I've also adopted my husband's passion for Roman baths, and take them once or twice every week.

My husband sends his regards, as does Schimmel, even though he does it by giving you his paw. And I think that one should tackle the new year with good courage: believe me, it will make a difference. If you could read your letters with my eyes, that's what you'd read there.

Lou.

[RMR to LAS in Göttingen]

Rome, Villa Strohl-Fern
January 21, 1904

Now, dear Lou, I have your letter, which I had so longed to receive. I thank you for its dear news about you and your quiet, spacious world; that I might see it again and have it around me, if only for a single day: *see it again*: for I feel as though I knew it, as though all of it had been around you forever and had received life from your life; it has merely grown simpler now, grown quieter and more inward, because reality always makes everything simpler and every natural fulfillment only fulfills things of weight and importance. Such things are around you, and even as far away as I am I can feel their peace and happiness. And I know, Lou, that all of this grounds life, grounds my life too; it's just that I am separated from this good ground by a murky surface and a restless depth; it's just that I don't know how to hold myself without churning up my water and can't find the place where the ground remains steady beneath the current, like a picture beneath the safehold of glass.

But I love everything you write about, and my awkward, blundering life is forever striving toward such modest days, and whenever it manages, with great quietness and however briefly, to come close to actual things as it passes them, I can feel it grow. Here much is just as it was in Schmargendorf; often I don't go into the city for days, and live on what I myself prepare: on groats, eggs, canned vegetables and milk; *Sanatogen* has replaced *Tropon* (which seems to have disappeared), because some supplement seems to me necessary as long as one can follow a vegetarian diet only in such unbalanced, piecemeal fashion. At the inn (a sad little *trattoria*) I even have to eat a meat dish now and then, much as I would rather not; for vegetarian life appeals to me more and more, and I still avoid any drink with alcohol in it, preferring instead herbal tea and coffee I brew myself, which have become great pleasures.

My wife brought with her a device for making steam baths (she had grown used to them), and we have reassembled it here in the garden, where one can enjoy it along with sunbathing without fear of being disturbed. Days and nights I am often in this garden (it is quite overgrown but one section of it is specifically designated as part of my little house), where, wearing my old Russian shirt, I clear and trim, plant and pull weeds, and end up fretting because even work such as this I perform badly and awkwardly and feel at every moment that my strength or knowledge will fail me. Walking barefoot is the only thing I miss here; the ground is too hazardous and thorny for it, the meadows have been neglected too long and in the warmer months all sorts of unfriendly creatures go about in the grass; recently I took a two-hour trip to the sea, and, at a spot near Anzio where Nero's summer villas once stood, gave my feet a holiday in soft, wet sand; from now on they shall enjoy this occasionally.

On that trip I discovered that an old villa owned by the Borghese family stands on this nearby seacoast (the whole thing is up for rent, each room separately); with its grand halls, stairs, and terraces it looks out over its lush orange groves onto the sea so beautifully that "The White Princess" could have even more plausibly been conceived here than in that house in Viareggio. None of the house had been rented yet, and I walked through its many echoing rooms, whose windows opened at every turn onto always new vistas and surprises.

Perhaps, had I found this place earlier, before I had rented the place where I am, I would have wanted to live by the sea in this great eloquent house; but then again, it is doubtless best that I am where I am and thus all alone; soon other people would have arrived there, it would have become loud with voices and footsteps and I would have been only one among many, one who has the lowliest room in a disdainful house: while here I am everything to my little house, its entire life and heart and heartbeat; also "no one's master and no one's slave," since I do everything that I require myself—at least as far as my strength and knowledge permit. At first I wanted very badly to have a dog, and since my little house sits alone at the edge of this extensive garden, the owner of the villa himself encouraged me; but in the end I chose not to increase my family status this way: there had been expenses enough, disruptions as well, and for a long time it would have meant more of both, since one would have had to buy a very small dog (I thought of Wolff in Wolfratshausen); and then another new destiny would have arisen from this bringing together and imperfectly joining two lives—, unexpected things, difficult things, things at any rate much too complicated for a beginner like me.

(So Schimmel then remains my "closest" dog or better yet my dog-confidant and as such I send him my greetings.—)

My two windows are tall; I can see the park rising and widening and also much sky, and thus also much night. In front of the one is my desk; and the writing stand, where I spend most of my time, is placed in the middle of the room where the views from both windows can be enjoyed.— Each morning the translation of *Слово о полку Игоря* proceeds there slowly, since I have returned to it after a long interruption; and the most recent evenings have been taken up with the book *Ellen Olestjerne,* in which Franziska Reventlow has finally set down all the events of her life in the form of a novel. I am supposed to write a short review of this book for *Zukunft,* but I read and read and the right words just won't come. This life, whose principal value lies simply in its having been *lived* without disaster befalling it, may lose too much of its urgency when it is told by the one who steered it and underwent it without in the process becoming an artist. Suddenly it appears as if the person in question had not been the most important thing in this life and in its connections, —as if there, out beyond her, life had arisen that she didn't grasp at all . . . But perhaps I am biased and can't see clearly because the book itself turned out to be so much less remarkable than the fate through which its author lived; perhaps, on the other hand, this fate, crowded into a small, sickly countenance, heaped on a strange young woman and borne by her every day of her life [*in the margin*: as I once knew it], could not but appear larger, more imposing, and more extraordinary than it actually was; this book is so full of that frivolousness which always seemed to me only a mask, a form of mimicry behind which she could hide amid so many difficulties; but now, in this book, it seems almost a natural facility for what is easiest and most superficial, for what is perpetually amusing—and hence a kind of empty vanity. And when I call in my memories to check, I realize that as many of them will support this view as the earlier one, and her letters also from all these years can be read first one way, then another—so that the only way to say something about the book will be to read it free of all personal feelings and recollections, just as it is.

But evening is here and I must get to work on this task that has been waiting for me all this time. Just one more thing. You read my picture well: it actually is from the beginning of bad days; I am fond of it only because it has in it something of the room that was a fragment of home and restfulness, a small quiet spot for us, even if only for a moment; it lacked reality to the same extent that this little house about which I've written you various things today *possesses* reality; and I've told you about it so you'll know where and into what life your little picture will arrive; for yes, Lou, please, do send me one. I want to keep it with my fondest things and accomplish my days before its eyes; feelings analogous to those in your dear letter will be visible in it along with all the other things that I remember so often and that seem to me to reach all the way back into my childhood, —and I shall read in it as one reads in the Bible, never knowing what new realization will dawn and fade.

Rainer.

Many, many greetings to your husband and to your wonderful house beside the mountain forest.

[RMR to LAS in Göttingen]

Villa Strohl-Fern, March 17, 1904

Dear Lou,

It was January 22. That's when I wrote you. I told you about many mundane things in my life; I thanked you for your letter; I asked you for a little picture.

Since then I have not heard from you and circumstances are such that this worries me. Every day I must wonder if the Russian War has not brought terror and danger to your family—to your nephews, your mother, and yourself. That this disaster had to come, this heavy burden, this suffering for thousands who all feel the war the way Garshin felt it: as agony inflicted.

God, had one but strength, reserves of strength—did one not live, as I do even in this quiet, remote life, meagerly and anxiously on the daily bread of one's strength, —had one become something real (a doctor, which ultimately is what one should have been—), there would be only one place or calling now for someone who would put himself to use or bend to the task: those dressing-stations where Russian people are dying grievous and horrible deaths.

I think of young Smirnoff, one of the workmen we met at Schillchen's. Later I received two letters from him; he was a soldier in Warsaw. Perhaps he too is out there among the conscripted, suffering and thinking, thinking, trying to understand . . .

What is it like now for all those people who have been sent so suddenly to the East from their quiet snow-covered villages and suburbs?—

But finding out about you is of utmost urgency to me now. Are you at home, are you in Russia?—

Here (yes, here) the Roman spring is beginning; the city is filling up with tourists seeking out all the traditional enchantments; now and then a group of them comes through our park, and from behind the bushes one can hear approaching that terrible sound of German voices waxing enthusiastic. Then I creep deeper into my tiny red house I almost never leave. I am reading Soeren Kierkegaard. This summer I shall learn Danish so I can read him and Jacobsen in their own language.

The *Слово* translation is finished. Back in February I began a larger work, a kind of second part to the *Book of God* [*Liebe-Gott-Buch*]; right now I am stuck somewhere in the middle of it without knowing if and when it will continue and where it will lead. All sorts of troubles arrived—disruptions, chance happenings, everything that always distracts me so thoroughly no matter how involved in my work I am. But now I must return to it; its very difficulty persuades me that some day it actually will become something, something good.

It still appears that the *Book of God* will be published this spring in a shorter, simple, unadorned edition under its intended old title: *Stories of God* [*Geschichten vom lieben Gott*]. In May I will be able to send them to you, dear Lou.

I hope you are peacefully at home with your garden, which should be beginning to stir; the little migratory birds that are tuning their voices here now will soon be on their way to you.

Rainer.

[LAS to RMR in Rome]

[Göttingen,] Loufried, March 20, 1904

Dear Rainer,

What a comfort it is to hear you speak of our war this way! In Germany no one understands that Russia, however involuntarily, stands in for Europe against Asia in this conflict, —always forced into this middle position where it must endure the collision of East and West on behalf of all, as it did earlier in the time of the Mongols. All its fates have been shaped by this fact. But what is truly tragic seems to me: that its own deepest destiny—may it fulfill itself through the course of centuries (дай Богъ!)—is almost directly the opposite: namely, to fight through toward a synthesis, toward a spiritually fruitful union of Eastern and Western culture, instead of prolonging that fierce uncomprehending split which for the rest of Europe will probably last forever—and for good reason, since, you see, they pursue their mission elsewhere. And so this war that is murdering our people, however it ends, even if in victory, can only signify regression and delay. Up till now—and this seems so characteristic—Russia has proceeded in its unstoppable expansions into Asia with tolerance and as a force of direct cultural enrichment, in contrast to the other nations, which colonize only to unload their people and whose culture wreaks havoc and destruction as upon some totally alien region to which it is completely indifferent. It is true that these very virtues are now causing Russia to engage in a certain intolerance and cultural repression in her Western members such as Finland and the Baltic provinces, since in the end all the horses do have to pull together if they are to get the cart moving. But who is concerned with all this, who speaks of it? No one but the religious and reactionary slavophiles who for the most part regard these issues from a narrow and again one-sidedly anti-European perspective.

Especially in the case of this war, everything pointed in the opposite direction: the innate disposition of the people, the czar's love of peace (about which, at such horrific cost now, he was so sincere that he didn't even make preparations), the cultural endeavors of the progressives, all the most influential political voices; and yet against all this, Russia nevertheless *had* to want this war, had to want it because—England wanted it. Ah, how can one *not* hate and rage against this? The mere thought of it makes one want to scream! And so often it seems to me that only a single human being is marching off to war: Russia, like some one person, an intimate acquaintance whose soul one feels as one's own. —One knows only a few scraps of this vast country, and yet one has this overwhelming feeling of a direct human connection.

Among my two brothers' sons, three are waiting for their marching orders; my old mama, who turned 80 in January but is amazingly vigorous and alert, sits and sews for the wounded. I was supposed to visit her last month, but was ill for a long time. Which also explains my silence. Not that this prevented my selfishness from anticipating a letter from you, sometimes. Our winter this year was almost Russian, less by its coldness than by its whiteness and splendor, and there was constantly the most perfect weather for sleigh-riding; such magical jangling of bells all through the mountain woods! We ourselves bundled into a sleigh hung with strings of little chimes and took a wonderful ride toward the mountains, through silvery woods that stood there like tall, very quiet fairy tales. Now the snowdrops in the garden are coming up, but snow flurries are still gusting around them, and the hills remain white. My balcony has become like a giant birdcage extending all the way to the sky! Every day new little birds and new little sounds are added; and if one listens carefully, one can eventually hear everything that thrills the heart and makes life beautiful! So, early as it is, a greeting today from spring to spring, dear Rainer,

from

Lou.

[LAS to RMR in Rome]

[Göttingen, Wednesday, March 25, 1904]

Христосъ воскресъ!

[RMR to LAS in Göttingen]

Rome, Villa Strohl-Fern
last day of March, 1904

Христосъ воскресъ!

Dear Lou,

Ивановъ [Ivanov] and Гоголъ [Gogol] once wrote these words from here and many are writing them even today from here to their Easter homeland. But alas, this is not an Easter City and not a country that knows how to lie quietly beneath the pealing of great bells. It is all display without devoutness, charade rather than true festival.

For me Easter was one single time: back in that long, extraordinary, incomparable, excited night when everyone was out in the streets and amidst all the jostling Иванъ Великій struck me in the darkness, blow after blow. That was my Easter, and I believe it will suffice for an entire life; the Good News was given to me writ strangely large in that Moscow night, was given into my blood and into my heart, I know this now:

Христосъ воскресъ!

Yesterday they sang Palestrina in Saint Peter's. But it was nothing! Everything dissolves in the vanity of that huge empty house, which is like a hollow pupa from which some dark giant butterfly has crept. Today, though, I spent many hours in a small Greek church; a patriarch was there in grand vestments, and through the imperial gate of the *Iconostass* in a long file they brought him his ornations: his great crown, his staff of ivory, gold, and mother-of-pearl, a pyx with the host, and a golden chalice. And he accepted everything from their hands and kissed the bearers, and they were all old men who brought him these things. And later one could see them, these old men with their golden cloaks and their beards, standing around the large, simple stone table in the Holy of Holies, reading long and deeply. And outside, before the wall of icons, young monastic pupils stood in facing lines, right and left, and sang to each other with heads uplifted and throats outstretched, like black birds on spring nights.

Then, dear Lou, I said Христосъ воскресъ to you.

And then, immediately after that when I came home, waiting there was your card, on which those same words were written. Thank you, Lou.

And thank you also for the letter and the dear picture. They have fulfilled so much more for me than my request: things past that were irretrievably lost cling to them, and things future that were unable to come rise through their power, dear Lou.

The war—our war—is almost like a visceral unrest inside me, —but I read little about it since I loathe newspapers and do my best to avoid them; they only twist and distort everything. A few days ago in the "Zeit" (daily sheet of *Die Zeit*) there was a Russian officer's letter, which I am enclosing; needless to say, they couldn't resist prefacing this simple, tremulous piece of news with an annoying introduction. I also read somewhere that the war would probably last for years; Kuropatkin was supposed to have said that; but surely it can't be possible!

It is good that you are in your house, with the flowers that are about to sprout; and good too that you are so close to your family and yet are at home and are having the spring of the winter you've just passed. But to hear that you are ill . . . ?

Be in good health, Lou, —for yourself and for those who need you.

Rainer.

[LAS to RMR in Rome, color postcard depicting a horseman in armor—son of a czar—halted in front of a gravestone whose image depicts a scene from the Russian fairy tale of Ivan the Czar's son, the firebird, and the gray wolf]

[Göttingen, Monday, April 11, 1904]

Thank you, dear Rainer, for the words and flowers! The snowdrops have remained standing *until today*. I wanted to thank you more graciously, so I have waited until today, but can't: bedridden! You write in my place, tell me about yourself, won't you? Here winter has returned.

Lou.

[RMR to LAS in Göttingen]

Rome, Villa Strohl-Fern
April 15, 1904

Dear Lou,

When—as so often happens—you are in a dream of mine, this dream and its echo in the following day are more real than all daily reality, are *world* and *happening*. I am thinking about this because the night before the eleventh and all that day (the same day you wrote your card) passed thus: in your presence, which makes me calm, patient, good.

There have been endless interruptions these last few days, and I had a presentiment that they would come one after another when I began my new work back on the eighth of February; it became apparent then that my mode of working (as well as my more receptive way of looking) had changed, so that I would probably never again be able to write a book in ten days (or evenings), would need for each new one a long and uncalculated time; this is a good thing, it is an advance toward that state of continual work I want to achieve whatever the cost; perhaps a first preliminary step. But this change brings with it a new danger; fending off all external disturbances for eight or ten days is possible—: but for weeks, for months? This fear oppressed me, and may be to blame for my work faltering and breaking off around the first of March. And what I took for a brief hiatus has become, against my will, a burdensome vacation that goes on and on.

My mother came to Rome and is still here. I see her only rarely, but—as you know—every meeting with her is a kind of relapse. When I have to see this lost, unreal woman unconnected to anything and unable to grow old, I feel how even as a child I struggled to escape her, and I fear deep inside that after years and years of running and walking I am still not far enough away from her, that somewhere inwardly I still make movements that are supplements of her stunted gestures, pieces of memories she carries around broken inside her; then I feel a horror of her mindless piety, of her obstinate religiosity, of all those distorted and deformed things to which she has clung, herself an empty dress, ghostly and terrible. And that still I am her child; that some scarcely discernable concealed door in this faded wall that is not part of any structure was my entrance into the world— (if indeed such an entrance can lead into the world at all . . .)!

That is difficult and confusing enough for someone like me who has so much to make up and whose courage keeps failing. But there were other things too. People who were planning to visit Rome and (even though I have no social contacts at all) expressed their desire to see me or make my acquaintance. Some even tried to come with written introductions, and it cost me letters and excuses on all sides to keep them away. And Rome began to swell, became fat and German and enthusiastic through and through. At the same time the spring advanced in abrupt shifts of wind, and each day rose steeply from its chilly morning to its sun-scorched noon, so that of course a cold and the feeling of flu were soon upon me. Swarms of ants broke out of all the walls of my little house and attempted invasion after invasion. The first scorpions appeared, uncommonly large and early. And on top of everything, the painter who had loaned us furniture last fall (with the agreement, unfortunately verbal only and insufficiently explicit, that we could purchase it later if necessary) returned to Rome and, forgetting all previous arrangements, demanded that his property be returned posthaste, so that now, at a single stroke, my little house is almost empty. And I had taken care of these things all winter long, they were my closest connections, and I already had little roots in them. Now I console myself by remarking that for the time being I have been allowed to keep a bookcase and a bed, that my standing desk belongs to me, and that during the summer it is fitting anyway not to have many things around me.

For the season here, God knows, has for the last three or four days ceased to be spring and become dense, young summer. The hyacinths in my little flowerbed, which had long been hesitating, have now flung open their blossom-eyes like someone jolted awake by an alarm clock, and they are already standing there tall and erect. The elms and oaks next to my house are full of leaves, the Judas tree has shed its blooms, and all its leaves will be ready by tomorrow morning; and a syringa tree that only three days ago was stretching out its clusters is fading already and becoming scorched; the nights are scarcely cool any longer, and their voice is the busy croaking of frogs. The owls call less often, and the nightingale still hasn't begun. Will she now sing at all, since it is summer?

Summer in Rome. Another new affliction. I thought it was still far off and was looking forward, now that my mother will have gone again, to one or two temperate months of work. And I still hope that it is possible, still hope that spring will return after a few rehearsal-days for summer. (Moreover, I will probably have to stay on here throughout the summer, for there is scarcely any possibility of my traveling elsewhere, and, at any rate, I wouldn't know where to go. But that will only be the question after next; the next one is the question of work and self-concentration, and I want to see it soon decided.)

It is beautiful in the large garden, even if not much is blooming there, and even if what is distinctly Roman is perhaps too loud, too insistent to be called Spring. Even these meadows full of anemones and daisies are too thick, too heavy, too close-meshed; and in the sky there are none of those gray days behind yet empty trees, none of those vast, transforming winds and the softly falling rains that are for me the essence of all springs. It is, alas, a spring for foreigners who have only a little time—obvious and garish and exaggerated. But there is one tree in the garden that could stand in Tuscany, in an ancient cloister there: a tall old cypress, full of wisteria-trails whose light blue-violet pendants are now falling and rising everywhere, even all the way up out of the tree's darkness; —an emblem of happiness. And along with it the glorious fig trees, which with their upcurving branches stand there like altar candlesticks out of the Old Testament and slowly open their light-green leaves.

And that I am able to observe all this now and take it in calmly and patiently does seem to me a kind of progress and preparation; but, as you know, my "progresses" are somehow like the faint steps of a convalescent, improbably weightless, tottering, and beyond measure needing help. And there is no help. It would be a help to talk to you about many things and see you listening silently; to read to you sometime. . . . But writing you is also a help, dear Lou; I know that when I think of the years when I did not have this refuge.

Please: And now you must get well!

Rainer.

[LAS to RMR in Rome]

[Göttingen, Loufried, beginning of May 1904]

Dear Rainer,

Thank you for your letter. Perhaps by now your compulsory vacation days are already over, but of course one can't know about these things, any more than one can know whether a nighttime dream will recur. If this deep anxiety had not been made an ingredient of all creative work, the latter would probably be too undiluted a blessing for human beings; I always think of this and a few other sensations as requiring such additives to prevent them from working like concentrated and swiftly fatal poisons; they can only be life-enhancing if they are bound up with our inner inhibitions or with some other person (which is inhibition enough!). That's why one finds in all that has ever succeeded at life the processing of an almost infinite profusion, equally rich in truths and errors, triumphs and failures; from case to case ever anew an enigma; because *life*. At any rate it made the deepest impression on me when I read somewhere that chickens would grow sick and die if their feed were completely free of bacteria, and that overly pure water will cause stomach-trouble.

As different as it seems, you might try looking at your mother from a similar perspective: even if she were nothing more than a single thick bacillus in your meal of life or in your most personal makeup, her presence there might just as easily be enabling as disabling. Bacteria only bring to ferment what is already inside oneself and what, given that opportunity (illness), one *expels*. Many a perfect, most blessed mother is for her child *sterile* (germ-free nourishment!!). We know so little that we needn't entwine ourselves in imaginary arguments; a fig tree in bloom where you are, the blue violet-clusters here with us that are everywhere pushing out of the mossy cracks in the old stone wall around our garden: these are still the most *factual* things, the things most worth knowing, the true things one must experience.

But an entire summer in Rome would be gruesomely unhealthy. Most years Rome has already become a strain on one's nerves and a nest of fevers by early May. Are you settled in so firmly there that you can't take advantage of the inexpensive refreshments of the Italian mountains and sea? And the many beautiful things that lie beyond Rome?

Even we had a few days of summer heat; now a fragrance and freshness again that are intoxicating. One can't even look at the little leaves and the budding flowers without knowing: we are kin to them, it's just that we forget it over and over, but Spring says it so loudly that we too are Springs. For this at heart is why it so delights us.

The fruit-trees are starting to flower. And there are 43 fruit trees in our garden!

And as for myself, during the days of my illness I let slip from me a piece of work, a big, cherished work of which the larger half, 300 pages when printed, had fully developed, and it caused me to walk around week after week in a state of heady bliss. One must have patience.

Lou.

[RMR to LAS in Göttingen]

Rome, Villa Strohl-Fern
May 12, 1904

Your letter, dear Lou, I have read often; it was just and good. When it arrived, there was a quiet spacious evening over the garden and I read it slowly on the flat roof of my little house and pondered it for a long time. Perhaps, said something inside me, I will begin something good tomorrow morning—perhaps. And amid much subdued hope there was a bit of gladness in me—:

Which was not to blossom; for the burden of my vacation time increased with every day. The weather had gradually grown cooler and the disturbances had receded and nevertheless things wouldn't begin to improve inside me; just as last spring a strange frailty, sickness, and inertia took hold of my life, so now also everything became difficult and frightening once more. It stopped short of those feelings of anxiety out of which I began calling for you a year ago. I was lucid and recognized what was happening and saw everything around me without fear. But an incapacity that I understood as issuing from something physical reduced me to a minimum of existence, a continual exhaustion, an aridity from which the last drop had been drained, —and in doing so divided me from everything alive and living and made me as alone as something thrown away in disgust that no longer connects with anything. As if the premature heat of those brooding April days had remained in my limbs undiminished and stood in my nerves as in airless rooms, I went about weighed down and filled up, every morning beginning the struggle against all burden, every evening succumbing beneath it. Those strange fluctuations in the circulation of my blood that I wrote you about last year had returned, and amid excruciating headaches, toothaches (wherever the influx of blood is most violent, its presence pounds most insistently) were causing me days and nights that passed uselessly and with torturous slowness. All effort to accomplish something always ends on such days the same way, with all my blood finally gathering at the throbbing spot, trembling in my eyelids often far into my anxious dreams and filling my eyes with its close disquiet as with fearful images.

In times like these I long so much for a true physician, one to whom I could tell all my plight; such a doctor, I think, would have to have the patience to listen to me and hear me out. For even if it is hysteria, it is still a force against which my will is as powerless as against a wound that will not close. That would be so good for me: just once to find a doctor who does not categorize me the moment I start talking, who would have patience and time and friendship enough to accept my statements as the symptoms of my life, which even and *precisely* in its suffering accords so deeply with every life's desire: to outlast its sickness, to grow beyond it, and to slowly learn from it the unconscious processes by which such alien entities are expelled . . .

When I ask myself what may have precipitated my incapacity this time, three possible causes come to mind.

First, in the work I accomplished during the month of February there may have been a certain overexertion; I made an effort back then, in connection with my new book, to write down and give form to many things from my difficult Paris impressions, and occasionally I would feel, while I was doing this, a stab of pain in my soul similar to what one feels in one's back when one lifts something too heavy.

Second, during the entire time of this work I felt the impending arrival of my mother as a limit, a stopping-place, and this injected into my writing an element of rushed urgency, a hurrying that eventually caused it to break off. From this anxiety over something external that was impending, there developed premonitions of all sorts of disturbances, worries, and chance interruptions; and when this invasion of voices into all my quietness actually did come about soon thereafter (and in so many ways), it at least released me from the wavering burden of such forebodings, but it also consumed more and more of the time and strength and courage that I needed for *one* task.

The third is the Roman climate. At first I thought that I had come through this winter's many sirocco days relatively unscathed. But when the first attacks of summer warmth in my garden and in my garden-house (which soaks up much heat) decimated me so utterly, I realized that I must have been using up great quantities of strength all winter long in my daily resistance to this climate—so much so that now my reserves are practically exhausted.—

The clear experience of this necessitates new decisions, and before I set about making one or another of them I want to tell you, dear Lou, a few things about myself, as best I can during these ineffectual days. Perhaps you will want to respond to one or another aspect of what follows; that would mean very much to me; you know how much. (But if you are immersed in your work now, in the work that is dear to you, then put this letter aside, because it comes from someone restless, and he can wait; can wait as long as you wish.)

And now:

I have rented my little garden house in the park of the Villa Strohl-Fern through September. I had hoped to hold out there for the entire summer (or at least the greater part of it); but now I know—that is out of the question. Moreover, I had planned on keeping the house for yet another year: for where would I ever find another like it? Just a little house, all to myself, with large windows and a flat roof-terrace, inside it a spacious bright simple room, and situated deep, deep in a private garden, inaccessible and secluded, far removed from traffic and noise—: a feeling counseled me to hold on to this place where all of that can be mine, at least for as long as external circumstances, which are so disobliging and fickle, in any way permit it; but now this same feeling tells me that I should insist on such favorable living conditions only if I can find them under a healthier sky, beneath which one may live the entire year without fear and dread. The autumn here was bad, and the winter, with its frequent sirocco and its long periods of rain, was oppressive, and the spring which everyone praises so extravagantly is nothing but a hastening into the dangerous summer like a downward plunge without a stopping-place. The people who live here insist, moreover, that one endures the Roman climate best as a novice, and that with each successive year one actually fares worse, as the seasick-like atmosphere of its sirocco days gradually drains one of one's defenses.

In addition: I seem in the past few years to have moved far, far away from things Italian. (I already felt this a year ago in Viareggio, where I ascribed it to different causes—.) That I now experience everything so differently may be due to my being in Rome and not in some region of Tuscany, which spoke to me so quietly with sky-blue and marble-white, with Botticelli and the Robbias, with gardens, villas, roses, bells, and girls with a strange, distant allure—; but speak it did (and Rome speaks too), it didn't keep silent and it didn't scream: it *spoke*. It talked to me until my cheeks glowed—(and I sometimes wonder if *that* wasn't the good and important thing for me, and if my first Viareggio, concluding as it did with such empty fireworks, with so great an expenditure into nothing, was not already evidence that Italian influences are not among the things that truly advance me).

However that may be, —the fact is that more northerly and somber countries have since taught my senses to appreciate what is simple and understated, so that they now feel all this shrillness and the strong, schematic, uninflected quality of Italian things as a relapse into picture-book instruction. It happened quite by chance that I was able to absorb and study this whole obvious and ostentatious spring in a purely botanical manner, with the objective, quiet attention that is becoming more and more a part of my gaze; the season's movements and voices and the upward flight and course of its birds interested me in a completely factual way, without my ever feeling it as something whole, living, and mysterious—as soul vitally bordering on mine. I noted details, and since up till now I have observed so little and am a beginner in the simple act of looking (as in so much else)—such activity satisfied me, and I made progress. But if it ever happened that I expected or needed something from the *whole*, I opened up and closed again empty and felt a deep hunger. Like a lung in a used-up room my soul labored in an exhausted world, a world into which nothing new enters with the spring, nothing vast and unpredictable. I felt the great poverty that lies in wealth: how, with us, a flower, a small first flower that fights its way through and arrives, is a world, a happiness, the sharing of which one experiences as an infinite good, —and how here whole flocks of flowers arrive without anything stirring in one's own self, without anything taking part and feeling akin and divining its own origin in something else. Here everything is given over to ease, to the easiest side of ease. Flowers and blossoms come, anemones and wisteria bloom, and one says this to oneself and says it again as to someone hard of hearing. But it is all so pitifully blank and make-believe; colors are there, to be sure, but they always subordinate themselves lazily to some cheap tint and never develop out of themselves. The Judas tree bloomed, bloomed and bloomed, its endless unfruitful blooms even oozing out of its own trunk like blood-soaked mesentery, and in a few weeks everything, anemones and clover and syringa and star flowers, everything had taken on the mauve of its mauve, for God knows what reasons, —from indolence, from mimicry, from lack of inspiration. And even now the red roses are assuming this corpse-like mauve as they wilt and the strawberries have it after only a day and the sunsets throw it up in billows and it suffuses the clouds morning and evening. And the skies in which such cheap color-games take place are shallow and as if silted up; they are not everywhere at once, they do not, as do the skies of the sea, the plains, and the moor, play *around* things, are not an endless beginning of distance, are conclusion, curtain, end, —and behind the last trees, which stand flat like stage props against this indifferent photographer's background, —everything ceases. This truly is the sky over things past; drained, empty, forsaken sky, sky-husk from which the last sweetness has long been extracted. And as the sky is, so are the nights, and as the nights are, so are the voices of the nightingales. Where the nights are vast their note is deep, and they fetch it from infinitely far away and carry it all the way to the end. Here the nightingale is really only a small bird in heat with a shallow song and an easily satisfied desire. In two nights one has already grown used to its call and one registers it with an inward caution and restraint, as though one were afraid that any stronger response would injure one's own memories, memories of nightingale-nights that are quite, quite different.

The exhibition-atmosphere so typical of the city is also the most obvious aspect of the Roman spring. What takes place here is a grand display of spring, not Spring. The tourists of course are delighted by it and feel themselves honored like little monarchs for whose sake everything has been decked out and polished; for these reputable Germans, Italy always must have been a kind of royal journey with triumphal arches, gifts of flowers, and fireworks. And in a certain sense they are right: they come down, tired of winter and heated rooms and darkness, and find everything that is sunny and comfortable, ready and waiting for them here. That's all they ask. And something like this is probably what I too was experiencing back then in Arco or Florence when I would sometimes feel surrounded by well-being. But once one has seen, as a native, the entire winter here (full of the sullen persistence of what cannot die), then the miracle that ought to follow rings false. One knows that this is no real spring, for one has seen no spring *evolve*: these flowers have had as little difficulty arriving at their appointed place as decorations have in being put up somewhere. And one grasps so well the sham-life of this people whose time is past, the empty phrases of its descendant-art, the garden-flower prettiness of D'Annunzio's verses.—

It is good that I have experienced all this so slowly and with such physical immediacy; for Italy has always been a call for me and an unfinished episode. But now I can leave it in good conscience, for the end is here.

Of course it will be hard, because this little house stands on this spot and cannot be taken along and set up again in some different, more northerly garden; hard, because the new break comes unexpectedly and leads out into the uncertain; hard—, because I am weary of forever having to break off and start over again.

Yet all the same it must hapen. Just let me linger a moment over the question of where I will go now. Someplace, I answer, where once again a small house like this one stands alone in a large garden, useless for everyone else and fitting me like a good suit of clothes! But I know that such houses are rare, that one cannot seek them out but must come upon them accidentally. And so I don't even inquire about them.

But I do want to say what circumstances shall *not* play a part in my upcoming choice of a new place.

Clara Rilke, my wife, will soon leave here (probably even before I do) and try living in the country somewhere near Bremen (which she hopes will send her a number of students and portrait commissions), concerned for herself and devoted to the work that is her calling. —Little Ruth, our dear daughter, will remain with my wife's parents on the quiet country estate where her life has already set down roots and is growing fine and straight. —As to the question of income, which rears up again with each change, demanding and threatening, I can say this: that I am not closing my eyes to it and am not putting it off until it returns with even greater urgency; I see it and know that it is always there. If nevertheless I do not accord it the most important voice in this present choice of place, it is because of my ever-growing conviction that from my work must eventually come my bread. For it *is* work and as such necessary; and it *must* be possible (or become possible) to do it and to live, if one only does it well. Art is a way of life that stretches as far as can be imagined, and when I think how slight and elementary everything is that I have done up till now, it does not surprise me that this achievement (which resembles a strip of half-cultivated field the width of one's foot) yields me no sustenance. Plans do not of themselves bear fruit, and seed prematurely sown does not sprout. But patience and work are real and can at any moment change into bread. "*Il faut toujours travailler*," Rodin would say to me every time I tried to lament to him the conflict inherent in daily life. He knew of no other solution, and indeed it had been his own. For decades they denied him, and had he gone off with his plans and waited for better days, everything would have passed over him as over nothing; but since his world rose up in the midst of these people, it made them stop in their tracks and was an obstacle with which they had to contend. —To persist with my art and to put all my trust *only* in it: this I am learning from his great and greatly given example; just as I am learning patience from him. But experience has all too often shown me that I cannot count on any great reserves of strength; and so I shall avoid, at least for as long as it seems possible, doing two different things at once, shall not divorce earnings from work but try to find both in a single, concentrated endeavor; only thus can my life become something good and necessary, and all its inherited and immature disjointedness grow together into a single supporting stem.

Hence I want to set all other factors aside and choose my next abode strictly with an eye toward my work and its needs. This is all the more important since I now feel in the midst of developments and transitions (changes that involve perception and creation in equal measure) that may slowly be leading to a *toujours travailler* with which, at least in a certain sense, all difficulties, perils, and confusions, internal as well as external, would truly be surmounted. For the effects of my health (which is so fickle) on my work and the effects on my health of my inability to work could one day be made to reverse or cancel each other out; then the inner chasm would fill, and the outer hardship would be free of fear; for whoever *always works* can also live, *must* be able to live.

And so it is time to address my immediate intentions.

The works I have in mind and which shall occupy me by turns are:

1. The *Prayers*, which I want to expand.

2. My new book (whose firm, tightly woven prose is a schooling for me and an advance that had to come so that, later on, I could write all the other things—including the military novel.)

3. An attempt at a drama.

4. Two monographs:

The Poet: Jens Peter Jacobsen.

The Painter: Ignacio Zuloaga.

Both the latter require travel. The first a trip to Thisted and a stay in Copenhagen, the second a journey through Spain. (Zuloaga was, besides Rodin, the only person during my stay in Paris who affected me deeply and lastingly and whose importance and value I feel and can express. Or shall be able to express. Some day I will tell you about him.)

There is no hurry about these travels and books; I shall probably take up Jacobsen first. You can't imagine how crucial he has become for me: I have approached him on ever new paths, sometimes alone, sometimes with my wife (who reads him so well and with such empathy); indeed, no matter where one wanders amid things of real importance one can be sure of coming out in a place where he also is (if one walks far enough); and how strange it is to find his and Rodin's words often agreeing so exactly: one has that crystal-clear feeling one gets in mathematical proofs at the moment two distant lines converge, as from eternity, at a single point; or when two large complicated numbers which bear no resemblance to one another simultaneously withdraw in acknowledgment of a single simple integer at the heart of all. —Strangely inviolate joy issues from such experiences.—

I also have in mind certain studies to accompany and supplement these works. Already I have begun learning Danish, chiefly so that I can read Jacobsen and some of Kierkegaard in the original.

I also began something in Paris that I would like to go on with: reading in the big German Dictionary of the Brothers Grimm, from which a writer can,

I think, gain much provender and instruction. Ideally one ought to know and have at one's disposal everything that has ever entered into a language and is now part of it, rather than trying to make do with a chance supply that is so meager as to allow no room for choosing. It would be a good thing if such a project led me now and then to read a medieval poet; for doesn't it seem that the Gothic period, with its myriad and unforgettable accomplishments in architecture and the visual arts, must also have possessed and created a sculptural *language*, in which words were like statues and lines like rows of pillars? I know nothing of it, nothing whatsoever. Nothing, I feel, of all I would like to know. —There are so many things about which some very old man should tell one while one is little; for then one would simply grow up and know them. There are the starry heavens, and I don't know what mankind has learned about them, don't even know how to read the constellations. And it's the same with the flowers, with animals, with those simplest laws that are operative everywhere and traverse the world with just a few strides from beginning to end. How life originates, how it functions in the lower creatures, how it branches and spreads, how life blossoms, how it bears fruit: I need to learn all of that. To bind myself more firmly to the reality that so often denies me, by taking part in all that lives, —*to be there*, not just in feeling but in knowledge, always and always: that, I think, is what I need to grow more secure and less homeless. You feel that I don't want the scholar's sciences, since each one requires a lifetime and no life is long enough to master even their beginnings; but I do want to cease being someone excluded, someone who can't read through surface-events to his era's deeper tidings that lead out beyond the present and reach back into the past, a prisoner who has an inkling of everything but not even the certainty required to know if it is daytime or evening, winter or spring. I would like, in some place where such a thing is possible, to learn what I would probably already know had I been allowed to grow up in the country and among more basic people, what an impersonal and hurried schooling failed to tell me, and all the rest that has since been discovered and recognized and is now part of common knowledge. It's not the history of art or any other history I want to learn, not the essence of any philosophical system, —I only want the chance to acquire and earn for myself one or two of the large, simple certainties that exist for everyone; to ask one or two questions, questions as children ask them, random and disconnected to the minds of outsiders but full of family resemblance for me, who knows their birth and genealogy to the tenth generation.

*

May 13, 1904

Universities have so far afforded me very little; there is so much resistance in my nature to their ways. But it is also a matter of my own awkwardness, which never and nowhere knows how to receive or take in: I lack the presence of mind to recognize what I need, and lack even more that one most important thing: patience. Perhaps things have become better with me now; patience, at least, shall no longer be lacking in anything I do. And if I no longer try, as once I did, to follow lectures in disciplines where one can hold endless opinions—words about words, views about views—but listen instead to real things, new things to which all my instincts say yes, I will simply ignore whatever vexation my external circumstances invent for me, or else bear it calmly for the sake of what is important. A period of learning like this is what I need more than anything else—not only because there is such a wealth of simple and essential knowledge I lack, but also because I always imagine that this must be the path by which I shall ultimately attain the ability to help myself, all on my own, to whatever the case requires. That I am unable to do this, that I am helpless when left alone among books, a child who has to be led out again—this continually impedes me, leaves me baffled, saddened, confounded. If undertaking some scholarly study were slowly to result in my learning how to view the whole of any subject, how to sift through and read the existing bibliography (to say nothing of compiling one), if I acquired the ability to study older books and old manuscripts also, —in short, if I could appropriate to myself a little of the historian's craft and the archivist's patience, and hear spoken a few real truths and insights, —then any place with such rewards would suit me. I feel that without some acquisition of this kind I will be unable to take my next forward steps; after the Rodin monograph I considered one on Carpaccio, later one on Leonardo; what I lack for such projects is not art-historical knowledge (that is precisely what I want to avoid), but rather the simple craft of the scholar, the technical assurance and practice I often have to envy in quite young people; I lacked the key to the great libraries here and in Paris, the inner instructions for use (as one might say), and my reading was haphazard reading because, for want of preparation, it could not become work. Given my education, which no plan oversaw, and given the intimidation in which I grew up (everywhere running into laughter and disdain and being forced back by everyone into my clumsiness), it is no wonder that I failed to learn much preliminary material and most of life's technical side, which everyone later

A long, crazy, heart breaking letter

handles with ease. My feeling is filled with memories of occasions when all the people around me were adept at doing something and were doing it automatically and without thinking, while I, embarrassed, didn't know how to go about anything, wasn't even capable of watching them and secretly copying their gestures. Like someone who has stumbled into a game whose rules he doesn't know—, I feel on a thousand occasions like a knot in a length of thread. Then I am a hindrance to others and a cause for annoyance, —but these same defects get in my own way too and leave me bewildered.

Once I spent a whole summer on the Schönaich estate alone in the family library, whose archives are crammed full of old records and documents and correspondence; I felt in all my nerves the near-presence of destinies, the stirring and rising of figures from whom nothing separated me but the stupid inability to read and interpret old writing and introduce order into the uncatalogued disarray of these papers. What a good, industrious summer it could have been, had I only had some grasp of the archivist's procedures; the basic outlines of something like a *Maria Grubbe* might have been given to me; at the very least I would have learned and gathered a great deal from so intimate a contact with the still unchronicled events, —while as it was I only received every day new proof of my unfitness, of that excludedness which life keeps impressing on me when and wherever I try to approach it.

And not just for work on monographs, but for every work I take up, this lack of preparedness and overview shall become increasingly evident. For my plans concerning things Russian, for instance, it has always been a major hindrance and the reason I progress so slowly. But a schooling such as I have in mind (even though I can't picture it clearly)—would it not enable me to attack and hold onto my work with greater confidence, would it not also be a means of reaching that "*toujours travailler*" which is the crux of everything?

So a summary of my projects reads like this:

1. I want to read books on natural sciences and biology and attend lectures that will stimulate me to explore these areas. (Observe experiments and preparations, etc.)

2. I want to become more adept at archival and historical work, insofar as it is understood as technique and craft.

3. I want to read the dictionary of the Brothers Grimm, together with medieval poetry.

4. I want to learn Danish.

5. To continue reading Russian and occasionally translating from Russian.

6. To translate from the French a book by the poet Francis Jammes.

And to read closely the following books: Michelet's studies in natural history and his History of France; the *18th Century* of the Goncourts . . . and others . . .

I thought for a while of attempting all these things in Copenhagen; of traveling there in the fall and working there. But arguing against this:

—I will make my work more difficult by going to a country whose language I don't speak, where there is less to be gained by attending lectures, where practical matters (such as the use of libraries, collections, and laboratories) will become more complicated.

—Copenhagen is a very large city and perhaps not good for my health.

And so the question forms: could not everything I want to attempt be best and most simply achieved (at least in its first stages) in one of the smaller German university towns? It almost seems to me that it could. I don't want to go to a big city, especially not to Berlin, and even Munich (which of all the big cities is the most hospitable, civilized, and progressive) repels me in many respects. I tell myself that one is left more alone in big cities, but one is also left more unaided, and I shall doubtless at key points need aid and advice. And a mass operation such as Berlin University will only be a new form of intimidation for the awkward part of me (as I know from experience); on the other hand, the mere fact that I am older would, even in a small university where cliques form and close more quickly, isolate me and thus ensure me the solitude I shall require. So I am thinking (quietly for now, and confiding only in you) of looking for a smaller university town in Germany where one can hear competent lectures in the natural sciences, attend a seminar in history, and make use of libraries, etc. It would need to be one where all those rituals of student life are not too disruptive, the countryside would need to be close by (close enough perhaps that one could live inexpensively at the edge of town), and there would need to be access (if at all possible) to vegetarian fare. These would be the practical issues to bear in mind.

Dear Lou: now I ask you for your advice. Tell me what you think about all this and which of my plans meet with your approval. I won't ask if the place I am seeking might not be Göttingen? For you would tell me if this seems possible to you. Germany, the Germany of the small universities, is after all a small country, and it is not rash to hope that whatever town I settle on will be near you, perhaps only half a day's trip from your dear house at the edge of the woods.—

But I ask your husband's advice also. Once we have agreed on the feasibility of my plans and a place has been chosen, I will come to ask you and perhaps him too for whatever personal recommendations you can give me; such help could ease my way with much that I am going to find new and difficult; it might also allow me to learn certain things in a more private, person-to-person relationship than students normally enjoy. (For: having someone knowledgeable to turn to when certain questions arise would be an infinite boon to me, a vital enrichment and encouragement; but of course I will take this road which must be taken even if such a relationship is not easily obtainable.)

But if you think my plans would be better realized in a foreign country (and it is always good not to be among Germans), then Switzerland probably first comes to mind, Zürich perhaps, where you have done work, and where, if I remember correctly, Forel has a professorship. I am sure Carl Hauptmann would recommend me to him, and any recommendations you might provide would certainly be of great value there too. Of course a healthy place to live would be included in the choice, and nutritional food (with milk, eggs, and vegetables) is probably easier to find and more affordable there than anywhere else. Or am I wrong? You have lived there and would know—also if the university itself and its teachers are right for me. The fact that many Russians do research there along with people from all over the world would be another point in its favor; and the clear mountain air I hope to find there might be a good change after this sirocco year. Hence Zürich. Should I consider Basel also? (I lived here in Rome twice in the same place as Professor Woelfflin without ever getting to know him—a testament to my awkwardness around people.)

Copenhagen, of which I spoke first, would be the next possibility; I could continue there for one or two years with the studies already in progress (for which, I think, Denmark would provide favorable conditions) and then slowly move on to the work on Jacobsen, which I think of as calmly erected on very sound foundations. This monograph, especially, will require the kind of preparation and training I want to undertake; all the historical research that will have to substitute for personal contact with Jacobsen is hopelessly beyond my abilities; I even lack the skill and schooling to start up and operate the critical apparatus that I occasionally construct for myself.

Did you know, by the way, that just recently in Copenhagen (in the student club before a very full hall) someone spoke about my books? Yes, it actually did happen that Ellen Key, armed with a big lecture manuscript dealing exclusively with my works, traveled to Stockholm, Copenhagen, and God knows what other Swedish cities—all for my sake! There she told people about me, and now, she writes, many are beginning to buy my books and read them; and so she has in fact helped me and done me the practical service she so desired. But now she wants to publish a long essay that grew out of those lectures in a Swedish periodical and (translated) in a German one. She is a dear and capable person and has gradually become to both of us, to my wife and me (and also little Ruth), an indispensable friend. I do understand, with sincerest gratitude, what she is trying to do for me, —even while I feel strongly that such advocacy can in no way be justified yet; now that her project is gathering momentum, I view it (confidentially speaking) with alarm—: for in reality and to less charitable eyes nothing has been accomplished yet, nothing demonstrable. A little in the *Book of the Good Lord*, in *To Celebrate Myself*, and in the *Book of Images* (she knows nothing of the *Prayers*) could vouch for me; but I am afraid she has represented it all as much less patchy than it actually is and has given everything an aura of maturity that it doesn't possess and about which people will feel cheated now when they buy my books. Further, she has based much of what she said (or so it appears, —I haven't seen the lecture yet, only a small fragment of it) on passages from my letters of the last few years and so discovered things that are not properly in the work I have published thus far. —And over and beyond all this I feel: if anyone ever needed seclusion, it is I. (Every line and every perplexity of this letter, but also every place where it shows strength and determination, bears witness to this—.) All the same I realize that I must accept everything that might support my life and allow me to continue with my work. And for this, to be mentioned and proclaimed abroad is surely a good thing. Moreover, it all came from the mouth of a sensitive and discreet person and surely (even if what she said got out much too early) no harm can result from that. It also turned out that there was a smattering of young people in Sweden who already knew about me—they could even recite poems from my books by heart; and one of the young Swedish literati was currently engaged (independently of Ellen Key and unaware of her intention) in collecting material for an essay on my work.

You can imagine that some of my publishers would like more of this (which is scarcely to be feared). Nevertheless, aside from the beautiful new edition of the *Stories of the Good Lord* (which ought to appear soon), only the Rodin book is coming out (and not before fall) in a new printing, so that my means are not likely to allow me much movement. So as long as the worst heat still hesitates, I will hold out in Rome in my little house and slowly disburden myself of everything that weighs on my nerves in order to accomplish something worthwhile; at present thunderstorms are close by, and there are days and nights when the air cools off, and a good wind comes down from the mountains—: all of which makes me believe that it *must* be possible to overcome my exhaustion once again and accomplish something. For a while I thought of going to Ravello near Amalfi (this would have allowed me to see Naples, Pompeii, and the blue Mediterranean bays), and in June or July, when the weather becomes unendurable here, I still plan to take up residence in Assisi, where Saint Francis's eternal benediction lies over the entire landscape; if there is still time for this, it will only amount to a few week's stay, for to endure the whole fever-filled and perilous summer here would only make sense if I were going to remain in Rome for another winter. So I shall probably come to Germany after all; if you think Zürich is where I should conduct my studies, one solution would be to go there for the summer also. But I would still detour through Germany; it's true that I have no place there that invites me, (for there are many reasons that I can't go to Oberneuland to visit our little Ruth), —but I mustn't miss the exhibit in Düsseldorf. Just think: Rodin has sixty sculptures there (as well as 50 works on paper), and Zuloaga (as he wrote me recently from Seville) eighteen paintings [*in the margin*: and I need his and Rodin's art constantly]. Yes, if I can somehow arrange it, I shall travel (no matter how the other plans turn out) to Düsseldorf in July or August. And since I will be so close to Göttingen then, perhaps, dear Lou, I could visit you for a day—to see you and your house and your garden and talk to you about the many things that can't be included even in a letter of this length. My summer, which stands so forlornly between two periods that have specific and clear purposes (one summer too many), would thereby be suffused with my fondest and tenderest thoughts, and I would have even in my present straits something so great to look forward to with such joyful anticipation, that my joy would become the strength and courage for everything.—

But it may be that you are planning a trip and won't be home; I always fear that you could suddenly be in Russia and far, far away, beyond all my questions and requests, which at any rate would lose their voices in your homeland, where things of such incomprehensible weight are happening!

Dear Lou, if it were possible to meet you this summer, do, please, let it be possible. I see for miles around no other thought, no source of trust which I can truly believe might help me.

Meanwhile this letter arrives, its length running through two days, and it makes many selfish and indiscreet claims on you; treat it indulgently. Writing it helped me no end; it was like activity after all these weeks of a persistent inner paralysis. There are, I recall, certain small animals, beetles and insects, that fall into such states of frozen life whenever someone touches or comes near them; I have often watched them, have observed how they let themselves be rolled like objects, how they do everything to resemble inanimate objects as closely as possible: they do this when they see some huge danger approaching them—and want to survive. Could my condition have similar causes? Could this rigidifying and holding still that extends into my inner being all the way to my heart's chambers be an instinctive defense, a way of deceiving something that is capable of destroying me? Who can say?

I will be confident and not count the time and wait until this passes. But *then* I will bestir myself, for nothing has yet been done.—

Yesterday was the Feast of the Ascension, so Pentecost is not far behind; there with you, in your garden, spring will have survived all dangers and will now be starting to grow confident and perfect in its joy. How beautiful it must be in your garden!

Good holidays, dear Lou, and good workdays: good days.

Heartfelt greetings to your husband from me, —and whenever you find the time, write me his and your own reactions to all my plans and wishes. Then I will keep such advice in mind and will think some more about what needs to be done and will try to be of good cheer. And *thank you* for everything!

Rainer

I think of Schimmel too, and how the snowfall of blossoms from 43 fruit trees must intrigue him.

[LAS to RMR in Rome, postcard: Venice, Grand Canal, Palazzo Browning; date from postmark]

[Venice, Saturday, May 21, 1904]

Have been for the last few weeks at the seaside spa near Venice! Postal address Loufried, to which I shall soon return.

[RMR to LAS in Göttingen]

Rome, Villa Strohl-Fern
May 30, 1904

Dear Lou,

So you were that near. And I had been feeling the whole previous time that you would come to Italy. Then, when one day I saw a card—: your handwriting and the Italian postage stamp, —for a moment I hoped, I hoped too strongly . . .

Meanwhile a long, long letter from me had gone to *Loufried.* Now this short one follows it to greet you at home: for presumably you will soon return.

To my recent letter this should be added: Ellen Key's lectures in Sweden and Copenhagen and her influence have procured for me several attractive invitations to the North; a first one to a chateau in Sweden's southernmost province of Skåne, which I have accepted forthwith. I see that there is nothing further I need to wait for here, —summer is becoming increasingly intense and oppressive and my house is absorbing more and more of the long days of sun. And so I am preparing to depart. I will remain here until June 8 or 10 and then travel north (probably with my wife, who, when she has finished her work here, will go to Worpswede). I plan short stays in Assisi, Pisa, Milan, and, last of all, Düsseldorf; but I must be in Sweden at the appointed place by around the 20th, since the one occupant of the chateau whom I have yet to meet has to leave shortly after this date. So it will be a rather hurried trip through Europe from below to above.

But I am quite excited about the happy chance that calls me to the North, into a "nature of sea, plains, and sky" (as Ellen Key wrote). And the invitations, especially the first one, carry with them no social obligations; I shall only have peace and a quiet, out-of-the-way room and wind from the sea. As soon as I have arrived there and begun to settle in, I will go straight to my interrupted work and immerse myself in it for as long as possible. And what will come after that I shall only know when you will have written me; for all my next questions are waiting for you and your advice: as you know from that long letter. It may happen that you will find some chance to write me here by the 8th, perhaps just a brief word in response to my long letter. But if you can't write now then wait, please, for my next reliable address. If no longer here, perhaps I might find a message from you in Düsseldorf, before I head all the way north, on a course that passes so very close to Göttingen. —Greetings to your husband and your dear house *Loufried* and its springtime:

Rainer.

I am enclosing a few small pictures (snapshots I took myself—or at least tried to take—with the camera that went along with us to Russia). This is my little house (its inside and outside); now the heat has changed it and spoiled it for me, —but for a whole winter I was happy in it and lived my daily life there.

[LAS to RMR in Rome]

[Göttingen,] Loufried [beginning of June 1904]

Dear Rainer,

Still fully immersed in the joy of being back home, I must rush to make sure this letter reaches you! But apart from this it occurs to me: wouldn't it be better not to take up *just now* the difficult issues set forth in your first letter, since the second one (which I read at the same time) newly defines your summer? It seems to me that first you should let the impressions toward which you are now traveling have their effect on you, and then, in the fall, plot your next course. You will probably find only part of what you expect of a university town in any one place: this makes it all the more important that you know, when you must choose, where your main emphasis lies. And this will surely depend, in addition to these new impressions, on how successfully and on what you are able to work this summer. I'm glad you'll soon be living somewhere out of this Roman June! Are you as thin as you look in one of these three little pictures that are almost too hard to see? About Italy I feel almost exactly as you: so much so that I have discussed the same things almost verbatim several times now with Zemek, who had packed me up for the month of May and taken me down there, since he was worried that I was falling ill too frequently. One returns from there as from a theater into a reality! But it was lovely in the cabana by the warm blue sea.

And one of these days soon now I'll visit my poor Russia.

Lou.

Beginning of June 1904: RMR and Clara leave Rome for Sweden, where they have been invited for an extended stay at a country estate. En route they spend five days in Naples, then four in Düsseldorf, before Clara returns temporarily to Oberneuland while RMR takes a steamer north to Denmark. After a brief stopover in Copenhagen RMR arrives in the southern Swedish province of Skåne (Borgeby gård), where he resides for the next six months. Clara eventually rejoins him there, but only for five weeks.

December 1904: RMR rejoins Clara (and Ruth) in Oberneuland.

March–April 1905: RMR and Clara convalesce together in the Weisse Hirsch—an extravagant six-week "second honeymoon."

June 13–June 25: LAS invites RMR to Göttingen, where they see each other for the first time since their break of 1901. During long hours together, their friendship deepens.

September 1905: RMR returns to Paris, working until May 1906 as Rodin's private secretary. After a stay on Capri (December 1906 through May 1907) he lives in Paris until the first days of 1910. Various trips during this time take him to Prague, Vienna, Venice, Berlin, and again to Capri in March and April 1908.

December 1909: RMR first meets Princess Marie von Thurn und Taxis-Hohenlohe (1855–1934), who will become his most important patron during the next ten years.

Early 1905: LAS, amid a happily active life (friends in Berlin, Munich, Paris, etc.; longer trips abroad with Zemek and others; her writing; Loufried in Göttingen), had developed a heart condition from which she tended, after each episode, to recover very slowly. When her illness flares up once more after her return from a trip to the French Basque country (August and September 1905), a Kur *of several weeks at Bad Nauheim in Hesse is prescribed. Thereafter she makes it an annual routine to spend part of late summer in St. Petersburg with her family and two winter months in Berlin before returning to the rural seclusion of her house near Göttingen.*

May 1909: Accompanied by Ellen Key, LAS meets RMR (and the visiting Clara) for a few days in Paris. Over the years LAS and Clara develop a friendship independent of Rilke.

During 1905, it appears, LAS wrote only two letters (now lost) to RMR, while for 1906 the existence of only one postcard and one letter (both also lost) can be assumed. The absence also of letters for 1907, 1908, and for much of 1909 and 1910 may simply be due to the fact that neither felt a need to sustain their correspondence. This long lacuna, in other words, need not indicate a willful later suppression or distortion of the record.

[RMR to LAS in Göttingen]

Borgeby gård, Flädie
Province of Skåne, Sweden
July 3, 1904

Dear Lou, you were so right: first the time here had to come and now it must be lived; but as I begin to live it, I can't tell you how comforting it is to know that you are aware of all those other things and perhaps now and then ponder them. I thank you for your dear letter; yes, it did find me still in Rome; it arrived as I was about to depart for Naples and I read it during the trip. Naples was, unlike Rome, truly alive, truly a world and an ocean's nearness. But the many impressions I received there were nothing compared to the time just thereafter. Shutting down in Rome, packing yet again, nine crates almost beyond my strength, in the midst of it all a dear visit evoking many memories, bright godsend amid a Roman mood: Pasternak from Moscow. Then the journey: stopovers in Viareggio, Milan; the Last Supper, magnificent beyond words, an art of painting like that which produced the wall-paintings of antiquity, nothing else comparable; almost vanished, almost told only in the profoundly moved voice of someone invisible, and yet inexpressibly *there*, absolute presence and in its innermost being indestructible. The cathedral a plaything of the centuries, almost pure confection. —Gotthart Pass (and en route, in Bellinzona, suddenly Pasternak appears again), one continuous torture and exaggeration, with its long airless tunnels and the mountains weighing down on top of them, even more heavily from the human exertion (overexertion) that has expended itself in boring through them. At heart a sad labor, as there is something melancholy about traveling through all that blackness amid constant droning. The mountains far exceeding the scale of life, people and animals looking small and insignificant beside them, as in St. Peter's. The waterfalls beautiful and lively (Leonardo was right to love them). Then a night and in the morning: *Germany.* Düsseldorf, parlor atmosphere. Friendly and curious philistines; in their midst, wild like a quarry, Rodin's objects, and like a great garden: Zuloaga. A day in the house of a collector of Japanese art, perusing engravings and prints by Utámaro, Kionaga, Hokusai. A day looking through the 13 volumes of the *Mangwa* (Hokusai's sketchbook) and thereafter Düsseldorf again. Then at an ever faster rate: Bremen, Hamburg, Kiel: at 1:30, in the light dawn, leaving the port; strong wind on an open, blue-black sea, —sunrise. At 8 o'clock in Korsör, at 10 o'clock in Copenhagen.

A city like no other, strangely inexpressible, completely dissolving in nuances; old and new, mysterious and frivolous, —graspable everywhere, nowhere. In Ny-Carlsberg (the younger Jacobsen's collection) many magnificent Rodins, in the open air before the museum in splendid bronze: *The Burghers of Calais.* One feels J. P. Jacobsen, Kierkegaard, hears the language like an interpretation of all this. The next day a trip across Öresund. Malmö. Waiting there is Ernst Norlind, poet and painter, friend of Fräulein Larsson, the owner of this château, which is situated between Malmö and Lund, with an ancient gate tower adjoining which a modest home has been built. Arrayed like a palace, the high old dark park rises in broad meadows and pastureland. There I sit under an ancient chestnut tree and write. —The two people are simple, serious, energetic, good. Both of them with a solid grounding of old peasant stock, on whose foundations the archways of subtle knowing and feeling and understanding rest securely. Everything quiet and simple. For me: walking barefoot, sitting still, reading, listening to stories and now and then telling some myself. Eating fruit and groats of rye, drinking milk. Longing for work, but with patience and many insights. Above all resting, which is much needed. Ellen Key, to whom I owe all this, lives another 7 hours on from here. I expect to see her soon.—

And now farewell, dear Lou, —greetings to your beloved country when you go there. There is much that is similar here, in the people too, which makes me feel quickly part of it all and hopeful.

Rainer.

[RMR to LAS in Göttingen]

Borgeby gård, Flädie
Province of Skåne, Sweden
August 16, 1904

Dear Lou, I think of you, even though my thoughts don't know where to find you. I search for you in this great storm, which fills the old trees of the park and throws light and shadow across the paths and toward evening towers sky upon sky over the meadows.

I remain here with these Nordic people, almost always alone. There is no one in the house but an unmarried woman with a quiet, firm, self-contained presence and strength and a young man, a painter and poet but above all a person, her friend. And many legends live with us, perhaps also the ghosts of ancestors from great families—but they frighten no one, and one leaves them to themselves.

The days are long and quiet and expire slowly in many shades of twilight. Then under tall old chestnut trees that canopy a space large as a great hall I walk the whole extent, from one old weather-worn memorial stone which stands under a golden rain-tree to another around which the fragrances of phlox and poppy mingle in thick profusion. And on both stones one finds the same name, inscribed in Swedish: Brite Sophie Friherrinnan Hastfer. For Borgeby gård has always belonged to women.

I have not accomplished much: I have learned to read a bit of Danish from books by Jacobsen and Hermann Bang and from the letters Sören Kierkegaard wrote to his fiancée; translating these letters is almost the only work I have done. Then I was ill, badly so at that, and have still not fully recovered. And only wish that this great storm which is so majestic and wide as all autumn might never cease. I feel as if I've had much too much summer and too much sun. Everything in me is waiting for the trees to shed everything and reveal the distance behind them, with its empty fields and the long roads into winter.

I am considering leaving here early in September, first for Copenhagen or its vicinity. If I should feel well and find decent lodging, I would live there and work a while. For I would still want to accomplish something before I set in motion my next plan (of which not long ago my very long letter spoke to you). In general, I still think as I did then, but would nevertheless like to try Copenhagen first. In so many ways it is incomparably good here: almost all the people have reached that point of maturity where it is possible now and then to have sensible conversations. But for my further purposes (due to the language) a German city will still be necessary.

I dare not tell you or moan to you any more about myself; now that Russia is calling out woe after woe, everything that pertains to me seems so trifling, hardly worth mentioning. If you happen to be there in your great, burdened homeland, then her weeping and wailing will fill you utterly. And I would wish that she were my homeland too. And that I had the right to feel every lash and take on the pain of this great woe.

Rainer.

Postscript: I am sending you, dear Lou, the new (only superficially) revised edition of *Stories of the Good Lord,** since it is so much easier to hold and read!

[LAS to RMR, picture postcard from Copenhagen to Borgeby gård, Wednesday, August 17, 1904 (date of postmark), without writing, only an "X" on a townscape to mark her lodgings (Hotel Bellevue)]

[RMR to LAS in Copenhagen; written on the envelope: to be delivered personally upon arrival]

Copenhagen. Hôtel Bellevue
Rathhausplatz
Saturday, August 20, 1904

We receive mail on Borgeby gård only once each day. Late at evening. Thursday, the 8th, d. L., your card arrived. The next connecting train did not leave until the following morning. I took the very first one, was in C[openhagen] early yesterday (Friday)—you were gone. In the Hotel, nothing. That in eight days you would again be passing through—: only a rumor. And, if I understood correctly, Doctor Pineles is with you. On top of all the loss, this great

*With the inscription: For Lou, Borgeby gård, August 1904.

negligence. I am returning to B[orgeby gård] today. If you arrive, find this letter, and wish to say something to me, a telegram will have to be sent to Borgeby gård. How I wait:

R.

[LAS to RMR, picture postcard from Christiania to Borgeby gård: Norwegian landscape with the handwritten message "Christiania 20.VIII"; Saturday]

[LAS to RMR, forwarded to Furuborg, picture postcard from the mountains in Norway, Tuesday, August 30, 1904 (date from postmark), with the handwritten message:]

Dear Rainer! Greetings en route! The beauty here is that of some primordial world! On September 10 in Petersburg.

Lou.

Almost Russian little houses dot the Norw. countryside.

[LAS to RMR in Borgeby gård]

[St. Petersburg,] Офицерская 54
September 16, 1904
[forwarded to Copenhagen]

Dear Rainer,

I am sending this letter into the realm of Chance, since I am sure that you are no longer in Sweden but in Copenhagen. Our failure was my fault, and my card to you a monstrous stupidity. I received your letters en route, one of them at the Hotel Bellevue, where, however, there was no time left to linger, since I had to get to Stockholm and onto the Russian ship. In Copenhagen I sought constantly the impression this city made on you, but could not get hold of it during the few hours of walking about (most of the time I lay ill). The Danes are to me—this is my first fleeting appraisal—slightly disagreeable. I had this same feeling when 2 1/2 years ago my husband and I spent wonderful summer weeks at Skagen and got to meet all manner of Danes, since he speaks Danish well. Even their language reaches my heart only when spoken by Norwegian lips, as, indeed, the Norwegian countryside up in the northwest is among the great experiences of my life. It affected me like a union of Volga and Finland, and the people there seemed to me at times to have stepped out of an era when ancient Slavs and ancient Germans at the beginning of Russian history spontaneously recognized each other as brethren. It became hard for me to tear myself away from this! In Stockholm a few things reminded me of Petersburg, but the Russian impression was blurred, and Russia only stood before me—great, mournful, awakening love and pain—when I entered Kronstadt, slowly drifting past the Baltic Fleet, which was just then waiting for the czar to arrive and bestow his blessing on its departure. This image of the sun rising above the warships into a deep-blue sky, amid cannon thunder and festive commotion on all the boats, will remain with me forever. At home I found my dear eighty-one-year-old старушка vigorous and rosy-cheeked, as if she were a young girl, and I will stay with her until my last day here, without further excursions. And at any rate that day is not far off—my address here is good only until October. Where will you go then, where will you spend your winter? I can't think of any German city that would truly accord with your winter wishes, but perhaps I am not sufficiently familiar with any one of them. Even Göttingen is almost foreign to me, and *Loufried* would be out of the question, since I will presumably (if Zemek has his way) have to be laid up in bed there for two months. Let me know where you will be staying, Rainer, —and: forgive me the stupidity that has weighed on my mind ever since Copenhagen, and bear me no grudge because of it.

Russia greets you, and with her

Lou.

Write me about your health.

[RMR to LAS in Göttingen]

Jonsered near Göteborg (Furuborg)
October 17, 1904

Dear Lou, when your letter found me a few weeks ago in Copenhagen, I wanted to write you at once; but I could not. Your voice was there again, and that was good; for the postcards had passed over me like signs in the sky; the events they signaled took place as if in a different world, and I could not insert myself into them, however much I longed to do so. For weeks I lived only in this one thought: *your nearness*; in the rising and sinking expectation of meeting you; and thus it is hard for me now to write you, since everything, everything mine, had already changed into talk, into actual talk and reticence for you, into gazing, into reality—: and now it all must become writing again, and it cannot, cannot change back so quickly.

Dear Lou. I have spent whole nights asking myself: Why did this occasion pass me by like this? Other times it is my own lack of resolve, my worn-out, pathetic will, that *lets* things pass me by, foreign and familiar things, as if I were that old kobtsar on the Крещатикъ. But this time it was different. For all my impetus is *toward you.* I feel that it wasn't really your first card that changed my writing into talking and into audible silence; that transformation had in fact begun much earlier; my first letter to you (from Viareggio or Paris) was already filled with so much need *to speak* to you. And ever since those days I carry a letter with me and read it often and it always begins with the same words: . . . "at all times you can be with us, in bad as well as good hours."

I know that now I *cannot* come: you say so. And I am far away, it's true, in a foreign country, and would do well, before I depart, to absorb all that I had desired here.

But I can't help thinking so often that you are suffering greatly now and may be bedridden for a long time; and that, to my mind, is only one reason more for me to be near you.

Here in this great autumnal forest where I walk barefoot there are paths on which we might have walked together; they must be very much like certain paths in the forest near Schmargendorf, even in the sound with which individual leaves fall. I am in a country house [Furuborg] with friends of Ellen Key who are kindly disposed toward me. I came back here from Copenhagen; I couldn't find a good room for myself there, kept looking and as I looked became more and more homeless; went from door to door like a beggar. Here I have a lovely room and a large window that looks out into all the burning, glowing, blazing trees and into clumps of fir. But I cannot be sufficiently alone, cannot follow a vegetarian diet, and the living arrangement takes my evenings away from me: supper is at seven and conversation follows.

I am still not working. The book I began in Rome has not been resumed: I lack the heart and the spirit (and this in itself may have physical origins). In Copenhagen I consulted an insightful doctor, the head of a naturopathic institute. His diagnosis and his prescriptions (both of them difficult to adhere to) I received in writing, and am enclosing a copy for you.

For the time being my health is tolerable: only now and then intense facial pain emanating from all my teeth, without apparent cause, flaring up at any time, and lasting for hours. I am trying to find a way back into work. Ah, if only I were in my room in Waldfrieden with its good long evenings; if only such a time would return, if only I had it good for a while, as good as back then—

Aside from all that, I am still thinking about studying somewhere; since I cannot find the release from within to start working, it is most likely going to have to come from without. —Once more: Göttingen? Zürich?

Dear Lou, please read my letter again, the long one from Rome. How do you feel about it now? Isn't it right?

I also want to tell you that in the last few months I have been seeing more people. I was with the good Ellen Key for several days. In Copenhagen I frequently saw Georg Brandes, who is dear and good but old and in the end more an amusement park than a human being. I was at the Michaëlises (Sophus and Karin). Karin spoke often of Helene Klingenberg. Thus something came full circle. How is Helene? How good it would be to see her again . . .

I have been trying to find Therese Krüger. [*In the margin*: Do you know her address?] I thought she might be able to help me a bit with the technicalities of finding a room, perhaps might also know a few things. But I found only an elderly language-teacher who had the same name but could tell me nothing further.

For a while my dear wife was with me in Copenhagen; now she is in Germany, near Bremen, and lives and works close to our little Ruth.

When I left Borgeby, and rushed to Copenhagen, where I hoped you still were, I had pictures of Ruth with me for you.

I can well understand what you say about Copenhagen; I view it through J. P. Jacobsen and out of love for him. It is not spacious, but it is quiet, —it is old-fashioned, and, as for its atmosphere, altogether *intérieur*. And after Paris, where I was as if suspended in external space, there are moments when a certain feeling of close-fitting inner space can do me good. I was predisposed to react that way.

I am probably not strong enough now for the great vastnesses (for the Volga-world I often yearn for). Wasn't so even back then when all of it was lavished on me so freely . . .

And yet I still must make something of myself.

Dear Lou, help me with that.

Rainer.

Many greetings to your husband and to your dear house in autumn. Did you harvest many apples?

[RMR to LAS in Göttingen]

Furuborg, Jonsered, Oct. 19, 1904

Dear Lou,

This morning in a moment of great brightness it became clear to me: I have been living for years in bad conscience and shallow strength: whatever drifts into me rides on my current for a short while, sails along, but then suddenly hits bottom with a shriek and is stuck there.

If my life is to improve, I must concentrate above all on these two things: strength and conscience.

My strength (as a blood analysis has shown) is insufficient. A stay in Skodsborg or at Lahmann's could improve this. After that, life lived simply and according to nature.

But what about conscience? I see that I can't keep going on with my work this way; that I must open up new tributaries to it; not because the streams that flow into it from event and existence are too meager, —rather: because I can't order or unite them. I must learn to grasp and hold; I must learn to work. I have been telling myself this for years and yet go bungling on. Hence my guilty conscience; all the guiltier when others have confidence in me. [*In the margin*: My immediate family; my father, who is patient with me now in so sad a way; Ellen Key, the people in this house.] I cannot be happy when I look at myself and for *that* reason am never happy.

I lack perhaps just a few helpful hints. If only someone would open the first door for me, I think I would know how to work the mechanism of the next one. And if water, much water, would now suddenly rush over my wheels, some entering stream that knows how to rush and roar, perhaps the whole drudgery of these grinding millstones would be in the past.

You are no doubt thinking that I have said all this before. And that I merely imagine it. And that a fresh start will never happen there because it is impossible to coordinate all the haphazard workings of my will.

But that was not the enlightenment I received this morning in a high forest clearing while I was sunbathing. The clarity this time was truly clear, to wit:

I want to stay here as guest for a few more weeks, buy myself linen, clothes, and shoes (all of which I am almost out of now). Save up, which being a guest will allow. Put in order. Work, to the extent that I can.

Then I want to remain in Copenhagen for several weeks, pursuing two particular projects there.

Then I want to return home and have Christmas with Ruth. A long Christmas.

Then I want to go either to Skodsborg or Lahmann's and undergo a complete treatment, probably during February-March, when my flu has the habit of returning.

Then I want to take a short trip to wherever you happen to be.

Then for the summer semester I want to go to a university and study history, natural sciences, physiology, biology, experimental psychology, some anatomy, etc. [*In the margin*: not forgetting Grimms' Dictionary] This involves *two* things:

1. Finding the university most suitable for me.
2. Discovering some specific person willing to help me, so that the general process of education can become an affair between two people.

Regarding 1: I often think of Zürich. Because presumably I would be able to live in the country there and maintain a vegetarian diet. —Because it is a university with lectures in German without actually *being* German; because, I am assuming, one finds there more than elsewhere not students but people (and Russian people to boot).

But regarding 2: will I find there a teacher of stature to whom I can come personally with my questions and wishes, with my huge wealth of inexperience? (So that I don't have to be one among hundreds: in such contexts I get lost completely, collapse back into myself with full force . . .) There was a time when Simmel wanted to help me, though nothing good for me could have come of it, nothing but a monstrous complication of my conflicts. Kurt Breysig was also willing to provide this kind of help and would probably still be willing, even though at the time I turned away in a fit of rudeness. But I see him as insignificant and vain and merely diligent, not wise. —A humanist like the old Jacob Burckhardt would have been exactly right.—

Zürich, as far as I know, is the home now of Ricarda Huch, who, I have heard several times now, knows of me. She surely would be willing and able to help me in many respects, both as intermediary and advisor.

And isn't Forel still there?

Dear Lou, I am sending this letter on the heels of the one I mailed two days ago; it is, to be sure, just as ragged and piecemeal, —but I think it has a firmer structure and better supports my asking you to help me, since it shows more clearly where help might be given and lays out more foreseeable goals.

So it will be a matter of thoroughly weighing over the next few months the choice of a university; you mustn't trouble yourself with this, but it could well be that you will hear or read something that might help me along. And then you do have personal memories of Zürich. That's a great advantage.

Dear Lou, I thank you for everything, for your thoughts, for your patience.

And be well. Perhaps "the victory" will be on your side after all, and you won't need to be laid up for so long and will slowly, slowly regain all your health.

I think often now of the small Madonna inside the silver casing; after having completely forgotten about her for years, now I remember her again in every detail—as if I had held her in my hand yesterday, opened her shell and closed it. Farewell.

Rainer.

[LAS to RMR, letter from Göttingen to Furuborg, second half of October 1904, following her return from St. Petersburg]

[RMR to LAS in Göttingen]

Jonsered near Göteborg
Furuborg, November 3, 1904

Dear Lou,

At last, at last a great storm; there was such an unaccustomed stillness in this autumn. The leaves remained on the branches even though a mere nothing held them; they lacked the will to fall off. And one felt *oneself* affected by this and walked about among all this beech and oak growth with extreme caution, so as not to cause the slightest stir. But today a storm came, a great storm, and in half an hour everything was bare. And now one can see in all directions, can see the bright cold lake, can see white country estates and small red, red wooden houses; everything has crowded in closer, as if gathering and huddling for winter, while the world all around is vast.

And the storm!

Up on my solitary mountain I wrote a poem, it was almost like something torn from me: (the first one for a long, long while). I give it to you now, dear Lou, out of thanks for your good letter. It has shored me up at the deepest levels of my being. You know now from my previous letter what direction I am resolved to take. And I am mounted on the back of this resolve and clinging to its mane and hanging onto its neck and certainly not making a knightly impression. Still, we do progress this way, that's the main thing. And should I fall off yet again (oh old riding-school memories!), I am determined to run after this resolve for as long as my breath holds out. — That's how it stands now. And first the one thing shall come about, then the next. And so whether it will be Göttingen or Zürich in the spring may have to be determined later. From a purely practical standpoint, Göttingen is feasible, and I cannot afford to rule it out yet. What you urge me to consider has long been considered. Dear Lou, you are the holiday of my holidays, and believe me, I do intend to have workaday years. All the same I am yearning for a reunion, something I am missing everywhere: all my thoughts lack their initial letters. But it will come about, and when it does, it will work its effects on me, and I am confident that I can be very quiet, can be just another person on the outskirts of Göttingen who claims to know nothing about *Loufried* except that there is a profusion of apples there and a white, inquisitive, uncommonly wise dog.

Do you remember the *Cornet*? A limited edition has come out: do you think I could send a copy to Helene? I would very much like to. (Karin Michaëlis was often with Helene in Berlin, knows "the book" and everything else that is intimately related to Helene. How they came to be friends I don't know.)

I can well understand that the great war sounds to you like an anthem of fate: for you have just seen again the soul that in its great need sings this heroic lay, this deep hymn to God.

Here no one can imagine this, and as for myself, I am very quiet about it and pray alone in my room.

Keep well, Lou, I greet your dear husband and greet you and thank you for all your help.

Rainer.

[RMR to LAS in Göttingen]

Charlottenlund near Copenhagen,
Villa Charlottenlund,
December 4, 1904

Dear Lou,

Now at last I am on my way back after a long good time at Furuborg. Long, because it seems to me that I have had summer, fall, and winter there, and each of them fully: the last days of summer with which it began were such quintessences of summer, and then each autumn day was a festival of autumn, and finally a proper deep winter arrived with sleigh rides into the quiet countryside where everything had become distance, along the cold lake, on over toward strange blue-darkening mountains. And once there was a complete journey, white through white, seven hours by train into Småland, followed by a swift sleigh-run through a silently snowing afternoon, and finally arriving in early dusk at a lonely estate. Amid the jangling of ten small bells we drove down a long, old avenue of linden trees, —the sleigh swung out and there was the forecourt, flanked by the small side wings of the castle. But where four stairs climbed heavily and laboriously out of the snow of the courtyard up to the terrace, and where this terrace, bordered by a balustrade with ornamental vases, thought itself a preparation for the castle, —there was nothing, nothing but a few bushes sunk in snow and sky, gray, trembling sky out of whose twilight scattered flakes were falling. One had to tell oneself, no, there is no castle here, and then one remembered having heard that it had burned down years ago, but one felt nevertheless that something was there, that somehow the air behind that terrace had not yet merged with the rest of the air, that it was still divided into passages and rooms and in the middle it still formed a hall, a high, empty, abandoned, darkening hall. —But then from the side wing on the left the lord of the manor stepped out, tall, thick-set, with a blond mustache, and admonished the four long dachshunds to stop their shrill barking; —the sleigh drove past him and curved to a halt in front of the much smaller wing on the right, and out of its door stepped dear Ellen Key, black and unassuming but all happiness beneath her white hair. For this was Oby, her brother's estate, and in this side wing on the right is the old-fashioned room where, sitting on her grandmother's red sofa, she writes the second part of her *Lifelines* and answers the countless letters she receives from young girls and young women and young men, all of whom want to know from her where life begins. She asks me to send you her best regards; you know those quiet but deep regards she has for the people who are especially dear to her. That was a week ago, and now I am near Copenhagen where a great thaw is under way; I will be here only a few days, above all to see Hammershöj. Therese Krüger is staying with the very old man in Damgaar, —if possible I will see her during a stop on my trip in Fredericia. And then I will stay in Oberneuland near Bremen for the time being.

I have thought so often of you during these weeks, and there was so much that would have turned into a conversation with you, —it could not have become a letter; perhaps because there was too much I would have needed to write. —But today my thoughts are with you not in conversations but in all that silently ushers me into my thirtieth year. I have been alone this day so that I could reflect and write to those I love and to you.

Rainer.

[*In the margin*:] I will send you a little book of Obstfelder's which contains a few things that I have come to like very much.

[LAS to RMR, letter from Göttingen to Oberneuland, December 1904]

[LAS to RMR in Oberneuland, postcard]
[Göttingen, after Christmas 1904]

Dear Rainer,

Thank you for the greeting of carnations! Beneath the fir tree that we took from our garden they came into full perfect bloom and were so very beautiful!

Lou.

[LAS to RMR in Oberneuland, picture postcard, Russian icon-painter, outlines of Russian churches]

[Berlin,] December 31, 1904

Съ новымъ годомъ,
старой дружбой!

[RMR to LAS in Göttingen]

Oberneuland near Bremen,
on the day after
Epiphany
1905

Dear Lou, your card with the иконописецъ was postmarked Berlin S.W.; so I don't know if I will find you at home with this short letter. But I want to look for you nonetheless.

Christmas is over, and a year has begun with a high, clear, star-bright night; I scarcely noticed it, scarcely felt a trace of festiveness, and no rest. What I found on arriving here were mere external circumstances, incomplete and provisional. Add to that influenza and the constantly changing weather. And the adjustment and the rethinking and the being wrenched from the closeness to work which was what Furuborg was for me. And the torment of German surroundings. Amid all that it was hard to experience Christmas, to hear bells, distance, silence, childhood; hard to comprehend the new one who is Ruth, —hard to be tangibly there for her dear hesitant way of coming toward me; all too hard to *love,* to have all that attentiveness, strength, goodness, and constant devotion that make up love. At a loss—that's all that I was, incapable, amid all the external unrest, of being someone, of being who I am to become. I was elsewhere whenever the "little voice" spoke to me, not ready for it and not sufficiently secure. And so I have gained nothing from this [day] on which your dear greeting arrived. Изломай! I had written that to myself on a scrap of paper, and it lay loudly in front of me on my Roman desk for half a year. So that every day I would know it. But it didn't help at all. Again it was as always: the moment life nudges me with one of its realities, refers to me, demands me, —I feel only intruded on. Where others feel welcomed in and taken care of, I feel dragged out prematurely from some hiding place. The way children's hands would dig one out, take one out of the earth and look one over: ah, and I think they would find me completely worthless. One should not be permitted yet to look into me, I should not have to be ready yet, not for anything, because everything about me is unfinished, insufficient. What event in life, what actual happening was there that didn't force this realization upon me? What was there that didn't culminate in this monastic longing? Longing for years to be spent in the desert; completely dug into the earth, not blooming upward, only working down at the roots that no one sees.

Thus, dear Lou, and in confusion I lived this year's beginning. Wouldn't you like to see me for a short time as I am now? The thought occupies me for hours at a time: to begin the Russian year with you, —with both of you at *Loufried*—? To be with you on the twelfth and thirteenth? But your card arrived from Berlin and now I don't know myself if I can get away. Above all, though, whether you can accommodate me? There is much, so much to discuss. Concerning the middle section and the end of the *Samskola* piece. *The White Princess* was rewritten so extensively at Furuborg that it became a new drama. And I would like to read all the Prayers with you. And—: innumerable things for me to do while I am with you. I have been feeling for years: that all my next advances are in your hands. —And of course I also need to see Göttingen (with a view toward the possibilities of living and studying there) and discuss the next phase of my future. You must write and tell me if it would be better for me to come now or later; the place where I live here is available until the end of February, and I could stay here until then; but I might also, in order to be completely alone, leave earlier and head back north, or even change my mind and travel south beyond Germany. And this time I *must* not miss you in transit; a reunion with you is the single bridge to my future, —you know that, Lou.

For today just this; and what my friends in Sweden (as the people in charge of Samskola) made me promise to convey to you when they saw me off: their many, many regards and this message: that when you come back to the North you must consider staying at Furuborg, and not just for a day but for a long period, to work or to rest, as you may need.

And Lizzie Gibson wrote me recently: "Does Frau Salomé read Danish? I was so reminded of her when I came across the enclosed poem by Drachmann, and thought it might give her pleasure to read it. If you think it would be fitting to send it to her, please do so with many regards and the love of someone who has been a secret admirer ever since reading *Zwischenland*."

I am sending the poem (though it seems to me rather superficial and overwrought in that typical Drachmannian way), because it was meant to bring you something dear. Here and there (you will find the places) it does open up on moments with a bit of *Zwischenland*-feeling in them, albeit with too much bright light mixed in, too much elucidated twilight. —Among my Christmas books is Beer-Hofmann's new drama, Volinsky's *Book of the Great Fury*, and the appreciative book Luise Nyström-Hamilton has written about Ellen Key. All my love to all of Loufried from

Rainer.

[LAS to RMR, letter from Göttingen to Oberneuland, January or February 1905]

[RMR to LAS, letter from Dresden to Göttingen, regarding the publication of the "Prayers," March 1905]

[LAS to RMR, letter from Göttingen to Dresden, with violets laid in, March 1905]

[RMR to LAS in Göttingen]

Weisser Hirsch near Dresden,
Sanatorium Dr. Lahmann
the last day of March 1905

Thank you, dear Lou, for your words. Just as the fragrance from the little violets had dispersed so far beyond them that it seemed to come from an entire field, so a scent as from many words came to me from your few phrases.

Thank you for the Prayers: that I may receive them in order to give them to you again and again. That they, which are yours like a vast inheritance, may be a perpetual daily gift from me to you. I will lavish so much care on *your* book that you will love its every part. But I shall ask you not to send them until I have arrived in Berlin and have time and quietness for myself. Here all is in-between space and in-between time. At best reading goes well now and then. Frau Garborg's little book was the last one and now Weininger lies there and is sometimes opened. Only for the space of a few glances, and always with the feeling that a precious find has fallen into angry and unjust hands. Into an unprepared life. Thank you, dear Lou.

Rainer.

[LAS to RMR in Dresden, picture postcard depicting "Göttingen, Feuerteich"]

[Göttingen, Sunday,] April 16, 1905

Dear Rainer, from Loufried with Ellen Key—greetings to you

Lou

Dear Rainer Maria, Lou and I have had so many talks about you!

Your *E. Key*

[RMR to LAS in Göttingen]

Dresden-Neustadt, Railway Station
April 19, 1905

Dear Lou,

I didn't send thoughts to Loufried on the 16th, since Ellen Key's last letter from Vienna gave her address beginning the 15th as Amsterdam; thus I could not but think that her day in Göttingen had been cancelled. Now it turns out that it did take place after all. I wonder how it went? That certain aspects of Ellen Key's concern for me, indiscriminately well-meaning as it is, could after a conversation with you be *corrected,* is something I can well imagine—and hope for dearly. You must have discussed S[immel], about whom she has done nothing but warn me ever since her days in Berlin; but I grew wary of these warnings when I heard what she wished to give me in his place: a *Pole* in Vienna, Holtzapfel. "This," she wrote, "will be *your* philosophy"; alas, rather the philosophy most alien, farthest from mine . . . I am on my way to Berlin to see S[immel]—who isn't there just yet, is in Paris, will visit Rodin this coming Saturday. But even so, it's to meet with him that I'm making this trip. I'll call on Frau S. these next few days. And reside for the time being: in a small pension that adheres to Lahmann's principles: Westend, Kastanien-Allee 20. Would you send me the manuscripts to this address, soon, so that they soon may return to your hands? Copying is to begin forthwith, Insel-Verlag is expecting the book in early May. (Of its existence Ellen K. knew nothing; did she find out?) A touch of love, of Easter!

Rainer.

[LAS to RMR, consignment of the "Prayers" (manuscript of *The Book of Hours*) from Göttingen to Berlin, soon after April 19, 1905]

[RMR to LAS in Göttingen]

Worpswede near Bremen
May 19, 1905

Dear Lou,

From here I mailed the fair copy of the Prayers to the publisher two days ago; from here I am mailing back to you today the two books with which I have been living the past few weeks. Here, inside an empty, gray, cell-like studio where they were my only reading, and outside, under the great spring skies. It was good that I had time for these dear books, that I could be alone with them one last time before they undergo the next transformation, with which they will be taken away from me, even if only to be given back to me from a greater distance.

That I obtained this time and this place for the task, however, came about this way: It became clear (and my doctor supported me in this conviction) that after the labors of treatment, the initial effect of which is a certain exhaustion, I would not be able to bear the city (and above all Berlin) without some period of adjustment; any exertion that involved strain and endurance could have easily blocked a successful outcome, and so I made a quick decision to come here around Easter, with the idea of returning to Berlin when there was some improvement in my health; that I am still here is due to the absence of any genuine recovery, about which I had been so hopeful. There are many things I could lament, and I lament above all this incomprehensible tiredness; sleep is always impending, and it seizes me, as if I were some object it owned, in the middle of the day. And what was torment before is torment still, above all this: to observe that my confidence in myself, in my strength and soundness, has not increased at all, that I can't count on myself for anything: this is the greatest torment of all. These many attempts at a more natural life, these endeavors to set up more health-conscious regimens, which were actually intended only to make life easier and more conducive to work, have, over the course of years, God knows how, become work themselves, become duty, expense of strength and time, vocation; and a vocation to be pursued laboriously at that, one that makes everything harder and comes up against all sorts of external obstacles. At the *Weisse Hirsch* I threw myself into the work of treatment with boundless enthusiasm, but for one reason only: so that afterward I would never have to think about all this again. And now it turns out that it might go on like this endlessly? I think that one day I am going to have to forego this continual working on my health. It is like perpetually putting on one's costume and getting oneself ready while one is standing right there in the middle of the stage and the curtain has already been raised. Isn't there just one thing left: to do the play such as one is?

I still have not, as you see, dear Lou, taken that turn that is supposed to come now. But it *must* come, I am more firmly convinced of this than ever.

Berlin will have to be risked in any case; I'll probably go there for the month of June to see about being an extension student; I did not see Simmel during those days in Westend (he was in Paris). But his wife received me warmly. I shall be on my guard with him and at first say only the most factual and easily said things—.

(Ah, dear Lou, there is only one person to whom I could truly speak, one person alone; but this confused and stupid letter will give that one person no desire ever to call me.)

To hold the old black book in my hands again, that was true reunion; and woven as it was out of joy, discovery, desire and gratitude, submission and confirmation, it seemed like a heightened presentiment of that other reunion I keep thinking of.

The old Prayers rang out again (had I only been allowed to sound them for *you*!) in this gray cell; they rang out so steadfastly kindred, and just as back then I was the tower whose great bells began to peal: resonating so powerfully inside, trembling so far down into my foundations, reaching so far out of and beyond myself. Reaching so passionately toward you. How near everything was for me, how strong the sense of being face to face.

Farewell, dear Lou. How is your health? I hope to hear that it is following your garden into bloom. How one longs to be part of it; to feel just once the hand inside again that throws the larks so high into the skies.

Rainer.

[*In the margin*:] Greetings, dear Lou, to your husband and to your house.

[LAS to RMR in Worpswede]

Loufried, May 21, 1905

Dear Rainer, yes, I can have you here easily if it could be during Whitsun week? To travel to Berlin before Whitsun is scarcely worth the effort anyway because of the holidays. Write if you'd like. I rejoice.

That's all the letter I can write today. Imagine our heartbreak! Across from us a giant box is being built! For now at least, springtime is still bigger, and mercifully blocks most of it out.

Lou.

[RMR to LAS in Göttingen]

Worpswede, May 23, 1905

Dear Lou,

I don't read it, I hear it as tidings of great joy. I thank you, I rejoice, I know that this year is blessed and full of goodness since it *really is about to usher in this one thing.*

But my joy has so confounded me that I've forgotten what Whitsun week means. Does it include Whitsunday, or does it mean the days thereafter, or the days before? In brief: you must specify the day when I may come; I will arrange everything accordingly.

For the moment I'm not even able to summon up regrets about the "giant box." I feel only that nothing (not any thing) will prevent me from gazing far out into the world and into my life from your garden. I feel only that something wonderful is coming.

Rainer.

[*In the margin*:] (Tomorrow I will travel to Oberneuland for two days to be with Ruth, then I'll be back in Worpswede.)

[LAS to RMR, letter from Göttingen to Worpswede, toward the end of May 1905]

[RMR to LAS in Göttingen]

Worpswede near Bremen,
the last day of May, 1905

Dear Lou,

I need only a small place, so you mustn't give it any thought at all. Of course a cot, for which I shall bring everything necessary.

Yes, my itinerary: Hanover—Göttingen—(Berlin). But Göttingen (Loufried) looms so large right now that I can't think beyond it. My thoughts about Berlin are in brackets, which may drop away once we talk about it. But the closer summer gets, the harder it is for me to imagine Berlin. And when I read something by Simmel now, nothing summons me to him. Nevertheless, I do want to attend lectures somewhere for a few weeks as a way of preparing for fall, when I plan to begin in earnest. And two or three days with you will get me clear and point me toward the right decision.

I certainly have no desire to be here (where I have no "home") during the Whitsun days, but I won't let my impatience make my decision and will therefore (if this agrees with you) set Tuesday after Whitsun (that is, June 13) as the appointed time.

The letters I will bring with me.

I only still have to decide what I could bring Schimmel to serve as legitimation and unmistakable sign of recognition.

Do you also have such summer days? Here it is always the same sky over a countryside that grows denser by the day. All houses have been transposed and placed in deep clear shade, under chestnut trees, beside syringa bushes. And when one passes by a window and looks inside, one sees no interior space, only another window with a bright green lawn in front. The houses are growing smaller and smaller and summer is coming more and more into its own. The people who live here are glad of it; for me, though, everything summery is only a presentiment and a likeness of what shall come.

Rainer.

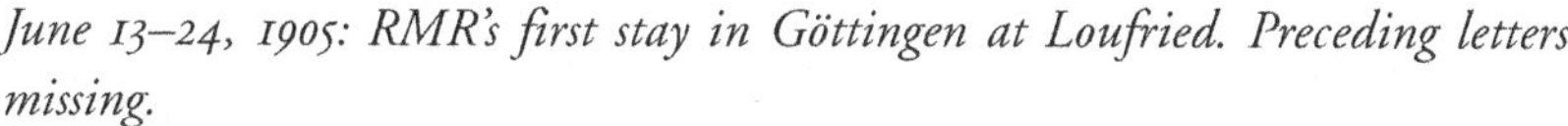

June 13–24, 1905: RMR's first stay in Göttingen at Loufried. Preceding letters missing.

[LAS, Diary]

Rainer, who was with us from Whitsun until Midsummer Day, and whose arrival was really little Schimmel's last great joy before he fell ill, helped dig the grave.

[LAS, *Looking Back*, "Epilogue, 1934," addressing RMR posthumously]

That manuscript [of *The Book of Hours*], which was in my safekeeping, became the occasion for our first reunion: in Göttingen at Loufried, as we named it after the inscription on that flag we had placed atop our peasant hut in Wolfratshausen.

I can still see you stretched out on the big bearskin rug in front of the open balcony window, while the restless leaves cast light and shadows across your face.

Rainer, that was our Pentecost of 1905. It became so in yet a different sense than you, in the turbulence of your emotions, suspected. To me it was like an Ascension of the *work* of poetry above the *man* of poetry. For the first time it became clear to me that the "work"—what it would become through you, what it would demand of you—was your rightful Lord and Master. *What further things would it require of you?* My heart skipped a beat as something in me greeted across decades the still unborn Elegies.

Ever after that Pentecost of ours, I read what you created not just with you—I entered into it and affirmed it as an expression of your future which now was not to be denied. And in so doing I became yours once again, in a second way—in a second maidenhood.

[RMR to LAS in Göttingen, first half of letter missing]

[Berlin, after June 26, 1905]

2.) would be satisfied—; Simmel could not imagine a state in which one's models, after many transformations, would achieve a supreme embodiment that could only be called *la nature* again, that one single very great name. *La nature* was for him merely the source of supply for the most boring, uninspired naturalism, whereas Rodin's model would necessarily have to be something different, some more complex amalgam . . . I don't know if you can understand how all this went? I would have to relate it more clearly, I know, but right now I can't.—

Seeing Helene was wonderful; I had dinner with them on Sunday. She has matured beautifully, and radiates warmth, easy self-assurance, and infinite kindness. They were very happy with your things. The pannier looked quite fetching with its many apple-faces crowded round the little basket of wild strawberries. Helene was out when I got there and so I unpacked my treasures before Reinhold and Alma and later when Helene had been back for a while she suddenly noticed all of it with delighted surprise. I urged her to read *Schluppes,* and she did so intently and liked it immensely. After dinner I told Gerda about you while her little hand rested in both of mine. Then she ate wild strawberries while Reinhold, beside himself with happiness, went in and out with the pannier on his back and carried all sorts of things around in it. They all greet you a thousandfold: I should have said that many times already, as well as how happy Helene was about the prospect of having you in Treseburg. Not in Blankenburg (which is two hours away), in Treseburg itself there is a very pleasant, quiet inn, ten minutes from Helene's house: that is where we would stay. They were all looking forward to a trip there already; they planned to leave this morning. And the air is said to be so light and high and glorious that every morning one wakes up joyfully.

Many warm and heartfelt greetings to you and your husband, dear Lou; be blessed. Now that I know *Loufried,* I can wish that for you so much better.

Rainer.

[LAS, Diary]

From Sunday to Sunday [16th–21st] in mid-July I was at Helene's in her little Treseburg farmhouse. Rainer came with me. Met in Halberstadt as agreed.

[LAS to RMR in Friedelhausen, postcard depicting the Pyrenees]

[Caption:] Saint-Jean-de-Luz
Falaises Sainte-Barbe
[August 18, 1905]

Dear Rainer, Greetings from the Atlantic Ocean!

[RMR to LAS in Göttingen]

Meudon-Val-Fleury near Paris
Villa des Brillants
November 14, 1905

Dear Lou,

Everything has changed completely; your card from Spain surprised me, as you can imagine, but at the time I didn't know yet that I would be answering with surprises of my own. —Not long after I came here from Friedelhausen, Rodin invited me to live with him. I accepted, and this stay has turned, unexpectedly, into something real and abiding. I am held here inwardly by his great friendship, and outwardly by the position he has given me to help me along a bit. Since the end of September I have been writing most of his letters (in a French for which there is bound to be a purgatory somewhere). He is satisfied with the arrangement and is very generous and insists that I allow time for myself. The afternoons are mine entirely, and around his art there is such an atmosphere of work and *capacity* for work that perhaps here I will learn all that I am lacking. In his garden on the hills of Meudon I have a little house to myself; on the card I have enclosed you can see it, small as it is, next to both his own house and the *Musée* where his wonderful sculptures stand.

Even when I failed to write, I sent thoughts your way often. Now, though, I am at a loss where to direct them. To Petersburg? Is your family doing well? And how is your health? Please, let me know. How was the trip to Spain? Now that I am living not far away, perhaps I too will be able to take a trip there. My first lecture tour (Dresden and Prague) is behind me; there will probably be a second one in early March, since I have been invited to Berlin (Verein für Kunst). Might I come by way of Göttingen? I could perhaps speak there also? I'm pleased with the Rodin lecture. I think it goes a step or two beyond my little book, —at any rate it is "spoken" to the same degree that the book is "written." —Now I also have two Russian friends here in Paris and through them an occasional Russian book. —But what is happening there, —isn't everything in chaos—? Please, dear Lou, give your husband my warmest regards and take the time to say a little word about yourself so that I can hear it and everything that resonates in it.

Rainer.

[*In the margin*:] From Worpswede the books I still had will finally get back to you; very soon now.

[LAS to RMR, letter from Göttingen to Paris, following her return from Spain and a subsequent period of illness, around November 20, 1905, probably with the "Ellen Key manuscript" enclosed]

[RMR to LAS in Göttingen]

[*Letterhead*:] *Villa des Brillants*
Meudon-Val-Fleury,
(Seine-et-Oise)
November 23, 1905

Dear Lou,

Thank you for your dear sign; now those loving thoughts that sometimes need to reach you will know where to find you.

So now I discover that for quite some time we were both in Paris? There *were* moments when I had the feeling I might encounter you, but the truth is I don't go into the city very often: can you believe that I have only been to the Louvre once? If it is not the work, it is my little house with its remoteness and proximity that holds and occupies me, it is Rodin's sculpture and the beautiful things from antiquity among which I wander, it is that out here everything, everything is gathered together, far beyond what other people could collect in a single place over an entire lifetime. To show you my little house (which I want to hold on to, insofar as it is up to me, for as long as possible), to stand with you at the window that looks out at the Buddha and onto an expanse which the Sèvres bridge seems to segment into a stanza of sonorous rhymes: it is a hope that I feed and nurture with many good thoughts. Perhaps, since you enjoy Paris so much, one day you will take a trip that passes close to me. No, I am going away in March for a short time only, but it will be a real tour with stops at the several cities which have already invited me and at those which, it appears, are about to send an invitation; dates have not yet been fixed, only a frame established by readings already scheduled for Berlin on the second and ninth of March. Everything else will be planned around these two dates. Perhaps I'll also get to Vienna.

Imagine: in Leipzig recently, at the very end of October, having just returned from my lectures in Dresden and Prague, suddenly I find myself in the same hotel as Beer-Hofmann, am with him for the Leipzig premiere of the *Count of Charolais* (which he chanced to attend), and spend a whole evening conversing warmly with him. What an unexpected surprise! —My Russian friends here (M. and Mme. Goloubev) have large estates in the Ukraine, and I get them to tell me all sorts of things about life there. But I rarely meet people, occasionally someone who comes to see Rodin; yesterday I was at Verhaeren's (Ellen Key had sent me there), and I felt a quiet intimate bond underlying our conversations. What beautiful poems he has made! Saturday I am seeing Zuloaga, who has finally come to Paris for a while to work. But how did you like Spain? Rodin came back from there rather repelled—by the food, by the postal services, alas, even by the Spanish themselves, who with their appalling slaughter of horses in the *Corridas* and the pleasure they take in it almost made him want to renounce them altogether. But his trip was rushed—though still relatively profitable for him. (What would not bear him fruit; even the daily walk to the train becomes for him a beautiful trip which leads each time through different lands.) Tell me: the beach from which you sent your card, could one go down there for a few days' vacation and be assured of living inexpensively and in solitude? Did you come back with good memories? I would guess that the richest memory is still Paris, with all its extravagance from the crudest to the most refined.

Rodin is in Switzerland now for a few days. I am using these days to get my backlog of letters written and to put my own things in order, books and manuscripts, for which there has been insufficient time. And then I start on Rohde's *Psyche*.

Did you—(but I should be telling you things, not asking—), to add just this last question: did you see any of Rodin's works during your journey? If you visit Berlin in the near future: Karl v. d. Heydt, the banker, with whom I enjoy a certain friendship, has just purchased with my help a beautiful marble piece of Rodin's, *Frère et soeur*, which I selected for him; he writes me that he wants to have it exhibited at Schulte's for 2 or 3 weeks once it arrives; please, take a look: Rodin himself feels that it is one of his most accomplished pieces—so much so that it was very difficult to get him to part with it.

Other than that, many good wishes for this vacation to you and your husband. I may take a few days around Christmas to be with my wife and child, but then I will be back here until the March tour, which isn't supposed to exceed two weeks, even if it takes me all the way to Sweden. I don't have time, then, to think of Naples, and at any rate the sister of Countess Schwerin didn't go to Capri this year at all, because the countess is seriously ill and must spend the winter in Heidelberg in order to be treated there (by Vierordt).

I thank you for the speedy return of the Ellen Key manuscript; I'm glad (but don't want Ellen to know) that it will disappear for the moment in *Deutsche Arbeit*, and my secret hope is that it won't materialize later in book form. Isn't it strange how little observation there is in all of it, how much preconceived notion, how much determination to prove certain things at any cost, how much friendly and well-meaning prejudice unmodified by any experience? [*In the margin*: And then it comes at such an inappropriate, premature time, with all those slightly slanted quotes from my letters.]

Or did you have a more positive impression? To me it seems glossy and somewhat saccharine, like a relief-portrait by some student of Thorwaldsen. The second part of *Lifelines*, by the way, just appeared in Swedish, the third is concluded and fully born, though Ellen is still carrying it around with her a while longer.

We too were snowed in completely here, virtually cut off from the outside world and lost, for three whole days. Yesterday it thawed, and today a tremendous storm is flinging the rain about so violently that it can barely fall.—

The shouting for joy is there; but I want to spread it out in very small portions over a long period of time so that it is only a steady breathing. And then it should be transposed, if possible, into something real and visible instead of expending itself in the air. To transpose joy: that is the goal of all artistic labor . . . Many good wishes and greetings for your husband, dear Lou, and for you in gratitude:

Rainer.

And Marie and little Marie? Is she already beginning to resemble the new pope?

[RMR to LAS in Göttingen, inscription on the dedication page of a copy of *The Book of Hours* (Insel Verlag, 1905)]

Returned—
[printed] LAID IN THE HANDS OF LOU
for all time.
Rainer.
Advent 1905.

[LAS to RMR, card from Berlin to Paris, shortly after mid-February, 1906]

[RMR to LAS in Berlin]

[*Letterhead*:] *Meudon-Val-Fleury, (France)*
(Seine et Oise)
France
February 21, 1906

Dear Lou,

My hope that you would be in Berlin increased when Frau Fischer wrote me recently that she had run into you; and now your dear card arrives before

I could mail you the news I've been meaning to send you for days now concerning the details of my tour.

Presumably I'll start speaking on the 26th and finish around the 12th. Elberfeld is first, then Bremen on the 28th, Berlin on the 2nd (my own work), Hamburg on the 4th, on the 9th Berlin again (Rodin), Weimar on the 11th and then also probably [Vienna. I will be in Berlin only very briefly], i.e. from March 1 (appr. noon) until March 3 afternoon; (I hope with my wife, who is going to accompany me for a short part of the tour). And then again from March 8 through 10 (probably alone). In a word, then, just long enough for the lectures, allowing myself only the smallest leeway. It is practically no time at all, I know, but I would all the more gladly stay in the pension where you are, if that is possible. (For without this closeness we would scarcely be able to see each other and talk during so short a time.) I hear from von der Heydt that all pensions are booked beyond capacity and don't know if accommodations can be prepared in yours for so brief a guest. If it can be arranged, then for the first stay a large two-bed room or two single-bed rooms with connecting door would need to be reserved. Send me word if it will work, but don't go to any trouble on my account. I'll be here until the 25th early; after the evening of the 25th, at Baron August von der Heydt's, Elberfeld.

Rodin went to London yesterday, and I needed that most urgently; for my workload has been heavy since I returned, and about all that remains for myself and my solitude are those minutes my watch sometimes gains for me out of pity by running fast. And just when I long more than ever to return to my own work. The *Book of Images* is going into a second edition (at last), and I am carefully adding to it a few new and old things that I think will please you. But "only time," and where to find it?

Yes: if only I could talk to you again some time and see something with you. I am looking forward to seeing Hofmannsthal's *Oedipus*, whose first act feels to me so full of glorious movement and in places composed almost in my own tonality.

But in Gerhart Hauptmann's *und Pippa* I don't feel any return of the old closeness; he almost seems to me on his brother's confused paths, taking them just as riddlingly and restlessly, stirring up a fantastic murk that would better remain sediment, since it clouds and obscures everything and makes it move with syrupy slowness. Or am I completely wrong? And do you grow skeptical when you hear me glorifying Hofmannsthal? All that, well, we'll just have to wait. (God, if we only had a year to hear each other out.)

Frieda wrote me not long ago; we will probably arrange to meet again in Weimar.

But I have other things to think of and the air outside is so springlike and wants to be felt and experienced too. Goodbye:

Rainer.

Greetings, please, to your husband.

[RMR to LAS in Berlin, picture postcard depicting Villa Wannsee]

Villa Wannsee, February 28, 1906

Dear Lou, thank you for giving Clara so kind a welcome. Tomorrow morning we move to our room at the *Hospiz*; at 2 o' clock we are having breakfast with Karl v. d. H[eydt], and for the evening the baroness has reserved seats for us to see *Tsar Fyodor*; I accepted because I was afraid we would not have been able to get tickets otherwise, and because nothing had been arranged with you. But I am hoping that you will be in the theater too and that we will see each other (if not before at the *Hospiz*) there and afterwards. I am, you can imagine, impatient for that.

Goodbye

Rainer.

[RMR to LAS in Berlin, written on Rilke's black-rimmed calling card, his father having died on March 14]

[Prague,] Sunday, March 18, 1906

Dear Lou amid sad tasks just the news that we hope to be in Berlin tomorrow for certain, whether at 12 noon or 9:30 at night. The lecture is on Tuesday. I am very tired, but it will refresh me to see you again. Until very soon, then:

Clara and Rainer.

[RMR to LAS in Göttingen]

[*Letterhead*:] *Meudon-Val-Fleury*
(Seine et Oise)
France

April 12, 1906

Dear Lou,

Your husband's birthday must be just about now; please express to him my cordial and sincerest wishes. How are you now after all the various things in Berlin? If your thirty-eight fruit trees are as far into flower as everything around us here, where a great show of blossoming and fragrance is under way, then I'm sure you aren't regretting the change and are happy to be able to see and feel yourself surrounded by all that splendor.

I have to listen constantly to my rational self in order not to take off blindly for Viareggio one day—: so much does this perpetual working at one's job and writing stacks of insignificant letters conflict with what is now my deepest need, viz., to take in this "everything around us" attentively, to give myself over to it for days, and be completely ready for things that are my own—. It would not be in vain. —But. . . . well, I did know exactly how this would turn out. And it did, and it is now not worse and not better.

Sunday I was in Versailles to see Alexander Benois, who is back painting the park again, just as he did years ago. And two days ago Herr v. Goloubeff wrote me that the Russians will be performing at the Chatelet theater in the beginning of May. Do you think you could give me some sort of introduction that would permit me to make the personal acquaintance of one or another of them, and that might also allow me to attend every evening's performance at not too great an expense? This is perhaps asked oafishly, but let me ask anyway, and you'll tell me if you think so. I have apprized Rodin of this group in some detail, and he intends to go also. But will it really happen? He and his wife have both been in bed with a "grippe atroce" (as I have affirmed now probably fifty times in various letters) and he feels tired and weak and is without his usual energy. —One more thing: could you lend me Harden's article about the Russians for a few days, or at least tell me which number of *Zukunft* it appeared in so I can find it myself? —Good news from home.

Happy springtime, dear Lou, and days like Easter. (Will you be spending the true Easter in Moscow?)

Rainer.

[*Written diagonally across the top part of the letter*:] Excuse the coarseness of this handwriting, which has been dulled by its daily chores.

[LAS to RMR, letter from Göttingen to Paris, after mid-April 1906, probably with the forwarding of "Harden's article about the Russians"; the corresponding issue of *Zukunft* was not among LAS's papers]

[RMR to LAS in Göttingen]

Capri. Italy
Villa Discopoli
December 13, 1906

Dear Lou,

My aversion to using postcards as practical aids to communication allows gaping holes to open up in my relationships, which is not my intention at all, and which in particular cases I try to prevent at any cost. In ours above all.

But I tell myself that even when for certain stretches you remain ignorant of a few of the details from my life, still no rift opens between us—isn't that so? I tell myself that and feel it and am convinced of it.

You do need to know, though, with a kind of fact-and-figures brevity: that I was in Paris until the first of August and worked there very well, consistently as scarcely ever before, day after day, for months. Then, alas, I let myself be talked into all kinds of traveling, which, since at times it involved the three of us and was very awkward, became so expensive that I was unable to return to Paris (though I had needed to badly), especially since after this summer of journeying there followed an unbearable stay in Berlin, which did not conclude until about two weeks ago and was necessitated by a torturous, seven-week-long dental treatment that has left me wretched and sick (*truly* sick: perhaps due to the antiseptics they used to treat a severe abscess). Then at the crucial moment the late Countess Schwerin's sister generously offered me this place of hospitality, into which I am settling now and in which I want to hold out and work (though I am not quite at that point now) until the next wave lifts me back to Paris, where I *do* need to be for a while longer yet. Clara has decided (and in this my Berlin days served a purpose), against inclination (or better: from disinclination), to see if she can somehow make her work more purposeful and productive in Berlin; she has set up provisional quarters there (Halensee, Westfälische Strasse 41), and in this several of our Berlin acquaintances, the Fischers above all, proved very helpful friends.

Ruth was with us for three months (during which time she got through a case of the measles quickly and energetically and without any aftereffects, but was also able to see and absorb much in her own little way: we were in Belgium; saw the sights of Furnes, Ypres, Bruges, Gent, and Ruth saw them with us), and now she is back in Oberneuland living her accustomed life.

So. Now nothing is left out. You can come across the gulf on these few solid stepping-stones and tell me something about you, about you both, which is something I very much desire. Your summer, your autumn? And how will your winter pass? Where? — (One day I walked up and down Heiligendammerstrasse, which is still very much the way it used to be. Walked for a long time. Simply couldn't stop, no reason to do so coming to mind.) Are you thinking now about going to Russia? How I wish I could! I'm not all that enamored of Capri, which seems composed from the misunderstandings of German admiration and is at the moment cold, in the midst of a storm and thus without anything real, necessary, simple. Ah! . . . —From time to time: Dieffenbach; Gorki lives here, half anarchist, half millionaire, throwing around money and threats against society, and corrupted by fame, so it would appear. Also Meta von Salis-Marschlins, who is friends with my landlady. She herself — But about that later.

Christmas greetings to trim your dear house! The most cordial greetings, please, to your dear husband, and share with him some of the many dear words which in my thoughts I send you, be they in writing or not.

Rainer.

[*In the margin*:] Have you written anything new? Please, tell me if there is something of yours to read, wherever! I was asked to include Clara's heartfelt greetings the next time I wrote you.

[RMR to LAS in Berlin, postcard depicting Capri, Piccola Marina e Faraglioni]

[Capri,] December 13, 1906

Dear Lou: just now when a letter for you has gone off to Göttingen, Clara writes me that you are in Berlin and had remembered her warmly. Many thanks! Now, when you see her, you will hear everything that my letter was trying so incompletely to catch you up on, and Clara will be the one to find out what I ventured to ask you about. So that my letter is almost superfluous, —though at least it tells you about my remembering, which surely has not been so intense these days for nothing. Are you perhaps on your way to Russia? Many regards to Helene and her husband and her children.

And to you above all.

Rainer.

Address: Capri, Villa Discopoli.

[RMR to LAS in Göttingen, dedication in a copy of *Neue Gedichte* (New Poems), 1907]

Lou.

Съ новымъ годомъ . . .

Rainer

End of 1907

During May 1909 together in Paris, along with Clara Rilke and Ellen Key. Preceding letters missing.

[LAS, in retrospect, from *Rainer Maria Rilke*, p. 43]

. . . we were sitting . . . in his splendid refectory of the Sacré Coeur (which Rodin himself had appointed with his own furniture), before the wide terrace across which the scent of flowers from the garden, empty of people and growing wild, embraced him—as it did during all those work-intoxicated weeks. He spoke of this rapture of creativity that had him under his spell almost to the point of confusing living people with the characters and episodes in his work—and he also spoke of the pressure that would not lift from him because, even so, "he had not accomplished his childhood" but had evaded it, had put things of fiction in its place.

[RMR to LAS in Paris, dedication in a copy of *Der neuen Gedichte anderer Teil* (1908; New poems: The other part), delivered by messenger]

for Lou.
Paris, May 1909.

[LAS to RMR in Paris]

[End of May 1909] Monday

Dear Rainer,

How beautiful was this second, even more unexpected "Christmas package" and the былина! How good of you to send me all this. Now I'll go back, and there, at home, among the trees that even here with us have retained a bit of spring, I'll be with you for long spells through your two books. It was a deep joy for me to see you again. Thank you.

Paris turned out to be no longer possible for me; quietness calls me too strongly. If I should nevertheless want to stand in front of something again, for a long time and utterly alone, it would be the *Balzac,* placed as it is now in the warmth of that wide, fragrant lawn of clover.

For Clara, all my heart; I feel more affection for her than she can possibly know.

Lou.

You must thank the woman for me once more; when she came I was in the buff and thus unable to react at all. Ellen Key will send the cooking utensils back to you before she leaves.

[RMR to LAS in Göttingen]

Paris, June 12, 1909
77 rue de Varenne

Dear Lou,

I've just mailed you the Bichat together with the little book *Requiem.* I've kept my annotations to the Bichat here; they were jotted down as I read and are too vague and half-formed to convey anything specific to you. I leafed through it again and remembered the extent to which this book served as springboard for the most wondrous leaps. The curves of this gymnastics, though, are still waiting to be traced, and when they are, you will see what comes of them.

The way the contour of each individual expression has accrued from so much experience, and yet the way that expression, for all its assurance, lays claim to nothing definitive; the presence of mind in the observation of the unexpected and unforeseen; a certain ordering of the facts by reference to large, overarching issues, so that they all, as it were, look out into the open—: this will (I think) appeal to you also when you look through this book that focuses one so acutely, since a passionate concentration was the atmosphere of its own origin.

The sharp distinction [this physiologist] makes between full, integrated animal life and a manifold life of the organs that somehow remains prehistoric made a very special impression on me. And how in the life of the organs one autonomous entity exists alongside another, organ by organ, each with its responsibility, its labor, pleasure, and aversion, its sleep, its death; how over all the dim individualities of this interior only a rumor of connectedness whispers, externally lulling them to sleep—: this and other such things seemed to me true even in their widest symbolic significance, —more so and more remarkably than I as yet understand and can say.

The other day I spent a quiet hour with Ellen, around the time when the lanterns outside cause the window slats to cast shadows that envelop the room in their strange lacework. I was reading there that your forest is lovely and that you begin your day, again a rustic day, very close to it and in its company. That must make Paris far away and improbable. As for me, when I returned from my little journey through sunny Provence, I was overwhelmed again by its immense reality. The pilgrimage to Saintes-Maries was strange; the small flat town by the sea from which only the church, sturdy as a citadel, rises so strongly and collectedly, its interior full of pilgrims, dogs, and gypsies; a shared long vigil by all these creatures in the dark inaccessible interior of the church, with ever more candles, with Provençal chants, with individual high-pitched shouts for a miracle; and outside perpetually the sea.

Clara moved to Hanover three or four days ago. I am scouring around for some place to live, but without much hope of success. Maybe I'll travel for a month during the summer; all the way up to Föhr, perhaps, to see your doctor: would he be there?

A cordial farewell for today.

Rainer.

[*In the margin*:] Many most cordial regards to your husband. I would like very much to send him a *Requiem* too; please tell me if you think he would enjoy having it?

[LAS to RMR in Paris]

Göttingen, June 17, 1909

Ellen has just told me that you are not doing very well, and for the moment I cannot picture this at all since I am still feeling the enchanting happiness that fills your poems. And these same poems are also all around you, so numerous, so near; how exceptionally life has favored you with this possession, Rainer. And, you know, this is surely one more reason why full human honesty in artistic matters is even more important than in relations with other human beings: without it, one would lose this refuge within oneself. The only undeceiving one.

I have been together with you so strongly during this entire time that it feels odd having to write. Did write, as a matter of fact, but in my diary—words you have none of. From the New Poems 1 and 2 I don't feel the same suggestion radiating toward me as from the Book of Songs II* and the

* *The Book of Images* (augmented edition) of 1906.

Requiem (about which I'd like to talk to you!) But I am still *searching* for you in them as in a very dense forest that contains many hiding places. And I am enjoying both finding and seeking.

Bichat's turn is not coming any time soon. But he sounds interesting.

Forgive the half sheet, Mariechen solemnly dropped her slice of buttered bread on the other half.

Föhr etc. packed with children and adults during summer; the doctors besieged then and hounded; I'd advise against it.

Lou.

Yes, my husband would enjoy having the *R*[*equiem*].

[RMR to LAS, letter from Paris to Göttingen, forwarded to Berlin, July or August 1909]

[LAS to RMR in Paris]

Berlin W. Margarethenstr. 12 (Baroness Seidlitz)
Monday [August 1909]

Dear Rainer,

Your letter found its way to me on roundabout paths: because M. Cl. was not quite sure of my address here, she had mailed it to Göttingen. I keep thinking: perhaps a bit of the summer that concluded in June may still come over you, for weather is so important, and summer reigns during that period, at least here, and therefore probably even more brashly and ebulliently there. But if not, then it has been reserved for somewhere else, and you will experience it in good time. But that doesn't change your present situation, which is hard, almost too hard, and to know of it and feel such affection for you leads most emphatically to arguments with Life; I feel this often now, when so much from last month is coursing through my mind and heart: every least bit you imparted from your thoughts and memories assumes importance for me and provides rich insight as I engage in these contestations. But as my thoughts keep returning to you I have no choice but to become again and again extraordinarily *happy*. (If you should ever feel like writing me out of old, childhood-oldest memories, then *do* so, even if you have to overcome a brief reluctance.) Ellen sends heartfelt greetings.

Lou.

[RMR to LAS in Göttingen]

Paris, 77 rue de Varenne
October 23, 1909

Dear Lou,

I don't want to put off writing to you any longer now, and wherever you are I want to find you and tell you things for the length of these two pages. Lizzie Gibson wrote me earlier that they were hoping to see you at Furuborg: are you reading this letter there, in the air full of autumn forests that blows off the lake toward the warm country house in which my "golden room," as word has it, often awaits me?

How was your summer, and how is your autumn unfolding? I have wondered often.

I have been traveling since September. First in the Black Forest, at the old mineral springs of Rippoldsau, where I took a kind of cure (aromatic pine-needle baths, nutritional meals, but best of all simply the clear pine-tree air and the sound and coolness of the pure springs from every hillside: that in itself was a strong change, and ought to have some effect). The local physician (Dr. van Oordt) gave me some attention; but not enough, and not quite the right kind, either. At the end, which came all too soon, he recommended a stimulant: *Phytinum liquidum*, which I have been taking now, three times daily, for about ten days; is it one of the two stimulants you mentioned to me? (Would you write their names down some time and send them to me?— I forgot them.) About my physical condition let me just say that for months I have been plagued by a tension that arises in various places in my muscles at even the slightest fatigue from reading—in my brow, in my cheeks, at the root of my tongue, in my neck; in the latter place often provoked merely by the slightest pressure from my collar; it is only a bit of foolishness but bothersome, and I am amazed that all the change that is otherwise bringing so much to an end in me and creating fresh starts has not allowed me to transcend these grievances. The feeling in my back and in my esophagus that I spoke to you about here was of the same kind. It is as if an alum solution had gotten into the fascia: they contract almost to the point of painfulness, bitterly as it were, and with this disagreeable sensation I could trace the entire course of all my muscle fibers—that's how clearly this inner torsion defines them. I write you this in case you should see your doctor (from Föhr). He would surely know how something like that is related to other things and how it can be made bearable and less frequent. I have been fighting it for so long now—. But enough of this; generally speaking, I am better and hope to budget my hours so that I can keep working in spite of everything.

These last few weeks, until about ten days ago, I have been living in Provence, in Avignon; it was one of my most remarkable trips. Almost daily, for seventeen days, I saw the immense Papal Palace, this hermetically closed fortress, in which the papacy, sensing that it was starting to unravel at the edges, thought to preserve itself by sealing itself up inside one last genuine passion. No matter how often one returns to see this desperate house, it stands on a rock of improbability, and one can only get into it by leaping across everything traditional and credible. From the other bank of the Rhone, seen from Villeneuve, the city made me think (God knows why) of Novgorod the Great, and I did not then suspect that in this landscape, a few hours further on, I would find the wondrous place that may have been your earliest home. Have you never heard of Les Baux? One approaches from Saint-Remy, where the soil of Provence bears field upon field of flowers, and then suddenly everything turns to stone. A completely barren valley opens up and, with the rocky path scarcely inside, closes shut behind it; thrusts forward three mountains, mountains stacked slantwise one behind the other—three springboards, as it were, from which three last angels, with a terrified running start, have leapt. And opposite, embedded in the distant sky like stone in stone, rise the edges of the strangest settlement, and the path there is blocked and diverted by such immense ruins (whether fragments of mountains or towers, one can't tell) that one imagines that one would also have to be able to fly to carry a soul into that open emptiness above. That is Les Baux. It was a castle, with houses around it that were not built but hollowed out of the limestone strata, as though the people had found space there through a stubborn will to dwell, like the drop from the eaves that only rolls away where it falls to the ground and does not give up and finally joins those like it and endures. Those who endured there most tenaciously were the first of that legendary race of the lords of Les Baux, which will expire with an eccentric in Naples in the seventeenth century, amid fitful flickering violence, like the end of a candle that goes out amid sooty smoke and strange melted accretions. But he who founded the house, ages earlier—he was, according to a tradition passed down to this last heir, the great-grandson of King Balthasar from the Orient, and the true progeny of one of the Three Kings of the Epiphany. And even the old crazy *Marchese* in Naples still used a seal with his sixteen-rayed star.

From the rocky lair of Les Baux this race arose, well-rested for the coming centuries. Their fame could scarcely keep pace with them, and in the impetuousness of their ascent the most brilliant names have attached to their crown. They became lords of seventy-nine cities and villages; they were counts of Avelin, viscounts of Marseille, princes of Orange, and dukes of Andria; and they scarcely had time to notice that they had become (at least by title) kings of Jerusalem. Their reality is so fantastic that the troubadours give up imagining it; they flock to this court and *describe* it—while, fired by their songs, the lords grow ever bolder and the women rise to that incomparable beauty which by 1240 in Cécile des Baux had become so great that she was famous in even the remotest regions and called everywhere *Passe-Rose*—she who surpasses roses.

But in those days the first Giovanna, queen of Naples, was the contested heiress of Provence; the dynasty, now for, now against her, kept increasing. It cast itself so high and far that it never fell back to itself and regathered. In Naples the court ate away at it and so did the jealousy of the San Severini; it extended only single wild tendrils now, tendrils with thorns, at the ends of which rebels sprouted, poisonous blooms without any desire to be fruit, their scent making even the emperor nauseous. But where it had fallen on tougher ground, it clung with the force of an untended fig tree, and fared better: in Dalmatia and Sardinia it formed robust dynasties.

At Les Baux itself, however, only governors now sat, first of Provence, then of France, after the countryside had fallen to the king. All their names are known and one recalls immediately those of the House of Manville, under whom Protestantism became entrenched in castle and city. Claude II of Manville was still protecting the Protestants of the Reformation when it had become dangerous to side with them: he reserves a chapel for them in his palace. But already his successor is faced with the choice of abandoning his religion or his post. In the end he chooses to renounce things external, and with him (in 1621) all Protestants are expelled from Les Baux. Among those banished, there were probably Salomés: grandchildren or sons of the notary André Salomé, who under the first Manville governor wrote his book of recollections; pages that have been used variously since and are now (so I was assured) in the safekeeping of a notary at Mouriès, Maître Laville.

Now you understand, dear Lou, at the very end, the point of my whole story, which has become so long-winded. I was in Les Baux for one day. The distant view from up there, about which the guide had told me, never cleared: it is supposed to open endlessly and spread out beautifully and extend all the way to the sea and the church tower of Saintes-Maries. But the near view became all the grander the more the day grayed and closed around it. I was soon rid of the custodian, the innkeeper also, after I had finished breakfast. And from then on my only company was a shepherd, who said little. We merely stood next to each other and gazed at the village. The scattered sheep grazed on the rocky soil. But occasionally, whenever one of them found a patch of wild herbs and nibbled at it, the fragrance of thyme arose and lingered around us. And I thought of *you*!*

Rainer.

[RMR to LAS, written on the back of a reproduction of a painting by Eugène Carrière: Christ on the Cross, with the lamenting Mary]

Christmas 1909.

Rainer.

[LAS to RMR in Paris]

Göttingen [December 28, 1909]

Dear Rainer, thank you! You know that Christmas for "grownups" can happen when a certain memory arrives all of a sudden—it is as if a piece of silver thread from some invisible Christmas tree had gotten caught somewhere and was igniting a multitude of little incandescent recollections, the kind of profuse disarray that usually hangs from just such a tree, but now turned all at

*LAS tried to make illegible "And I thought of *you*!"

once into pure unsupported festiveness. Do you remember how the Christ Legends were the first thing you read to me in the *Fürstenhäuser*? Yes, *this* Jesus I love, or rather this Mary-Woman who releases and relinquishes him to his cross, and stifles her scream in these hands, —herself remaining hale, remaining Nature, so that she might ever again bring forth the mortal body for its great achievement, an immortal deed. The picture, brought to my house today, is already hanging in my blue room with the bearskins. How were your holidays? Here, my husband (even though the poor man has to hobble about with a cane because of his sciatica) was kept busy being Father Christmas for Mariechen, pulling toys for her out of a glittering damask sack one by one, while she curtsied at the appearance of each one, almost all the way down to the ground to make absolutely certain he was pleased. Ruth has probably outgrown this!

Outside there is an unseasonable spell of gray, damp, stormy summer warmth; linden trees and lilac bushes are breaking into leaf. But in the very near future I may be traveling to colder regions to see my mother, who has been rather sick and, even though she is completely well again, wants me to come anyway. And imagine what I am currently doing and finding extraordinarily enjoyable, so much so that I want to continue with it from now on: writing children's stories. It started because of two children in particular, the Klingenbergs' Bubi and Schnuppi, as they are nicknamed. Three stories are finished now and they are as nice as you could ever imagine! One is called "The Real Father Christmas," another "The Tale of the Stone, the Daisy, and the Cloud," and another "About Birds, Foxes, Butterflies, Mice, and Some Other Horrible Thing."

This is the most impressive news I have to pass on to you. Tell me about yourself. Also, if you are feeling better now. Last time I forgot to write you that *our* miracle elixir is called *Lecithin*, but it is probably the same as yours, pretty much. If you can work, I'm sure you'll also be sound at heart; the final cause of all this is ultimately a displaced creative imagination which roams about exactly where there is no space at all for it, within the smallest bodily particles, so to speak, and thus throwing them all into confusion; not in any grossly literal sense, of course, but nonetheless so that they dream, as it were, of illness, of disintegration. This is far from harmless, I know: but, in the end, only *other* dreams, the different, strong ones in mental life, can drive them out. Those, true enough, cannot be prescribed by any physician, but when they are entrenched as the decisive factor in a person's disposition, as his second, proper soul, they will fight this battle again and again all by themselves.

Isn't it exactly this, by the way, that one understands by "ghost"? A something *that acts as if it had space*, while there is really none at all for it, other "positive" things occupy this space completely: therein lies its eeriness. This is the contradiction: that this eeriness is nothing more than its non-reality, its being-nothing, and that this lack of being, through the errant behavior of the imagination, through, as it were, a mistaken identification, is being supplied with ever so small a droplet of life-blood, —just enough for delusion, for sustaining the contradiction.

Good night, little heart, it's way past my bedtime.* My room smells wonderfully of little pieces of charred pine. And I am feeling very gay and would like to have something beautiful for you. Out of gratitude and joy. Something beautiful for 1910.

Lou.

Since I don't know if you are still at 77 rue Varenne, I sent this letter as registered mail so that it may find you in the South.

*[*In the margin*:] I'd say time for me to go to bed with the chickens if they hadn't all been butchered!

[RMR, mailing *The Notebooks of Malte Laurids Brigge* from Paris to LAS in Göttingen, probably in June 1910]

[RMR, letter from Paris, early November 1910, to LAS in Göttingen (forwarded to Berlin), presumably with a poem enclosed]

[LAS to RMR in Paris]

Charlottenburg, Suarezstr. 22 Klingenberg
November 6 [1910]

Dear Rainer, it was almost like a voice out of my own very earliest times! and yet so much *your* voice that said it and *your* eyes that saw it, —in cases like this I always feel that the whole of lyric poetry with its capacity for meaning and expression is but a small sector of that realm in which it is your task to make things come to life. But then I also know of no other "art form" that has so wide a scope, and perhaps therein lies its magic. And you are going to go so far in it, you dear fellow. If you could only shake off that physical discomfort; the way you describe it, it is certainly and absolutely beyond doubt neurasthenic. Are you going to stay at the cloister until Christmas? Isn't it up for sale? I have and have had no travel plans, was detained in Göttingen (where your letter had been kept unforwarded all this time due to some postal foul-up) by happy work, by happy things in general. Much to tell, much to query! Never mind. At some bend in the road we are sure to look back at each other.

Lou.

[*In the margin*:] Bichat from Göttingen

Late 1910: Following the May 31 publication of The Notebooks of Malte Laurids Brigge, *RMR begins to experience a severe creative crisis, and his life for a time becomes almost nomadic. His travels take him (for the last time) to Rome, briefly to Princess Marie's Duino Castle near Trieste, then back to Paris and on to Bohemia to stay at château Janowitz with Sidonie Nádherný von Borutin. In November, embarking at Marseille, he sets out on a four-month journey through North Africa, from which he returns to Paris via Venice. After another stay in Bohemia, this time at Princess Marie's estate at Lautschin, he returns to Duino (in October 1911 for a stay of over six months), where the "task" of the Elegies is given to him in a burst of inspiration (the first and second elegies, fragments of the third, sixth, and ninth, and the opening lines of the tenth all in a few days in early 1912). After a summer in Venice, RMR spends four months in Spain before returning to his Paris home (or home base) at the end of February 1913. For the next year and a half he travels constantly, often to Berlin and Munich, always returning to Paris.*

July 1914: RMR leaves his Paris apartment for a short trip to Germany. The outbreak of the war surprises him in Munich; a period of productive work there ends with his call-up for military service, which he spends in the War Archive in Vienna.

June 6, 1916: After his discharge, RMR returns to Munich.

October 25, 1912–April 6, 1913: LAS, accompanied by her "adopted daughter" Ellen Delp, resides in Vienna. There she immerses herself in the study of psychoanalysis under Freud, with whom she develops a close cordial friendship that will last until her death. Back in Göttingen she has a brief but heartfelt reunion with RMR in July 1913, and thereafter they spend much time together in Munich: from September 8 until October 17, 1913; again in 1915 (March 19 until May 27); and, for the last time, between March 26 and June 2, 1919.

1915: LAS begins working as a lay analyst at her home.

All eight letters (and one telegram) LAS sent to RMR in Duino early in 1912 have been lost, and no letters from her to him during his subsequent stay in Venice are known to have existed.

[RMR to LAS in Göttingen]

Duino Castle near Nabresina, Austrian Littoral
December 28, 1911

Dear Lou,

Let me cling to the thought that you are expecting a letter from me about now, else there will be no excuse at all for this big sheet of paper, and I really can't take a smaller one. There is a good chance that around now you are at home and at peace, since it has always been that way between the two Christmases, —so let me tell you this and that for a few pages.

I heard about you through Gebsattel this autumn, but as you can imagine, he gives back no complete pictures, he is like one of those mirrors that doctors use for examinations; thus nothing whole could be gleaned from him, but I gathered nonetheless that things are going well with you, and that agrees with everything that I, apart from all reports, know to be true of you.

You notice that I am, as always, in a rush to get to myself, that I still assume this topic can be of interest: would you care to find your way in yet again? Please, please do, I will help you as best I can, it may be badly—but at least there is a clue: *Malte Laurids Brigge*. I don't need responses to my books, you know that, —but now I need fervently to know what impression this book made on you. Our good Ellen Key, of course, promptly misidentified me with Malte and had nothing further to say; yet no one but you, dear Lou, can make the distinction and judge whether and to what extent he resembles me. Whether he, who doubtless *is* in part created from my perils, is destroyed by them, in order to save me, as it were, from destruction, or whether with these journals I have finally gone all the way out into the current that will sweep me away and plunge me over the edge. Can you understand that in the wake of this book I have been left behind like a survivor, stranded high and dry in my inmost being, doing nothing, never to be occupied again? The nearer I approached its end, the more strongly I felt that it would be an indescribable division, a high watershed, as I always told myself; but now it turns out that all the water has run off toward the old side and I am walking down into an arid world that stretches on unchanging. And if it were only that: but the other one, the one who was destroyed, he somehow used me up, funded the immense expenditure of his destruction with the strengths and materials of my life, there is nothing that was not in his hands, in his heart, he appropriated everything with the intensity of his despair, scarcely does a thing appear new to me when I discover the break in it, the rough place where he tore himself off. Perhaps this book needed to be written the way one detonates a mine; perhaps I should have jumped far away from it the moment it was finished. But I probably still cling too desperately to possessions to have done so, and for the same reason cannot achieve boundless poverty, much as that, I expect, is the crucial task that awaits me. It has been my ambition to invest my entire capital in a lost cause, but then again the true values of the investment could only become visible in the loss; thus for the longest time, I remember, *Malte Laurids Brigge* seemed to me not so much a downfall as a strange dark ascent into a remote and neglected part of heaven.

It's been almost two years; dear Lou, you alone will be able to grasp how falsely and wretchedly I have spent them. When they began I thought I had a long, long patience, how often since then have I patched it up, what have I not unraveled and tied onto it. I have gone through so much bewilderment, experiences like watching Rodin, in his seventieth year, simply go wrong, completely wrong, as if all his endless work had never been; as if something small and idiotic, some sticky trifle such as earlier he must have kicked from his path by the dozen, not taking the time to be thoroughly done with them—had lain in wait there and overwhelmed him tauntingly and now day by day is making his old age more grotesque and ridiculous—, what am I to do with such experiences? All that was needed was a moment of lassitude, a few days of slackening, and his life rose up around him as utterly unachieved as around a schoolboy and drove him, just like that, into the nearest pitiful trap. What am *I* to say, with my little bit of work I set aside so many times, if *he* was not saved? Should I wonder that life-sized life treats me with utter scorn during these intervals, and what in all the world *is* this work if one cannot learn and undergo everything in it, if one hangs around outside it and allows oneself to be shoved and pushed, grabbed and let go, getting oneself entangled in luck and injustice and never understanding anything.

Dear Lou, I am in very sorry straits when I wait for people, need people, look around for people: that only thickens the dark cloud hanging over me and makes me feel myself a villain; they cannot begin to know how little trouble I actually take with them and of what ruthlessness I am capable. So it is a bad sign that often since *Malte* I have been hoping for someone, *anyone*, who would be there for me: why is that? I had a ceaseless longing to lodge my solitude with someone, to put it under that person's care—you can imagine that nothing came of it. With a kind of shame I think of my best time in Paris, that of the *New Poems*, when I expected nothing and no one and the whole world streamed toward me increasingly as pure task and I responded clearly and confidently with pure achievement. Who would have told me then how many lapses were ahead of me. I wake each morning with a cold place on my shoulder exactly where the hand ought to be that would shake me. How is it possible that now, ready and trained for expression, I am left in fact without a calling, superfluous? In the very years when Ilja von Murom rose up, I sit down and wait and my heart knows of no occupation for me. What will you say, Lou, when you read this? Could you have foreseen it? I remember a passage in your last letter, which I don't have with me: "You are going to go so very far," you wrote. And if not, —what to do to keep from stagnating while I stand still? What to do?

I think less than I used to of a physician. Psychoanalysis is too fundamental a help for me, it helps once and for all, makes a clean sweep of things, and to find myself swept clean one day might be even more hopeless than this disarray.

On the other hand I do still occasionally think of pursuing a few things uninterruptedly at a small country university. —You smile, you've heard that before, yes, there is little that's new with me, and the worst of it is that certain of my plans and perhaps even my best and most deplorable qualities only make sense up to a certain age and beyond that become absurd. Indeed, it is almost too late even for the university, but you know what I mean by this; the terrible thing about art is that the further one advances in it, the more it commits one to the extreme, the near-impossible; then there enters in psychologically what in another sense the woman in Baudelaire's poem refers to when in the great silence of the full-mooned night she suddenly bursts out: *Que c'est un dur métier que d'être belle femme.*

Here, Lou, is another of my confessions. Are these the symptoms of the long convalescence that is my life? Are they the signs of a new illness? I wish I could be together with you sometime for a whole week, telling and listening. It's been so long. I get about so much, should it not be possible for us to meet just once?

Do you know that last winter I was in Algiers, Tunis, and Egypt? Unfortunately under conditions so little suited to me that I lost my seat and my grip and finally only followed along like someone who had been thrown by a runaway horse and was careening along by one stirrup. It wasn't the right thing to do. But a bit of the Orient rubbed off on me anyway, on the Nile boat I even tried my hand at Arabic, and the museum in Cairo may have made something of me after all, confused as I was on entering.

This year I am a guest in this old sturdy castle (for the time being all alone) that holds one a little like a prisoner; it cannot do otherwise with its immense walls. And at least the practical disorder in my affairs will benefit from my being looked after here for a few months. Beyond that I know nothing and want to know nothing.

Adieu, dear Lou; God knows, your being was so truly the door through which I first found my way out into freedom; now I still come from time to time and stand up against the same doorpost on which so long ago we marked my growth. Let me keep this cherished habit, and hold me dear.

Rainer.

Cordial greetings to your husband. Is the little one still young enough to keep him busy during Christmas, Mariechen I mean, (wasn't that her name?)

One thing more: do you have Kassner's latest book, *The Elements of Human Greatness*? Some time ago I acquired a copy for you; may I send it?

[LAS to RMR, letter from Göttingen to Duino Castle, beginning of January 1912]

[RMR to LAS in Göttingen]

Duino near Nabresina, Austrian Littoral
January 10, 1912.

Dear Lou,

The elder Prince Taxis was here, I have only been alone again for a few days, now at last I can thank you for your good letter. Believe me, I have gleaned much from it, I walked up and down in the garden with it as with something one wants to learn by heart; what would I do without this voice: yours. I can't tell you how warm and comforting it was. I am the single small ant that has lost its direction, but you see the anthill and assure me that it is undisturbed and that I will find my way back into it and make myself useful. And on top of everything came the surprise that you know this coast, so that your letter, as it were, concerned not only me but my surroundings, was addressed to everything and attuned to everything.

You are right, it has probably always been like this with me, but, you see, I am exhausting myself in the process; as someone who walks on crutches always wears out his coat under the armpits first, so my one-sidedly worn-out nature will, I fear, one day have holes in it and yet in other places still be new. These last few years it has often seemed to me as though many people working as artists have got themselves in hand by outwitting and exploiting the inadequacies they recognize in themselves, much as they would have made use of a weakness they perceived in someone else. I side too strongly with my nature, I have never wanted anything from it that it did not give forth greatly and happily out of its own innermost impulses, almost like something beyond me. And the most one can arrive at by the other road is the assurance of always being able to write; that doesn't concern me. What distresses me this time is perhaps not even the length of the pause but rather a kind of dulling, a growing old, if one wants to call it that—as though what is strongest in me really had been damaged somehow, were a little bit to blame, were atmosphere, you understand: air instead of world-space. It may be that this continual inner distractedness in which I live is partly physical in origin, is a thinness of the blood; whenever I notice it, it fills me with reproaches for having let it get so far. No matter what awaits me: I still get up every day doubting whether I shall succeed in doing so; and these misgivings have grown to their present size through the actual experience of weeks, even months going by in which I produce only with the greatest exertions five lines of an utterly insipid letter, which, when they are finally there, leave an aftertaste of incompetence such as a cripple might feel who can't even shake hands any more.

Can I, despite everything, move on through all this? If people happen to be present they offer me the relief of being able to be more or less the person they take me for, without being too particular about my actual existence. How often do I step out of my room as, so to speak, some chaos, and outside, perceived by someone else's mind, assume a composure that is actually his and in the next moment, to my astonishment, find myself expressing well-formed things, while just before everything in my entire consciousness was utterly amorphous. To whom am I saying this, dear Lou, indeed it is almost *through you* that I know this is the way things are, you see how little has changed, —and in this sense people will always be the wrong thing for me, something that galvanizes my lifelessness without remedying it. Ah, my dear, I know so very well that my earliest instinct was the decisive one, I don't want to act against it in any way, but I can't escape the fact that I have been placed among people and have felt real influences from them and have worked my way in as though I were one of them. I won't even speak of that one special year when, as things were not progressing at all, or better yet, not getting started anywhere (for there *was* nothing there—), *you* came: that can happen but once, just as there is only one birth, —but I have other individual memories of human companionship to which I cling, —when one puts them into words their content seems completely unremarkable, and yet, would you believe me, in the long complicated solitude, often pushed to the extreme, in which *Malte Laurids* was written, I felt absolutely certain that the strength with which I paid for him derived in crucial ways from certain evenings on Capri when I did nothing except sit with two elderly women and a young girl and watch their needlework and sometimes at the end receive an apple that one of them had peeled. There was no hint of destiny between us, I have never wondered to what extent precisely *these* people were required for what was born there to come about; name it has none, but I experienced from it something that was almost like the mystic nourishment of the Eucharist; while it was still there I knew that it was giving me strengths and later, in my arduous solitude, I recognized these strengths among all the others; it was strange: they were the ones that held out the longest.

Dear Lou, when I wrote recently that I was almost hoping for people, I meant that I have not felt *this* again and that I need it infinitely. Can you not imagine that there is a human being who can give this, spontaneously, without even knowing, and who would be content to radiate sheer presence and expect nothing in return? There *are* special people who do this for the sick, where all care leads, at best, back to health; whereas here it would as it were *begin* at the peak of health, and extend God knows how far. It wasn't in times like these bad ones that this need of mine developed; it acquired contour during the immense concentration that pushed the *New Poems* on to completion, and I wrote *Brigge* through to the end as though on condition that it would be there. Let me explain to you with a specific example. Can you imagine that I am gripped with the same anxiety when I consider whether to take a little furnished room in the rue Cassette again, or to return among my own furniture, which over the last few years has been transformed completely into the scenery designed for the last act of *Malte Laurids*? Absurd as it is, I undergo all these phases the way one undergoes destinies, and that is why one day they are fundamentally over and done with and never to be recommenced. Do you understand that I imagine some presence that would make the things I have blown out of all proportion ordinary and harmless once more? Is there no such thing? One might think that the fable is playing out in me: that I had sung instead of built and that now, when it is getting cold, I find myself without shelter. But no, you see, what I have in mind could not have been built anyway, it would be completely miraculous, and I would have no right to count on it had not every decisive turn in my life also been independent of my storing up and impossible to plan out or lay foundations for. Perhaps anyone who hears this will immediately ask what I, for my part, propose to contribute towards such a relationship; and here I must admit that I have nothing really to respond with, save perhaps my own warmer and happier being, as it may have manifested itself to those women on Capri. I believe it was in Naples once, as I stood before some antique tombstones, when it flashed through me: I should never touch people with gestures stronger than the ones portrayed there. And I really do believe that sometimes I am far enough along that I can express all the surge of my heart, without detriment or disaster, by placing my hand lightly on a shoulder. Would that, Lou, would that not be the only progress thinkable within that "restraint" of which you remind me?

It is half past three, I have eaten almost nothing, I have spent nearly the whole day writing you and yet it is so difficult to make anything understandable that my head is buzzing; I am making scarcely any progress, I keep wanting to start over again and say everything differently the second time around—; but to persuade you of no particular point. I merely want you to know what I meant by "people": not any forfeiting of my solitude; only that if it were a little less suspended in mid-air, if it were to find itself in good hands, it would lose all its suggestions of morbidity (that is bound to happen eventually), and I would finally achieve some sort of continuity within it instead of carrying it around like a pilfered bone from one bush to the next amid loud hallos.

Well look at this, your old mole has been burrowing again and has thrown heaps of dark soil across a perfectly good path. Forgive me. To you I speak my inmost heart like the people in the Old Testament, an entire scroll of sayings: for what stands there in your life's burning thorn bush is the very thing that should also have power over me.—

Dear Lou, if things work out, I shall probably stay here into the spring, although neither the house nor the climate is quite right for me; this continual shift between bora and sirocco is not good for my nerves, and I exhaust myself going through first one and then the other. All the same, when I add up the individual advantages of this retreat, it comes to a sizeable sum, and I must count myself lucky to have it at all. In my present state any place would have been hard for me, but not everywhere could I have so plumbed the depths of my condition as here. It is only too bad that Nature here elicits almost nothing from me, even the sea leaves me indifferent; as if this gross Austrian mixture of languages stripped even the landscape of its unified, straightforward expression. I can scarcely find words for how repugnant everything Austrian is to me. I long for Naples, or I would like to walk for hours in the snow through the woods and afterwards drink delicious coffee with you. But it will be all right the way things are.

Another thing occurs to me: I'm sure you know that some two years ago *To Celebrate Myself* was reissued (substantially in its old form) together with the *White Princess* in a single volume called *The Early Poems*; in a letter that came day before yesterday the publisher urges me to consider doing the same thing with my even earlier books, so that they would return to life in a similar volume called *First Poems*. I once mentioned to him, unfortunately, that there are *Visions of Christ*, and since Kippenberg naturally thinks it important to include unpublished pieces in these reissued editions, he has been rather insistent about adding these weighty poems (that I myself have not looked at for several years now) to the new volume. On no account do I want to do this without knowing what your thoughts are. Do you think there is something else from that period which might be more appropriate, or should it really be these things' turn? *Inselverlag*, by the way, has been unwavering in its friendship and support, I can refuse it anything I would rather not do, but on the other hand it has helped me so loyally during these barren years, and I realize that it means to serve both our interests by putting old and oldest things back in circulation. I have asked my wife, in Oberneuland, to look for the *Christ-Visions* in my chest, meanwhile will you write me briefly what you think of publishing them in a volume where they would be surrounded by *Advent, Crowned by Dreams, Sacrifices to the Lares,* etc.?

The *Bichat* please consider yours, I received another copy of it some time ago. I am sending you Kassner's *Elements* with this letter. It will be very important for me to learn what impression this little book makes on you. Kassner himself one cannot see without being struck by him. Perhaps it is only the extent to which he has come to terms with his massive bodily infirmities (that in itself would be quite enough), but I've always suspected that he threw a great many other things into the process and thus vanquished them as well—, how else explain the clear serenity that shines in his eyes; only you can be as radiant as he is at times.

Farewell. I would just as soon write for another year (but: eight pages of this: what will you say!)

Rainer.

[LAS to RMR, letter from Göttingen to Duino Castle,
around January 18, 1912]

[RMR to LAS in Göttingen]

Duino Castle near Nabresina, Austrian Littoral
January 20, 1912

Don't be startled, Lou, that I am back again so soon: it will only be a little visit, if it doesn't suit you, put me aside until tomorrow, day after tomorrow—whenever you wish.

Chance decreed that I should find your letter on my writing table this morning alongside one from Gebsattel, which I am enclosing. I beg you, read it; here quickly are the bits of information that will make it comprehensible to you.

You understand that the thought of undergoing an analysis comes up in me from time to time; what I know of Freud's writings is, to be sure, uncongenial and in places hair-raising; yet the central insight, though it runs away with him, has its genuine and strong sides, and I can well believe that Gebsattel employs them with prudence and to good results. As for myself, I have already written you that I tend instinctively to shy away from this getting swept clean, and that, my nature being what it is, I could scarcely expect anything good to come of it. Something like a disinfected soul results from it, a non-thing, a freakish form of life corrected in red ink like a page in a schoolboy's notebook. And yet: dear Lou, the way things are with me I scarcely have the right merely on instinct to cast suspicion on a help once it has been offered and is ready and waiting. I more or less knew that Gebsattel would be prepared to perform the whole excavation on me, but I had never actually asked him whether, insofar as he knows me (and there was a time in Paris—a desolate, wearisome time for me—when we had detailed, intimate conversations), he thought psychoanalytic treatment seemed appropriate in my case. The letter I sent him on the 15th of this month contained this question along with some of my misgivings. The enclosed is his reply. He seems to me wrong on several counts; nonetheless it is time, given his readiness, to seriously consider this way out. The fact remains (so far as my body is concerned) that I find myself quite unbearable, certain bad habits, through which in years past one would repeatedly fan one's arm as through bad air, are gradually thickening, and I can well imagine them someday shutting me in like walls. The hypersensitivity of my muscles, for instance, has become so great that a little exercise or any strained posture (as in shaving) will immediately produce swellings, pains, etc., phenomena upon which then follow, as if they had merely been waiting, fears, torments, rationalizations of all sorts; I am ashamed to admit how wildly this vicious circle dances around in me, often for weeks, each misery doing the other every favor.

Perhaps you know, dear Lou, that Gebsattel has been treating my wife, starting some time last spring—; with her the situation is different, her work has never been a help to her, whereas mine has in a certain sense been from the start a kind of self-treatment; but as it evolved and acquired independence it has lost more and more of its therapeutic and solicitous qualities and makes demands; a soul which has no choice but to find its harmony in the immense exaggerations of art ought to be able to count on a body that in no way mimics it and is precise and the very opposite of exaggeration. My physical being runs the risk of becoming the caricature of my spiritual being.

Dear Lou, if this is not becoming too much for you, give me a few words to help me mull it over. (Possibly I could go to Munich, do a few things there at the University and at the same time attempt the analysis.) Your letter I will answer soon, thank you for it, you see how things go up and down and back and forth with me: what to do?

Rainer.

[LAS to RMR, telegram and subsequent letter from Göttingen to Duino Castle, around January 22, 1912]

[RMR to LAS in Göttingen]

Duino Castle near Nabresina, Austrian Littoral
January 24, 1912

Dear Lou,

Kind heart, you *speak* to me while you write, I am so at home in the reading of your letters that, the ink's blackness notwithstanding, I don't for a moment doubt that those little stars you mentioned the other day still shine—; and furthermore I have been so prepared for what you say by my own feeling—that first, ever anew strongest feeling to which you lend credence—that I find myself already persuaded. I paved the way even before your telegram, thanking Gebsattel with a few lines for his letter full of friendly willingness, and pledging him a quick reply. And one of these days now I will write him, without undue haste.

I know now that analysis would make sense for me only if I were truly serious about that strange thought at the back of my mind—*no longer to write*—which during the finishing of *Malte* I often dangled before my nose as a kind of promised relief. *Then* one might have one's devils driven out, since in ordinary bourgeois life they are really only bothersome and awkward anyway, and if by some chance the angels left with them, well, one could view that too as a simplification and tell oneself that in one's new, one's next occupation (but which?) there would certainly be no useful place for them. But am I the person to undertake such an experiment with all its consequences? Or is even this just another piece of cunning fabrication—to imagine, as it were, a different person, not inside an ongoing work but living at home in one's own moth-eaten skin, beginning tomorrow? For a time it comforted me in a general way to think that one could after all take up something different at any moment, in case the work one had been doing until now should cease. But to tell the truth, long as the present hiatus has stretched on, nothing has occurred to me that I could take hold of subsequently, saving of course the analysis, and that of course would only defer everything yet again, present issues as well as those to follow. You mustn't laugh, but for weeks, toward the conclusion of *Brigge,* I had the feeling I could still become a doctor afterwards, could study and then be a doctor somewhere in the country—

It is a shame, a shame that we cannot meet one another now out on a walk. I would tell you a great, great many things. But that will happen sometime. Meanwhile it is fine, glorious for me that you know analysis so intricately and moreover that you have also seen Gebsattel (who indeed practices analysis only "for a limited time and in certain cases," as you say).

Your letter I shall read often.

Adieu, I want this to get off today and therefore am closing quickly. And *thank you.* (I hope I didn't barge in on you too violently while you were at work?)

Rainer.

P.S. I have quickly copied, so that something more would come back to you along with this hasty scribble, two poems from an entirely new little *Life of Mary.*

Visitation

She still took her way easily at first;
only sometimes on some steep slope did she
become conscious of her wondrous body,
and then she stood, breathing, on the high

hills of Judea. But not the countryside,
her abundance spread all around her;

as she walked on, she felt: no one will ever
surpass this greatness stirring in me.

And suddenly she craved to place her hand
on the other body, which was farther on.
And the two women swayed towards one another
and touched each other's garments, hair.

Each woman, filled with her holy treasure,
found protection in the other's shade.
Ah, the Savior in her was still a flower,
but the Baptist in her cousin's womb
was already making joyful little leaps.

Before the Passion

O if you wanted *this*, you should not have
chosen to come forth through a woman's body.
Saviors must be quarried in the mountains,
where hardest things are chiseled from what's hard.

Do you yourself feel no regret for ravaging
your beloved valley? See my weakness:
I have nothing but brooks of milk and tears,
and you were always rich in everything.

With such display you were announced to me.
Why did you not just exit from me wildly?
If you need only tigers to rip you limb from limb,
why did they raise me in the women's house

to weave for you a cloak of softest white
in which not the slightest trace of seam
presses against you: that's how my whole life was,—
and now you suddenly turn Nature inside-out.

———

[RMR to LAS, "jubilation" letter from Duino Castle to Göttingen in connection with the genesis of the first Elegies, toward the end of January 1912]

[LAS to RMR from Göttingen to Duino Castle, probably beginning of February 1912]

[RMR to LAS in Göttingen]

Duino Castle near Nabresina, Austrian Littoral
February 7, 1912

Yes, dear Lou, Дай Богъ жизнь! And may the truth be ever more confirmed which Christ so gently helped the blessed Angela of Foligno understand: that at every moment he was so much more prepared to give than she was to receive. The only bad thing is that for me now, from a purely bodily standpoint, the receiving takes just as great a toll as the not being able to receive. Ah, old calash that I am, once my ride was so smooth, and now—if the miracle opts to enter me for half an hour, I am amazed that it doesn't immediately climb back out: I bump and rattle about like the poorest telyega and in the process almost come apart myself.

Enough. For the third day now I have been trudging about a little in the snow with bare feet that long constantly for spring; the snow did start thawing two days ago, but such a quantity of it had fallen that, despite the sirocco, it still hasn't all been licked up out of the garden. (Sometime soon, I believe, I need to have a regular winter again, one with a real bite to growl back at.)

Today, to return to your third letter ago,* I wanted to tell you a little about Kassner's ideas. But it is hard for me to leave the man himself out of consideration, indeed, I can't do it at all. What I had read of him before I knew him was "too difficult" for me; I have only begun reading his work with real understanding now that I feel him behind it, often even directly before it. Increas-

*The (lost) one of January 18.

ingly isolated as he is now, he has placed a strong trust in me and considers me unreservedly his friend: and he is certainly not wrong in that, he is in fact the only man with whom I can make any headway at all, —or perhaps better: the only man who knows how to draw out a bit of the feminine in me, to his own advantage. Even when I saw him for the first time years ago in Vienna I felt, with extraordinary clarity and directness, the serene radiance of his being, which *shines*, which instantly is a light, a brightness in the room. He has something that the others, seen next to him, do not have, he must have succeeded at something that eludes the rest. (By the way, as to background and origin there is nothing Jewish about him or in him—you seem to take him for a Jew? —No.) He is certainly—as he himself would acknowledge—a spiritual child of Kierkegaard. Kierkegaard comes to an end in him and makes a full turn and goes on. I suspect that Kassner's bodily infirmity is for him what "melancholy" is for Kierkegaard. And as it was a kind of advantage for Kierkegaard always to have, instead of so many unforeseeable hindrances, only this one immense, superhuman melancholy, before which he ranged himself in ever new battle formations, so Kassner too somehow prevails by virtue of the fact that all resistances coalesce for him in *one* hindrance: that procures for him concentration and assuredness; nothing can, so to speak, attack him from behind. But his indescribable admiration for Kierkegaard may owe just as much to the fact that Kierkegaard's adversary was more mystical, more inexhaustible, more perilous, handed down from the Beyond, as it were, through the Father's agency, whereas that which *he*, Kassner, overcomes by force of mind and spirit at every moment is, from the divine perspective, not a disability at all but a well-earned distinction. (Whereas Kierkegaard's melancholy is still an impediment even in heaven.) Do you know Kassner's earlier essay on "Indic Idealism"? I think it may be his best. If you like, I'll have it sent to you sometime by Bruckmann (where, if I am not mistaken, it was published). In the beautiful chapter on the chimeras (the best in the whole book, it seems to me), I *may*, incidentally, have been painted in at the bottom, very small and perhaps even lower than on my knees, as the "little patron": in Paris, back when we saw each other often, I once casually suggested, without knowing what he was currently working on, that he climb up again to the chimeras on Notre Dame and take another look, without saying anything further—; but that must have been impetus enough, and it obviously came at just the right time. I can imagine, by the way, that what I felt in reading his books before I began to factor the man himself into them — is actually quite similar to your reaction upon seeing him in person. But to what is it due? —If you spoke with him, you would, I believe, hit upon it in half an hour; he always prejudices me in favor of his own meaning, but you would enjoy watching him and would form your own opinion.

A few evenings ago I read the *Chamber Plays* of the old Strindberg: they are frightening, frightening: it is dreadful that old men should come to their end this way, like the little twenty-three-year-old dauphine whose last words were: *Fi de la vie, —ne m'en parlez plus.*

The old Michelangelo who writes in a sonnet: What does it profit a man to have made so many puppets? (Or something like that; I know only the Italian text, and it is difficult to translate.) But in Strindberg there must be strengths, the massive concentrations of strength in a landslide; to live in *this* kind of world, and nevertheless to exist, to achieve, —it is beyond all comprehension. For he doesn't just *speak* of this terrible despair to which everything gives rise, he *makes* something out of it, and he makes it magnificently, that one must grant him. (Have you read these pieces? *Chamber Plays*, published by Georg Müller, Munich-Leipzig; especially the second, third, and fourth!)

I could not help thinking that life lived under Clara's parental roof would have to be portrayed in just these terms. Her father was horrible, her mother is so thoroughly broken inside, and kept outwardly almost young, like dolls with an exaggerated child's face when they are old, impossible—and yet something still plays with her, —but *only* plays. Clara's psychoanalytic treatment is expected to end around Easter, then she wants to take Ruth with her to Munich, enroll her in a school that Ricarda Huch's daughter and several other children I saw there also attend. That could, if it works out, be very good for the little girl as well as for Clara. Clara said, as you, I believe, learned in Weimar from Gebsattel, —that she wants our divorce, I understand this very well, unfortunately the thing will be lengthy and drag on. There is no ill will between us, but as my wife she does, so to speak, go around falsely labeled, is not with me and yet cannot move on to anything free of me. It is strange: our relationship consisted of her infinitely and unreservedly affirming and accepting me, and then, as she realized how much she had signed onto there that is absolutely alien, even hostile to her, reversing into wholesale rejection. If behind all this one looks for *her*, for what she has become since the end of her girlhood, one finds (her motherly care and her relationship with Ruth excepted) nothing tangible, nothing but this alternating function of ingesting me and expelling me, and if, as I hope, the analysis succeeds in completely getting rid of me (apparently a pest in her nature after all), then she will presumably have to start up again at that point where I entered and interrupted her . . . Gradually (under the pressure of her decision and my need for someone who can help me, stand by me, offer me protection) I have come to understand why nothing real could become of us living side by side: because she was either my double with all her strengths and thus too much for me, or else my antagonist and thus of course an advocatus diaboli, a pale reverser and endless opponent, without personal background of her own. The many things she herself may have suffered in this are almost impossible fully to identify, but at any rate it was for both of us futile and hopeless. The beautiful letters she sometimes wrote me were *mine*, *my* letters, letters in *my* key, or else she did not write at all. I remember when she was in Egypt, a few accounts of her trip arrived, I read parts of them to our intimate circle in Capri: all were amazed, were certain: this could have been written by me. Then she returned, I was full of anticipation, but my mouth dried up, aside from a few inconveniences and mishaps she brought back nothing to tell me, absolutely nothing, because she could never quite make herself echo my way of *speaking*. How often did I ask myself in sorrow: who *is* she, by what means does she express herself, through what joys, desires, hopes does she recognize herself? For not even her work is a genuine means of expression for her: this was, when I discovered it, quite early on, so immediately bizarre to me—that someone should be working in art without having come to it through her own inner expansion; I often teased her about this enigmatic origin of her sculpting, which was there without anyone knowing where it had come from; was simply there and got better and better, but without being necessary to satisfy some inner urge or demand. Once it reached excellence it was simply carried on industriously and rigorously and honestly, somewhat like a well-maintained dépendance for which cooking is done in the main house—; but it never became that for which something inside her screamed, screamed in order to plunge herself into it head over heels no matter what the cost. Later I stopped teasing, I saw the impending doom in these accomplishments into which nothing ever entered except strength, pure, as it were colorless strength, never a heart-surge, never anything that achieved its equanimity there, —always only this equanimity itself. Thus finally the exhaustion after all, the feeling of an unending repetition, the Buddha-idea that came as such a relief because, in a manner of speaking, it discharged the rhythm of these monotonous exertions.

I am sure that I lurk among the circumstances that have so delayed this person's finding herself; when I think about it now, she gives me the impression of a personality that never got round to proving itself at something. As a woman she would of course have had to be loved, for in being loved the feminine achieves its realization, and it is true that in certain years she went about with a look on her face that struck me as a reproach; it reminded me of Madame Rodin's expression, about which a young girl, quite frightened, once said to me: "My God, was it really necessary for her to make herself look so unloved?" —But on the other hand she was also an artist and had to be able to help herself. —How will she fare? I think about it not without great concern. Living together with Ruth (if, as I hope, that proves feasible), which both of them are looking forward to, might draw her out of herself quite naturally and allow her within a certain circle of friends to move about at ease: I almost expect more from *this* than from her art, although with a recent bust of Dehmel, for which she had traveled quite suddenly to Blankenese, there are signs (this was my impression) of an inner involvement with her subject that is new for her. I am sending the photographs of it and of the (unfinished) bust she did of Hauptmann the year before in Agnetendorf.

But now прощай, how much did I write!

Thank you for your letter.

Rainer.

P.S.: Please show the busts to your husband as well, I am anxious to hear his reaction. And cordial regards to him. There is *no hurry at all* to return the photographs; they are mine and I have no further use for them.

[LAS to RMR, letter from Göttingen to Duino Castle, mid-February 1912]

[RMR to LAS in Göttingen]

Castle Duino near Nabresina, Austrian Littoral
February 19, 1912

Dear Lou,

Thank you: I've been living on in quietness with your support, and even so things have been bumping along as over a newly furrowed field; how long it's been now since I was on a level road!

Yesterday I was delighted with the little portrait you made me of your mother. How wonderful it is to be able to observe those qualities in her that your writing almost perfectly describes: one reads and cannot be mistaken. It made me realize so clearly how vivid a picture of her I have retained inside me; only the blue of her eyes needed a bit of touching up and now it is again like new. Please do mention to her sometime in a letter how delighted I am that she still remembered me, and assure her that I will not forget her.

Just recently I wrote a few words to my grandmother (on the maternal side), who was beginning her eighty-second or eighty-third year; what a coarse fabric: it just doesn't wear out, simple as that. I saw her briefly this summer in Prague: like children at dinner with their ravenous appetites, a rough, almost Flemish joy in being alive brims in her flesh—, there is no other way to put it; she simply must keep going. Life has played violent jokes on her, but like circus clowns she never registered anything but the bang, —and so it did her no harm. It's amazing how even now, when my mother, who at times can barely walk, orders herself a carriage in Prague, my grandmother manages to hurry down on foot—and in the gayest mood—from her faraway miserable tenement rooms to experience the sheer physical joy of going along for the trip, no matter where. How alien she is to me in her cheerful durability—just as, even in my childhood, everything in her then still rich and well-kept house felt like a different world. (I still remember how at occasional family dinners the spoons full of soup passed into one's mouth like unknown objects.)

Which makes me think that in my mother's almost completely frayed nature a few of these same firm threads must still be holding; it is almost incomprehensible how, with that existence half defined by lengthy maladies and devout acceptance and half by distractions, she retains a taste for life, is in fact beginning to get trustfully attached to it. If one could ever achieve some peace and composure, I'm sure that even this and her whole unenlightened appearance could be fathomed, described, possibly even admired; but in my situation this too, as so often happens, becomes a cause for anxiety instead, and I behold at this natural place a figure so vague, that even now, in my more experienced heart, no real feeling at all can take shape.

Dear Lou, yes, after the "enough" of recently there was a flood of "more" in thoughts and circumstances; then in the course of the week some comfort came from an unexpected direction: curious to see how Goethe actually took in Venice, I suddenly found myself reading, amidst the most remarkable impressions, the whole Italian Journey, the Campaign in France, the Siege of Mainz, and would have had no objection to things continuing that way. The spell that had enforced my distance from him had already been broken back in July, when I came upon the youthful, wondrously spirited letters to "Gustgen" Stolberg; but now the "Journey in Italy" became downright moving to me as I experienced the seriousness, the foresight, the sheer effort with which a person almost divinely favored with productivity, at the edge of youth and surrounded by things sorely missed before and now experienced as exactly what was right for him, seeks to win for himself new, less contingent incentives to happiness. I sometimes sensed in the reading that this precocious learning and appropriating of everything Italian was not without melancholy, not without a feeling of farewell, thus perhaps not without despair, and that here in his own way he was undergoing the very thing I always felt was missing in him. I am amazed at how everything comes in its own time and is not to be forced, but then is not to be held back either. For the rest I read Venetian history all day, sometime I'll tell you to what end. Unfortunately this too begins with the disgrace of having forgotten absolutely everything I'd read about it earlier, gone, not a trace. Adieu now. Greet the sandals for me, those good sandals, —tell them not to give up on me.

Rainer.

[LAS to RMR, letter from Göttingen to Duino Castle, toward the end of February 1912]

[RMR to LAS in Göttingen]

Duino Castle near Nabresina, Austrian Littoral
March 1, 1912

Ah Lou, when I think that through all of this I am finding my way back into life again, my heart takes on such high ambitions; it is dreadful to have come to a halt (for the second time) and to have stalled for so long at the very point where returning should have become easy. And I have still not crossed, I know, but even so I cannot watch the people working down below in the garden without being seized by the notion that I am secretly doing what they do. My soul must, after all, have grown more spacious, but why do I not live in it if there is room where the spiritual things dwell peaceably, why am I alarmed by every noise in my body and diverted and scattered by it and so entangled in the misery of the smallest matters that it is as if I were living among petty relatives who do nothing but squabble. This becomes truly wretched and shameful in those moments when a dash of animation glides through my feeling and wants to go on and on endlessly, but my feeling doesn't concur, it remains behind in some rough area of my body, stands there stock-still and rots. Now, when most of what I do is read, I feel like someone who has sat down to a pleasurable meal and is digging in, but who, every time, as more and more of the plate beneath begins to show through, is dismayed by this cheap, scratched, chipped tableware and asks himself, why? I used to be amazed at times when I read about the diligence with which saints submitted themselves to bodily evil, but now I understand that this eagerness for pain, extending even to the torments of martyrdom, was a haste and impatience to be no longer interrupted and disturbed by even the worst that can come from the bodily side. Many a day I look at all of created life with the fear that some pain may erupt in it and make it scream, so great is my dread of the abuse that the body in so many ways inflicts on the soul, which finds peace only in the animals and safety only in the angels.

I am reading (and Goethe is to blame that these last few days I have become so immersed in it) the *Annals of Italian History* which Muratori [*in the margin*: (who is not dry at all but full of zest and good humor)] compiled in the eighteenth century from all sorts of chronicles, many of which he himself discovered; I am deep into it—, but, Lou, I am seriously troubled by my lack of memory, troubled not only because I retain practically nothing from earlier readings, but also because things I do know slip out of my mind from one day to the next, despite all my exertions; there is something in my way of absorbing things that consumes them without a trace. This happens not only with books but with any other intake of knowledge, so to speak: it passes into my blood, mixes there with God knows what and is in danger of being as good as lost. A plant would read this way but it has its calm, pure sap and would push into bloom without trouble; no one, however, knows anything about blood, I am constantly alone with mine, I lack that concrete entity between it and myself. If only I could begin now to create one!

I marvel, marvel at this fourteenth century, which has always been the most remarkable era for me, so exactly opposite our own time, where increasingly everything internal remains internal and plays itself out there without any real need (and before long without prospect) of finding equivalents outside for its states and degrees (hence the artificiality, insincerity, and self-consciousness of present-day drama). The world is retracting into itself; even the things themselves are complicit, transposing their existence more and more into the vibrations of money, and nurturing there a mode of spirituality that even now is outstripping their tangible reality. In the age which I am studying, money still was gold, still metal, a beautiful material, the most malleable, most easily graspable of all. And a feeling set no store by behaving nicely in some "interior" and becoming part of it; scarcely was it there before it leapt out into the next manifestation and overfilled a world already replete with visibility, a world in which the Great Death of 1348, intoxicated with so much pure life, no longer exercising discretion, went wild. I am studying Venice, but the Venice of those days stretches so far that I jump about constantly, am now in Avignon, now in Naples, myself a bit familiar everywhere, only with Constantinople, alas, do I have to take the events on faith, sight unseen. Adieu, dear Lou. (If only I could find one or two people from whom I could learn something more. Once there were always such people, and Goethe was well provided.) If things go on like this I will have to take up Latin also; had one only been taught earlier that the porridge gets cold if one has to make a spoon first, nay, has to learn how spoons are made. Such is my situation. What to do?

Rainer.

[*In the margin*:] (((is it Metschikoff's Lactobacillin?)))

[LAS to RMR, from Göttingen to Duino Castle, toward the middle of March 1912]

[RMR to LAS in Göttingen]

Duino Castle near Nabresina, Austrian Littoral
March 16, 1912

Dear, dear, Lou, a shout of joy cannot be revoked, and so I kept quiet; granted, it might almost have been as you thought, the difference is no more than a hairsbreadth—, and yet it was *not* as you construed it, on the contrary. As for me, I suffer from a malady that turns everything, everything into an affront, I have made myself sick feeling offended so infinitely, I take all these things to heart: but, fortunately, none of this gets inside me, instead it is like some child feeding a doll, the food is held right there in front of its face and in the end it looks quite sated anyway and weary of the whole enterprise. During days like these you have no idea how high and steep a path each morning confronts me with when I wake up, an indescribable fatigue through every limb all the way into my last finger-joints trying to put off the first steps—, were it not for the excuse the climate offers I should be utterly demoralized during such periods. But tell me, can so much evil be the fault of the air, be abetted by the air? It is true that Duino has never agreed with me, as if it had an excess of direct-current electricity that was overloading me, quite the opposite of what I usually feel almost immediately when I am at the sea. For two days now the weather has been milder, and I've resolved to take twice-daily sun baths below on the shore—I have a keen desire for them, and when I am undressed I have as well a kind of confidence directing me into the open. My nature really *is* eager and willing, but I don't provide it help, that is the wicked thing, I am on the side of the tempter, under his tutelage I am employed to do all those most contemptible things for which he can find no one else. Sometimes I see myself as if on the path to a joy (just recently before a golden wallflower blossoming out of the old rampart here)—but as if I could no longer make it all the way there, no sooner do I delight in the prospect of joy than the joy suddenly scatters, dissolves before I can grasp it, and everything is reduced to the nostalgia of once having been capable of doing so, reduced to what is left: being no longer young and not being older. Strange, Lou, how by contrast I *do* reach death and decline, wherever they signal their presence, with so powerful a bond of understanding that there is not even pause or hesitation along the way; recently I happened to read the letter in which Montaigne relates the death of his friend de la Boëtie: afterwards I couldn't fall asleep for crying, but to my shame this crying returned the following evenings with no apparent cause: you can imagine that I did not give in to it easily, I had books in front of me—but alas, these books: one sends me back to the other, basic knowledge is everywhere lacking, soon I will be sitting back behind the first vestiges, and what will I do *there* without memory?

This tension in the nerves of my forehead, my temples, all the way down into my cheeks, which so often torments me now, does not get any better during reading (: it is as if a few drops of lemon juice had gotten into my blood, were twisting and tightening everything wherever they happened to drift; last year I was free of it for months). And if occasionally I don't wake up into this irksome condition, then looking into the mirror while shaving (in the course of which, clumsy as I am, I expend an inordinate amount of effort positioning and surveying myself) is sufficient to reestablish it.

Lou: had I but written you then, the very moment *Malte Laurids* was completed, we might have exchanged these letters back then, and things would have never arrived at that difficult stage which I had to go through last year, and which I could easily believe did some internal damage to my soul, not because it was difficult but because it was wrong, not because it overstrained my body but because it warped my spirit. On that great journey, when in Kairouan, south of Tunis, a yellow Kabyle dog jumped up at me and bit me (for the first time in my life, throughout which the response of dogs to me has held great importance), I felt that the dog was *right* in what it did, it was only expressing in its way that I was wrong, completely in the wrong, with everything. Since then I have to a degree come back from this detour and started out anew, but I really have no idea how things will proceed, not even the external things. When I wrote you last, as I was about to resume my great task of reading, I thought I would wind up settling next in Venice, or at least stay somewhere in Italy; but these last weeks have again severely drained my resolve. Hotel life there is a dreadful prospect, it isn't at all the way it was ten years ago, when one received beautiful quiet rooms in the pensions, now there are two beds in every larger room, and if one comes alone one is stuck away into a corner which will barely hold one person. The last time two years ago in Rome I had bad experiences and for a great deal of money got almost exactly the opposite of what I require. I also asked myself again if when I leave here I shouldn't first go to Tobelbad near Graz, where Prof. von Düring, who had the Weisse Hirsch for a while after Lahmann's death, runs a sanitarium—? I know him a little (nonprofessionally), he is a remarkable man who has spent much time abroad, especially in Turkey, from whence he returned as pasha of I don't know how many horsetails—. (Besides that he is a cousin of my publisher's wife, who is a née Düring.) For the time being I carry on here as best I can with the help of sun baths; Prince Taxis, the one who was here in January, is expected again sometime in the next few days, and it is said that Kassner plans to come with him.

You read *Malte Laurids* again, I too looked at it the other day, read about John XXII, about Charles VI, because all of that is intimately connected with my current pursuits. In the meantime *Magdalena** arrived, I sent you the first

**The Love of the Magdalene. A French sermon transcribed by the Abbé Joseph Bonnet from the manuscript Q I 14 in the royal library of St. Petersburg.* Translated by Rainer Maria Rilke, Insel-Verlag, 1912. —Handwritten dedication in the book: "for *Lou* (a kind of *supplement* to *Malte Laurids*, found in Paris Easter 1911, shortly thereafter translated.) Duino, March 1912."

copy, even as I was opening the package. The people who claim to know attribute this discourse to Bossuet, which is possible, —but should it not best remain, as do certain paintings, under the rubric: "Unknown Master"?

Enough, dear Lou, here I've shown up again, certainly not as you'd expected me, and am perforce wearing your patience thin; but it was you yourself who counseled me not to hold back, and so I didn't. Even so send your good thoughts down to warm me here (where there really isn't much continuous spring: the fickle moods of this stretch of coast take precedence over every season).

Rainer.

Clara is having her exhibit now at Heller's (in Vienna); I don't know if I mailed you a catalogue the other day when I sent the *Magdalene*; in any case, I'll send you one today.

[LAS to RMR at Duino Castle, two letters, the first from Göttingen prior to March 21, the second from Berlin around March 21 or shortly thereafter]

[RMR to LAS in Berlin]

Venice, Grand-Hotel. Sunday
[March 24, 1912]

Thanks, Lou, for the two letters: they did as much good as possible. Kassner did not come, is no longer coming now, but I have made use of the most unexpected opportunity and have rushed off to Venice for three, perhaps four days; unfortunately the German emperor with his "*Hohenzollern*" is arrayed in world-power proximity before the Riva, as if it were the whole German Reich. You are lucky not to have him in Berlin.

I will write from Duino and send you news when there is news to send.

Прощай.

Rainer.

[RMR to LAS in Göttingen (forwarded to Vienna)]

Ronda, Spain, Hotel Reina Victoria
December 19, 1912

Dear Lou,

Quietly, without a stir, Christmas approaches, here also, —let me write to you. Once again there is something on my heart: myself, with all my weight and with the heaviness of I know not what things—. The last picture you had of me was through Gebsattel, but I doubt whether he provided you with quite the right lens; the peculiar refraction that occurs in him is always interesting, since it leads to new points of reference, which then themselves immediately become polar, attract and repel, that is, make sense of things—; as a metaphor, then, this new configuration yields every time a perfect truth, but as mere news it is not to be taken verbatim.

It seems natural to survey the year now, and when I look back to its inception, which is also when I began writing to you, it honestly seems to me that I haven't moved an inch since then, unless I have been going around in a circle—, God knows. A passage from the *Instructions* of the blessed Angela da Foligno serves me as a kind of tidemark; I underlined it a year ago, and when I chanced upon it again here day before yesterday it applied to me just as much now—so much so that in writing it out I reveal the whole of my condition: "*Quand tous les sages du monde et tous les saints du paradis m'accableraient de leurs consolations et de leurs promesses, et Dieu lui-même des ses dons, s'il ne me changeait pas moi-même, s'il ne commençait au fond de moi une nouvelle opération, au lieu de me faire du bien, les sages, les saints et Dieu exaspéreraient au delà de toute expression mon désespoir, ma fureur, ma tristesse, ma douleur et mon aveuglement.*"

The good, generous sanctuaries, such as Duino was and immediately thereafter Venice, did not help me very far along; in addition, these so singularly configured surroundings always require too much adjustment: they have their existence in such strange and multifarious conditions that when at last one feels that one belongs to them, all that has been accomplished is the lie that one has been accepted. Till well into autumn I was in Venice, supported by kind and friendly connections, but at heart merely staying on from day to day, from week to week because I did not know where to go; finally, from confusion, from instinct, from impulses dragged along for years, the decision took shape in me to make this journey through Spain, actually just to stay for a time in Toledo, and on arriving there, breathlessly exposed to this something that was infinitely anticipated and yet infinitely surpassing all expectation, —I believed myself almost torn out of my doldrums already and on the path to a wider participation in the ultimate realities, —there are no words with which I could tell you how supremely this city rose before me amidst its untamed landscape, through and through *the very closest thing*, something that only a moment earlier could not have been endured, at once intimidating and uplifting, like Moses when he came down from the mountain with horns of light—, and yet also little by little recalling to me everything that was ever necessary, strong, pure, and dependable in my life. But from the very fact that I did not stay (I was there four weeks), that the cold, that my old pains, the rush of blood to forehead and eyes, that various discomforts sprang up alongside so great and to me so eloquent a presence, preoccupying and distracting me, you can see how badly I failed what was perhaps meant to bring about "*la nouvelle opération*," —my path turned southward, I stood marveling in Cordoba, I had time to see that Seville held nothing for me, something drew me to Ronda—, and here I am now and in these no less incredible surroundings am hoping primarily only for a better distribution of my tormenting blood under the influence of the high pure air that everywhere comes wafting over, out of the mountains pitched all around, into this city that is itself held steeply aloft.

When I wake up in the morning, there before my open window, risen in pure space, refreshed, lie the mountains; how can it be that this does not move me inwardly? Even four, five years ago a sunrise on the crossing from Capri to Naples could transform me from head to toe into pure joy, into completely new joy that hadn't existed there before and leapt out of me and flowed into everything like a new-found wellspring; and now I sit here and look and look until my eyes ache, and point it out to myself and say it over and over as though I had to learn it by heart and still hadn't got it and am truly one in whom it does not thrive.

Dear Lou, tell me why it is that I ruin everything—sometimes it seems to me that I strain too hard vis-à-vis my impressions (indeed, this is almost literally what I do on so many occasions), I remain too long before them, I press them into my face, and yet by their very nature they *are* impressions, aren't they, even if one just lets them lie for a while very quietly, *au lieu de me pénétrer, les impressions me percent—*

I go for long, long walks outdoors here, sometimes for a few hours the sun is such that one can rest beside an evergreen oak, then a little bird-voice favors me with a song or else the roaring from the deep river gorge makes everything that has been and everything that can be seem superfluous. But as I walk I ponder so many things, —beginning January 1st a studio in Paris is mine, I foresaw that the most important thing for me, however this journey turns out, would be to have an independent place of my own to move into immediately afterwards, and I was certainly right. And whether Paris, which has sapped so much of me, is still necessary or even beneficial, time will have to tell. I know one mustn't leave a bandage on all one's life just because it once did some good, also if possible I would rather not go back to Paris before the worst of winter is over.

I must tell you, Lou, I have a feeling that what would help me most would be an environment similar to the one I had with you in Schmargendorf, long walks in the woods, going barefoot and letting my beard grow day and night, a lamp in the evening, a warm room, and the moon, whenever it suits her, and the stars when they are out, and otherwise just sitting and listening to the rain or to the storm as though it were God himself. As you travel about, dear Lou, keep this in mind and take note if you see a place where it might be done. Sometimes I think of the Black Forest, of Rippoldsau, of the area around Triberg, then again I think of Sweden, what it would be like for instance at Ellen Key's (though I would rather not be "at" anyone's)—or near her by a lake in the woods or near a small university town in Germany; for to have books, preferably some person also with whom one could study something, would naturally suit me. Do you know if it is true that the Books of Moses in the original text are something completely different from what both the Greek and Latin translations contain? I have been reading some remarkable books by this curious Fabre d'Olivet (beginning of the nineteenth century), who was spurred by this discovery to reconstruct an entirely new Hebrew grammar (just as he used up his whole life on the preliminaries for a gigantic master-work that he never started—): here I am reading the Koran and am amazed, amazed, —and again I want to learn Arabic. Could I undertake that with your husband, would Göttingen, for instance, be totally out of the question? —I am spinning fables, you see, and of that there is no end.

Where are you, dear Lou? In Vienna? Do you see Kassner? Where will you spend Christmas? There will be a full moon exactly on Christmas night; include me in your good thoughts.

Rainer.

(In Toledo our evenings in Новинки with good old Ник. Толстой and his Spanish diary became so vivid to me that I sent him a greeting, which he answered warmly.)

[LAS to RMR in Ronda]

Vienna IX Pelikangasse 14 Hotel Zita
[December 30, 1912]

Dear Rainer,

What thoughts must have passed through your head by now: after your letter had commissioned Father Christmas to carry the reply, not even the New Year's Messenger brings it to you! But I am not to blame: your letter was left undelivered in Göttingen, and I did not receive it until today. Full of joy! For even though you judge yourself so harshly as you look back on the year just passed, it did not go by without the essential accomplishment, —I heard talk of it this very day, from Kassner, at Beer-Hofmann's. He spoke of the two elegies. As highly as you regard both the man and his judgment, must he not somehow be right about this? Of the man himself I must say that I didn't gain much sense of him, —I'm not sure if he was tired or if it was something else, but at any rate everyone agreed that he had not been like Kassner at all. We are often at Beer-Hofmann's—I say "we," because I am here with a young girl, one of my adopted daughters—and even spent Christmas Eve there. For the rest, I am deeply engrossed in Freudian matters and many human aspects relating to them, have been *living* in them since October and have in mind to continue into March. Then it's back to Göttingen via roundabout paths. Perhaps summer will somehow bring us together there? Your plans concerning Arabic,* small university town, way of life, possible forest-stay in Sweden, etc., will by then either have taken on firmer outline or dissolved completely. I don't know whether being near Ellen, in Alvastra, would be possible for you; the house is always full of people, and the workaday routine there is rather taxing, I don't know if it would be good for you. For now at least Paris is still waiting for you: it may have an entirely different effect from back then when you had to learn how to endure it and put it to use. And keep in mind the one crucial thing: it was *there* that you learned how to observe external presences—so penetratingly and in such depth and detail and with so little reference to yourself that the two *New Poems* came into being; that attainment was an ongoing consequence of your close contact with Rodin, and *now* you are, on the contrary, still suffering the aftereffects of what undoubtedly was a necessary development, when you write that it feels to you as if you are exerting "too much force vis-à-vis your impressions," are "remaining too long before them," are "pressing them into your face," —"au lieu de me pénétrer, les impressions me percent." Don't you think that this is merely your way of getting through what comes immediately after the harvest, the feeling of autumn on the stubble fields, the appearance of dearth that has to be waited out? I am trying to form a picture of it: but I am as yet unable, I will have to wait to see if you want to say more, from time to time, as you did back then. This must be as you wish: but I reach out my hands to you not only for the good old greeting but also with my palms turned upward, —in case you may want to give me something for 1913. Yes?

Lou.

Moissi's letter, age-old, from Easter [1912] in Berlin, when you were on your way to Venice.

*[*In the margin*:] Your question about the Books of Moses will have to wait until I can ask my husband.

[RMR to LAS in Vienna]

Ronda, Epiphany 1913

"Actually he had come free some time ago, and if anything kept him from dying, it was perhaps only that somewhere he had already encountered it full force, so that he had to go, not on ahead to meet it, as other people do, but back towards it. The vital part of his life was already outside, where it lodged in those persuaded things children play with, and perished in them. Or it was rescued in the glance of a strange woman passing by, —at least clung there in its jeopardy. But dogs also ran past with it, anxious and looking round to see if he wouldn't snatch it back from them. Yet when he stepped before the almond tree that was in its bloom he was startled nonetheless to find it so fully there on the other side, completely crossed over, completely self-occupied, completely apart from him; and he himself not facing it precisely enough and too dulled even to mirror this his own life. Had he become a saint, he would have drawn a serene freedom from this condition, the infinitely irrevocable joy of poverty: for it was thus, perhaps, that Saint Francis lay, consumed, having been so partaken of that the whole world was a delectable savor of his being. He, however, had not extracted himself cleanly from his shell, had ripped himself out of himself and had given away pieces of his husk as well, often also had (as children do when they play with dolls) held himself up to an imaginary mouth and made smacking sounds with his lips, and the morsel was left lying there, uneaten. So that now he looked like garbage and was in the way, —however much sweetness might have been in him."

I wrote this in my pocket-book this morning, you will observe to whom it pertains. Yesterday your good letter came. Yes, the two elegies are there—, but I can tell you in confidence how small and sharply riven a fragment they form of what was then delivered into my power. Had circumstances and forces been as they were when the *Book of Hours* began—: who knows what could have been achieved! *If only we could see each other, dear Lou,** that is my great hope now. [*In the margin*: my support, my everything, as always.]** I keep repeating to myself that it is you alone through whom I am linked to the human, in *you* it is turned toward me, senses me, *breathes on me*; everywhere else, sad to say, I come out behind its back and cannot make myself known to it.

Greet the Beer-Hofmanns warmly for me (and Kassner) and wrap me in your heart, —*You.*

Your *Rainer.*

[LAS to RMR in Ronda]

Vienna IX, Pelikangasse 14
January 13, 1913

Dear Rainer,

Your letter, just delivered, lies before me, and I feel as though this first wintry snow scene that spreads out beyond my window and across the adjoining gardens is a part of it: so vividly does it symbolize for me that distance from

*These words are underlined twice, "dear" three times.

**LAS tried to render the words in the margin illegible.

you of which you write: it should not exist. I feel them strongly, Rainer, both this purely spatial distance and the senseless fact that it *will* not be bridged. Or if so, only through railways and every conceivable expenditure of energy for the briefest meetings whenever they can be arranged. Instead it should be possible for us to be together quietly and without any effort at all on invisible paths—not as one locus of experience set next to the other and altered by that proximity, but present to it without displacing it and having to adjust to its boundaries. This ought to be possible, and perhaps one day will yet come to pass. For me it already does exist—or something close to it—and I have mentioned it to you more than once. When I read your letter, and the passage from your pocket-book, and those words which suddenly give expression to what otherwise remains mute and formless even in the most personal and penetrating moments of human conversation, —then, yes then, I *do* have you with me. I hold this profound unique experience that is *you*, and nothing in the world could persuade me that even the smallest piece of you has in the interim crumbled away, for you are fully preserved in it and hale, i.e., are he who most deeply experiences all that defines the *essence* of being human. Yes, that's when I have you, reunite with you, and it is truly my solace to know that you can undertake such a secret journey all the way here to me and into all my thoughts about life's innermost mysteries. But how should I now for my part *convey to you yourself* this indescribable closeness? How make available to you this strange capacity of yours, for which it makes almost cruelly no difference whether it comes from the bliss of feeling yourself given over to all things, or from the horror of being mixed up with everything isolated and unclaimed? How persuade you of this confident joy that in *both* cases the same person expresses himself, —just as assuredly the same person as the man on the cross and he who was resurrected are One, *—the same person,* who, between the bliss of total possession and the torture of becoming possessed, could do no other than renounce what other people call their "development," that steady efficient furthering of their existence. I believe profoundly that for this *no* correction is possible, and I am glad of it, because with the correction would come the most heinous termination. I believe that you *must* suffer, and that it will always be so. No one at your side could rectify this, but it is possible, —yes, this is possible— that it would be healing (though also hurtful) to have someone next to you at times who knows this also, and who would suffer through it and live through it together with you. I have the strange feeling that I would now be much *harder* with you than before (even if in a completely different sense than would have been possible before), but also that a thousand maternal tendernesses are ripe inside me now for you and only for you, who alone could see them and make use of them. The two, furthermore, would really be one and the same thing: and it is strange how clearly I feel the hardness to be an element of them and that it would be big and that I would not want it to be smaller. Do I turn you away from me when I write to you like this? I do know with such certainty: however long it may take to happen, we *will* rejoice in being with each other again, and will revel also in all the dangers that life, for each of us individually, has in store.

I must write to you today of another dying, one different from the passage in your pocket-book, but which for me also is not a death. My mother has quietly gone to sleep. Not wanting to cross over into her ninetieth year, she went away. She did this gently and as in a dream. I tell no one here about it, I don't want to have anyone speak to me of this as a demise. For that reason I will try also not to succumb to the perfidious and ugly custom of "being dressed in mourning." But I would gladly wear white for her.

Lou.

[It is assumed that RMR sent the following poem to LAS as a letter from Ronda to Vienna, around January 10, 1913.]

Mary's Assumption

Exquisite one, precious oil that wants to rise,
blue ring swung from smoking censers,
long-prolonged note fading straight upward,
milk of the terrestrial, pour forth,

nurse the heavens not yet weaned, nourish
the weeping kingdom at your breast.
You are gold now like the tall gleanings,
and pure as the image in the pond.

As all night long in our deserted hearing
we hear the fountains as they run:
you, in your ascension, alone occupy
our sight. As in a needle's eye

my long gaze wants to thread itself to you
before you flee this visible sphere,—
to be drawn by you, even if left mere white,
through the dazzling colorfast heavens.

(Ronda.)

[RMR to LAS in Vienna]

Ronda, January 14 [1913]

To the Angel

Strong quiet candelabrum, placed
at the verge: above, the night becomes precise.
We spend ourselves in unillumined
hesitation at your base.

Ours is: not to find any path
out of these mazelike inner regions;
then you appear on our hindrances
and they glow like a high alpine range.

Your pleasure knows itself *above* our realm,
and we scarcely glean its precipitate:
like the pure night of the vernal equinox
you stand, partitioning day and day.

Who could ever infuse in you
that mixture which secretly clouds us:
you have glory of all magnitudes
while we excel in things most petty.

When we weep, we are no more than piteous,
where we observe, we are at best awake,

our smiling exerts no power of attraction,
and if it does attract, who pursues it?

(Anyone.) Angel, do I complain, do I complain?
Yet what could my complaint mean to you?
Ah, I scream, with two wooden sticks I pound
and don't delude myself I'm being heard.

My clamoring won't pierce that quiet around you,
if you didn't feel me because I *am*.
Candelabrum, shine. Make the stars strengthen
their gaze on me. For I am fading.

Dear Lou, let me add this to what I sent recently, written down outside in the meadows, while on a walk, this afternoon: and felt immediately that you should have it.

Rainer.

[LAS to RMR in Ronda]

Vienna IX, Pelikangasse 14
[probably toward the end of January 1913]

Dear Rainer,

I have been having daily encounters with your Angel, and he has told me many things about what you, even in your times of trouble, have to keep you company.

At first I didn't write about him, so that my words wouldn't cross paths with a letter already en route here from you, —even now I am scarcely writing, really only keeping silent out loud so as not to disturb you in the event a letter from you is having trouble getting under way.

My dear, dear, boy! Greetings to you, heartfelt greetings, and whatever the case, from

Your
Lou.

July 9–21, 1913: RMR's second stay in Göttingen. Preparatory communications are missing, as is the letter of condolence RMR sent to LAS when he learned of her mother's death.

[RMR to LAS in Göttingen, inscribed in a copy of his *Life of Mary* (1912)]

Mary's Death

Not just from the gaze of the disciples, who
have now only your robe's light sadness:
ah, you've withdrawn from the calyxes of flowers,
from the bird, who reenacts your flight;

from the complete openness of children,
from the udder and the chewing of the cow—,
all has become less by a *mildness*,
only the heavens, deep inside, increase.

Enraptured fruit from our ground,
berry that stands ripe with sweetness,
may we feel it, when you dissolve
in the mouth of that enraptured bliss.

For we remain where you departed. Every
place here below wants to be consoled.
Bend mercy toward us, strengthen us as with wine.
We need so much more than understanding.

for Lou, Loufried, July 20, 1913.

Rainer.

[Written on two pages that LAS pasted into her diary]

Narcissus

And so this: this emanates from me and dissolves
in the air and in the aura of the grove,
leaves me gently and becomes something mine no longer
and gleams, because it meets no enmity.

This rises incessantly away from me,
I want to stay, I wait, I linger;
yet all my borders strain impatiently,
rush out and even now are *there.*

In sleep also. Nothing binds us in.
Pliant core in me, kernel full of weakness
that can't control its fruit-flesh.
Fleeing, O flight from all places on my surface.

What forms there and so resembles me
and quivers upward in tear-stained signals,—
it perhaps took shape just this way
inside a woman; it was beyond attaining

(however hard I struggled for it pressing into her).
Now it lies open in the indifferent
scattered water, and I may gaze at it
no end beneath my wreath of roses.

It is not loved there. Down there is nothing
but the equanimity of tumbled stones,
and I can see my sadness.
Was this my image in her eyes' flashing?

Did it surge up like this inside her dream
as sweetest fear? I can almost feel her fright;
For, as I lose myself to my own gaze:
I could think that I am deadly.

[LAS, Diary, around July 20, 1913]

One day Rainer was standing there in the evening twilight and even before we spoke our hands were clasped across the garden fence.

Something behind all this is continuing, calmly growing to perfection, while he, to whom it is happening, suffers almost without respite and is forced to doubt. For me it was a daily source of happiness and made me as free of worries about Rainer as I have ever been.

[RMR to LAS in Göttingen]

Leipzig, Insel Verlag, July 22, 1913

Many a moment I feel deep inside me as if, strengthened by everything You know and are, I were slowly beginning a new life; I could not repeat any one particular thing even to myself nor find words to make anyone else understand how thoroughly everything has been put in order, but this feeling courses through my blood night and day, full of love.

Oh if I could make a good start now, late as it is, or at least let things take their own course, quietly. If, instead of all of time's outward aspects, which perpetually distract me, I could keep in view the serenity of this crystalline inner world, which no chance convulsion shakes, and whose only movement is the pure rotation of the heavenly bodies as they turn inward to sustain the dynamics of a rapt contemplation.

To look off and gently let one's gaze fall where it may, facing certainties.

On the train I read Worringer, agreeing wholeheartedly. What a relief to see this question of "style," with which I had been acquainted superficially, at last thought through and put to rest, simply and elegantly. I can follow his essential ideas, though not some of the turns they take—sometimes my mind just can't keep pace. His final summing-up is, I think, a bit hasty, since surely "style" continues to appear even after the Renaissance—how could it not play a part, for instance, in El Greco?

Spoke with Kippenberg first thing yesterday about the question of money; it turns out (something he hadn't told me before) that a group of friends of my work has formed and will contribute to the monthly five hundred until the publishing house can grant me these payments from its own resources. (I am astounded at such beneficence; if only, love, I could turn all these friendly strokes of fate to my advantage; if only I were not so prone to squandering, like a parrot scattering everything left and right with its beak.)

I am entertaining the foolish idea of leaving here at the end of the week and spending eight days at the sea (Heiligendamm—the Nostitzes are there, and I'd very much like to see them) before going on my way to Berlin (two or three days there at the dentist's) for a somewhat shorter stay at Krummhübel, which I am sure to find quieter if I don't arrive until two weeks from now—. I hear they have beautiful beech-tree forests there—, and already I can feel the sea spreading out before my soul. So perhaps I will take this route.

Cordial greetings to your husband. I hope he is in excellent health. I'll not send the translation of *Omar Khayam* (by Gribble) that Insel published. Kippenberg himself considers it inferior, but he knows and admires Rosen's version, also knows Rosen personally and will add the translation of *Tuti-Nameh* by Rosen's father, Georg Rosen, to the Insel list.

We are leaving presently to spend today and tomorrow in Weimar, craving a touch of Goethe. —Let me thank you, dear Lou.

Rainer.

[*In the margin*:] Were the *Visions of Christ*, inside a yellow folder, left behind at your house? If so, please do feel free to read them!

[LAS to RMR in Leipzig (forwarded to Heiligendamm)]

Göttingen, Thursday [July 24, 1913]

Yes, I did indeed read the Christ Visions (they must be the same ones I keep copies of in my safe-deposit box at the bank) and they have made me see for the first time quite wonderful connections. So difficult to describe in detail in a letter! They read far differently from your two recent poems, the present elegies—and yet everything you have created has advanced along the same steady course between these Christ visions in the past and the approaching Angel visions. Your whole work opens out before me now like a vast landscape, everywhere revealing paths I had never seen before, and receding into horizons one knows will open, because light comes from there and spreads across the landscape, and because it is the light of dawn.

This came about, needless to say, through your being here, but the whole picture coalesced so suddenly. (On the wet Rupprechtsweg, where one climbs toward the little forest and then on the other side of the slope sees sheep grazing: it happened there all in a flash.) And now, as a consequence, I don't feel in the least that you have gone away—on the contrary, never have I felt *less* like that—rather as though Rupprechtsweg passed over into a country in which I would with greatest joy find you again every good morning—and all this on your very own ground. (Which you never left, not even in Egypt, even though for a moment only a single small candle cast light for you on what is yours and made it recognizable.)

The fragments of the elegies, though, don't forget them when you find time for copying: for there is much about them that becomes difficult or vague over time, and then it is as if my longest panoramas were blocked by an insurmountable wall.

Regarding what the friends of your work have set up for it: they have actually created the ideal situation, merely an anticipation of what will come about of its own accord, only more slowly, as your books find buyers. And yet not as an advance on the future, as with some beginner; each installment leaves the future open before you, free and unencumbered, —for your work is receiving thanks from its friends and is being valued for its achievement.

The two books: Bibesco and also the Doctor's Diary (especially the first half)—beautiful! I've always thought more of Worringer's grasp of oriental than western art; so please don't bother to return the book, that would be as annoying to it as to me: you can see that it was obviously waiting for the chance to leap into your hands!

My husband is in a jolly mood and sends his greetings. Also the two Maries. And also the wren who hopped onto the balcony tabletop today and glanced around for your hair and called loudly with its all-important little tweet.

Farewell, dearest.

Lou.

Nothing arrived from Prague, so all's well. May I ask you: do not send a money order but cash in a registered letter.

[RMR to LAS in Göttingen]

Seaside Resort of Heiligendamm, Mecklenburg
Grand Hôtel
August 1, 1913

Dear Lou,

My apologies, that was stupid of me, before leaving Leipzig Saturday, I mailed the money order, and day before yesterday your letter came telling me how I should have done it. My apologies.

If only your "daughter" were still in Arendsee, it would have been so easy for me to visit her; letters to me must also be addressed now to "Mecklenburg" —who would have thought that?

This town is Germany's oldest resort, attractive for its seaside forest and a clientele limited almost entirely to the landed gentry of this area. The Grand Duke has his villa here, otherwise only a spa with a beautiful portico, a hotel, and about a dozen villas—everything still relatively unspoiled in the good taste of the early nineteenth century—even a few salons dating from around 1830. On the gable of the spa a clock with a blue dial and a strikingly old-fashioned voice. The people come driving over from their estates in the most elegant carriages; that causes wonderfully animated reliefs to stand out against the ocean's backdrop. On Monday morning I had the good fortune of watching a Count Alvensleben, who drives the best four-in-hand, demonstrate his skill with great bravura—. For all that there is much stillness in the woods and even on the beach (which is pebbly), all in all a serviceable little place, —I am glad, at any rate, to know of it.

It was good to find the Nostitzes still here, along with (something I hadn't anticipated) the mother of Frau von Nostitz, who is a daughter of the former ambassador in Paris, Prince Münster. She was famous for her beautiful voice, and even now, in her old age, it has lost scarcely any of its strength and timbre (as if in a voice so gifted with all manner and nuance of expression nothing transitory could have ever perished)—, she sings to me almost every afternoon—Beethoven and long-ago Italians.

The Nostitzes will depart next week, but I may stay on a while longer, in the end even spend some time swimming if August turns out well. I'll have to see what I'll do about Ziegelroth, but I don't think I'll cancel just yet—unless, of course, by some surprise I suddenly feel well. I wrote him that I would be coming later.

It occurred to me that in Munich I can stay with Clara's Swedish friend Ingrid Stieve, so that my stopover there would cost little. If not before, we will *definitely* find each other there in September. (Performances in Hellerau have been scheduled for as late as November.) Traveling through Berlin, I saw the recently discovered head of Amenophis: a miracle, I tell you. In Leipzig I spoke frequently with Prof. Steindorff, the university's Egyptologist, and raised the possibility of accompanying him, together with the Kippenbergs, on a dig in the Nubian desert (then you would have to come too!). As soon as the Nostitzes have left, I'll make the copies for you. Farewell, and thank you for all the good and confident words in your letter—but I do need to hear them out loud as well, *so very much.** Regards to your husband, also to Marie and little Marie. (Enclosed a handkerchief.)

Your *Rainer.*

[LAS to RMR in Heiligendamm]

[Göttingen] August 4 [1913]

Dear Rainer,

Aren't we the proper ones, —down to the little hanky! but please to observe with what proper diligence I darned that one tiny hole for you.

Ellen [Delp]'s address is Villa Seerose on Waldstrasse in "Mecklenburg," and she will be there until September. Wish you much good sun at your sea! It was a guest here for one week, a few unbelievable sunsets which turned the first city lights into a perfect emerald green—something I had never seen before.

Someone else was our guest just now, and it was a powerful experience for me: Сажа, passing through from Switzerland. Tell you about it in person; many beautiful things.

Read Goethe—yours. But you still haven't given him to me, not completely. (Due in part to the hastiness that marked your departure.) That remains for this autumn, along with much else that I am so looking forward to.

Wrote a little story for Ruth, it's called "Seelchen" [Little Soul]; have it typed neatly and will bring it along for her in the fall.

Lou.

---

*Underlined three times.

[Rilke to LAS, letter from Heiligendamm to Göttingen, probably with the "fragments" of the Elegies, August 7, 1913; envelope survives]

[LAS to RMR, letter from Göttingen to Heiligendamm, around August 12, 1913]

[RMR to LAS in Göttingen]

[*Letterhead:*] *Baltic Sea Spa Heiligendamm*

[August 15, 1913]

It was with your letter yesterday, dear Lou, the way it sometimes is with letters I deeply cherish: I'll be in the room with them for a long spell without noticing them, and then suddenly I'll reach for them as if I *knew* they were there.

Shortly before, I wrote Werfel telling him how much pleasure his various pieces give me; I'll show you many more of them when we see one another, this time from the first book too, which I am enjoying now as much as the later one—. This poet has had so clear a rising, completely unobscured by clouds; his very first rays struck a world and brought that world into the light of day—. This is what I wrote to him; there truly is in his earliest poems a kind of beautiful morning, which lifts one's spirits and makes one's whole heart feel more pensively.

At the end he even turns to the reader directly, almost as in an apostrophe, addressing him as someone for whom he longs (in this respect he proceeds from the human, as *you* rightly perceive it), —but, in confessing this emotion so openly, he also creates the freedom of expressing himself without holding back before anyone else's sensibilities. And in knowing everything the other could possibly be, knowing it beforehand and long after, knowing it infinitely, utterly, more completely, irretrievably, and blissfully than the person who *is* this, he also becomes his own, singular self again, the locus above them all, where his transformations easily merge with the view from God's vantage.

How beautiful all this is, beautiful, and it means much to me that I can have so clear an impression of the young generation personified in this emerging voice and can, as if it were my own, concur with it.

We have a storm, rain, the sea torn open by squalls and then quickly covered again, departures everywhere—, I'll perhaps leave on Sunday to see the Woermanns outside of Hamburg, where Ruth and Clara are just now, —then to Berlin on Monday, *Hospiz des Westens*, 4 Marburgerstr.; there I'll give the dentist all the time he needs and hope there will be a chance to see Ziegelroth for a couple of weeks in order to achieve a bit better perspective on myself and find out to what extent he and Krummhübel are realistic possibilities for me. That certain malady has (under the influence of a medication I brought with me from Göttingen's apothecary) completely gone away, but on the whole I am not quite well, my body is prone to little mishaps and very easily frightened and thrown out of balance by any one of them. —On September 10 or 12 I expect to be in Munich and will most likely stay there until the end of the month; thereafter Leipzig once more.

Farewell, dear Lou, I am very, very much looking forward to Munich.

Your *Rainer.*

Tell your husband I have become a votary of Natura-Werk products and make a delightful repast here of *banana-pap* and fruit purees.

[LAS to RMR in Heiligendamm]

Göttingen, Sunday [August 17, 1913]

Dear Rainer,

Your letter just arrived, and, with my suitcase packed, I am sitting down between tartan strap and handbag to write you, since in 3/4 of an hour I'll be on my way to the train station. But I can't tell you how wonderful it is to live your experience of Werfel along with you. The *way* you experience him. It is beautiful: just as Rodin was Old Age as dreamt by you and came to exert its powerful hold over you, so now Youth as you dream it is unveiling itself in the Other; at the very moment Rodin was fleeing from you into the fourth room, frightened and timorous, this Youth was preparing to step up before you, trustful and strong, as a new warranting of life. And to *you* it *had* to happen that way: since everything within you so inescapably must become image, an externality, something perceivable, a work of art almost, precisely *because* of the inwardness in everything that happens to you. That is what makes it so very much *yours*, —your destiny taking shape there, primal necessity as much as personal fulfillment, coming to you in the form of gifts, free offerings, which are really nothing but your own deeds returning to you, —and which consequently will turn into the enormous riches that you, at the same time, bring into Werfel's life. In all the world only you could so concur with his words as to make them resonate with life's highest truth: *We are.*

I am very happy. I want to take your face in my hands and gaze at you: even though you were here just a short while ago, gaze at you as if with altogether new eyes. Everything is so good, I say to you. All the things that lie before you are revelations, and they are without end.

Now in Berlin try to be tolerant of all those quirks of the body that are not to be avoided, the body being what it is: i.e., ignorant and easily frightened and at the mercy of everything imaginable; and try not to blame it either when it sometimes seems intent on subverting what your innermost being is trying to accomplish, namely *outward* articulation in signs and realities. Then here comes your body with its torment, —by which it says: all this far surpasses poor ignorant me.

It will go on tormenting you, many things will, and many things will cause you pain, but be calm, be calm, dear, dear Rainer.

Lou.

Address as of today: Vienna IX, 14 Pelikangasse, Zenit Hotel.

September 8 through October 17: Together in Munich, in Dresden-Hellerau, in the Sudeten Mountains, and again in Dresden-Hellerau. In Munich meeting with Freud (September 9), Gebsattel, Clara, and Max Scheler; in Dresden-Hellerau performance of Claudel's Annunciation, *meeting with Franz Werfel; in the Sudeten Mountains consultation with doctor; in Dresden-Hellerau Jaques-Dalcroze dances.*

[LAS to RMR in Munich, postcard, written in pencil and sent by pneumatic dispatch]

[September 10, 1913]

Dear Rainer, Dr. Ferenczi says just now: if for tomorrow, Thursday, in the afternoon, a mediumistic session could be arranged, then he would stay to take part. If so, please write by pneumatic dispatch or porter to Bayerischer Hof, room 402, to Dr. Ferenczi, where I'll be also, ok?

Nothing to be undertaken together before noon anyway. After lunch, and from then on completely, free. Come!

Lou

Wednesday evening.

Call Ebersbacher.

Lou.

[RMR to LAS in Munich, note]

[September 19, 1913]

Dear Lou,

A pity!

I don't want to risk intruding, you may be catching up on sleep. If you need something, have the maid telephone me (33313). I'm bringing you Mereschkowsky's *Gogol*—and (enclosed) the article I spoke to you about yesterday.

Tomorrow morning please have the maid tell me how you are and take good care of yourself and I do mean it. The weather outside could not be worse anyway.

Rainer.

[LAS to RMR in Munich, postcard, written in pencil]

[September 20, 1913]

Dear Rainer, I'm not completely well and would rather stay in bed during the day. Would you like to come for a bit in the evening after 8 o'clock, if you're free?

The rain spoiled yesterday, but it was still interesting on account of Scheler.

100 greetings!

Lou.

[RMR to LAS in Munich]

[September 20, 1913]

Dear Lou,

Eight o'clock it is!

Have a restful day, I heard nothing new yesterday, despite *voyante.* Rega [Ullmann] will be with me this afternoon. Enclosed the article about Rabindranath Tagore, the Bengal poet about whom van Eeden spoke. Important, it seems to me.

1000 greetings

Rainer.

[RMR to LAS, by messenger]

[*Letterhead*:] *Hotel Marienbad*
Munich,
Friday [October 3, 1913]

Dear Lou,

The doorman just informed me that if we could leave an hour earlier (8:25 instead of 9:25) we would have a more comfortable train and gain a great head start; this train is almost two hours faster, we would be in Dresden by 5 o'clock, shouldn't this be just the thing?

You'll let me know at the *Ethos* this evening, —but perhaps you might have the messenger carry the small suitcase and the books over here now? Till 7 o'clock tonight.

Rainer.

[RMR to LAS in Dresden]

[October 16, 1913]

I spoke, summoning my best persuasive skills, with a not quite identifiable Someone who told me that the artistic dance presentations are now, at the beginning of the school year, no longer open to guests; at best, if one stayed, something could be arranged for *late* in the morning. But I would be very welcome out there, Dr. Wolf D[ohrn] has left for Berlin, Harald Dohrn and Hegner are present and are expecting us, if we wished to come, around 5:30 at the Institute. Do we want to take them up on this, drop by Anna Münchhausen's briefly, and have dinner at the H[ellerau] Pension? In any case, whatever it is to be, I'll expect to see you here, *Europäischer Hof*, very soon.

R.

[LAS, Diary]

On September 4 departure [from Vienna to Munich. On Sept. 8] missed Jung's and Bjerre's lecture, went to meet Rainer at the station, with him . . . to see Freud at the Parkhotel. [Oct. 4] With Rainer and little [Sidi] Nádherný by auto to Hellerau for the performance of Claudel's *Annunciation.* Rainer and I made Werfel's acquaintance here. [Oct. 11] We consulted Ziegelroth in Krummhübel, but Rainer of course could not really open up to him. During our return trip from the mountains we conducted a dream analysis during which among other things many distant childhood memories came back.

[RMR to LAS in Dresden]

Am traveling, with your blessing inside me, Paris.

Your

old *Rainer.*

Greetings for Ellen [Delp] and good wishes for Dresden!

Oct. 17

[LAS to RMR in Paris, Telegram]

Dresden 10.17.1913, 5:05 pm.

As from a garden my thoughts reach toward you

Lou

[LAS to RMR in Paris]

[Dresden, October 18, 1913]

When your words arrived, I felt terrible, and I got up quickly to see if I might still meet you; then it occurred to me: you may be on your way to the station already, in a hurry to finish all those last-minute arrangements, and I stayed, and then greeting upon greeting arrived from you; I thought, and Ellen [Delp] felt the same way: if only *you* could see it, this huge blossoming crown over the head of my bed (standing on the edge of the desk behind it), arching over me, and beside me the white carnations extending out so high—as if they were our old white carnations and had been growing taller and taller. I telegraphed Kippenberg for your address, of all the people you gave it to only I had failed to write it down! Now you have been in your rooms a few hours; but to me it is as if you were still here, as if I could see you: and I believe that it will always remain this way for me. My poorest darling, dear old Rainer.

Lou.

On the last day it was so terrible, almost as if I were chasing you away there [i.e., to Paris]: but you know how it really was, and that I only wanted to help you. But that's something people can't do for each other. Only remain loyal in the deepest, most fundamental sense.

[RMR to LAS in Dresden]

Paris, 17, rue Campagne Première,
October 21 [1913]

Dear Lou,

I cannot be entirely unhappy, given all the things you've helped me to understand, things reaching so far beyond us, so deep behind us; but to the extent that I can be, I am, with all my heart. You have shown me that I am still somehow the same, even the same in a more consolidated way, that actually none of my old advantages has been laid waste or lost, that they may in fact still be there, all of them, but that for the time being I don't know how to make use of them.

Paris this time was exactly as I had anticipated: difficult. And I feel like a photographic plate that is being exposed too long, in that I continue to lie open to everything here, to this burning influence. My room was full of last June, waiting, threatening to make me live out everything begun back then. Out of fright I went straight to Rouen that Sunday. I need a whole cathedral to drown me out. Provincial France always has a soothing effect on me; so many of the old houses there I imagine living in as I pass them by—and then when I stop and take a good look, most of them actually are for rent.

Would you believe that the glance of a woman coming past me along a quiet street in Rouen so moved me that I could see almost nothing afterward, could not collect myself for anything? But then gradually the magnificent cathedral did assert itself, with the legends of its densely filled windows where earthly experience becomes translucent and one sees the lifeblood of its colors.

I believe I can hold out in Paris only if I convince myself that I have come here for a few days completely on whim, to take in whatever opportunity presents itself: in my neighborhood some of the most venturesome young people have opened a theater that intends to put on both old and new things in an honest and unadorned way, so I can keep up my interest in the Hellerau métier; if only I can manage to remain as hidden away as possible, so that I can grow used to myself again, in the good old sense: contented. A little reading, resting, gazing outside, —I would be satisfied with everything if only it were wholly mine again, without seeping out into longing. I am frightened when I think of how I have been living outside and away from myself, as if always standing at a telescope, ascribing to every woman who approached a happiness that was certainly never to be found with any of them: my happiness, the happiness, long ago, of my most solitary hours. Time and again I find myself thinking of the poem from the *New Poems* whose title, I believe, is "The Stranger," —how well I knew what it all comes down to:

> To let all this slip past without
> desiring

and I, who did nothing *but* desire—.

To begin anew. Indeed, even in the old school exercise-book days it helped to turn to a new page; this current one, Paris, is truly full of the most humiliating mistakes, red marks one on top of the other, and where the correct answer took its own good time to arrive or had second thoughts at the last minute, it is written across a spot erased almost completely through, on the thinnest skin of a hole.

Dear Lou, somehow you really have helped me infinitely, what's left to do is now up to me and the Angel, if only we stick together: he and I, and you from afar.

I will copy for you the Stefan George poem that Werfel spoke of, the one he recited, and the "Murderer."

(For Ellen a most cordial word.)

Rainer.

[LAS to RMR in Paris]

[Berlin, October 28, 1913]

Dear Rainer,

During the coming weeks could you send me the various Freud brochures? (Freud, Jung, Grosse, etc.)? Did you enjoy reading Tausk's Spinoza? But answer only if you're inclined just now to write. Tomorrow morning I am finally returning home; my husband joined me here, you know, and in addition I have been kept here by the analysis I am conducting, three hours every day, which has yielded up splendid insights. Now I can scarcely imagine ever being without at least one ongoing analysis. Ellen [Delp] went back to Leipzig yesterday. And I am looking forward *more than words can say* to my rooms and woods; to the wanderings and exploratory side-trips one undertakes so deep within oneself while trees, tiny animals, clouds, mountaintops look on in silent sympathy. It is almost divinely beautiful that life knows and can embrace this alternation from the outside to the inside and vice versa. Often, often, often I am with you in all my thoughts and discover there again and again such *fullness,* which I ever so gradually relive, since in the actual moment of our being together there was not nearly enough time to experience it.

Lou.

[RMR to LAS in Göttingen]

[*Letterhead*:] *17 rue Campagne-Première. XIVe.*
Paris,
Dec. 2 [1913]

Dear Lou,

Welcome back to your own home. (If only I had such forests and pathways—, Paris seems to me like a poultice that has been allowed to soak too long—). I am sending you the brochures, will keep only the Worringer and the two volumes of Bergson unless you happen to need them right now. (I've enclosed an issue of *Weisse Blätter* with Werfel's "Visit from Elysium," a dramatic scene that underlies, so to speak, the poem we'd intended to explore.) The Spinoza dialogue by T[ausk] is beautiful, I agree, but somehow not self-sufficiently beautiful: more like an essay to be imposed upon a complete structure of already defined premises, so that I wouldn't know where it might be placed. It is too short for Insel-Bücherei, and also not suitable for other reasons. But about Spinoza a request: you know about my plans for a talk on how and whether God reciprocates our love. A note I recently read somewhere brought to mind the wonderful relation that Spinoza (I think) established through his insight that the act of loving God is independent of any reciprocal motion on God's part: so that I might not have to go any farther than this one path would take me. What part of Spinoza would I need to read to achieve a better understanding? Would you have the relevant volumes? Could you lend them to me? — ("the alternation from the outside to the inside," yes, if one only remained in the "inside," seeing how terribly the opposite movement has gained dominance!). Farewell, many thanks for your good memories and thoughts of me: I am sure they are working wonders.

Rainer.

(Did Rosen play the Maiden of Orleans?)

[*In the margin*:] read Simmel's *Goethe* with continuous pleasure and agreement!

[LAS to RMR in Paris]

Göttingen, Friday [December 5, 1913]

Dear Rainer,

It is strange about the Spinoza: twice this summer I thought about talking to you about him, precisely in connection with the idea of "God's not returning love," and yet both times the idea seemed to slip away from me into something far too abstract. Even now I don't know where *specifically* in his work you could read about it, for this idea is a stimulus present in everything he wrote and yet present only as the ardor that inspires everything, even the coldest inquiry into epistemological content and method. (Which is why he is interpreted as godless as often as divine, and why I almost worshipped him from the time I was a child.) My old volumes, purchased secretly back then with money I got from selling my jewelry, are not much good as translations, the best by far, which I will send you soon, is the Reclam edition. Thank you for the letter and its enclosures; *this* Werfel also strikes that very deep chord: one knows instantly that one is dealing with the same poet as before. Simmel's Goethe I am reading resolutely, whenever I can catch a little time for it; for I have already parceled out my days according to as strict a schedule as possible. The first morning hour here is especially wondrous (and it comes early indeed, since I also go to bed early), despite the wintry harshness: it emerges in the absence of artificial illumination between the red pulsing of the coals in the stove (which fortunately is always lit!) and the almost equally rayless red disk of the sun, which slowly glimmers upward out of a damp, stormy, dark shroud of weather and then finally breaks through outside, —such that this hour becomes the harbinger of far more than just a "day," of . . . I can't say what . . . but an hour for miracles nonetheless; perhaps only because thoughts get into it as through a wrong door, thoughts that had meant to visit a dream in the empty bed of the adjacent room.

My husband meanwhile has (in October and unbeknownst to me) come up with a bizarre therapy: for ten days he went *absolutely* without food and now walks about with a veritable astral body of not quite 131 pounds—which however leaves nothing to be desired in the way of agility, capacity for work, and overall vigor. The doctor in Kassel who advised him to try this adhered to the same regimen for 20 days, with equally surprising success and without having to interrupt his extremely demanding practice. But for the likes of you and me this would be as imprudent, I think, as the glass-eating or sword-swallowing of the dervish, and I can only be glad that I had no hint of it.

At the moment I am finishing something about which I occasionally wonder: what would *you* make of it? It grew out of a correspondence with little Reinhold Klingenberg and is called: *Three Letters to a Boy*, with the letters separated by three-year intervals. Only the last two are relevant, since the first is a fairy tale: would you, sometime or other, care to read through them in typescript? Had I not known of so many similar cases, I wouldn't have let this matter pass beyond the specific personal situation that it originally addressed. But here too Freud's attitude regarding this issue seemed to me the right one: especially this total distancing from every previous soft-coloring of things—whereby paradoxically, I believe, the genuine hues of life are for the first time allowed to shine.—

What a lengthy piece of scribbling this has turned into! So many things have piled up. Nevertheless I won't end with a question, since you might not want to write. But you do know how it is.

Lou.

Lia Rosen did play the *Maiden of Orleans*; a number of papers praised her performance highly, but I couldn't go. For Clotilde von Derp I looked and looked until my eyes turned red, but never found a notice: her dancing in Berlin must have dropped from the program.

[LAS to RMR, picture postcard, with V. E. Gebsattel, from Würzburg to Paris, beginning of January 1914]

[RMR to LAS in Göttingen]

[*Letterhead*:] *17 rue Campagne-Première. XIVe.*
Paris,
February 9, 1914

Dear, dear Lou, since when! for how long! I counted on your entering the New Year through *double* doors, wanted to stand at the inner, Russian one . . . Now it is almost a month later, one can no longer keep wishing, already the year is no longer bright enough for that. —I did receive the Würzburg card from the two of you, —before that and afterwards much reading, daily attempts at work, trying to coax it into the realm of possibility through regularly scheduled translation of Michelangelo's poems, aside from that much correspondence, one (among it) beautiful, hopeful somehow, often engaging me outwardly, much more often inwardly; not writing you, because *that* letter would begin where those others leave off and because whatever of one's own situation one chose to speak of would ring false out in the light of day. Will send you new poems by Werfel, which I copied for you out of *Weisse Blätter*; never heard from him, but did write him of the joy they gave me. —(I have learned just now, from Thankmar, of Wolff Dohrn's death!) Don't forget to send me the boy's stories, I long for them often. Are you happy? (Cordial regards to your husband) Your

Rainer.

[*In the margin*:] Will send you in a few days a book by Marcel Proust, 2nd part mostly just novel, but the rest wonderful, full of inexhaustible ideas and relations and for psychoanalysis very interesting!

[LAS to RMR in Paris]

Göttingen, Friday [February 16, 1914]

Dear Rainer,

How welcome is your letter, dearest, I have found myself thinking of you (more accurately: conjuring you up) so often, especially during this present stretch of time. Most often, I should immediately add, on account of the weather. That sounds odd, but *such* weather! Never before have I experienced anything like it in German lands. For over five weeks the most radiant sun, sun, sun, at first with absolutely windless frost down to 14 and 15 degrees, such that one could walk about hatless and almost without a coat, and then, between one new moon and the next, the glittering snow-white landscape turned to spring, snowdrops burst out, the hanging catkins reddened, the moss greened as never before, the birds went wild with jubilation, and all this happened without the interference of a single cloud, in nothing but sun, sun, sun. When I went out for walks, many hours every day, your yearning for a "real" winter always came to mind. When I saw your envelope bulging with poems a huge joy befell me at first, I thought it might be the Michelangelos, but of course that was not to be, and I shall soon find the new Werfels to be just as splendid as no doubt they are; how admirable it is that you can appreciate them without that recently suffered disappointment interfering; I'll be able to manage it now only gradually. Do you know that after a reading one evening in Berlin, when Scheler heard Werfel's poems, he was completely spellbound? And this both by the poems and by him personally; he told me: Werfel is as a poet exactly what he, Scheler, wished to be as a philosopher. The ultimate explanation of this may reside in the: "wished to be." For behind the intellectual import and greatness of Scheler's philosophy lies an impulse to withdraw into it, seek refuge there. Scheler by the way is just now in Göttingen, came yesterday, missed me; before long he will spend an evening with us, together with Thankmar and my analysand from Berlin, a woman who lives up at the Rhons. Along with the sun she has been the vital part of this winter for me, due to the way the analysis has confirmed and extended earlier insights. I just remembered, by the way, something important I forgot to write you about in November re. our visit to the Egyptian Museum in Berlin. My husband, Ellen and I were there together; all three of us were quite beside ourselves, and we spent a long time inside engrossed with everything. They have acquired several new pieces since your stay in Berlin; among them a mouth with a small fragment of nose above it, so magnificent that I felt I had suddenly gained an unforgettable friend in this unknown person who once spoke through a mouth such as this. My husband tried to have a cast made of it, but to no avail, since all these works are sculpted of a sandstone that would be harmed in the process; and besides, the replicas, simply by being of a different material, turn out very poorly, as you yourself have already seen in the head for Clara. You will have no doubt noticed how many Amenhoteps IV resemble you? The one dark relief placed opposite his wife is especially like some dream-portrait of Rainer.

How irrepressible your "*r*" has suddenly become?! this way: "*r*", —no, can't get it right. But it has this flag-waving quality about it, or as if you were rising heavenward. You dearest you.

Lou.

The book just arrived. I thank you very much and will read it when I am good and relaxed, which is not likely to be soon. In the wake of this letter I will send you the letters to the boy; perhaps also the introductory fairy tale, so that you can tell me if it sounds too silly; it *is* the chronological onset of the whole thing. Any marginal or epistolary remark from you would be of value to me, any number of things can still be added or removed. I didn't send anything so as not to risk disturbing you.

[RMR to LAS in Göttingen]

[*Letterhead:*] *17 rue Campagne-Première, XIVe.*
Paris,
February 18, 1914

Dear Lou,

Yes, my "*r*"s are simply inimitable, I don't know myself what's gotten into them. Thank you for your good, good letter, here the weather was just as splendid for a time, but I'd just as soon remain up here with myself, going out somehow vexes and shames me and then also, truth be told, Paris has become for me (and seems likely to remain) roughly what that "luminous" Gothic arch was for Salzmann when, behind us, he carried on about its falseness. And the more light and color play their effects there, the more I find myself detesting it. Thus must it always be, I suppose, in a love that has run its course. This morning your manuscript arrived; it is lying here and can feel, I hope, how much I am looking forward to it. —I am enclosing a touching little Russian letter with translations, the last one, "И вотъ одинъ . . . ," I read with special fondness, I believe it is good (?), and at any rate the entire letter is such that it could have only come from there. Please, send it back to me by and by, it has not been answered yet. —And farewell for now, and keep up all your kind thoughts and dearest wishes.

Rainer.

[RMR to LAS in Göttingen]

Paris, 17 rue Campagne Première,
February 20, 1914

Dear Lou,

I have just read your three "Letters," completely gripped by them, I had no idea that one could say *so much* to someone this age, and yet it is, as a letter to a boy, only the starting point for the beginning of true utterance. Many things pass though one's soul as one reads—, could I, at Reinhold's age, have grasped it the way you present it to him? Can he grasp it only because he grew up in these days and not back then—, above all, you yourself could not have said it back then: and so one finds oneself where one is, and one's own childhood seems more puzzling for having been outgrown.

The arguing away of the miraculous for the sake of the miraculous begins beautifully with this old Father Christmas who is not at all reluctant to become obsolete, one almost feels a shudder at how he strikes back out into nature [*in the margin*: and I know the place], taking just one little thrush's wish with him into its silence. And that, indeed, is the common theme that runs through all three letters: this onrush and subsequent receding of Nature, which however never really recedes but only observes us intently from one flood to the next.

In place of anything coherent I shall only jot down a few notions as they came to me while reading, all of them pointing beyond the frame of the letters at us, at me.

It was beautiful to grasp, in a way that I had never before envisioned it:

how the creature, as it evolves, is transposed further and further inward, out of the world and into the inner world. Hence the exquisite position of the bird on this inward journey; its nest is indeed almost an external womb granted it by Nature, a womb it only furnishes and covers instead of containing wholly within itself. Thus it is the one creature that enjoys a very special feeling of familiarity with the outer world, as though it knew itself to share in that world's innermost secret. That is why it sings in it as if it sang in its own interior being, that is why a bird's note glides so easily into our own inner depths, we seem to be translating it without residue into our feelings, indeed, for a moment it can turn the entire world into an inner space, because we feel that the bird does not distinguish between its heart and the world's. —On the one hand animals and humans gain greatly by the transposition of the ripening life into a womb: for the womb becomes more intensely world when the world outside forfeits its share in the maturing processes (and then, having lost this share, grows more insecure—); on the other hand (you will remember that question, from my pocket notebook, written last year, in Spain): "Whence comes the intense inwardness of the simplest creatures" (those other ones): from the fact of their *not* having matured inside the body, such that they never really have to leave the sheltering body at all. (Remain in lifelong contact with the womb.)

Very beautiful is the passage about the "two secrecies": the one secrecy protecting what is within, the other secrecy excluding what is without.

And what's shown there so beautifully about the plant-world—how it makes no secret of its secret, knowing, as it were, that it could exist no other way but *in perfect safety*—that, can you imagine, is exactly what I felt in Egypt standing before the sculptures there, and what I have always felt since then standing before things Egyptian: this *open* mystery, this laying-bare of the secret which is so through and through, so at every point secret, that there is no need to hide it. And perhaps everything *phallic* (how strongly this entered my mind in the Temple at Karnak, though I could not at that time *think* it) is only the human "privately secret" translated into the terms of the "openly secret" of Nature. I can never call to mind the smile of the Egyptian gods without the word "Blütenstaub" [pollen] occurring to me.

Splendid is the part about the two "eliminations" or "discharges," —love and revulsion (as in El Greco's *Ascension of Christ,* where the guard with a sword in his hand clatters downward, allowing the Savior to ascend all the higher into Heaven): the one jettisoned as no longer ours, comprehended as already no longer "life" even when it was still *inside* us; the other—wherever it may be, however far outside of us by now—affirmed, acknowledged in the child, in the grandchild, in all who are to come, in all who have been.

Ah, dear Lou, doubtless you *could* have said it back then, and had one been allowed to hear it, one could have found a way to cry about it and absorb its lesson. But if nothing else, it's good to find such things out before it's too late.

R.

You can see that I am writing all this (really as nothing more than very preliminary thoughts feeling their way along the edges of one corner) more poorly than if one were to say it, for then the other's presence and demeanor would be there to prop up one's expressions. Even so I'll send this piece of paper just as it is, since at least it has the virtue of being written immediately after reading; by tomorrow some of it will already be deep inside the blood, and thus even farther beyond reach, while other parts will have been expelled outside; —and so this might be, between us, the right moment after all to push a few half-words, murmurish as they are, out onto the old accustomed leaves.

—Imagine, this *Cornet*: they are printing the thirtieth to fortieth thousand: translations have been offered to us in English, Polish, and Hungarian; an Italian one, excellent, recently passed through my hands, and I just heard that a French one is under way. (Who could have persuaded us of this back then in Schmargendorf!)

(Do you ever hear from Sidie? —Karl Krauss is spending much time with her in Janowitz, which makes me happy for Sidie, given her despondency; but Clara, I notice, views it with disapproval and indignation.) —Now farewell, for today.

Rainer.

Is there in Würzburg a nice, slightly old-fashioned hotel where one could enjoy a few days of peace and quiet? And if you know one, do you by chance remember its name? Someone has asked me.

Do you have Kassner's new book *The Chimera. The Leper.*? (The whole thing only about 60 pages and very curious.) Shall I have it sent to you?

[LAS to RMR in Paris]

Göttingen, March 1, 1914

Dear Rainer,

Your "murmurish" words murmured *so many things* to me—thank you for them! In fact listening to them precluded any swift reply. It became so clear to me: *you* should have written these three letters to a boy, only then would each single seed that a Reinhold is meant to find lying there for him be surrounded by the rich springtime that creates the desire for this, that *is* the delight in this. At the very least the little bird should be fluttering around in it, your little bird, the way *your words* interpolate it. I confess to you that I can't bear this absence: *do* permit me an "epistolary quote" in the text or in a footnote! Without this special chirping the rest will become for me mere chattering. After the third letter, the one already conceived from a Freudian point of view and sent off to Reinhold only this winter, I found myself still writing, for, regarding this strangeness one feels toward one's own body, I was much concerned with what I remarked when you spoke of the idea that was to inform the "Phallic Hymns." The phallus as a sign of the body seems so ridiculous next to the intricately purposeful arrangement of the body's other parts (which in their own way seem to express us at least to "ourselves" reasonably well), *because* it exists as a self-contained entity that defies description and thus has so little range of expression that whatever it does express becomes something "other" and in almost no other way than symbolically. This deep purpose—to be only an image for the totality (a cow understandable as eternity, etc.)—is what ancient art attributed to *material reality* in general, and as a result the phallus rose in the midst of it as an integral presence: the obelisk pointing upward in much the same way as our church steeple, —whereas for us, who are accustomed to making purely practical use of material reality and regarding it as mere basis, a lowest "step" toward the spiritual, the sexual becomes a contradiction, something oddly simplistic and yet strangely fateful—our attitude toward it is part giggling and part dread. It has always been my fondest notion: to come to understand that finally everything we call "materia," everything objectively placed outside, everything opposite (and this includes our own bodily self), is at heart nothing but the borderline that marks our arbitrary singleness, the point where our ability to keep pace (in either feeling or understanding) with *essential* life fails us, so that we cease saying "I" to it and in our helplessness fence it off from ourselves. In doing this, however, we only admit to its omnipresent splendor, which extends above and beyond our individual singularities, and in which we all repose, so that we are able to reach through everything surrounding us, even including our bodily nature, trustfully, the way one hand reaches in the dark toward another, and are meant to do it calmly, with the "intense inwardness of the simplest creature" for whom this relationship has never been obscured.

I am sending this with pictures Scheler hopes will interest you in the Maniasco exhibition soon to open in Paris. M[agnasco] is close to El Greco, and a friend of Scheler's (von Heister) has recently acquired 70 of his works for twice 100,000 marks. I am also enclosing the *dear* Russian letter! It does make you a bit of the Orthodox slavophile in accord with the current dogmatic political climate there, but its intent is very sympathetic; the literary value of the translation I dare not judge. Strange to know it's the *Cornet* who is riding ahead of you! How very different the characters toward whom he leads those readers who follow him; and yet, that is what he does, even though one overtakes him and moves beyond, as new editions of your subsequent works will show, each more clearly. But some part of you *is* lodged in this advance rider. Ellen [Delp] wrote just now aghast at Werfel and his reading, her every feeling being exactly the opposite of Scheler's. From Sidie [Nádherný] I had a number of infinitely warm letters, but in response to my second letter merely a New Year's Greetings telegram, which is why I don't know anything further just now; I do find her so appealing. And Würzburg? We lodged at "Russischer Hof," the rooms old-fashioned in the hotel-style, but the whole place agreeable, prices moderate, fare as in all of Bavaria not overwhelming. Where will you be in the spring?

Lou.

[RMR to LAS in Göttingen]

Berlin-Grunewald
Hubertusallee 16
Pension Bismarckplatz
March 9 [1914]

Dear Lou,

Every day I have wanted to write and let you know *where* your letter found me: it's inscribed above; beautiful walks through a very early spring storm in a Grunewald that was so like the old one to me, so very like it, that it was almost as if I were still young after all. And the strangest chance happenings, and music—divine, by Busoni. And the Egyptian Museum. All manner of unanticipated, good things drew me here, I stay only until tomorrow, will then leave for a few days of Munich, Hotel Marienbad. At first I wanted to ask you for Scheler's address here, so that I could talk with him in person about Maniasco: but it would have been too much. These reproductions also came my way so unexpectedly, they're marvelous, I have looked at them again and again, would love to take them with me all the way to Munich, the journey there would be such a perfect time for studying them. Without doubt the finest are the portrayals of monks, they're tremendous. —And yes, love, of course you may quote, only on Ellen Key's desk was it written *Du skall ikke citerer!* —But *You* may. More from Munich.

Rainer.

[RMR to LAS in Göttingen]

Paris, 17, rue Campagne Première
June 8, 1914

Dear Lou,

So here I am, back again after a long, broad, heavy time, a time in which once more a kind of future became past, not lived out strongly and reverently, rather tortured incessantly till it succumbed (a skill of mine no one will easily imitate). If sometimes during these last few years I was able to plead my case by saying that certain attempts of mine to gain a more human and natural foothold in life had failed because the people concerned did not understand me, had inflicted on me violence, injustice, and pain, one after the other, and had left me stunned and bewildered—, now, after these months of suffering, I stand condemned in an altogether different sense: having to admit this time that no one *can* help me, no one; and *were* someone to approach with the most unfeigned, spontaneous heart and prove his worth to the very stars and endure me no matter how stiff and difficult I made myself and maintain his pure undeterred path toward me though I broke the ray of his love ten times over with the murk and thickness of my underwater world—: I would still (this I know now) find a way to isolate him and leave him exposed in the fullness of his endlessly fertile help, to cut him off from me inside a realm of suffocating lovelessness so that his support, rendered impotent, would hang past ripeness on his own branches and shrivel and die horribly.

Dear Lou, I have been alone again for a month and this is my first try at getting a grip on myself—: you see what a state I am in. In the end certain things will have been learned, —at present of course I observe over and over but this: that yet once more I was not equal to a pure and joyous task, one in which Life stepped up to me again, guilelessly, with no hard feelings, as if it had never had a bad experience with me before. Now it is clear that this time too I failed the exam and will not be promoted and will be kept sitting for another year in the same pain-class and every day, all over again, have those words written for me on the blackboard, those same words whose dull accent I thought I had learnt already to the very depths of my being.

What finally turned out so absolutely to my misery began with many, many letters, light, beautiful letters that came rushing out of my heart: I can scarcely remember ever having written such letters before. (That was the time, you will recall, of my exuberant “↗”.) In them (I realized ever more clearly) a spontaneous liveliness welled up as though I had tapped into a new eager reservoir deep in my most genuine being, which now, released in inexhaustible communication, poured forth over the most serene slope while I, writing day after day, felt both its joyous streaming and the mysterious repose that seemed almost naturally prepared for it in the recipient toward whom it flowed. To keep this communication pure and transparent and at the same time to feel or think nothing that would be out of place in it: this suddenly became, without my knowing how, the measure and law of all I did, —and if it is possible for someone inwardly turbid and muddied to become clear, that happened to me in those letters. The everyday and my relationship to it became to me in some indescribable way sacred and accountable, —and with that a powerful confidence seized me, as if now finally an alternative to my sluggish drifting had been found in a current of steady fatefulness. How powerfully, from then on, I was caught up in some process of change I could also observe from the fact that even the past, whenever I talked of it, would surprise me in the way it made its appearance; if, for instance, it involved times I had often talked of earlier, the emphasis would fall on places formerly unheeded or scarcely known, —and each assumed, with the innocence of a landscape, something like pure visibility, was there, enriched me, belonged to me, —so that for the first time I seemed to become the owner of my life, not through any exegetical appropriation, exploitation, and understanding of things past, but simply through a new truthfulness that flooded even through my memories.

June 9, 1914

I am sending you, dear Lou, this sheet I wrote yesterday; you will understand that what I describe there is now long past and lost to me; three (unachieved) months of reality have placed something like a strong, cold plate of glass over it, beneath which it becomes as unpossessable as in a museum's display case. The glass reflects, and I see nothing in it but my face, the old, earlier, long-ago, once-again face—, which you know so well.

And now? —After a fruitless attempt to live in Italy I have returned here (two weeks ago today), resolved to throw myself headfirst into some project; but I am still so dull and numbed that I cannot do much more than sleep. If I had a friend I would ask him to work alongside me a few hours each day, no matter at what. And when, in the meantime, with heaviest heart, I think of the future, I imagine that what might best succeed is some kind of labor regulated from without and as removed as possible from true creation. For I no longer doubt now that I am ill, and my illness has spread through much of me and even lurks now in what I used to call my work, so that for the present there is no refuge in it.

I am reading slowly in your Bergson and from time to time can follow; am reading Stefan George's strange new book (*The Star of the Covenant*),—spent an afternoon recently with Maeterlinck's essay on the Elberfeld horses. (Have you read it? *Neue Rundschau*, June issue) In this connection I'm reminded that in Duino, where I also stayed for a while, another experiment was made in mediumistic writing, through the same person, —and the result this time also was extremely remarkable. After several manifestations in foreign tongues—Arabic, Greek—the same Spirit seemed to appear and indeed with so vehement a return that the medium could finally bear it no longer and walked about for three days with pains shooting through her arms.

But now I'm also sending you—finally—the Magnasco photographs. If you think I should write Scheler a word myself and try to apologize for my outrageous delay with these pictures—, then please, give me his address. In the interim I have seen some Magnascos here and there, most of them in Milan, and I arrived here just in time for the exhibition. It may in part be due to how unusually open and receptive I was back then, but the impression made by the reproductions was not heightened or significantly altered by a single painting; even the portrayals of monks, beautiful as they are, had already been conveyed to me completely in the photographs. Several pieces are here that Scheler did not send reproductions of: a monks' warming room, wonderfully fantastic, with all those bare feet and begging hands hanging out of the habits, far around a gloomy fire; a workroom with clusters of busy nuns; and, above all, two of his earlier, more colorful works, interiors of a guard room, one of them with a very few grotesque figures who leave the center of the high hollow room empty, so decidedly empty that they seem to have forgotten, every single one of them, to take their place there; and in this emphasized emptiness a woman and a small child dance side by side. —He has a way in all his paintings, even his earliest ones, of distributing figures and linking them together as if they formed constellations—, this may be his most notable characteristic. Other than that I feel in the paintings themselves a kind of disproportion between the smallness of the image and the overly drawn-out brushstrokes, and then again between this fluent, almost rote contour that usually predominates and certain details where both tempo and acuity of vision change dramatically. (Certainly not a great painter, but a free observer and reproducer such as any period can use, and for this painter his own shot-up and tattered time must have been just the right era.—)

I have thought often, Lou, of your *Three Letters*, have talked about them at great length, and have made a list of three people who should have the little book as soon as it is published. Let me know then when it appears—, and, when you can, write me whether in the meantime there has been more from you along this line, and if so, where some of it can be read. And anyway please do write me.

Your old *Rainer.*

Did you find my "Dolls" essay in *Weisse Blätter*? —What plans are you making? I'll be going to Leipzig in July.

[LAS to RMR in Paris]

Göttingen, June 11, 1914

My dear old Rainer, — you know I had to weep horribly over your letter, it was stupid to do so, but sometimes Life really does treat its most precious human beings in such ways that one simply must. I had been accompanying you with all my thoughts, —insofar as “accompanying” can take the form of wondering every day where a certain Someone is: whether flown up into the skies and pushing at the very boundaries of our human atmosphere, or fallen into a crater and embroiled with all the fire that has ever burned inside the earth. When you had written me about the letters, with all your “[illegible]”s turned so giddy, —then it seemed to me conceivable that a creative period was about to begin in response to your new human experiences, and at such moments a terrible danger is as close as a great victory. Life is easy for those people who are granted a very small portion of creativity to go along with their strong experiences and can expend the former entirely on the latter; and now and then those others, the ones who are creative by nature, succeed the other way around; but much more often the two as it were meet somewhere in the middle and die there, since they collide on their one path rather than proceed along it together. But—even if it is true that in *this* death you alone are completely to blame, have no excuse, no palliation, still *one* thing cannot be doubted: the manner in which you bring it to life again in your words, resurrect it there, is exactly exactly exactly the old undiminished strength that makes life out of death, —and further: the grief over how things turned out is that of a person whose most delicate, innermost feeling could not be *less* guilty of all those things of which you accuse yourself. And yet it *is* you, —the same *you* who at other times cannot work or wastes some attempted work. And certainly it helps you nothing, can help you nothing, to be told that it really *isn't* you, because standing before bread in a locked pantry does not still one's hunger and neither does waiting for sheaves on fields that have not been mowed yet. That's why, when I cry about it, I cry differently, because I cry as another person, as someone looking on who at the same time sees so heartrendingly that the bread itself and the fruit of the field *are* there. And is it not the same with what now lies there before your glance under “the hard, cold glass of a display case”: you do not possess it and the glass mirrors you to yourself; nonetheless it served as proof of the importance of your possessions; and just as you had not known this side of them—their deep, rich belonging to you as part of what you are—, in the same way they still have sides to turn toward you of which today you may not even have an inkling, and from whose perusal you may be separated by a partition even thinner than a sheet of glass. But alas, what can all this help; for now you will feel only: that something, be it thin or massive, *separates* you from life; and every, every word said against this is inept, stupid, weightless.

The photographs just arrived along with your letter; I'll have them returned to Herr Heister today along with a few words; Scheler was really only a go-between in this matter (you may have even been meant to keep the pictures, but this I don't know). What's this in *Weisse Blätter*? Which issue contains the "Dolls" essay? And how long ago did you write it? The Maeterlinck article I also read: and I *must go there,* to see these dear singular steeds. Tell me: do we want [*the rest of the letter is missing*]

[RMR to LAS in Göttingen]

[Paris, around June 13, 1914]*

(Written, I believe, late January or early February—)
Just now your *good* letter. *Thanks* dear Lou.

[LAS to RMR, letter from Göttingen to Paris, middle of June 1914]

[RMR to LAS in Göttingen]

[Paris, Saturday, June 20, 1914]

Lou, dear, here is a curious poem, written this morning, which I am sending you at once, since I instinctively called it "Turning," knowing that it represents *that* turning which surely must come if I am to live, and you will understand its meaning.

Your letter about the "Dolls" essay I sensed in advance; I could feel that one was on its way with something comforting, with a reaction that would somehow make sense of things. And so it did. Yes, I understand exactly what you

*Written into the March 1914 issue of *Die Weissen Blätter,* regarding the essay "Dolls: On the Wax Dolls of Lotte Pritzel." Underlined twice in pencil at the end of the essay: *Thanks.*

discern there that the "words" do not achieve, including the last sentence about the doll's having become one with the body and its most hideous undoings.

Yet is it not terrible that one should unsuspectingly write down something like that, under the pretext of a memory about dolls treating material most primordially one's own, and then swiftly put one's pen aside, only to live out the eeriness yet again, this time without limit and indeed as never before: until every morning one's mouth was dry from the tow with which one, stitched hide and nothing else, was stuffed to the very lips?

Your *Rainer.*

Turning

"The path from inner intensity to
greatness leads through sacrifice."
KASSNER.

He had long prevailed through gazing.
Stars fell to their knees
under his grappling up-glance.
Or he gazed kneeling,
and the scent of his urgency
lulled a Force immortal,
until it smiled on him from sleep.

Towers he gazed at with such force
that they were startled:
building them up again, abruptly, as One!
While often the landscape,
overburdened by the day,
would come to rest in his quiet gazing, at twilight.

Animals stepped trustingly
into his open gaze as they pastured,
and the caged lions
stared in, as into unthinkable freedom.
Birds flew straight though it,
feeling its welcome; flowers
gazed back into it
hugely, as they do with children.

And the rumor that a *gazer* existed
stirred the less clearly,
more questionably visible ones,
stirred women.

Gazing how long?
How long inwardly lacking,
imploring deep down in his glance?
When he, forever waiting, sat far from home; the hotel's
disinterested, turned-aside room
sullenly around him, and in the avoided mirror
again the room
and later from the tormenting bed
again:
there was argument in the air,
beyond grasping there was argument
about his still feelable heart,
his heart which through the body, painfully buried-alive,
could nevertheless be felt
they held argument and passed judgment:
it does not have love.

(And forbade him further communions.)
For gazing, you see, has its limits.
And the more gazed-upon world
wants to prosper in love.

Work of the eyes is done,
begin heart-work now
on those images in you, those captive ones;
for you conquered them: but you still don't know them.
Behold, inner man, your inner woman,
she who was won
from a thousand natures, she
the till now *only* won,
as yet never loved creation.

(June 20th.)

[LAS to RMR in Paris]

[Göttingen, June 24, 1914]
Wednesday

Was away 2 1/2 days (to talk with someone), am back today, and so am *fully* in the company of your words and with them alone. With this "Turning," which *is* one, and yet scarcely one any longer, since it has been on its way for so long, has been prepared for, indeed has already almost arrived. Your body knew of its coming, as it were, before you yourself did, yet in the way that only bodies know of things, —with such infinite innocence and directness that in the end this knowledge could temporarily create for it a new misunderstanding with the mind. Do you know by what sign this revealed itself? By the eyes, —those *gazing* ones, those wresting to attain that being "as yet never loved," one and the same in a thousand different guises; *they wanted to love,* they blasted the boundaries set for them, and (do you remember what you told me about it?) plighted their troth in a gaze, —not just figuratively, but in the most immediate corporeal sense, all the way down to that turmoil in your blood, as if more had occurred in such moments than merely a glance. (Thus in the one instance of the girl who saw herself mirrored in your eyes as she was making herself beautiful; thus also in the other, more personal instance.) But they, these eyes, left only to themselves in their arduous searchings, beyond the bounds of that which, in their normal function, they needed only to convey to the mind, —they could in their gazing only become ever more corporeal and—confusing, as it were, the more subterranean processes with those consummated at the visibly open and observable body surface—lead only to strange forms of torment; for the "heart-work" to be done on what had previously been only artistically gazed upon would have to occur in some innermost region were it to succeed. That's why, for example, things like this happened: your blood, with a stronger onrush, pushed against your eyes, bringing pressure and pain—as if it had misguidedly wished to turn the eyes into sexual vessels, into those parts from which the *bodily* procreative miracles issue. And they suffered in their honest effort, which only brought them into *conflict* with the body instead of achieving its deliverance. Until the full heartbeat entered into this rhythm of the great love that transforms outside and inside into a completely new union, that comprehends suddenly its entire treasure and leans over it as over a bride.

What love does in this union is dark and difficult and glorious—and stands on the side of life; who would dare or even want to guess more about it than that; and indeed, you will *experience* it. Certainly not without interruptions and doubts. Dear, my dear old Rainer, I can't help feeling that about such things I shouldn't really be *writing*; but, after all, this isn't just a piece of mail, rather it's as if we were sitting somewhere right next to one another (a bit like the way it was in Dresden, with the book of train schedules, when we suddenly wanted to return to Munich), pressed close together like children, the one as tightly as the other, whispering into each other's ear about something woeful or reassuring. And I would like to write more and more and more and talk and talk, —not because I know all that much, only because (even if quite differently from you, and probably only because as a woman one somehow is at home in these regions) I hear your heart-sounds, these deep, new ones, with all my being.

Can we, shall we, don't we want to meet during your trip before you have to be in Leipzig, —halfway if you like, on the Rhine?

Lou.

[LAS to RMR in Paris]

[Göttingen, June 27, 1914]
early Saturday morning

Dear Rainer,

It was only after my letter to you had gone off a few days ago that I began to live with the *poem itself*; I couldn't do so at first because its personal immediacy had overwhelmed me too thoroughly. And now I read, or more accurately: *say* it out loud to myself again and again. There is something in it as of a newly conquered domain, one whose boundaries are still out beyond one's ken, its compass extending farther than one could walk: one senses more terrain; senses many trails and long wanderings along paths that until now had always been shrouded in fog. And adding a little daylight, just enough so that one can see where to take the next step, would be, from one poem to the next poem, like a real advance of footsteps, one never as yet achieved, on grounds where (in contrast to "mere" art) illumination and action are still as one; this domain can indeed only be made into poetry insofar and to the extent that one has conquered it and thus made it part of a new experience. Somewhere in this realm, deep down, all art *begins* again with renewed force, arises as from its primordial origin, where it was magic formula, incantation, —a calling forth of life in its still concealed mysteriousness, —yes, where it was at once prayer and the most intense breaking-forth of power.

I do not tire of contemplating this.

Then I reached suddenly for the *Narcissus* poem that you had written down for me here last summer. And discovered in it the prehistory of the "Doll." For there is something about its effect, as if the melancholy of Narcissus (the melancholy in the myth itself and in this love collapsing back into itself) were being mysteriously intensified through the (one could say) inorganic, non-living medium in which he finds "himself" mirrored. ("Now it lies open in the indifferent scattered water—Down there is nothing but the equanimity of tumbled stones") What is fleeing out of him, not held in by the "compliant center," gains its full effect only through the dead *materia* in which it comes to a halt so as *thus* to change into its own opposite. But at the same time this out-fleeing contains the full suggestion of *why* things should be that way—why this experience full of melancholy is so inescapable: because he is also in the *creative* sense dissolving ("in the air and in the aura of groves"), because he "meets no enmity," —because he, *of his part,* gives life to what they say is dead, is outside, is opposite, —because his life *extends beyond* all that. And third, there is also this suggestion: how these two aspects at a certain point incomprehensibly intersect, and in doing so necessarily produce *erotic* melancholy; "what forms there and so resembles me and quivers upward in tear-stained signals, it perhaps took shape just this way inside a woman; it was beyond attaining." This running up against the inorganic, this becoming doll, in other words, this running up against our body, which for us (even though it is organic life) is yet the outermost outside in its most intimate sense, the first partition that differentiates us from ourselves, makes us the "inner being" lodged in it like the face in a hedgehog; and yet: our very body, with its hands, feet, eyes, ears, all the parts we enumerate as "us"; this perplexing tangle generally unfurls only in response to the loving comportment of an other, who alone legitimates, in a manner we can bear, our body as "us." In a "creative person," though, these components perpetually loosen *and* renew their ties: which is why, instead of repetition, new reality emanates from him.

You are in pain: *I*, through your pain, feel bliss.

Forgive me for that.

Lou.

[RMR to LAS in Göttingen]

Paris, June 26, 1914

Dear Lou,

You *know* and *understand*; could I but see for a moment on my own what, once you have described it, I invariably believe to be true, could I but be the insightful Other, I would return with renewed strength into my entanglements, which are unforeseeable and so long in the making. God knows how far the poem "Turning" precedes the onset of those new circumstances, I am far behind, God knows if such complete turns can still be worked at all, since the obstinate inner forces continue to abuse and exhaust each other in the most horrific misunderstandings. That's why I did put so indescribably much hope in at last achieving the proper loving attitude toward a human being, because with that all distances would have been put in proper order: the one toward the world would = ∞ again, the one toward one's own body would = 0, and in between all numbers in benign gradation. As it is, an exaggerated attentiveness has moved myriad separate details up close to me in larger-than-life proximity, and on the other hand interposed relationships between me and my body (probably the same as those aberrant ones I have with the bodily in general) that keep it in a state of continual excitation. In this way the havoc has gotten into every little vein, every muscle has received a spurious bulge. It occurs to me that a mental acquisition of the world that so fully utilizes the eye, as is the case with me, would pose less danger for the pictorial artist, because with him it achieves a more tangible calm, comes to rest in more corporeal results. I am like the little anemone I once saw in the garden in Rome; it had opened so wide during the day that it could no longer close at night. It was terrible to see it in the dark lawn, wide open, still *taking in* through its calyx, which seemed as if frantically flung open beneath an all-overpowering night that streamed down on it undiminished. And next to it all its prudent sisters, each of them closed around its own small measure of abundance. I, too, am as hopelessly turned outward, thus also distracted by everything, refusing nothing; my senses, without asking me, attach themselves to anything intrusive, whenever there's a noise I give myself up to it and *am* that noise, and since everything, once it has been *set* for stimuli, wants to be *set off* by stimuli, so at heart I *want* to be disturbed and *am* so without end. From such exposure to an existence in public, some sort of life inside me has taken refuge, has retreated to an innermost place and lives there the way people live during a siege, in deprivation and perpetual worry. Makes itself felt,

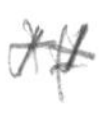

when it believes better times have arrived, through the fragments of the Elegies, through a first line, then has to retreat again, since outside it again and again finds itself completely exposed. And in between, between this uninterrupted outward-addiction and that interior existence I can barely reach any longer, are the true dwelling-places of healthful feeling: empty, abandoned, cleared out, an inhospitable middle zone whose neutrality also explains why all the kindnesses of people and nature are wasted on me.

Today, according to the day's date, it has been a month since I arrived here. I have spent it under a strict vegetarian regimen, with the great task of sleeping every night from 9 until 6 o'clock in the morning, which I've mostly been able to accomplish, catching up on missed portions during the day (so moved that my nature at least in the matter of sleep does not yet subject me to that *incapacity* of which in everything else I provide myself with countless examples). Otherwise before every sheet of paper and over every kind of book held back like a goat on a very short tether, and, in becoming aware of this constraint, getting myself so clumsily tangled up in it that most of the time I don't even have use of the rope's whole length. Within such a periphery, wandering about among books left unopened a hundred times before, nibbling at them listlessly, a bit here, a bit there, scarcely recognizing the various herbs from one time to the next; for *this* also I have in common with the goat: of what I have previously eaten there remains absolutely no evidence that would link me to that earlier meal: it simply turns into goat; and for the goat, once he has begun to get frustrated, that is no source of relief.

On how wonderful and inexhaustible a foundation would a life have to be built that, later on, finds its raison d'être in the construction of artistic edifices. The young Goethe becomes ever more amazing to me in this respect; how there is never any doubt that his harvest will be the full measure of what he can endure, but the full measure also of his great good fortune. To take in hand nothing that is not usable and to use *well* what is; from early on to collect in oneself memories of capability and of achievement, the most various and contradictory ones: so as to be armed with a hundred things when one comes up against that unending stretch of dearth that the gods can prepare for one at any instant.

Today (29th) after your second letter.

Perhaps, dear Lou, perhaps.

But is my situation not all the worse the more it has been prepared in the innermost part of me, since I have indeed turned out to be something so inwardly constrained? Between *Narcissus* and the recent poem lies a year, a dull year, and when I look back over it, I feel, from where I'm standing now, yet another degree heavier, harder to get through to, deader. How much time I require merely to lift my arm for a task like this, and how quickly it falls again—and I just can't do it any longer. My body has become like a trap; in the places where it earlier absorbed and transmitted, it now snaps shut and imprisons; a surface full of traps in which agonized impressions slowly die; a rigid unconducting terrain, and far far away as in the midst of a constellation growing cold: the miraculous fire, which can't emerge any longer except volcano-like, here and there, amidst occurrences that to the indifferent surface are, like outbreaks of havoc, bewildering and full of danger. Is that not the pattern of a true illness, this separating-out of life into three zones, of which the uppermost demands stimuli to the same degree that it is no longer being reached and shaken by the inner powers? Oh how in my youth I was *One*, amid all my need, in every aspect unknowable, but then also in every aspect *known* again and taken up and to someone's heart. And thus worthless enough to be thrown away and yet again cryptic and mysterious enough to be healed. How a joy, flitting about my face, would already be orbiting my most secret soul; when I felt the morning's air, it went through all of me, the morning's lightness and outset diffused through all the gradations of my nature; when now and then I tasted a piece of fruit, as it dissolved on my tongue, it was already like a word of the spirit I felt dissolving; the experience of what it had indestructibly accomplished, the pure savoring of it, already was rising high in all visible and invisible vessels of my innermost self.

And now journeys and powers and changes that should have the most dramatic effects—: and it is all being lost to a desperately fervent way of making my face and limbs available, which exhausts and so to speak overcharges my bodily self, while my soul, turned aside, otherwise occupied, withdrawn into itself, does not relieve me of my tensions. I *offer* myself, but my soul does not; it's the same in gazing as in loving, and so my body becomes contorted by this gaunt imploring intensity into which the sap does not spread that would make twig after twig of the gesture green and supple. The reason, the more I look into this, must be that I have one attitude (the one I have trained myself to assume in certain moments of work) and my soul has a different attitude—the subsequent one, the one further on—and so I serve it no longer and there is no one who *does* serve it. My soul is the bell-metal, and God again and again stokes it to white heat and prepares the tremendous hour of casting: but I am still the former mold, the obstinate mold that has done its job and does not want to be replaced—, and so there will be no casting. —Can a person understand so much and still not help himself?! And for years.

Renewal, change, hallowing—and the soul would plunge across toward it—, I know. But who would make himself new and not first shatter himself? And I treat myself like a delicate flower, all my life, lest some tiny little piece of me be broken off. Ah Lou, how much is sense, how much nonsense in all of what I'm scribbling here, don't pay it too much heed.

That we might be together in rural and yet comfortable surroundings for a few days and talk: that seems to me beautiful and important, perhaps more so even than a year ago. Only I am afraid of leaving, the closer my day of departure comes, again that whole overturning of effects, the preponderance of the external, the necessity again of making an outward show of oneself, of saying to other people "I" . . . , with this one word obliged to be well prepared and ready again, a tea perfectly steeped, whereas I have been steeping now so quietly (this whole month) from the ground up, silent, beneath an unlifted lid, and it is no one's business whether I turn a gold color or black and bitter. That is invariably the state of affairs which gives me the greatest sense of security, even where, half as someone sick, half as someone imprisoned, I can barely endure it and (as now) more give myself up than over to it—.

Are you free enough that we can decide as changes may require? (Please think about the Where *you'd* most prefer.) From mid-July on I'll be welcome at the Kippenbergs' house, and I should arrive there not much later, since I have other plans for August—about which I'll tell you. Farewell, dear—finally beautiful weather! But Paris so aggravates me that I don't want to see it, —only walk in the early morning through the magnificent avenues of the *Observatoire*, and then at noon go to my little vegetarian restaurant where salad and *yogurt*, in their slightly overdeliberate way, strengthen my sense of the good, the difficult good. I can scarcely describe to you how badly I manage to look beyond myself; the neighborhoods here around me are my ruination, since they have become, in part, witnesses to other days lost and wasted with self-recriminations, and have helped, in part, to mislead me into many a hopeless, uncontrolled, and irresponsible thought. And how should that not be the case, since during the last years I have managed to spoil for myself every other environment so quickly, have imposed on each one of them an obligation and made it oppressive and ambivalent—, the high forest last summer, the sea—, there was scarcely an hour when they meant World to me and not somehow an excuse and temptation—, and the good thing about this place is that at least I don't have to crawl into a hotel room but can draw around myself four high white walls that occasionally do stand by me a little.

Is it beautiful where you are, with many roses?

Rainer.

[LAS to RMR in Paris]

Göttingen, Thursday [July 2, 1914]

Yes, —and yet! However strongly you yourself may perpetually experience complete inhibition, it is simply not true that only now and then, in brief moments apart from, as it were, your actual continuity, that which creates the impression of plenty and strength erupts in the form of an isolated poem; no, —it is *not* that way, for while you are perpetually feeling sick and miserable you are also perpetually finding expressions for that experience, and those expressions, in the distinctive form you give them, would be quite impossible unless somewhere inside you there is a flowing together, an experiencing in unison, of what you feel as so torn into one impulse fleeing outward and another burrowing inward, with only an empty, self-deserted middle space between them. Those words with which you articulate this condition, and that passage, for example, about the anemone—they are nothing if not *works*, works accomplished, the coming about of deepest *unities* in you! A great deal of poetic work has arisen from various despairs, certainly; but if it arose out of *that* despair, the despair of not being capable of just such poetic syntheses, there'd be a contradiction, don't you think? To your *consciousness* of yourself it appears that way, your consciousness finds itself on the side of what is being blocked, and therefore is not party to those moments which show again and again that you are *not* so lacking throughout in unity as you feel and think "yourself" to be; you suffer yourself as a person blocked, and that piece of happiness which is lodged in this situation remains hidden from you, withheld, even though all its requirements are inside you and *express* themselves; for one *cannot* write about the anemone the way you do without some store of happiness (which is just not fully working its way into consciousness!). Certainly nothing could be further from my intentions than trying to pour you a serving of sugar water, —you, of all people, you know how, in earlier years, I would always exhort you to *know* the "Other"; but now it seems that your knowledge of him overreaches him, would become a knowledge of yourself rather than solely of this other one, so that you, in an exact reversal of that earlier time, now no longer notice, absorb, emphasize yourself at all, simply overlook yourself and *know* only him; but just as back then this "Other" really *did* exist in spite of your not wanting to know him, so now *YOU*. This may not factually change anything, since one has nothing of that which eludes one's feeling and thoughts; yet proof that it *is* real and *is* present remains important, —somewhat the way an insensate limb does not stir the same terror as an amputated one: the paralysis may be connected with processes that can at any moment resolve, and that do not block the flow of food and nourishment, etc. And yet I say to myself, again and again: it is of no help to the present moment, and truly I am leading you by the nose between grain fields while you are in need of your daily bread. Perhaps more could be accomplished in an actual conversation. But *on no account* should you consider it before you will have to think about traveling anyway—especially not in this midsummer heat that has finally arrived and is wonderful to be in but painful to journey through. I had thought of Elberfeld; it's half the distance,* and you'll have to pass by there anyway. But only if you're still interested in seeing the horses there (I mean before going on to Leipzig); I'm also free to meet you some other place or time. Here it is splendid now, yes, many, many roses and berries (strawberries and raspberries and gooseberries), and yet I'm afraid staying here will stir up too much for you; there are many people in the house where your little room was; it might be emptier much later. Where, geographically, will your August lie? You said: only during the summer is Paris possible for you, —will you return? Throw a word my way however it suits and pleases you.

Lou.

[*In the margin*:] One could surely find a rural place to stay along the Rhine? And ask Krall about a visit?

[RMR to LAS in Göttingen]

Paris, July 4, 1914

Five weeks of a steady pulse of living along and going to bed, and no benefit from it, not the one which should have resulted after only two: the steady horizontal rhythm of one's bodily existence, in relation to which fatigue, pain, disquiet, listlessness are only vibrations above and below the natural, and do not destroy one's feeling for and confidence in that steadiness as the string on which one is being played, however well or badly. If I were briefly to articulate it to a doctor: I have lost the bodily *level*; the least influence, a single exertion (whether the mental one of reading and writing or the alternating submission to and control over a productive moment, —or whether just some simple physical effort of the stupidest kind, the opening, say, of a somewhat difficult door) now no longer gives rise to this or that in my body but creates a general wavering in all its relationships: and as such it forces itself on my consciousness as something disrupted and disturbed, overwhelms everything that would like to exist there, colors it through and through with one of its needs and withdraws only to flood back at the slightest provocation with yet a new color of need. Even sick people are able to gauge during the pauses in their illness the mean-level of their bodily situation and rely on that, whereas I, so to speak, am constantly being moved out of one matrix into a completely different one. Even as I am accepting the present condition *tant bien que mal*, fitting myself out in it and, painful though it is, crediting it as the neutral, it takes on such strikingly different accents and emphases that I'll recognize it next time only by the cleverness with which it works its transformation. To say "I" and mean by this something constant in which the bodily as a matter of course and almost imperceptibly conducts its arguments with itself, to have the confidence that one can get this steadiness through a single day unchecked and unsubverted, to carry it safely across one (even the friendliest) night: that is something that I have not succeeded in doing now for years. Had this compliant nature been balanced by an intellectual occupation that is continuous and mostly documentary, it would not have gotten so far out of hand. But in my case, where everything depended on maintaining the intellectual in the most precarious balance, on exposing it to heaven and earth with no predictable outcome, it was only to be expected that the body, in its dullness, would draw from this attitude the worst possible lesson, mimic the mind and within its own conditions, given the slightest cause, become "productive" in *its* manner. One might think of an embroiderer whose pattern constantly keeps changing beneath her hands, its mesh expanding or contracting or demanding threads of ever different strength, while she is supposed to continue taking pleasure in the most beautiful cross-stitch or the most touching design.

This horrendous reaction I have come to understand quite clearly again in the course of these hot days; I did not spend them foolishly, and yet even so the heat (it concentrated fiercely in my rooms, which are located directly under the roof) caused me the most torturous nights, and yesterday, when the weather rebounded, I remained in a state for which "exhaustion" is not even close to the right word. The exaggerated tightening and slackening of the tissues, which I know so well at my temples and gullet, had spread through my entire body, in such a way that I felt as though a yawning-spasm had come alive in my every limb and were trying to bring forth a thousand little mouths, which would then finish what it started. I forced myself to remain at my desk as long as I could, but in the end I had to lie down; the strain in my body lessened, but in the afternoon it returned in my head and neck with such vehemence that I had to abandon the day as half lost and could not even keep my mind on reading.

Thus the heat's effect. But tomorrow it will simply be another influence, since influences are constantly intruding, from the atmosphere, from people, from objects, and my body answers even where no one asks its opinion, and thus the whole affair is hopeless. —My barber's hand, with its mixture of scents (every morning combined differently) can make such an impression on me that I leave him in a completely changed mood; but in my current state this annoyance has reached physical proportions: the trying to keep at a distance from it, the forced economy of breathing whenever it is in front of my face, eventually produces tightenings in my forehead and throat (this being only one example—), in short, it is the most piteous and ridiculous sight of someone being tortured.

To take this body, filled as it is with perturbations, it and my false behavior toward it, to take them to a doctor: in the end that will be the only solution after all. Not to a psychoanalyst, who assumes original sin as his point of departure (—for to *confront* original sin with its counter-magic is the very essence of my innermost calling and the motive force for all lives lived in the name of art)—but to a doctor, who, starting from the physical, would be able to venture far into the mental—, I can tell you, dear Lou, that I am thinking of Stauffenberg (how this came about, how my leanings toward him were recently confirmed, more about that when we talk). He wants to take time for me in August, and so I will probably be near him next month (in Munich or out in the country near Munich). I regret that I can't go now, for here I suffer like a dog who has a thorn in his paw and limps and licks and with every step he takes is not a dog but a thorn, something that he does not comprehend and that cannot be.

It is unimaginable that there should not be good, simple forms of help to remove from me, little by little, symptoms that so to speak extrude themselves toward the bodily surface like the swallowed needles of the hysterics. It is not a matter (Stauffenberg should understand this—) of helping me in places that are innermost and primordial—help is being kept in store there; but only of freeing my hands so that I can reach for that help. Just eight, indeed just three days of that state one calls "well-being," i.e., of physical neutrality (of the non-partisan body)—and the power inside me would prevail and would attend to me, instead of my having to drag this power around with me like a sick bird the weight of its wings.

Dear Lou, the Kippenbergs (he wrote me yesterday) could put me up in their house starting the 20th; I would thus, if need be, remain in Leipzig from then until August 1; then go to Munich. Before? If the least good could come of it, I would prefer to stay on here, at least until the 15th, which would also accord best with my meager funds (in a month when rent is due). If only things were not at times so completely unbearable in my muggy body and in my sullen heart.

As you can see, I am as timid about going as I am about staying; if you detect anything more definite in my scribbling, then please, advise—; if some deciding factor occurs to me, I'll write you on the spot; it would be quite good to see the horses; but whether it "appeals" to me, I don't know; for where (alas) *is* my own place of appeal?

Take this as merely a few annotations for which your letter this morning gave me the heart; such complaints are about all there is; when I try anything weightier, I'll wrench a muscle somewhere and lift it half way and drop it again.

Greetings to your roses and berries; God knows how these things happen, but the avenues here are changing into their best brown, and three times a day they have to sweep out of the way the autumn that the poor chestnut trees (which this year almost didn't bloom) keep scattering down.

Rainer.

[RMR to LAS, letter from Paris to Göttingen: "Rainer's letter," diary entry by LAS, July 8, 1914]

[LAS to RMR, letter from Göttingen to Paris, probably inviting him for a stay in Göttingen or assenting to his request to visit there—middle of July 1914]

[RMR to LAS in Göttingen, telegram]

Cologne, VII 19 1914 9:34 am

Arrive Göttingen this evening Hotel Railway Station Will come to see you tomorrow morning

Rainer

July 19 through July 22 (23), 1914: RMR's third stay in Göttingen.

[LAS, Diary]

Evening of the 19th went to pick up Rainer at the station amid the gymnasts' milling around. Murderous heat. We lose our way laughing.

While I have my meeting with Gebsattel, Rainer wants to see his publisher in Leipzig: then we'll meet in Munich, —but I'll travel there ahead of him.

[Entry by RMR in LAS's Diary]

"One must die because one has known them." Die
of their smile's unsayable flower; die
of their light hands. Die
of women.

Let the youth sing those deadly ones
as they come spiraling up through his heartspace.

Out of his burgeoning breast
let him sing to them:
unattainable! Ah, how strange they are.
Over the peaks
of his feeling they rise and pour
sweetly transfigured night into the desolate
vale of his arms. Breeze of their
rising leafs through his body's boughs. Glistening
his brooks run forth.

But may the grown man
keep silent more shakenly. He
who, pathless, at night on his feelings'
far ranges has strayed:
keep silent.

(Paris, July 1914)

[LAS to RMR, postcard from Munich (shortly after her arrival) to Leipzig, July 24, 1914]

[LAS to RMR in Leipzig, July 24, 1914, picture postcard, Portrait of a Girl, drawing by the young Goethe]

[RMR to LAS in Munich]

[Leipzig, July 26, 1914]

Thanks for your card: the "traveling weather" was good but not being by myself was very tiring. Here also much tiredness, went over business matters, everything hopeful; unfortunately it is true that Princess L[ichnowsky] committed to Kurt Wolff, but even that can be straightened out. Kurt W. is away

The War →

on a trip until Wednesday, which is why I haven't been able to talk to him yet about your little book. I saw Werfel yesterday, even in his manner of appearance this time he caused me no discomfort, but beyond that: he recited a wonderful poem for me; is leaving for Forte-de'-Marmi today. Clara wrote me a good letter, is in Munich until Aug. 1, has a good doctor, the right one, she valiantly believes. —The first thing I read here was a manuscript of Carossa's. —How is Munich!? —I will leave, I think, on the first or second.

Greetings Greetings

R.

[LAS, Diary]

Letter to Rainer [August 1], who is expected at the hotel the next day but now will probably not be able to come.

[LAS, *Rainer Maria Rilke*, p. 72]

At the outbreak of the war I assumed he would no longer be able to leave and took the last possible train home. But he assumed the same thing about me, rushed away, and so we traveled past one another.

[Telegram from LAS in Göttingen to RMR in Munich, probably in response to news from Rilke]

[RMR to LAS in Göttingen]

[*Letterhead*:] *Pension Landhaus Schönblick*
Irschenhausen—Mailstation Ebenhausen
Isar Valley RR Bavaria
September 9, 1914

How often, dear Lou, in this monstrous August, have I known that there is but a single place where one might truly survive it: with you, in your garden; for if one can imagine two people to whom this unlooked-for time brings exactly the same pain, the same daily horror: it is us, —how could it not be?

Thus I felt and inexpressibly understood your telegram, but even now I stand helpless in the face of its questions, —so little thought have I given yet to what else one should do now on one's own initiative.

During these fifteen days out here in the country I have been vacillating, from the very beginning, between what are really only two choices: moving back into the city, or, if getting well is the foremost purpose, going to take the cure at Ebenhausen, where at least spas, sun baths, etc., would be available to me. Merely staying on in the country is, this year especially, a tepid prospect, since one lacks the innocence to be with Nature; her influence, her quiet insistent presence, is outweighed from the start by one's awareness of the nameless human doom that is grinding on day and night, unstoppably. I was on the verge of going back to Munich; but then Clara wrote that she planned regardless to return with Ruth for the opening of school, which would be around the end of this week—, and so I hesitate, for she is almost penniless, and if I am to help her I can do so best from here, where I need little for myself and each week the same amount. My arrangements with Insel Verlag, which appeared so secure, have not exactly been canceled, but they remain valid, as Kippenberg told me in the end, only "while possible." That of course does mean a great deal, since how many things have not become simply *im*possible. Freiburg, for instance: as we were weighing everything in Leipzig, a glimmer of likelihood finally fell on the prospect of my attempting certain studies there, in the Black Forest air, not too far from Paris, near Colmar and other lovely places. And I would still like, even now, to make my next choice of abode with these aims in mind—which, by the way, if you can imagine, caused Stauffenberg the most unexpected pleasure, since he privately had been planning and desiring something quite similar for me. He was prepared for me, good old Stauffenberg, as honestly and prudently as my books and his power to empathize with them would allow—, so that our talk seemed really only the continuation of all the inner intercourse with me that had long been natural to him. It was not easy against this background, in the perpetually shattered present, to find the calm for our conversations, but he always did find the time, whole hours, even when work in the hospital was mounting around him on all sides; then he would come to me or we would hastily arrange for a walk together—. The outcome? He kept trying to reach that area where he believes his greatest power lies, and we did traverse it now and then; it was just that all digging and weeding and real work there remained out of the question. With terror I felt at times a kind of mental nausea which he was doing his best to bring on; it would be horrible to vomit up one's childhood like that in lumps, horrible for someone who is less concerned to resolve its unmastered aspects *within himself* than to expend it transmuted (and this *as the very thing he does*) on felt and imagined matter, on things, animals, and yes, even if need be, on monstrosities. —At one of his thorough examinations Stauffenberg discovered an old pulmonary lesion, harmless and insignificant in itself, and from then on there was at least a basis for dealing with me in mostly physical terms, which made things easier for both of us. (Sils Maria, where he would have liked to send me, was for the present impossible, and so it became—Irschenhausen.)

Dear Lou, this is about where things stand with me. Write me about yourself, what you might be thinking. Enclosed a few pages from August: to be in harmony with the prevailing voice. How one's *own* part beneath it looks, what will become of it, I am very slow to understand—, I keep thinking, with something perilously like gladness, of those who have died in the last few years, and how they would be spared observing all that we are now seeing from our vantage. —Write me, meanwhile I shall form a better estimate of what is to be done.

Your old

Rainer.

Wolfrathshausen, which I went to see on my very second day here, is beyond recognition; especially up in our neighborhood there must have been much planting and building and altering, —I couldn't even find my way. —Will there be lectures at the University in Göttingen? —Many regards to your husband.

I

For the first time I see you rising,
faintly rumored most distant incredible War God.
How thickly among our peaceful fruit had
terrible action been sown, suddenly sprung mature.
Small even yesterday, in need of nurturing, now it stands
tall as a man: tomorrow
it overtops all men. For the glowing God
in a single sweep tears his crop
out of the nation's roots, and harvest begins.

Human sheaves are heaved up into the human thunderstorm. Summer
is left behind among the games on the green.
Children remain, playing, old men remain, remembering,
trustful women remain. Tender fragrance
of flowering lindens pervades the general farewell,
and for years to come it will hold meaning
to breathe this, to keep this consummate scent.
Brides walk more auspiciously chosen: as if not some *one*
had joined lots with them, but the whole nation
had ordained them to feel. With slowly measuring gaze
boys surround the youth who already extends
into the more hazarded future: he who moments ago
was prey to a hundred voices, not knowing which was right,
now that *single* call has lightened him; for what
would not be caprice next to the joyous, the positive hour of need?
At last a God. As here the peaceable one so often
eluded our grasp, suddenly the God of Battles grips us,
hurling his bolt: while over the heart full of home
there screams his thunderous dwelling, his blood-red sky.

II

Hail, to see men in the grip of something! It's been so long
since the spectacle seemed real to us
and the invented image cut through to our hearts.
Now, beloved, the time, like a prophet,
speaks to us blindly, possessed by age-old soul.
Listen. *This* you've never heard before. Now you are trees
in which a mighty wind grows louder and louder;
over the level years it storms toward us
from the fathers' feelings, from loftier deeds, from high
heroic ranges that soon now, in the new snow
of your jubilant glory, will shine fresher and nearer.
Behold the living landscape in transformation:
a youthful fragrant coppice passes, and the older trunks
and recent saplings bend toward those moving on.
Once before, as you gave birth, you felt separation, mothers,—
feel again the happiness of being also those who give.
Give as if you were infinite, give. Be to these burgeoning days

a rich nature. Bless the sons as they leave.
And you, girls: to think that they love you, that in *such*
hearts you are felt, that such fearsome impulse
walked beside you, disguised as mildness, you so like flowers.
Prudence restrained you: now you may love more lavishly,
embrace your passions like those maids in the legends of long ago:
she who hopes, standing as though in a garden that hopes;
she who weeps, kneeling as though in a constellation that high above
is named "Weeper"..
....

III

Three short days ago, and what now? Am I really hymning horror,
really the God whom I'd wondered at from afar, believing him
one of the earlier, now only remembering gods?
Like a volcanic mountain he lay in the distance. Sometimes
flaming. Sometimes in smoke. Godlike and sad.
Perhaps only a nearby hamlet, one built into its side,
felt tremors. But we raised the hallowed lyre
to other—oh, to *what* other future's gods?
Then up he stood: stands: higher
than standing towers, higher
than the air breathed during our once billowing days.
Stands. Overstands. Stands to stay. And we? Annealed into One,
into a new creation, fired to life by his deadly force.
So I too exist no longer, my heart beats
with the beat of the general heart, and the general mouth
is what forces my lips apart.
And yet, at night there howls within me like a ship's siren
the perpetual question: where, where, does this lead?
Does the God from his tall shoulder perceive the path beyond?
Does he blaze like a lighthouse beacon out into a struggling future
that has long been seeking us? Is he a Knower? *Can*
he be a Knower, this rapacious god?
Since he destroys everything known. Everything known by us
so long, so lovingly, so trustfully. Our houses
merely lie strewn about now like debris around his temple.
Standing up, he shoved it scornfully aside and rose into the skies.

A moment ago skies of summer. Summer skies. Summer's
tenderest skies over the trees and us.
Now: who can feel, who can sense their infinite solace
over the meadows? Who
doesn't stare into them like an alien?
We've been changed, changed into sameness: like a meteor,
One heart plunged into our suddenly no longer personal breasts.
Hot, an iron heart from an iron cosmos.

IV

Our older heart, oh friends, the intimate heart
that stirred in us even yesterday: who could have thought it
irretrievably gone? No one will
ever feel it back again. No one who still exists
after the high transformation.

For a heart of time, an older age's
more distant heart, beating with residual rage,
has displaced the near one, whose intricate difference
we so slowly achieved. And now
bring to a close, friends, this suddenly
reassigned heart, consume the violence left in it!
With *praise*: for it's always been glorious
to live not in the caution of private cares, but in *one*
adventuring spirit, in those holiest sharings
of supremely felt danger. In the field
Life stands equally tall in innumerable men, and in each
A newly crowned Death walks with princely strides.

But amidst your praising, oh friends, praise pain as well,
praise without wistfulness the pain of not being those to come,
but of being, even now, so much more nearly related
to all that is past: praise and lament it.
Don't be ashamed to lament. Shout out in lament. For man's
destiny, which is unknowable,
which no one can comprehend, becomes true only
when you lament it without restraint and yet, unrestrained, *live* it,
this most deeply lamented fate, behold: like something craved.

V

Rise, and terrify the frightful God! Confound him.
For ages he's been pampered by Joy of Battle. Now let
Pain, let a new, astounded Pain of Battle impel you
ahead of his rage.
Even if a blood usurps you, a blood coming high
from the place of your fathers: let the feeling it fosters
be yours alone. Don't strive
for earlier stances, don't practice obsolete moods.
Ask yourself only: are you Pain. Pain entered into action. For Pain
also has its Jubilation. Oh and then the flag unfurls
above you in the wind from the enemy.
What flag? Pain's. The flag of Pain. The heavy
beating cloth of Pain. Every one of you has dried his sweating
hot imperiled face on it. The face common to you all
coalesces there and imprints its features.
Features of the future perhaps. So that hatred would not
permanently abide there. But an amazement, but a resolute Pain,
but an imperious rage that the blinded nations around you
should have suddenly disturbed your contemplation:
they, from whom you gravely, as from air and excavation,
won yourself breath and earth. For to comprehend,
to go on learning, and to honor inwardly
disparate things, even *foreign* things, was your heartfelt task.
Now you're confined once more to what's your own. But
it has grown greater. Even if it is far from World,—
take it as World! And employ it like the mirror
that catches the sun and turns it, aims it
upon the Erring. (May your own error
burn itself out in the painful, the terrible heart.)

———

[LAS to RMR in Irschenhausen]

Göttingen, Saturday [September 12, 1914]

Dear Rainer,

This is how I took in what came from you today: the way someone reaches hold of a fruit-tree branch and pulls down to his lips the sweetness that alone of all food he has all this time been thinking of. For my solitude has become something now in which I suffocate: because, as never before, it seems to have been annulled, suspended, declared irrelevant; because the "general mouth" does indeed "force open" one's own lips that have been keeping silent and one's own voice does shout within: "Hail, to see men in the grip of something!" —and yet somehow remains flat and listless in a sobbing contradiction. This present unity is *neither* the simple unquestioning kind, such as when a people unites in the face of a natural catastrophe to wrest victory from death, *nor* is it that almost supernatural bliss of the: "All as One!": it is made true and real only at the cost of one's closest fellow-humans and only by virtue of their deaths. (Even if the most natural-seeming causes for hostility may issue from those fellow-humans we know only as aliens and outsiders, that hostility is nevertheless rooted in matters that have everything to do with politics and nationalities—much more than with race and ethnicity—, as one can see from Ukrainians and Poles against Russians, Teutonic English against Teutonic Germans, etc.).

The most deeply horrifying thing, which causes me such trepidation, I can barely put into words: it has to do, I can tell you at least, with this: that "the War" has elements in it of (in our sense) "the Doll." The other day I read that they had hung an enemy uniform with all its accoutrements at the head of a locomotive like a quivering effigy, and I thought to myself instantly: "There's the image, there's the metaphor!" It's at heart the same misidentification that results from the compulsion to delimit oneself, to establish one's own boundary lines, and for which children are given dolls so that they may "learn" this. Such substitution must have gone on for long periods of archaic time in anything but a spirit of play—rather as a spontaneous, enmity-fueled dissociation from a world felt to be hostile to a particular tribe, a world over against which that tribe was united as a single creature. Today it is as if at some point one forgot that over the course of time it became a mere doll's body, and was meant to retain its function only until one was sufficiently mature to be allowed to embrace the unity of the world again unpunished and alive;

instead of shooting into the stuffing, one is suddenly shooting into breathing bodies, shooting at one another, as if in war games one had accidentally been given live ammunition. And the misidentification goes unnoticed: the doll, like all dolls, has its horribly realistic aspect, and this causes the blood to heat up and talk itself into any sort of reality. You see: this deed arising from the blood is *not* quite genuine after all, *cannot* be so, —not genuine in the way that all the primordial reality that is eternally alive in us is genuine and can break forth because it has an everlasting connection to the present and is in fact nothing but the eternal present of that which *is*. One only pretends that these bloody doings have an organic connection with the blood of life: every war is elaborately draped, aside from its flags, in almost everything that has ever been utilized in the way of big words, convictions, ideals, etc., and only *this* instills that tempestuous, jubilant courage; but how thoughtlessly has it all been picked up here and there, trotted out from how much narrow-minded thinking, dust-covered morality, —just as there are any number of scraps left over to sew into the glittering finery of dolls: and if, using the stuffed effigy as one's guide, one pursues this line of thought to its very end, one will inevitably arrive at what you, describing Lotte Pr[itzel]'s creations, so revealingly discovered to be the doll's *un*reality.

And I must say: this, this! —not the horrifying reality but the secret unreality, the insidious spectral "life" in it that must first sate itself, like a vampire, with blood of our most deep-searching and high-reaching thoughts in order to work its effects, in order to achieve credibility, in order to obtain sacrifices, —never has anything in all my years horrified me more than this, and thus if my mouth *were* to come open, it could only start screaming senselessly, —but not join in with the collective voice. At no previous time in my life could I have read your remark: "I keep thinking, with something perilously like gladness, of those who have died in these last few years, and that they have been spared observing all that we are now seeing from our vantage," with such intense agreement.

And yet one does not turn away, no, nothing would be more impossible; one ventures out and learns, learns, laboriously and with deep obedience toward these days and nights and what they have to teach, and does not grow tired and almost forgets to sleep as on the field of battle. And I must also share with you—though I can express it even less clearly than the previous matter—a chilling notion whose obviousness I have come to feel with full force: that there can only be war-murder because we are all continually murderers of ourselves and of one another. That is probably inescapable, but it makes the guilt an enormously general one; through the world there is passing a single unfolding action, which one has no choice but to enter: it is as if the only possibility of liberation lies in doing so, in understanding it this way, and in feeling, through the unity of blame, through that all-too-human guilt, the "heavy, beating cloth of pain" in which "the face common to you all coalesces and imprints its features," and because of which no feature which once was excluded and exposed will any longer remain uncovered and without its active, harmonious inclusion in the whole.

When I had reached this point, I realized with amazement: that for precisely these reasons, if I were a man or had borne sons, I too would have fought and sent sons off into the fight.

But it is more than time now to stop; and so I'll refrain from telling you about how carefully I've read again everything you said about yourself and Stauffenberg. That key point of ours: *why and by what means* analysis is disastrous for all creative production—I've only become clear about during the past month; the areas in us that are left unmastered—and there are really just a very few and specific such areas—are exactly those needed for productivity, and it is equally necessary that they remain inviolate, no matter what the danger. This is enormously important. Munich now, because of Clara's presence, will not be without its dangers: since it appears that she construes wrongly any encounter with you and any show of the most natural interest (such as your postcard on the bells-of-Chartres-day), as if you wanted to come back and just hadn't quite become conscious yet of that desire. In his new analysis with her, Gebsattel tried out an idea that probably suited Clara well; but he also suddenly saw everything through her eyes and from her perspective. This results from his own insecurity, which seems to me to have intensified; I am left feeling much concern for him and basically nothing but that, since his thinking, for all its abstractness, can no longer counter what is neurotic in him. There were moments when he himself felt that his analyses of others were merely a substitute for a self-analysis that had not been taken far enough, and that precisely as such, they were likely to be incorrect.

When, how, where will we be able to see and talk to each other again? My fondest thought: to have you *here*. There is a deathly quiet everywhere now, even up on the Rhons, but Thankmar's room is also vacant, as are the other rooms at the Keudells. The University? Yes, it will be opened as scheduled in every discipline, all the head lecturers no longer being green enough for war.

Right now I am going to Leipzig for a few days. My mailing address there will be: Grassistrasse 14, c/o Prof. Dr. E. Spranger.

Anything you propose will be fine with me. Aside from any *other* personal need, I bear it *as if under a heavy burden* that I am not living through this present time with you.

Lou.

Suddenly from everywhere splotches on these pages, —all on their own, it seems, dabbed directly from the inkwell.

[RMR to LAS, letter from Berlin to Göttingen, December 13, 1914. Only the envelope survives. "January 16 (1915) Rainer's telegram" (probably from Munich to Berlin): LAS, Diary]

[RMR to LAS in Berlin]

Munich, Finkenstrasse 2, iv right
last day of January 1915

Dear Lou,

Never to let anything call me away unexpectedly, no matter what its source, unless it makes itself felt as an absolutely *inner* prompting: how often have I promised myself this. And yet this time that is exactly what happened; otherwise I would not have made this trip, would be in Berlin, would have seen you, would see you now, we'd be talking, sometimes I think, would perhaps be working together a little . . .

I came here for three or four days, so I thought; after some eight I really could have left again. But then, despite numerous annoyances, Munich prevailed, due to its easier environs and—this was really the deciding factor—the chance it gave me to move into my old rooms and live in them all by myself; my lady friend, with whom I had rented the apartment in the fall, is temporarily away in the country (only her little daughter—a child of three and a half years who does not bother me—and the maid who takes care of me are here). I have actually had a week now without having to see anyone or say a single word, have spent it reading, i.e., pouring words into myself, the way I imagine someone gets drunk to escape where he is. What I have just gone through is the ever-relapsing fate of these recent years: the entering into a dear heartfelt connection, then, more and more, the painful certainty that every closeness exposes me to violence, then terror, flight, retreat back into the forfeited solitude, —though this time so many different external factors were also in play, and they caused so much damage, that who knows whether without them some sort of quiet supportive togetherness might not have come about in spite of everything. The apartment here was a wonderful start, and at first everything seemed so simply to happen as it should; indeed, none of the most likely difficulties materialized—Clara, for instance, who since she has been under regular medical care (for an intestinal problem) seems a different person, friendly and open without ulterior emotions. But then wicked things approached from a different direction, and even my weeks in Berlin were darkened by the shadows they cast, for they went on tirelessly working their effects.

Many things there did fall in place wonderfully: Frau Marianne Mitford (the daughter of Friedlaender-Fuld) lodged me in her beautiful, practically empty little house (in Bendlerstrasse) and extended me her most helpful friendship; at her home I saw Schleich and spent many lovely hours at her parental house (Pariser Platz), which (since her divorce two months after the wedding) she has made into a wonderful world all her own; my rooms in Bendlerstrasse are still available (since I only intended to be away for a few days); however, I was so little capable and composed that I have no idea *how* things would have turned out there or might still turn out—if, that is, I decided to return there after all. But Berlin seemed to me so unmanageable: there was, to begin with, all the trouble of eating out every day, and eating bad vegetarian meals at that, much too far away from where I stayed, and requiring that whole laborious effort of making one's way through Berlin's atmosphere and mood; on top of that, people were constantly announcing themselves (here all that is simple and straightforward). And even though I had been prepared (to a certain extent at least) with Prof. Loeschcke's help to make use of the University, that opportunity remains unexplored. (In this respect too, all those long distances to walk and those expenditures of time!) So here I am again, you see, trapped in between everything, with everything too far away because my own center shrinks back from everything. I don't know how to live, even when I ignore the things going on outside, much less when I see myself caught up in them all. Tell me now how you are doing, Lou; I think, given all this uncertainty of mine, that you shouldn't wait for me in Berlin; but if you think we need to talk now, I might be able to come to Berlin with Stauffenberg early in February; he wants to go there to take a short break from his duties. If in the meantime I decide to continue living here, I would come on my own to fetch my things that are still at Bendlerstr. and stay three or four days. (But I must be very careful with my money, since I have incurred the most foolish expenses!) Write me a word. What would your further plans look like, completely apart from mine? Enough; can you make any sense of these scribbles? In heart's confusion your old

Rainer.

Have you read Annette's *very* beautiful letters? (*Enclosed.*)

[LAS to RMR, letter from Berlin to Munich, probably beginning of March 1915]

[RMR to LAS in Berlin, telegram]

Munich, 3/4/1915, 10:55 am

Suits perfectly Anticipate your arrival Sooner the better Can probably let you have the room Please telegraph exact time of arrival

Rainer

[RMR to LAS in Berlin, telegram]

Munich, 3/7/1915, 10:20 am

Went to look at pension Fürstenstrasse 18 Good But think it better you try here Finkenstrasse 2 first thing Room ready If you arrive here at 6:14 leaving Berlin 7:08am could attend an interesting lecture that evening Please telegraph time of arrival Greetings to Druzhok Won't he be coming?

Rainer

[LAS, Diary]

Rainer's letter and telegrams: but I *cannot*— [Death of her oldest brother, Alexander von Salomé, in St. Petersburg on February 20; thereafter trip repeatedly postponed]

[LAS to RMR, letter from Berlin to Munich, probably on March 8, 1915]

[RMR to LAS in Berlin]

Munich, Finkenstrasse 2 iv
(with Frau L[oulou] Albert-Lazard)
March 9, 1915

Dear, dear Lou,

How strongly have my feelings been with you since your letter arrived—now you only need know that *each day* your room awaits you—, but also *can* wait. As can I; only my friend Lulu can scarcely manage any longer; she has been looking forward to you with such unbridled impatience, and yesterday evening she felt saddened. To what extent (if at all) she might find her own place among your daughters—is, I know, impossible to foresee, but if you *were* to grow fond of her, her life would once more enter a good season. *I* have not, all things considered, brought her anything good at all, after the first joyous weeks of giving and hoping (you know how I am) I have taken back most of it, all those revocations of my heart, which withdraws so quickly from human contacts, and now it is clear between us that I cannot help and that there is no help for me. Nevertheless she does still need me a while; when you see her you will understand immediately; her little daughter is with her, Ingeborg, even though for the time being the child is still being treated as a boy and called Nuckel. The path of her life has been strewn with the most unspeakable tribulations, and regrettably even last fall, when we, as far as our own relationship was concerned, were still all wonderment and hope, she herself had to undergo the very worst of them, at the very same time, in intimately nearby regions of her heart . . . Back then we had secured this apartment for ourselves, looking beyond the expected closing of Pension Pfanner (which, by the way, has since come about). It is the fourth floor, thus perhaps too arduous for Druzhok's needs, though there is a lift that could take him upstairs; Lulu also asks me to tell you that for certain emergencies there is a quite large terrace, which indeed could almost pass for real, all-embracing nature. Therefore if separation would be unbearable for Druzhok or if his upbringing as a good middle-class dog would suffer from it, he would not be lacking here in licenses and liberties. We will then each have a bedroom and a room where we can work, except that yours would have to serve as the dining room whenever we decide to take our meals upstairs. There is a vegetarian restaurant close by, most of the time we eat there, though in the evening it is often pleasant to have yogurt and some additional little something brought to us. We each arrange this, by the way, according to our own particular needs, without any regard for household schedules or restrictions, and you too, love, should avail yourself of all the solitude and quiet you desire, just as in any pension. This to give you a general idea of the external circumstances in which I await you here; as for the internal ones, —I am sure you feel them.

Yesterday's third (the final one) of Schuler's lectures will, when you arrive—and even if that should take weeks—still be resonating in us; an eccentric who has gained insights into the world's fundamental mysteries through his studies of Imperial Rome; a man who is important first and foremost because the hellish events taking place now have not damaged his ability to perceive the deeper inner connections —(and who can say that of oneself?)

I saw Gebsattel recently—by now probably four weeks ago—at my place; he seemed overly preoccupied, and in general seems to have all but disappeared from view.

Now give your heart time, love, don't think that I am impatient. A terminus only exists insofar as poor Austria, as I have just heard, is now ordering further call-ups of those previously deferred and considered unqualified; of my age-group, those between April 6 and May 6 are in line next—, and since there is a tendency to enlist anyone, it's quite possible after all to imagine that one will be whisked off to who knows where. In which case we would have to see each other before! —Goodbye.

Your old *Rainer.*

[RMR to LAS in Berlin]

Munich, Finkenstr. 2 iv
March 13, 1915

Dear Lou,

Even a few days ago it seemed to me that a disconcerting gap might open up in Druzhok's biography were you and he to separate at this present time; now I learn on top of everything that yours too would be burdened with an otherwise quite unnecessary trip [from Charlottenburg] to Berlin. Beyond all doubt, then: Druzhok must come with you. We have held counsel once more and have decreed that the terrace shall belong to those mythological processes in which his nature is still entangled. This terrace is a vast open space, yet at the same time there are a number of objects standing around there that allow for a certain discretion—.

And besides, your little friend is advancing in his upbringing, and he will, after all, be able to come down to the street occasionally with one or the other of us. And at any rate we are sure that the innocence [*Unschuld*] of his occasional duties [*Schuldigkeit*] will teach us important truths about our earthly indebtedness [*Verschuldung*] and that its lessons will not be lost on us.

You must, of course, so far as living here is concerned, be our guest, since the apartment is vacant anyway, and if Lulu (since I am already paying rent to her) has one fear, it is of sinking so low as to become a Munich landlady; you would not want to inflict *that* on her.

Board and everything else is, given Munich prices and our own vegetarian diet, very affordable; so you will be able to settle in quite frugally.

Just come soon now, love, with you will come comfort, help, and future, even though you yourself are still burdened with a heavy heart.

Goodbye.

Rainer.

P.S.

You will notify me of your arrival, won't you?

Sidie, in Rome, became engaged to Count Carlo Guicciardini, will marry in April. I'm very glad!

[RMR to LAS in Berlin]

[Munich, March 13, 1915]

Postscript:

Our very proper housekeeper, Helene Frank, says with reference to Druzhok: "He may do on the terrace whatever he wishes."

Nuckel, even, when he heard of the impending visit, implored his mother: Druzhok, oh, please, telephone him, he must come today.

So there . . . read that to him and then let yourself be persuaded by his own response.

(Saturday)

Rainer.

March 19 through May 27, 1915: Together in Munich. Time with Loulou, also with Clara. Long spells reading Hölderlin. Meetings with Gebsattel, Scheler, Hans Carossa, Karl Wolfskehl, Ricarda Huch, Regina Ullmann, Annette Kolb, Hertha Koenig (to see Picasso's Saltimbanques*), Lotte Pritzel, Paul Klee. Séances, excursions to Herreninsel.*

[RMR to Carl Andreas in Göttingen]

Finkenstr. 2 iv Tuesday, April 13 [1915]

Dear Professor Andreas,

For tomorrow, since this year I know [it is your birthday], most cordial greetings and all my sincere wishes! I am munching happily (as are we all) on the beautiful Göttingen apples, and the liverwort from the Loufried garden (since it recovered in water) has been a feast for my eyes. We have had few traces of spring here (Lou will probably not find it until she returns home), but all sorts of remarkable people keep us occupied—though none outdoes Druzhok, who with his pranks and turns and all his curiosity and zest is a source of perpetual amusement.

When you see him what will you say?! He is growing rapidly, has, since he arrived here, already passed through various stages, will, by the time he arrives in Göttingen, be all but definitive and complete. I hope that before long I too can be there once again. I make no plans; perhaps Time will make some in the absence of mine, and thus help itself beyond my impasse. All my things are in Paris, —but I will gladly consign them to the past, if only the future will come soon.

Cordially
Your
devoted
Rainer

[LAS, Diary]

February 20. Sasha's telegram [death of this brother]. Most of all, to see no one. March 4. Rainer's telegram. *Still* can't do it. March 13. Rainer's dear new call to come. Will travel soon. March 19. With Druzhok at Rainer's. Then with Lulu A.-L. in her studio. How good and wonderful to be with him, again-to-be. [Many evenings] at home with Rainer, reading aloud. March 25. Another delightful long walk on *Herreninsel* with Rainer, Clara, and Ruth. . . . Two dreams of Rainer in Munich, May. . . . One of the most radiant Munich memories will remain for me Clara and how well she has taken herself in hand.

[RMR to LAS in Göttingen, in a letter from Loulou Albert-Lazard]

[*Letterhead*:] *Pension Pfanner*
Finkenstrasse 2
June 9, 1915

LAL

It is a senseless undertaking, dear Lou, to sit down at the desk to write at a time when every spoken word breaks apart in my mouth. I do so only to thank you, to tell you how beneficial your good words were to me. I very much wish at some point in my life to stand before you not quite so poor, without merely a negative effect.

Meanwhile we have read together the book van Eden recommended. Its initial impact is devastating. If there is just a fragment of truth in it, then it seems horrible to go on living here without some huge revolt. We lent it to Hausenstein, but haven't heard yet what he thinks about it.—

Yesterday, after long unintended detours, I went with Rainer to Holzhausen on Ammersee to look over a small villa for him owned by Professor Erler. A beautiful quiet park at the lake, a delightfully furnished little house seemed to us an obvious choice. He is wavering only because he would have to commit himself for the summer months. I think being alone in nature will do him infinitely good.

We are looking for a vegetarian cook. Starting tomorrow, housepainters and carpenters will be rampaging about here.

A truly strong joy: the new book by Franz Werfel. Even in these present days he is strong.

Lou, forgive me for closing already, I can't continue.

Nuckel says: a little birdie has called Druyock. He talks about both of you often and sends greetings.

Soon I will write again.

(Kätie says to thank you.)

I kiss you

Loulou

Dear Lou, tired, so tired. You must be glad to be at home, tucked in amid your laburnum bushes. Will send you these next few days Ropshin and soon a new Werfel (*Einander*) that I received yesterday, a splendid book. And then more soon, just as soon as I find quietness somewhere and solitude finds me. If only it would!

Your old

Rainer

[LAS, Diary]

April 1916: News about Rainer! In Vienna judged to be fit for field duty, drills for a month, then taken sick and sent off to the War Information Office where he sits until three in the afternoon. May 1916: Rainer exempt from military service.

[RMR to LAS in Göttingen]

Munich, Keferstrasse 11
before Epiphany 1917

Dear Lou,

There is now, in spite of everything, a little tree standing in my room and it sends its greetings and shines over to you around this Russian Christmastime. How are things with you?

About myself it is difficult to speak; time has greatly reduced the portion allotted me for communication, and rest and work are still nowhere to be found in me following the Vienna rupture.

At least the unrest of the past month was one of restless angels, due to the presence of a beautiful beautiful young girl who was with me here. —When I was sorting through things at New Year's I found the Russian photographs that I had held back all this time but that are properly yours, and yesterday I had them sent off to you. Most cordial regards to your husband—and confidence in this year and that it might bring a good long reunion.

Прощай!

Your
Rainer.

[LAS to RMR, letter from Göttingen to Munich, June 1917]

[RMR to LAS in Göttingen]

Chiemsee, Herreninsel, Schlosshôtel
June 28, 1917

Dear, dear Lou,

I have been walking for the past two weeks on trails you know well (Druzhok knows them also!). This time living on Herreninsel itself, at the Schloss-Hôtel, which has beautiful rooms and a board that is still quite affordable. On Saturday I'll be back in Munich, on Monday at the latest a photograph of my portrait (luckily one is available) will be sent to you for Ilse [Erdmann]. I'm glad that you are happy in her company. That I cannot say anything about myself, you will understand; I must truly hold myself rigid and unresponsive, else the knowledge will suddenly break in on me of how terrible a time and future we have been allotted. If I can keep summer free, I might come to Westphalia in July to stay at Frau Koenig's estate and would then, I believe, be more or less in your vicinity for a few weeks.

Greetings to your husband and all who are with you, dearest.

Your *Rainer.*

[LAS to RMR in Munich]

Göttingen, July 9, 1917

Dear Rainer, I thank you: a few hours ago the picture arrived. For me it is not you. It does show some person inside you, but—I know this sounds crazy—he is there like a person in whose look* you are somehow reflected, who would gaze over toward you, gaze out to find you—; and so you are there and yet not there: for me, who may not be the best judge of art. When I look at the two little Russian photos on my desk which have captured you so poorly and in random moments, it is the same as when a single little blade of grass has been plucked from an entire garden: but it did grow there.

I am so very happy about the surprise awaiting Ilse! She is finally, though only after weeks, going to be called back to her vocation here as nurse, so I won't let her know anything yet. I am enclosing part of a letter from her brother (a sociologist): will you return it to me by *registered* mail? I hope it won't be an imposition. I want you to read what a *true* German writes there. For the rest I well understand if you don't want to hear or say anything now. We both surely know *this*: that what Russia is doing now has little relation to what revolutions at other times did; that even all her negating is only (again) a kind of governing by her God. Even if in practice she should come to ruin because of it—as indeed those are easily destroyed in whom a feeling of the unity of God and Earth is lodged too deep (too deep for "*Real*politik"!), —it is in the end only the *land* of Russia that lives now and "is victorious" for all.

When I suddenly envisioned you walking about on Herreninsel as in the old Whitsun days [of 1915], this whole pocket notebook became fully present to me; though its words are little more than abbreviations, it brings back to me *all* the conversations, *all* the impressions of those Munich days, almost without loss. And little Druzhok, —ah, how in the meantime he has proved his name! All the solace of the animal world is in him, —knowing *nothing* of war, of peace *everything*.

Westphalia? a reunion, whether from your or my direction? You will let me know in good time? The thought of Frau König has become for me inseparable from little plum cakes; give her my regards. And farewell, you dear.

Lou.

*[*In the margin*:] But I *do* like looking into this eye, and it *does know* of you.

[RMR to LAS in Göttingen]

[Munich, July 14, 1917]

Thank you, dear Lou: what a good letter and what a good brother! I had no idea that he is still so close to Ilse and in such intimate correspondence with her. That must be a great help to her.

Lulu's portrait seems to me also more like a question searching for me and for a bit of information. At first it surprised everyone who saw it evolving (Kassner, Hofmannsthal), but Lulu's portraits do not ultimately win through; in the end they fail to *contain* what appeared to enter into them with such intensity—that intensity would have to be *upheld* in order to truly "fill" a painting, and that would require a long, uninterrupted, imperturbable strength.

I don't remember if I wrote you that I am giving up my Keferstrasse apartment? Therefore indescribable packing. But the worst is done, and I hope finally in two or three days to travel via Berlin to Böckel, where I have long been expected. From there I will write you soon about how we can best see each other again.

Прощай!

Rainer.

In *Politiken* there are some very touching letters from the literary estate of Amalie Skram, who had been so completely forgotten.

[RMR to LAS, two unsent fragments*]

Munich, Continental Hôtel
February 20, 1918

Dear Lou,

Like a sleepwalker I went into Jaffe's a few days ago and headed straight for your little book, even though it was lying inconspicuously among many things with its title downward.

Since then I have read the *Three Letters* again and again, and they are still important and relevant to me, just as they were back then in Paris: as if at any moment I could instate in myself in all three stages of growing up and at each one of them, the rest of my life notwithstanding, be receptive. But this time, even more clearly than before, I find myself wanting you to treat the same material for my own present age and for each subsequent one. For this imagining oneself a child and young boy, however strongly it may bring the issue to the fore, also seriously limits it: for it cannot make the experience of death weigh equally alongside the experience of love. In this regard the remark about the plant's fruit and its twofold (white and black) birth seemed to me this time especially provocative. Were you the first to observe this process in such a light?

. . . that a host of creatures which are born from seeds left exposed outside have *that* as their womb, that wide, excitable freeness, —how *at home in it* they must feel their whole lives long, since they do nothing but leap for joy in their mother's body, like little Saint John; for it is this very same space that conceived them and carried them through to full term, they never leave its security at all.

Until in the bird everything becomes a bit more apprehensive and cautious. His nest is already a little maternal womb lent to him by nature, which he only covers instead of fully containing. And suddenly, as if it were no longer safe enough outside, the wonderful maturing process withdraws wholly into the creature's darkness and emerges only at a later turn back into the world, which is then regarded as a *second* world by this creature that will never be fully weaned from the conditions of the earlier, more fervently inner one.

(Rivalry between Mother and World . . .)

---

*"Sent to me by Ruth and Dr. Sieber end of Nov. 1927": note written by LAS on the envelope in which she kept this unfinished letter from RMR along with the subsequent passage, contemporaneous with the letter, that he had copied from his pocket notebook.

[RMR to LAS in Göttingen]

Munich, Ainmillerstrasse 34 iv
January 13, 1919

My dear Lou,

Can I be sure you have this address that has been mine since last May? You can imagine what a drought there is inside me, since I went without writing you for both German and Russian Christmas: seeing you, talking with you, has been an absolute necessity for so long now, but picking up the pen is hard for me, and it is made even more difficult by this accumulation of postponed letters; and the blockage which these years of waiting in line have created in me has become even worse now, instead of changing at the war's end, as was my hope, into outflow and surge.

Recently I happened once more on the letter I had begun to write you about the *Letters to a Boy*, back then when in the bookstore here I had walked straight to your little book even though I could only see its back cover: I turned it over with a feeling of certainty, and behold: miraculously it was by you. Such surprises you have effected but rarely during these most recent years and the ones behind them. At that time (I was still at the Continental) I began immediately to write you, —now I find it again, a leaf turned yellow—, and I don't have the heart to go on with it. Dear, dear Lou, how completely I am without composure, my inmost being has withdrawn and erected safeguards and gives out nothing, and my desire not to admit anything from outside grew so extreme that finally neither the War nor even the purest and most innocent manifestation of Nature could work its effects on me. Never have I been so unreachable by the wind blowing through from space, by trees, by the nightly stars; ever since I was forced to stare at all this out of the evil costume of the infantryman's tunic, it has retained a quality of estrangement, that non-relatedness I forced upon it back then in order not to ruin it for me. Awareness of this made actually spending the summer of 1918 in some familiar place impossible: i.e., my apartment here was new, I planned to become its resident, but that was really only a pretext for the sentence of immobility to which I had inwardly condemned myself. During the first days of the revolution, perhaps indeed only on its first morning, I thought that I'd been stirred out of inaction; and even if I weren't more mobile in any actual direction, I still felt moved as a whole, in one piece as it were, toward some sort of future! But the storm was not there, and thus it became obvious that one had no right to give up one's private future for a collective one—to which, so it seems, no one was compelled by pure impulse anyway. Now one sits yet again and singles out one's own existence and ponders it and plans it and holds it up against the murky background. And everything one was lies in the past—when one begins to count, six years back and farther. How this disaster has squandered us!

Imagine: I have a studio apartment, a few pieces of my own dear furniture, a second growth of books, —a complete household. Only it's not really Munich at all; but perhaps someday, someplace or other, I'll possess the calm to erect it around myself as something whole and coherent. But where? And when? —I desperately need some close-fitting sense of place—instead of all these approximations, this constantly adjusting to what never quite precisely and suitably fits my needs. The expanse of space I left unfilled in my time and employment here was filled many times over with people whom the great vacuum of Munich's streets was only too happy to squeeze into its cracks and interstices. Only with the beginning of the new year, which at least helps bring things to a close, have I resolved to be more energetic in refusing dates and appointments, —even if only to catch up on at least a hundred letters and a few long

[*half-page gap in the text*]

star falling without haste, beneficent and intense, through night-space and my own innermost being simultaneously—. These would be the two experiences that, along with the experience I had leaning against a tree at Duino, would come together like a first design for *inner* being. (As yet tentatively.)

Greetings to all, your husband, your dear room which in my imagination I always set before my own as the example from which it would have to learn ——— well, what else but this: to be both space and inner space!

Will you write some time?

Rainer.

From the pocket notebook, following the entry titled "An Experience":

"Later he thought he could remember certain moments in which the strength of this moment already gestated as in the seed. He thought back to the hour in that other southern garden [*in the margin*: Capri] when a bird's call sounded outside him and deep within him in perfect simultaneity—so that it did not break off, as it were, at his body's boundary, but merged both sides into an uninterrupted space in which, mysteriously sheltered, there dwelt only a single region of purest, deepest consciousness. With that he closed his eyes, so as not to be dissuaded of so all-inclusive an experience by the external contour of his body; and the infinite passed over into him from all sides so trustingly that he could believe he felt within his breast the gentle composure of the stars which one by one had been appearing.

"He also remembered the times when, leaning against a fence and similarly disposed, he would grow aware of the star-filled nocturnal sky through the gentle branches of an olive tree: and how then the universe would look back at him face-like inside this mask—; or how, if he but submitted to it long enough, it would be absorbed so perfectly in the clear solution of his heart that the savor of creation would be dispersed throughout his being. He thought it possible that such moments of ecstasy might be found as far back as his heavy childhood; he had only to recall the passion that always seized him whenever he had to venture out into the storm—how, striding across the wide plains, moved to his inmost core, he would break through the wall of wind that perpetually rebuilt itself before him—or how, standing at a ship's prow, his eyes closed, he would let himself be borne through thick distances that closed even more tightly behind him. But even if from his earliest days such things as the elemental onrush of air, the pure and infinitely varied conduct of water, the sense of the heroic in the march of clouds, had moved him beyond all measure (or better, since he could never comprehend them in human terms, had confronted his soul like Fate)—it could not escape him that now, with these last influences, he had been delivered over totally to such relationships. Something whose function was to keep things gently separate maintained between him and people a pure, almost luminous interspace, and though individual elements might reach through it from one side to the other, it soaked up every relationship and, saturated with it, obscured like thick mist figure from figure. He still did not know how far the others had any impression of his separateness and seclusion. As for himself, this lent him for the first time a certain freedom vis-à-vis people, —the small beginning of poverty by which he was lighter gave him among those bound to one another in hope and worry, in life and death, a mobility that was uniquely his own. He felt the temptation to hold his lightness out toward their burdenedness, even though he realized that he would be deceiving them in this, since they could not know that he (unlike the hero) had arrived at his kind of overcoming not by fighting through all their bonds and commitments, not in the heavy air of their hearts, but outside, in a spaciousness so little furnished for human comfort that they would call it only "the void." Perhaps all he could turn to them with was his simplicity; it was left for him to speak to them of joy whenever he found them too much ensnared in the contraries of happiness, perhaps also to share with them some of the particulars from his dealings with Nature, things they overlooked or only attended to in passing."

[LAS to RMR in Munich]

Göttingen, January 16, 1919

Dear Rainer,

Your letter entered my life during a moment of death, while I was holding my little dead Druzhok in my lap. (Isn't it strange: you here during Schimmel's illness and death, and now after all these years here again; you and I together in Meiningen when Lotte-Moppelchen fell ill, and then rushing home to find her dead.)

Ah, Rainer, it was such a help. And will continue helping, and I need such help so very badly, for it is my dear little Solace who lies here dead. It was he who bore me through the war on his small white shoulders so that I remained alive.

(Fit as a fiddle his entire life, he was suddenly struck last evening by tetanus-like seizures, and then at nine o'clock this morning—was murdered by them, I want to say, since in the intervals between them (shorter and shorter) he would become perfectly fit again, finally taking his leave with an inner intensity and depth of awareness that was incredible, incredible, incredible.

How much forbearance and love you showed back then in the face of his youthful transgressions!)

Rainer, so many times I've wanted to write you. It seemed to me that we should see and talk to each other before it will be too late. All these months you have been so intensely present to me, and in the way you always are; especially as regards my writing, which during the last three years has suddenly become, along with my professional work, as important to me as it was in my early youth. And then came a wish: from among the books (eight by now) that are kept in a safe-deposit box, to send you the one that rightly belongs to you: *Rodinka*, many pages long, admittedly, but at least neatly typewritten. When I read it again (read it to Ilse, who is in Bonn now), I still felt close to it; but even that feeling will not last forever, and once it's gone I'll no longer be able to send it.

At two places in the passage from your pocket-book I almost cried out in a burst of agreement. But my eyes and my soul are so mist-shrouded today, that I can't bring myself to verbalize it or write it down. So I can only thank you today,— so much, so much!

Where exactly is Ainmüllerstrasse? Is it an area I know?

Be careful about Ellen. There is something not right about the way she laughs. I could only explain it in person—and why, for all that, I still feel attached to her. But try not to poetize her.

Dear, dear Rainer, that today I should suddenly see you again! That I can greet you! And my husband (who is very, very old now and yet not at all the typical "old gentleman" but a character uniquely his own) also greets you, —from the wind blowing in the garden where he is digging a grave, deep and dry and lined with roof tiles and arched over by them like a treasure chest.

Lou.

[RMR to LAS in Göttingen]

Munich, Ainmillerstrasse 34 iv
January 21, 1919

My dear Lou,

Given the sluggish pace of my correspondence, it was only thanks to a set of peculiar and stubborn exigencies (among them a visit to the pension in the "Fürstenhäuser" which I set foot in again for the first time since . . ."back then") that I was able to be with you more intimately during this hour of death. Your letter moved me to recall your boundless loyalty to this little friend. And now you are suffering through long days of grief—; and yet I know how you and only you are able to experience in such moments a certain intimate confiding.

To be privy to these small heart-planets as they move through their whole course and fulfill their orbits: is it not also to be initiated into one's own life? And even though these serene moons reflect for us only purest world-sun, it was perhaps (who can say?) their always averted other side that linked us to the unending life-space behind them.

How splendid that you have accomplished so much work and with such youthful vigor: eight books securely in your bank-safe!—

I am newly resolved now to sit at home and—excepting perhaps occasionally Kassner and two or three others—to see no one; so that I could indeed ask you now to send me *Rodinka.* I only hesitate when I think how much better it might be to have you read it to me (as you did to Ilse). For there have been so many occasions when it was urgent that we see each other, and yet always, because everything I took up was weighed down by ever so many inhibitions, the moment passed. Are you by chance thinking about coming to Munich?

Ainmillerstrasse you should know if you ever visited old Keyserling (I can't recall if you did). It is a side street of Leopoldstrasse, left, the third one past Georgen- and Franz Josefstrasse. The view from my workroom (a studio) extends across roofs above which in the middle distance the steeple and cupola of Saint Ursula rise: toward evening the whole scenery is apt to turn into a bit of Italianate pastiche, somewhat like those intarsia made of little marble pieces that tourists would bring back from Florence.

I see Ellen Delp very rarely and always with an instinctive sense of caution. She thrives, I think, on having things "turn out well," and for that reason cannot be quite trustworthy.

Thanks, Lou; this little epistolary closeness has helped me immensely.

Rainer.

Last night I finally translated the Lermontov poem I had copied into my pocket-book long ago:

Выхожу одинъ я на Дорогу:

When I step out alone onto the path
that winds through mists, gently shimmering;
I can see the Void and God whispering
and every star conversing with other stars.

Solemn miracle: quiescent Earth
suspended amid the heavens' majesty . . .
Ah, why then my melancholy mood?
Whence this expectancy? Whence this pain?

I have nothing to demand of life;

things past I don't regret:
let freedom and repose wrap me
in the oblivion of sleep.

But not the cold sleep in a grave.
For centuries I'd like to sleep and sleep
feeling every strength inside me
and in my calm breast the steady pace of breath.

And hearing day and night the sweet, fearless
voice sing to me that rises out of love,
and knowing how the solemn oak
keeps whispering, darkly turned my way.

Прощай!

[RMR to LAS in Göttingen; inscribed in a copy of Insel-Almanach for 1919]

[Munich, mid-January 1919]

Lou
(in time for the Russian New Year's at least!)
съ новымъ годомъ!

[LAS to RMR in Munich]

[Göttingen, February 4, 1919]

Dear Rainer,

—had started to write you at once about the Lermontov, also about that tremendously moving continuation in the Almanach of the passage from Spain (the original passage I remember vividly from listening to you read it, but not the continuation), but I want to leave all that aside, want only to answer your question: yes, I would like to try that, to be in Munich, if not just now, then sometime in March. Any time closer toward summer and I won't be able to leave here, but this year could conceivably be my last chance to travel to Munich. And so as I think about it: Two such age-old confidants as we are should be able to take that risk, —if then at assorted hours their individual paths converge, they can be sure that these meetings always take place purely of their own accord and at any time may take a different turn. This way, without in the least violating your freedom, I could enjoy a short stay where I feel most at home.

I'm not familiar with Osw. Spengler's book *The Decl. of the West*; should I read it? Or anything else you've read lately, just the title. Also—was Schuler's book ever published?

Auf Wiedersehn, Rainer: how odd that sounds to me; for my own deepest being tells me that I have always lived where you are, and have always seen you.

Lou.

And there were times when I was scarcely able to keep something most deeply experienced to myself alone—and yet, conveyed in a letter, in the language of the approximate, it couldn't reach you directly enough. Especially last spring.

[RMR to LAS in Göttingen]

Munich,
Ainmillerstrasse 34 iv
February 7, 1919

—by all means, dear Lou, if there exists the slightest chance that you could come in March, then the trip to Switzerland, which has become a constant preoccupation, could be kept on hold a while longer (perhaps April might bring it about) . . . I feel anyway as if my mind and mood could not yet tolerate the impetus from new impressions and changes, since for the last four years I've done nothing but stand and wait and grow inwardly stagnant. Behind closed doors that are truly sealed off this time from anything outside, I am trying to set my inner life in motion again, slowly, and restore it to innocence: for which task the Spengler is proving in part to be quite an advanced school-for-walking. You will see! I am still reading it, so I had another copy sent to you today special delivery: for I'm eager to know us both immersed in the very same thing.

Aside from Spengler, only Hamsun's *Growth of the Soil* has meant anything to me. Ruth was inspired by this book to hire on as a "maid" with a farmer in a village near Fischerhude, and now she sometimes writes, sweating and exhausted, a little word to assure me how much she relishes all this hardness, all this work in which one grasps things with one's hands, and how fully she is up to it, how she has always wished to find something exactly like it.

Now again, in the midst of writing, as so often these days, I am overwhelmed by the joy that you will be coming here, dear Lou: we need only consider sufficiently in advance the question of your dwellings, since I just now heard again that there is not a single room available anywhere. In my neighborhood there is really only Pension Elvira, where the Kaysslers always stay; but they scarcely ever have a vacancy. Would you consider Gartenheim, Ellen D[elp]'s lodging? It is easily the best and quietest pension in Munich, and Ellen might be able to use her influence to secure space there. Or would you rather not live in the same house with her?

Farewell for today.

Is there anything, tell me, that could begin my future—if in fact one still remains—more honestly and deeply than our reunion?

Rainer.

Schuler has not published anything; revising and polishing his lectures, I hear, is slow work-in-progress. I never see him.

[RMR to LAS, note from Munich to Göttingen,
mid-February 1919]

[LAS to RMR in Munich]

Göttingen, February 17, 1919

Rainer,—

The thick wonderful Spengler arrived the morning of my birthday, and this day which I have never observed before shall henceforth be remembered; I spent all of it reading, reading and nothing else, from its morning well into its night, and have continued ever since as if even today were birthday without end. Does one's heart not exult that such broad, deep minds still exist?—minds that can completely enwrap and undergird one's own and yet also permit the most intimate affiliations. I did of course have to leave the printed page again and again and get out into the open, where I could absorb in yet a different way what a hundred hasty notes could not retain. And that too was like a birthday gift: since it was the first time that I had actually managed to feel myself again in the landscape, which without Druzhok had become inaccessible to me, veiled and blocked off. Even now, without having finished the book, I am looking forward to reading it a second time, no doubt through different eyes, —but a little time will have to go by first. And how all these pleasures combine with the foretaste of seeing you! Just now your note arrived; what is to be done about a place to stay (and about heating it and eating)? —all of this further complicated by a nearly empty purse! Here we have practically gone hungry these years (I'm quite thin and gray), I even resorted to medical certificates for milk and butter; would bringing such things be useful there also? I don't like it at all that you are out looking for a place for me; it is the most miserable of all occupations, and any of the engagements which you are now refusing would seem all glitter and gaiety in comparison.

I am completely at a loss and can only hope that the Good Lord will show us favor of his own accord; just as we, on our part, love him even without requiring from him any assurance that he exists.

Hard to finish today, but otherwise I will begin again right where I started.

Dear Rainer, thank you, thank you!

Lou

Too bad I won't see Ruth in Munich this time. But how lovely and to my liking what she has undertaken: I can imagine her picture so vividly in this sturdy frame.

[RMR to LAS in Göttingen]

Munich, Ainmillerstr 34 IV
February 21, 1919

Of a sudden, Lou, I've come to believe that the Good Lord has already done his share—for in the interim an unusually large royalty draft has arrived from Insel, completely unexpected and undeserved. In these present circumstances it must, must, must mean that you are to be my guest here! It's true, Lou, I need to invent no ruse to persuade you of this reading of God's intentions!

I have in fact been wondering all along if I couldn't set up my bedroom here for you and move myself into the studio. But no—that just won't work. The more I think about it: it must be the Gartenheim, except that your room there would have to be considered strictly as an annex to my apartment, as my guest room.

For I already know from Ellen that you would have no objection to the Gartenheim. If one looks for a room just anywhere, so many things are sure to be unsatisfactory: going out to eat is now a torture—irksome and inconvenient and in the end disappointing. Board at the Gartenheim, on the contrary (judging from the few times I've tried it), is first-rate; and in addition Ellen constantly has her hands on the most wonderful "extras" that come from a farmwoman she's friends with. One eats at small tables, undisturbed, and the company is such that one may actually enjoy turning around occasionally for a brief chat if one happens to be in the mood for it. So all that's important now is that you do get a room; I asked Ellen yesterday to make sure of that for you. Considering the favor and fondness she enjoys at the Gartenheim, she will, I hope, succeed; she is going to write me at once how things stand.

And if then a small room does await you there, will not preparations be complete? When did you want to come? It would probably be wise to wait and see how the old parliament here holds out, so that you don't, on arrival, find the station at the center of gunfire, as was the case again the day before yesterday.

It's splendid that the Spengler came at just the right time: and indeed, it is quite the thing for a birthday! I am now in the final section, after having been sidetracked by Goethe's *Metamorphosis of Plants*, then by Charles Louis Philippe, and most recently by Blüher. (Do you know Hans Blüher's books? In his second, just-published volume of *The Role of the Erotic in Male Society* there are some wonderful things—: well, you will find it at my place.)

But by your coming you will bring me so much more than you will find here! The Spengler is the first thing in a long time to focus me and knit me together again—but not to the point yet of giving me back the *landscape*. That whole realm has still not become mine again, my circulation is still too weak to incorporate it—and perhaps for that to happen there will have to first be a change, a trip, in the end wholly different surroundings.

When you write back, I will read it also as a confirmation of your coming, dear Lou!

Rainer.

I almost forgot: I spent two long evenings this week in *Rodinka*, indescribably received in all of it. The childhood-chapter does not have quite the same power as the rest, it seems to me, but everything thereafter is full of life experienced and also *is* experience! Thank you.

[LAS to RMR in Munich, middle of March 1919, preceded by a short note]

[RMR to LAS in Göttingen]

Munich, Ainmillerstrasse 34 IV
March 19 [1919]

(my father's name-day, on which as a child I always went out for a walk with him in my new spring outfit—, at the cost of an enormous cold)

But quickly to what's most important:

When, yesterday, your letter arrived, I was just on my way to consult with Ellen D[elp]; she hears much more in her pension about the general circumstances than I do, since I scarcely ever see anyone. Our conclusion was:

You really should travel as soon as possible, perhaps on the 22nd or 23rd; whether a "general strike" on the 25th really will come about, no one seems to know; if the room at the Gartenheim is not vacant by then, I can certainly arrange for you to stay at the Marienbad for the first few days. But do telegraph your arrival time the moment you have scheduled it, so that a place may be reserved there. I have already spoken with the doorman. That would be the nearest *dépendance* in Ainmillerstrasse, the next and certainly more comfortable one being the Gartenheim.

Concerning your arrival: Ellen or I will be at the station; but one can only wait, I hear, at the main exit, as the platforms have all been barred.

But now the most frustrating news: visitors are allowed to remain, everyone tells me, no longer than two weeks; only for this period does one receive food coupons. Otherwise one must have official papers documenting the necessity for a longer stay. They are being very strict and precise about this, since they want to make moving to Munich as difficult as possible. Two weeks! That seems out of all proportion to your long trip—, but we who need not make this trip have it easy; we simply say: come! The rest will take care of itself.

That the fare at the Gartenheim is good and plentiful I was able to confirm again yesterday; this really should become a reinvigorating vacation for you.

What else? Two letters arrived: one from Helene Stöcker, the editor of *Die Neue Generation*, and another one today from Munich; I think they may expect you here.

Spengler lives in obscurity in Munich, had earlier, so I heard, taught mathematics as a professor at middle schools, —I've met one person who visited him (though it wasn't someone from Munich), and he was received rather gruffly and grudgingly, even though the man had invaded his place in a spirit of pure adulation.

Many many greetings also to your husband, and now on to our reunion.

Rainer.

My trip to Switzerland, for which I still lack the all-important official permit, would have to begin immediately after April 15.

After an almost three-day-long journey by LAS, RMR and LAS together in Munich from March 26 until June 2, 1919.

[LAS, Diary]

Monday [March 24] left early. Wednesday at night Munich. Ellen and Regina in my room, with flowers, eggs, milk and crackers. Flowers and letter from

Rainer. April 7: The deposed University at dinner. May 16: Rainer read the two elegies, discussion of the phall[ic hymns?]. April 27: Around noon Frau von Hattingberg here with the permit; at the same time Regina. Frau v. H. very gracious and beautiful. [Notations:] Regina Ullmann. About Regina's way of writing poetry. With Rainer at Walt Laurent's. About Mallarmé [and Rilke]. June 4: Telephone with Rainer, his passport business.

[RMR to LAS in Munich, card in letter envelope]

Tuesday [March 25, 1919]

Dear Lou,

When is your train scheduled to arrive? It appears that there is no way of finding out the hour, they say it's often late by five or six hours: I hope you won't have to endure that! Under these circumstances I did *not* go to the station, everyone advised against it. But I welcome you, with many, many greetings, from my bed, and tomorrow, mid-morning, you can tell me, I hope, that you arrived at the hotel without complications. Good night, Lou, how wonderful that you are here!

Rainer.

[RMR for LAS in Munich]*

I
I held myself too open, I forgot
that outside not just things exist and animals
fully at ease in themselves, whose eyes
reach from their lives' roundedness no differently

*This poem, probably written in November or December 1911 at Duino, was found among LAS's papers only in a copy by Rilke's hand from the time of this stay in Munich. Because she cut off the top part of the (folded) sheet, the upper two lines of the second sheet are also missing (though they might conceivably have been the *reason* she cut the page); they have been restored here from Rilke's pocket notebook.

than portraits do from frames; forgot that I
with all I did incessantly crammed
looks into myself: looks, opinion, curiosity.
Who knows: perhaps eyes take shape in space
and watch intently. Ah, only as it rushes down to you
does my face cease being on display, grows
into you and twines on darkly,
endlessly, into your sheltered heart.

II

As one puts a handkerchief before pent-in breath—
no: as one presses it against a wound
out of which the whole of life, in a single gush,
wants to stream, I held you to me: I saw
you turn red from me. How could anyone express
what took place between us? We made up for everything
there was never time for. I matured strangely
in every impulse of unperformed youth,
[and you, love, somehow had
wildest childhood over my heart].

III

Memory won't suffice here: from those moments
there must be layers of pure existence
on my being's floor, a precipitate
from that immensely overfilled solution.
For I don't *look back*; all that I am
stirs me because of you. I don't invent you
at sadly cooled-off places from which
you've gone away; even your not being there
is warm with you and more real and more
than a privation. Longing leads out too often
into vagueness. Why should I cast myself far,
when, for all I know, your influence falls on me,
gently, like moonlight on a window seat.

March 25, 1919

. . . . *Elegy**

Someday, at the end of the nightmare of knowing,
may I emerge singing praise and jubilation to assenting angels.
May I strike my heart's key clearly, and may none fail
because of slack, uncertain, or furious strings.
May the tears that stream down my face
make me more radiant: may my hidden weeping
bloom. How I will cherish you then, you grief-torn nights!
Had I only received you, inconsolable sisters,
on more abject knees, only buried myself with more abandon
in your loosened hair. How we waste our afflictions!
We study them, stare out beyond them into bleak continuance,
hoping to glimpse some end. Whereas they're really
seasons of us, our winter-
long foliage, meadows, ponds, innate landscape
where birds nest and animals live among the reeds.

High up there: doesn't half the sky arch
over the sadness in us, over disquieted nature?
Imagine you no longer walked through your thicket of grief,
saw the stars no longer through the more acrid boughs
of black pain-foliage, and that the magnifying moonlight
no longer displayed fate's ruins for you so supremely
that among them you felt like a bygone race?
Smiles would also exist no longer, the consuming smiles of those
you lost to the other side—, with how little force,
as they were wafting past you, did they purely enter your grief.
(Almost like the girl who has just said yes to the suitor
who for weeks has been urging her, and she brings him, startled,
to the garden gate, and the man, jubilant and unwillingly
takes his leave: then, amid this newer parting, a step disturbs her,
and she waits and stands: her glance in all its fullness
meets utterly the stranger's, her virgin's glance
which infinitely grasps him, the outsider who was meant for her,

*The Tenth Duino Elegy (in its original form), followed by the Sixth and the Fourth.

the wandering other, outside, eternally meant for her.
Steps fading, he walks by.) Thus you always lost.
Not like someone who possesses: like someone dying,
leaning forward into the moist oncoming breeze of a March night,
Ah, and losing spring to the throats of birds.

. . . . *Elegy*

(Hero Elegy)

O fig tree, how long I've pondered you—
the way you almost skip flowering completely
and release, unheralded, your pure secret
into the sprigs of fruit already poised to ripen.
Like a fountain's pipe, your bent boughs drive the sap
downward and up: and it leaps from sleep, almost
without waking, into the joy of its sweetest achievement.
Like the god into the swan—

But we, for our part, linger,
ah, flowering flatters us; the belated inner place
that is our culminating fruit we enter spent, betrayed.
Only a few feel the sap of action rise so strongly
that they're stationed and glowing in their heart's fullness
when the allure of flowering caresses their eyelids,
touches their lips' youthfulness, like soft nocturnal air—
heroes perhaps, and those destined to leave early,
whose veins gardener Death twists in a different fashion.
These plunge on, in advance of their own smiles,
the way those teams of chargers precede the conquering
kings in the gentle bas-reliefs at Karnak.
Oddly, the hero resembles the youthful dead. Permanence
does not concern him. Ascent is his existence; time and again
he annuls himself and enters the changed constellation
of his unchanging danger. Few would find him there. But Fate,
which wraps us in mute obscurity, grows ecstatic
and sings him into the storms of his tumultuous world.

I hear no one like him. But suddenly I'm pierced
by his darkened music, borne swiftly by the rush of air.
Then how gladly I would hide from that longing! If only,
oh if only I were a boy with the unknown yet before me
as I sat propped on my future's arms, reading about *Samson*,
how his mother bore nothing at first, then—everything.
(Mothers of Heroes)

(Fragment:)
Even as the hero stormed through love's arbors,
each heartbeat meant for him bore him upward and on, —until,
turned away already, he stood at the end of the smiles:
someone new.

From one of the *Elegies*/
(written in Autumn 1915)

O trees of life, how far off is winter?
We're in disarray. Our minds don't commune
like those of migratory birds. Left behind and late,
we force ourselves abruptly on winds
and fall, exhausted, on indifferent waters.
Blooming makes us think: fading.
And somewhere out there lions still roam, oblivious,
in all their splendor, to any weakness.

We, though, even when intent on one thing wholly,
already feel the cost exacted by some other.
Conflict is our next of kin. Aren't lovers always
reaching boundaries, each in the other,
despite the promise of vastness, royal hunting, home?
Then: for an instant's virtuoso sketch
a ground of contrast is prepared, laboriously,
so we can see it; for they're very clear
with us. We don't know our feeling's contour,
only what shapes it from outside.

Who hasn't sat anxiously before his heart's curtain?
It rose: the scenery for *Parting.*
Easy to understand. The familiar garden,
swaying slightly: then—the dancer.
Not *him.* Enough! However light his entrance,
he's in disguise and turns into a burgher
who enters his kitchen to reach his living room.
I loath watching these half-filled masks;
give me the puppet. At least it's real. I can take
the hollow body and the wire and the face
that is pure surface. Right here. I'm out in front.
Even when the lights go out, even when someone
says to me: "It's over—," even when from the stage
a gray gust of emptiness drifts toward me,
even when not one silent ancestor
sits beside me anymore—not a woman, not even
the boy with the brown squint-eye:
I'll sit here anyway. One can always watch.

Aren't I right? You, father, for whom life
turned so bitter when you tasted mine—
that first murky influx of what would feed my drives—
who kept on sampling it as I grew older, and,
intrigued by the aftertaste of so strange a future,
tried looking through my vague upward gaze,—
you, father, who since your death have been here
often in my hope, far inside me, afraid,
forfeiting that equanimity the dead possess, whole
kingdoms of equanimity, for my bit of fate—
Aren't I right? And you women—aren't I right?—
who loved me for that small hesitating
love for you I always veered from,
because I felt the realm in your faces, even
as I loved it, changing into worldspace
where you were absent . . . : what if I do choose
to wait in front of the puppet stage—no,
to stare with so much force that finally, to counteract
my stare, an Angel will arrive here as an actor,

and jolt life into these hard husks.
Angel and Puppet: then, finally, the play begins.
Then what we keep apart, simply by our
presence here, conjoins. Then from the separate
seasons of our life that one great wheel
of transformation arises. Above us, beyond us,
the Angel plays.
The dying—surely *they*
must guess how full of pretext
is all that we achieve here. Nothing
is what it is. O childhood hours,
when behind each shape there was more
than mere past, and before us—not the future.
True, we were growing, and sometimes we spurred ourselves
to grow up faster, half for the sake of those who
had nothing left but their grown-up-ness.
And yet, off alone, we were happy
with what stayed the same, as we stood there
in the space between world and plaything,
upon a spot which, from the first beginning,
had been established for pure event.
Who shows a child just as he is? Who places him
in a constellation and hands him the measure
of distance and interval? Who makes a child's death
out of gray bread that hardens, —or leaves it
in his round mouth like the core
of a beautiful apple? . . . . Murderers are
easily understood. But this: one's death,
the whole reach of death, even before one's life is under way,—
to hold it gently and not feel anger:
is indescribable.

(Transcribed for you, in Munich, May 18, 1919.
R.)

Beginnings and Fragments / from the Material of the Elegies

Shall I once again have spring, once again
accept her earthly domain's close, assured future
as my own destiny? O fate more pure

———

But whoever is seized by the *zeal* of suffering, how little
does he remember how from time let go
to retrieve what is truly his? He, for whom a god
cuts up in little pieces the meal
that feeds him meagerly.

———

Unknowing before the heavens of my life
I stand in wonder. O the great stars.
The rising and the going down. How quiet.
As if I didn't exist. *Am* I part? Have I dismissed
the pure influence? Do high and low tide
alternate in my blood according to this order?
I will cast off all wishes, all other links,
accustom my heart to its remotest space. Better
it live in the terror of its stars than
seemingly protected, soothed be something near.

———

What, what could your smile force upon me
that Night did not freely give me

———

Assault me, music, with rhythmic fury,
lofty reproach, hurled up high before the heart
that didn't feel so surgingly, that spared itself. My heart: *there*
behold your glory. Can you almost always make do
with lesser pulsing? But the arches wait,
the uppermost, to be filled with thundering onrush.
Why do you long for the unknown loved one's withheld face,
has your craving not breath to blast echoing storms

from that angel's trumpet who announces the world's judgment:
then she too does not exist, is nowhere, will not be born,
she whose absence you parchingly endure.

You sing *me*, nightingale:
here, in my heart, this voice becomes pure force,
no longer evadable
Here, where we, pressing into one another, never *fail*
to find each other: here the angels begin
to sense each other, and through the deeper closeness
with sacred hastening endlessly approach

Ah, women, that you are here on earth, that you
move here among us, grief-filled,
no more watched over than we and yet able
to bless like the blessed.

Again and again, even though we know love's landscape
and the little churchyard with the lamenting names
and the terrible reticent gorge in which the others end:
again and again the two of us walk out together under
the ancient trees, lay ourselves down again and again
among the flowers, and face opposite the sky.

Look, I am living. On what? Neither childhood nor future
lessens. Superabundant existence
wells in my heart.

[RMR to LAS, letter from Munich to Höhenried,
June 3, 1919; only envelope survives]

[LAS, Diary, summarizing entry about what was to be hers and RMR's last time together]

When I think back on Munich, I see no one but Rainer. As if he were still standing there, as if I were still standing next to him as I did during those months.

[LAS, *Rainer Maria Rilke* (1928)]

No one was thinking about his moving to Switzerland: he was simply accepting an invitation for a few summer months. We agreed on a rendezvous in Germany for as early as October. And we talked about it even at the last moment, on the station platform, when I left [for Höhenried] shortly before his departure. His wife, a few friends were standing there with us. Everything seemed so propitious. But even as we spoke and joked and the train was slowly beginning to move, worries came over me, and a heavy word from one of his old Parisian letters cast its shadow across my thoughts:

> but I move the way the animals move
> when the hunting season is upon them.

June 11, 1919: RMR departs Munich for Switzerland for a planned reading in Zürich and a stay at Nyon on Lake Geneva as guest of the widowed Countess Mary Dobržensky. After a few days he travels again, to Bern, back to Zürich, Geneva, Sils-Baseglia, finally to Soglio, a town in the mountains near the Italian border, where he stays in a small hotel through August and September.

October 27–November 28, 1919: RMR's lecture tour: Zürich, St. Gall, Basel, Winterthur. In Zürich he meets Nanny Wunderly-Volkart ("Nike"), who will become his dearest friend and the person to whom he entrusts himself in the last weeks of his illness. Upon his return he rents two rooms in a pension in Locarno, where he lives alone from December 1919 through February 1920.

June 11–July 13, 1920: RMR resides in Venice (after June 22 as guest of Marie Taxis in the mezzanino *of the Palazzo Valmarana), where he had spent several months in 1912.*

August 1920: Back in Geneva, RMR seeks out the painter Baladine Klossowska ("Merline"); their friendship quickly develops into a passionate love relationship that will endure until RMR's death in December 1926.

End of October 1920–mid-May 1921: RMR briefly visits Paris (alone) before taking up residence (at first alone, then in the spring with Baladine) in Schloss Berg am Irchel, an eighteenth-century manor house near Zürich.

Late July 1921: RMR and Baladine, traveling together in search of a place for RMR, find available ("for sale or rent") the Château de Muzot, a tiny medieval castle-tower near Sierre (Valais). It will become RMR's last retreat, and Baladine, though she spends time with him there, will perpetually be frustrated in her attempts to join him there in something like a marriage.

February 9–February 23, 1922: RMR, alone in Muzot since November, experiences his great poetic breakthrough, writing all the remaining Elegies and both parts of the Sonnets to Orpheus *in a single two-week deluge of inspiration.*

December 1923: The symptoms of RMR's final illness become noticeable, then more pronounced, and he commences a back-and-forth existence between Muzot and the Sanatorium Valmont above Lake Geneva.

Beginning of January–August 18, 1925: RMR visits Paris for the last time.

December 29, 1926: RMR dies in Valmont at the age of fifty-one.

❖

February 12, 1921: LAS turns sixty, is fully absorbed in her psychoanalytical work—both her lay practice and her theoretical writings. Her correspondence with Freud continues.

End of 1921: LAS visits Freud for five weeks, staying in his house for the first time. There she meets his daughter, Anna, with whom she forms a lasting friendship.

October 4, 1930: Andreas dies in Göttingen at the age of eighty-four.

February 5, 1937: LAS dies in Göttingen at the age of seventy-five.

[LAS to RMR in Munich]

[Höhenried near Tutzing, June 6, 1919]

Dear Rainer,

Now it's over, and I won't see you anymore. I must always remind myself that the magic of our subterranean connection does remain with me, and that it would persist even if neither of us were to be aware of it. But I didn't tell you even once what it meant to me to feel such connectedness enter my bright day, such hour-by-hour reality of knowing you were only a few streets away. When we went to the dance-recital that morning I was so close to being able to say it, and yet even then I *could not.*

May these last days in Munich not roll away from you too furiously, may all difficulties and whatever is sure to pile up at the end work out smoothly. Even so, you'll lose some time on my account, for Frau Purtscher's sake, and in getting *Rodinka* to Franz: but he can come and fetch it himself. I shall talk to Rosa in person after all, but I wanted anyway to write down her grandmother's exact address, and if she can still get the "sugar package" for me she should go ahead by all means. Here everyone is disappointed about your not coming,* and all send their warmest regards.

Прощай, Rainer, dearest, and спасибо эа все. As your gift you presented me with a piece of life, and I needed it more fervently than you can know.

Lou.

P.S.: The name of Baba's people is "Dittweiler," right? Friday morning. Tel. Tutzing 26.

*[*In the margin:*] Frau Heyseler's birthday is today, and she really did think you'd be the candles on her cake.

[LAS to RMR in Munich]

[Höhenried near Tutzing, June 7, 1919]

Dear Rainer!

I am ashamed of myself to be pestering you again as I did just yesterday, but surely if you were in my place you'd think no differently: it was too beautiful to see how much Frau Heyseler delighted in your telegram, —like a child, and equally so on behalf of her husband in Russia! Now: Sunday is Bernt's, her younger son's, birthday; and though she finally managed to purchase the *Cornet* somewhere, she couldn't muster the courage to ask you in Munich to inscribe your name or that of her son in the book. Wouldn't it be possible to write a little something on a piece of paper (smaller than the Insel pages) and send it to me by registered mail? Then I'll paste it in. The boy himself would charm you. He'll very likely someday be in the company of those for whom you, in the truest sense, came into this world; he is (along with the doe!) my every hour's joy. And so please do forgive me. To make the woman a present of this will be quite wonderful (in many ways I am just now really getting to know her).

Today only this!

Lou

[RMR to LAS in Höhenried]

[Munich, June 10, 1919]

Dear Lou,

Here is my little rhyme for Bernt Heyseler; I wrote it just now as the next-to-last thing before going to bed; the last is thinking of you: of the fact that before long you will be staying here for a few days (Rosa is anticipating this with the best intentions), —that the weeks in Munich were as heartfelt for you as, in my own heart, I was hoping to make them; that you, despite all my inhibitions, were able to draw comfort from me, directly and unequivocally—: this latter gives me some confidence in my own strengths, for which there is often such questionable evidence. Thank you: for being here, and for being here that way, with so much closeness and presence and belief in me.

My final days here have been wicked: as if to test with all sorts of perverse labors whether I really did want to take this trip (I do). Unfortunately the last hours today have not been as leisurely as I would have wished; I did not find the time to go by the Dittweilers (that is their name, you spelled it correctly), something I didn't want to leave to Franz, since I wished to see Baba before departing: but there was no time left. Perhaps you can write them about the student not coming and make a reservation there for later. By the way, Baba is now officially yours; I paid the agreed-upon price for her, Frau May Purtscher had a hard time deciding, sends her best regards, and asks you to write her sometime how "Eli" is bearing up and accustoming herself to her new surroundings in Göttingen. (May Purtscher lives at Türkenstrasse 52, in the adjacent building—Studio-house in the courtyard right, third floor. All business matters with her have been settled.)

On Friday, Franz and Fräulein Richter were here with me at what was still a relatively quiet hour, —but ever since there's been little time that I can call my own; I had to give up on reading *The Devil's Grandmother*: that play and the two issues of *Imago* are in a large envelope on my desk where they await you. It's a pity I had to spend so much time working to leave the apartment in decent order—though the majority of it passed while I "stood in line" at all kinds of desks, doors, and counters—the Swiss consulate proved especially wearisome and time-consuming in this regard. I have never really been up to this sort of waiting, and now all these endless difficulties seem even more surly and insurmountable. Poor Be de Waard: on Saturday, when I tried to take her passport to her, after it had finally been obtained (and considerably in advance of mine), —I saw an ambulance at her door and she was just that moment being carried down and now lies, somewhat weakened, her patience strained but otherwise calm, in the Schwabingen hospital: men's section, room 114: I would have waited had there been the slightest prospect that she could travel on the next express train, —but there is no chance; in a week at the earliest, but even that isn't at all likely.

Now I have to get some sleep, for I'll need to be up at five o'clock tomorrow. Прощай: enjoy many good things where you now are and then back here and be always at home.

I would very much like for everyone in Höhenried to believe that my coming there has really only been postponed; especially since during so many moments I am almost there with you: on this late evening, for instance.

Rainer.

The next address is Lesezirkel Hottingen, Zürich; then I hope quite soon: Nyon, Villa Ermitage. (c/o Countess Mary Dobržensky.)

[RMR to LAS, presumably from Bern, received in Höhenried July 14, 1919]

[LAS to RMR, letter from Höhenried to Zürich, middle of July 1919]

[RMR to LAS in Göttingen]

Zürich, Baur au Lac
July 20, 1919

My dear Lou,

If these lines, these few hasty words, find you already in Göttingen, then may they welcome you home.

Your letter reached me very late, since it first went to Bern, from which I had just departed, and then had to turn around and come here.

First the matter of Franz above all: nothing of course could more please me than for Franz and Lotte [Richter] to take over my place; I hope that by now they have already moved in and not for too short a time. As far as the apartment itself is concerned, it will actually be an advantage to have someone live in it and for it not to be occupied by strangers. Unfortunately I forgot to write down Rosa's address, but presumably you will have had it and therefore were able to notify her quickly. I relied on Else Hotop as an intermediary: she was to keep a few keys in Rosa's absence so that she could send me things I might unexpectedly require. But now Else, after a falling-out with her parents, has left (which was not all that unexpected), and I am not sure how often she will get to Munich; she is living with the Seilings in Söcking (Starnberg), so far as I know.

Dear Lou: I won't start a long story today; that will come later. You read "Baur au Lac" and can well imagine that this doesn't mean I've settled into a really restful place; on the contrary, I've been on my feet this whole time. Nyon, offered with the friendliest of gestures, proved on the very first day, even by the second hour, to be the wrong place—at least for now. Later, should there be fewer visitors and the Countess D[obrženský] be alone, it might be more feasible. And so I went from spot to spot, to Geneva, to Bern: where, through Swiss connections, I was granted fourteen truly beautiful days that I absorbed into an admittedly still quite irregular inner life. It is not an easy matter to readjust to life lived in the open, and the worst confusions that result from this change tend to be purely physical. The idea of taking a short cure (based on diet and sun baths) at Dr. Bircher-Benner's brought me back to the not very welcome Zürich; but now, after an examination and a subsequent consultation, it appears that I should go from here to the Engadine (because after five years of having been closed off inside, the regimen of a sanatorium might be unnecessarily oppressive for me). My first destination is Sils (Baseglia), so that I can go through *Malte Laurids* with its Danish translator, a woman who has already sent me the most beautiful flowers from the high alpine meadows there; but my stay is only to be for a few days. In the Bergallon, on the terraces that slope down from Maloja toward Italy, I hope to come upon some place that seems so perfect that it will be as though I had found it neither by plan nor accident. Then from there I will write you in the way you deserve.

My first letter to Marthe (from Nyon to her old address in Paris) came back undeliverable. But of course that could not be the end of it. Now random chance has brought here to me one of her closest friends, a young Parisian painter—: she is doing well, and, imagine, in a few weeks she is coming to Tessin, to see friends who have invited her to stay several months.

By now little Baba will have grown well acquainted with her new home. Give her my regards! Have rich summer days!

Rainer.

[LAS to RMR, letter from Laubach (Hesse) to Zürich, August 26, 1919]

[RMR to LAS in Göttingen]

at present Locarno (Tessin) Switzerland
January 16, 1920

Dear, dear Lou, if it is possible let me hear from you again, —it's been a long time since August 26—, now you'll always have my address so that what comes from you won't have to take the roundabout way through Zürich, —mail from Germany being so excruciatingly slow as it is.

Christmas, New Year's, Russian Christmas: I have thought about you often. How are things with you?

And myself? I can't even begin to tell you now—perhaps later, in person. You'll notice that I am still Swiss, too cowardly to come back to the old gloom and doom. Several times since November I was close to returning—now because of my difficulties with my German money, now for other reasons. But again and again I managed to delay, and now I am hoping to hold out on Swiss soil throughout the two winter months of February and March, and then return with early spring. If only it were not Munich! How weary I am of this homelessness, of this forever readapting to conditions half-agreeable or just barely so: for once now the fit needs to become *exact*. How dramatically I saw again in Soglio last summer the effect that good, genuinely intimate external circumstances can have on me: the small old library there, the garden, and overnight I was fitted snugly into myself; yes, the rest was lacking, solitude, quiet, the benefit of a wholesome diet—; and yet, *how* happy even these few circumstances made me. I had originally intended to remain abroad during the winter only if a kind of "Soglio" could be found for these months also—. But I was drawn here by false expectations. Tessin's atmosphere is fatally akin to that of Capri: there's that same effusive German admiration and that certain softening of German emotions under the influence of a scenic "beauty," like bread-rolls in water. Many things here *are* lovely and unspoiled, even though all of it feels a bit cramped: it was wondrous to hear the pealing of the bells in the myriad country churches, beginning around Christmas and continuing into the new year up to Epiphany: all striking of the hour was absorbed into it: how often one would take the event seriously, begin to count—and then it was not an hour at all, it grew into the bells' pealing and out beyond into the pure play of the celestial. And the quiet in the deserted churches. I often sit in one of them all alone, and tears come, simply out of happiness for this intense inner quiet. Outside a scrawny village rooster will crow and the whole place becomes even quieter, fills with the quiet of a rustic holiness . . . Ah, dear Lou, might I be granted to fold this about my heart for half a year! Even during these few moments it transforms me, gives me back to myself, and one receives oneself strengthened and intensified. Dejected at the thought of breaking off.

All through November I was among people; after my first evening of reading in Zürich, there followed a second one and then five more in St. Gallen, Lucerne, Basle, Bern, and Winterthur. Thus many new connections, some good and enduring. Each time I understood better how to do this, and the one at Winterthur I got just right, but that unfortunately was the last. I recited only a very few poems, filled the time (often *two* hours) with a *discours* adapted to the specific place and moment, through which a factual connection and a shared foundation was established for the individual poem, which then often stood among us with an exactitude that was startling and deeply moving even to me. A beautiful experiment, and that it could succeed with the Swiss, who are so difficult to penetrate, is evidence on its behalf.

When you last wrote, dear Lou, you spoke of Marthe: I have seen her three times! First we were together alone for three days in Bégnins above Nyon, then I found her, for a stretch of hours, again in Geneva, and then, for the last time, unexpectedly, in Zürich. That this is only an "episode" in my time in Switzerland! I had forgotten so many things; how little we had seen of one another during our last year; that she had lost her voice, so that I often didn't understand her! In general, I felt as if something had died out in her, she came from the *milieu* of her mother, whose poverty she once tried to describe to me; she started, broke off, said briefly: *c'est même pas laid, puisque ça n'est pas* . . . I did feel that spark of genius in her heart whenever she told me about things in her past: how *wonderfully* she told such stories, first about a circus and what she had experienced there—, no, I can't convey it in writing, you'll have to hear it directly from me. *Marthe*: everything still resonates in that name for me just as before, but it didn't go straight through to my heart again, even though her feelings were so strong and unequivocal, so childishly breathless and at the same time a bit older and more knowing than before.

Dear Lou, so write me! How is it in Göttingen? How is your husband getting along, and Baba, does she remember me a little? Have you been away at all? Several times I asked Rosa if you had not announced your arrival at Ainmiller-Strasse; the apartment has been vacated again, except for Rosa. — Did you read my suggestion for an experiment in *Insel-Schiff*, number 1? The second part doesn't really fit—Be [de Waard], with her pragmatist's severity, drew my attention to the fact that in it incompatible categories of experience are being brought to bear on one another, and I think that she is right. Nor can I really say that I expected from the original experiment a result that would extend into those spheres. Only because I can't at all imagine the experiment actually being performed did I feel free to suggest a certain direction in which it might be taken. But that path, no doubt, leads to the realm of the purely inaccessible, and Be says quite rightly that none of our wishes actually desires such attainment anyway. But the experiment itself! Koelsch, with whom I've had many enjoyable conversations, takes it very seriously and expects from it who knows how many discoveries.

Are you reading his new book?

And aside from it, what have you picked out for your reading? Kassner? And: the Aksakovs' family chronicle. (How wonderful it is!) What has come of your negotiations with the people at Musarion? I took it upon myself once to write [Johannes von] Guenther concerning the matter of Prince Alexander Hohenlohe (whom I visit whenever I am in Zürich); they have taken over his writings from his previous publisher without giving him a contract, without having even the least discussion with him about business matters, in short, behaving not exactly in a manner that would be of help in my laborious little effort to build up trust with them. I wrote G[uenther] a long, urgent letter, requesting a reply, which never came.

Is Ilse [Erdmann] in Laubach? (By the way: your stay in the Laubach château, where you wrote so happily: might something similar be arranged for me?)

And Ellen: has she drawn yet again on our "extraordinarily close relationship" to pass on to you some better understanding of me? How *does* she get her information! She wrote me around Christmas—, back then when everyone in Munich thought I would be returning (there were even claims that I had been "seen," writes Kassner angrily). He sits in Oberstdorf, not exactly by choice, and laments the "quality" that has now finally appeared, from among so many, as Austria's own: homelessness.

Прощай, dear; turn your thoughts toward me, write!
и всего хорошаго.

Rainer.

[LAS to RMR, letter from Göttingen to Locarno,
around January 25, 1920]

[RMR to LAS in Göttingen]

[Locarno,] January 28, 1920

[A note on the cover of a copy of *Inselschiff* for October 1919 reads: "Page 14," where the following words are written above the title of Rilke's essay "Primal Sound":]

Lou!

At the same time as your letter, a few copies of this issue also arrived!

[RMR to LAS in Göttingen]

Schloss Berg am Irchel
Canton of Zürich
Switzerland
Last day of December, 1920

Dear Lou,

This time between the two Christmases (with the Russian one now approaching) mustn't pass without our having reached each other again more demonstrably—, first of all there are questions: where are you now? When, during this past year, were you in Munich and Höhenried—? And *I* failed to arrive; and Rosa, even though I seldom hear from her, must have behaved rudely, I fear, toward those I love most—, word has it that she is getting married very soon, and I'll breathe a sigh of relief to be rid of her. The apartment on Ainmillerstr. has been sublet to a Dr. Feist (I don't know him personally) who has stayed on there without ever knowing when I would return—for until the beginning of October, from month to month, even from week to week, I constantly thought I was on the verge of returning . . . , seeing no other way out and yet deep down filled with a voice warning me not to come back and with a kind of determination to keep myself in Switzerland at any cost since I had not yet received that peace which had been the sole reason for my journeying here. To continue my life in Munich seemed futile to me—, it was no different for me than a time of war and felt in so many ways unusable. Beyond that, Lautschin was waiting for me; I had seen Princess Taxis in Venice toward the end of summer, it had been agreed that I should live in a small house in the park, separate from the château—, but the closer the time came to implement this, the more uncertain I became about finding peace and undisturbed seclusion in Czechoslovakia, especially on a princely estate where no day passes without complications that the proprietors themselves would be the last to know how to prevent. Yes: Venice: it was my first contact with the days before; I was there for five weeks, resided, after the departure of the Prince and Princess T[axis], as I had years ago, alone in the beautiful *mezzanino,* was served exactly as before by my Gigia with her exuberant rushing about, and was received above at the Valmaranas with exactly the same friendship and indeed familial warmth as back in the days of 1912. That was wonderful, —but my desire to find everything unchanged, as unchanged as possible, was fulfilled so literally that I perpetually found myself standing at the edge, experiencing across the unspeakable years *pure* repetition, the *yet again,* and in the most uncanny manner: for while circumstances were constantly *appealing* to me as still the same as before, my heart, whose stagnation and arrestedness during the war years had turned "being unchanged" into *its* utmost and intensest attribute—, kept taking all this sameness in the old spirit: and when it did I would feel setting in that sense of *nothing but repetition,* which filled me almost with dread if I but glimpsed it in the distance. When, to make matters worse, I learned that Eleonora Duse had arrived, ill, to look for a place in Venice, the fact that even *this* was now to repeat itself seemed so horrible to me that in one day's time I fled from it and traveled back to Switzerland!

How different Paris! For just think, Lou, *I was there*! Six days, end of October. Repetition was not even an issue. My heart, to be sure, encountered the old place there with *its* fractures, but the healing was accomplished in the first hour, and from then on the stream of the hundred thousand transformations, new and old, unheard of and unnamable, rushed through the great circulatory system of consciousness restored at last. What days! It was autumn, the sky was suffused with that light cast by Parisian splendor, which heightens this season of nature with the season of a city that long ago *became* nature: what profusions in the light, what penetrability of objects, which allow the atmosphere to swing and vibrate through them and then pass this vibrating on; what unison of object and opposite, of nearness and profundity of the world, —what newness in the mornings, what age in the waters, what tenderness and fullness in the wind, even though it comes blowing through streets. And these streets: oh they had not lost anything, nothing had been suppressed, disfigured, diminished, or selectively rearranged—: they had retained their old completeness, their flow, their ceaseless activity, their invention at play everywhere and in no place failing. People walked toward me: I recognized them, one and the other, as those whom I had encountered at the same spots, for example on the *rue de Seine*, so many years ago: they had survived. One of them was wearing the same cravat. I recognized the merchants in the stores, barely any older—, the women selling newspapers in their kiosks, —even the blind man on the Pont du Carrousel, about whose life I had been so concerned back in the winter of 1902—, *he* stood there, rain-soaked and gray, at his spot: I can't tell you how strongly at this moment the joy of healing flooded through me and rose beyond me, —only then did I understand that nothing had been lost, and that continuing would be possible, in spite of these deep interruptions in my heart. —The books in the *bouquinistes'* boxes were still the same books, small items I recognized, specific ones, in the display windows of the antique dealers, and where a small, less dusty circle revealed the place from which something had been removed, I thought I could surmise *what* had stood there. There was a feeling in my heart that needed no sentiments. An emotion that could scarcely be taken up, so perfect was it in itself, so untouchable: instead one stood continually at the entrance to this first heaven that was filled with its haleness, —it was Malte's Paris in all its aspects, and now at last it seemed to recompense me fully for all that I had been forced to bear on its account, —now it bore me, I scarcely made the movements of a swimmer, the element bore me and spared my rapt volition all expense. —You can imagine that I sought no one out, not even Marthe. No place in my being was untouched, contact was absolute, I was wedded everywhere, and this being received and taken in from the first moment was so incredible that it would have cost me no effort to leave again after an hour: I was already fulfilled and assured of the whole inexhaustible reconciliation. In such a state six days were an incomprehensible abundance, especially with all of them lit by that same autumn splendor. Even the moon, with which my relationship has always been uncertain: I could swear that throughout the course of all those nights it remained full and round, high up in the skies until the dawn's paleness passed it on, dissolved, into the radiance of the sun.

And now imagine: scarcely had this wondrous experience returned me to myself, to my widest awareness—, when the next favor, for years hoped for and now all the more essential, was to be granted: this small old château Berg was offered to me, to *me alone*, as a retreat this winter, and it was so completely ready and prepared for *my* special uses that after the second day of being here I didn't have to change or rearrange anything nor say even the slightest word to make my wishes clear to the reticent housekeeper. Suddenly, much as with Duino, my world and I were solitary and in agreement (though at Duino a long period of acquaintanceship and mutual adjustment had first been necessary), something that I'd always sought but that in recent years had become the single most necessary thing, a need felt all the more urgently since the convulsed and adulterated world scarcely seemed able to offer any longer such remoteness and stillness anywhere. Berg, far away from all train connections, is difficult to reach, and now it has been cut off even further by a strict quarantine imposed to prevent the spread of hoof-and-mouth disease. I myself have for many weeks not been allowed to leave the area of the park; but every restriction of this sort only fortifies my shelter and safety.

Dear Lou, I won't go on today telling you about everything, about the region, about the park (its fountain, the measure of my quiet, will have been my only companion for this winter!), the old sturdy little château and my beautiful rooms in it—, or else this letter will grow and grow beyond all measure. In comparison to all you *didn't* know about me, now suddenly you know so much that this may well suffice. Now it's your turn to let me read the most important things about you—, how are things with the two of you, with your husband—, with little Baba (—did you find her the March bridegroom you were looking for in Munich?).

You gave me just now a dear present for Christmas. I received several issues of *Litterarisches Echo* in the mail, read your essay on Bonsels, thought I had seen both books (*Indienfahrt* and *Menschenwege*) in a bookcase here—, found them and spent my evenings reading them—, engrossed, completely amazed yet deep down on easy terms with them. Several individual passages in *Menschenwege* mean more to me than *Indienfahrt*—, what poise to seize on pure life in the midst of all this confusion and look into its face or into the lines of its hand. Who is this man?! And about Hermann Keyserling's foundation I hear contradictory news; were you in Darmstadt, is something taking shape there that could be of interest to us, or that would at least welcome our occasional participation? —Rumor has it that Hermann Keyserling and his sister Léonie Ungern spent considerable time in Bökel with Hertha Koenig, but I don't have any more detailed news from her either about these Darmstadt ventures.

And now farewell for today, dear Lou. Have you made many new Freudian discoveries and written and published them . . . ? You know that Thankmar [von Münchhausen] started a publishing house together with his friend Dr.

Erich Lichtenstein (Lichtenstein Publishers in Jena): I heard about it several weeks ago, one of the few pieces of news that came my way from Germany when I received proof sheets of the beautiful poems by a young Baltic poet, Veronika Erdmann.

Please, write.

And I would so very much like to read you while my little tree is still with me; that should be until Epiphany! —Greetings to your husband, to all and everything that is part of *Loufried*, of which company, mentally stepping into my sandals for a while, I count myself a member!

Rainer.

[LAS to RMR at Schloss Berg]
Göttingen, January 5, 1921

Dear Rainer,

It will not have been my fault if the Three Kings arrive in advance of me and snatch the little tree away before I'm there with my reply: I've been hurrying to get to you since this morning, but your letter took six full days to make its way here. And just listen to how strangely and palpably I received it: having gone to sleep very late at night for a change, I had the early morning mail tossed to me in bed, —was reading, —was reading your letter and unbeknownst to me was already dreaming it: that you yourself were standing there, even though you were saying the same words as those written on the page, that you were *showing* me what you were writing, —showing me Paris until I saw it in all its distinct details, the end of October had materialized here just as vividly, and in that strange unceasing moonlight which *actually* existed, which I too was experiencing back then full of wonder, for I could have sworn that the moon against the sky "would never end." But at the same time that you were speaking to me so intimately, we were off together in the park of your Berg château, near the fountain, and this now is the strangest part of all: the park behind the château was not that park at all but a spacious garden into which, when you were a child, you would run very early in the morning, before your parents were awake, until you came to a kind of grotto with a water basin. And now you had come back to it, and you called it the "primal castle" [*Urschloss*] and said that not even all princes and kings (referring to Duino and T[hurn] and T[axis] and Lautschin in your letter) had been able to give you this refuge for your deepest needs, meaning this place within which one is taken back completely into what is deepest and most protected in order to be "born into the world," —and then you were pointing again to Paris as if to a picture. And when I awoke, with your letter in my hands, I was so filled with knowledge and joy through what you had said—as if one could find written there not just what is most important about this intervening time, but what is most important about *you*. For you are without a doubt the most symbolical person I know, and what you experience are ultimate things, key confirmations, for which the lax stuff of material existence only now and then pulls itself together with sufficient concentration to make them visible; that is why so often you find yourself unable to live. From early childhood on, life happened to you only as such a symbol; as early as back then even your mother did not suffice, and you longed for a deeper secret stillness from which you would emerge into plentitude. And to this day, in your alternating need for solitude and sense impressions, you are still struggling "to achieve childhood again": once more, completely, resurrection, work accomplished. Ah, you need worry about nothing, what is yours will happen to you, and at a time, I can absolutely assure you, when you are feeling helpless and perplexed, for it happens to you completely independent of your intentions, in signs and miracles. The way you experienced this return to Paris is a perfect example: it was *all* miracle and sign, and as such it required no temporal unfolding, those few days were from their outset abundance and overflowing, were in themselves consummation, completed at the instant of the event, whereas in Venice the personal demands made on you thwarted this; indeed it *had* to be utterly personal in your "recognizing again" [*Wiedererkennen*] those most particular instances of human kindness and persistence and imperfection, —and yet at the same time far removed from anything like real human interaction; it is incredible how the two experiences of "seeing again" [*Wiedersehen*] can be so closely akin and yet as dissimilar as horror and the uncanny are to bliss and being at home again in life. But also: that you can *find words* for such things! One might well ask what in all the world one is living for if not perhaps, just once, to experience something of this kind, and to experience it with such consciousness that it can find expression: but no doubt this scarcely ever happens, not even to those one calls the Blessed. And thus the pleasure you take in Bonsels comes to mind; for in spite of all his great abilities I've come to feel somehow that he is *not* blessed; his less accomplished books are the result not of an inability, but of his stumbling over himself, over his most banal personal feelings, and on such occasions slipping into the deepest kitsch, —since to hash these things out in books is an abuse of art no matter what (and of course the added dollop of kitsch has greatly enhanced his fame). His latest book, *Eros und die Evangelien,* is again not much good. *Your* copies of *Menschenwege* and *India* (the ones you loaned me) are being kept for you in Munich. I was there from February until the end of June, stayed with the Schönberners whenever I was not in Höhenried or at Frau Heyseler's beautiful farmhouse in the mountains above Rosenheim; but Frau Heyseler, unfortunately, is pathologically disturbed; you couldn't talk to her for long these days. I'd *very* much, terribly much, have liked to see Ruth; but the totally unvirtuous Rosa thwarted that with the most willful malice. Who would have thought that she who reminded me so vividly of my first wax doll could change so much that now, the moment one sees her, one is reminded of those oldest primers on morality with their warnings against the "devastations wrought by sensuality." That someone is actually going to take her off your hands by marrying her seems to me scarcely credible; is that the only way you can be rid of her? Marriage is also turning out to be a problem for dear virtuous Baba; first of all, I can't find her a husband whom I approve of; secondly, she is in her little heat every other month instead of twice a year. I didn't take her to Munich with me for fear of breaking my husband's heart; when I got back she (as he explained) had grown into a princess and was a lazy lump of fat; for instance, when it was too hot where she was lying in the sun, instead of simply moving to a cooler spot she would whistle very specifically for my husband (so he says) to come and push her chair into the shade. In little time I had her slimmed down and bouncing around again. For spring I'll probably go again through Munich—to Vienna: for years now I've felt the urgent need to be there due to everything coming from Freud, but haven't found a way to make the trip; now such an opportunity has arisen in the form of an invitation (I have no idea who arranged it) to visit Hilmstreitmühle near Vienna, a "welfare institution for working people" owned by a certain Frau Dr. Eugenie Schwarzwald. Until November I had several patients over quite a long period; among them a case you especially would have found interesting. (If only it weren't so rare that a Someone finds himself stranded here!) It's remarkable to see the interaction that almost every time sets in between these treatments and the rest of my work, which I always completely abandon and set aside; it's as if the one makes me thirst and hunger for the other; and so in the end it is the *practical person* who feels the need to do work as a physician; listening fully passive, helping fully active, and yet drawing the true healing drink from the ultimate spiritual sources, as *from those my twin activities hold in common.* In this, no doubt, there is a certain evening-out, a compensatory rectification that here and there protects one from the sense of exhaustion and emptiness that follows the outcome of that other kind of work. And probably *my* only means of compensation, since I have certainly never been up, as one tends to say, "to the demands of life": apparently I never quite got around to giving it a try, and only this cheeky slice of infantilism has kept me cheerful. Incidentally, I'd like to come back once more to the way you experienced things in Paris: if you imagine this as an ongoing, perpetual mode of living, you'll see that it's got everything we think of as divine consciousness, a timeless containing of everything, without "sentiments," as you write so tellingly, —for all that is within would also be the outside and would be borne by it, "sparing its rapt volition all expense"; when one has chosen a reclusive way of life, in the "château," in the primal womb [*Urschoss*], one is sustained by the strength that comes with having experienced this and with knowing it to be the true essence of all that exists. That there exists *one* person who has met with something like this provides sustenance for all the others! It warrants them, as the fact of Heaven vindicates the believer. Dear Rainer, how splendid that you are among us! I must close with this quick and fervent prayer.

Lou.

[RMR to LAS in Göttingen]

[*Letterhead:*] *Château de Muzot*
sur Sierre
Valais

September 10, 1921

My dear Lou,

It would be—has been for so long now!—time for a letter, but this won't become one, not yet, —today I just want to send you, as quickly as possible, a book* that during the past week has almost exclusively occupied me: it belongs emphatically, given the kind of book it is, among your store of materials, and will be so much more pertinent and provocative to you than to practically anyone else, that I can't wait to know it is in your hands.

You'll find enclosed here what "Koe." (Koelsch, that is) has written about it in *N[eue] Züricher Zeitung*: it may give you some inkling. The book then will doubtless surpass whatever expectation the review creates. As you can imagine, I myself was affected by it very strongly.

Apparently that organizing urge, which among the artistic powers is the most constant and indomitable, is summoned most urgently by two contrasting inner conditions: by the consciousness of overabundance, and by complete inner collapse—which will eventually, in turn, produce its own kind of overabundance. And how deeply innocent are all these events, all these "transgressions," brought about by a person's flight into a paradise of his own creation before he was expelled from it at the age of eight. And then the innocence of illness as well and how it creates out of itself its own means of deliverance: the case of Wölfli will help to provide further insight some day into the origins of creativity; it already reinforces a curious and apparently growing recognition that there are many symptoms of illness (as Morgenthaler "conjectures") which would need paradoxically to be *supported,* since they summon up the rhythm through which Nature attempts to recapture for itself what has become estranged from it and to weave it into the soothing music of a new harmony.

Enfin: read, read—

How is everything with you, with both of you? —did I see a new book announced recently?

I am in the Valais: do you remember the powerful impression it made on me last fall through its affinity with Spain and Provence? This time, over a longer period, I am experiencing it on its own terms (which does not make it any less astonishing) and from an old indigenous place in the landscape—such that suddenly I found myself living *inside* the picture, instead of standing receptively across from it. This turned out to be no small matter, especially during the hot days of this exaggerated summer (Valais being the hottest canton in Switzerland as it is!). I came here to see if this old *manoir* of Muzot could provide me with a refuge for the coming winter: but it is, I fear, too rugged for me; living in it is almost like standing in a heavy rusted suit of armor. And through the hard slits of the helmet one looks out into a defiantly heroic land. —In May, when my time in the château Berg had run out, I went to the area around Lausanne; at that very moment the Princess Taxis was passing through, and I missed by a hairbreadth traveling on with her! Then I came to Valais, meaning only to see it again one last time—, and here the opportunity presented itself to "try out" Muzot. And now it seems likely, if I don't dare stay here for the winter, that another "Berg-like" refuge in the canton of Aargau will be prepared for me—and with that yet another (the third!) Swiss winter. Because elsewhere, much as I searched, no place turned up that was removed and dependable enough for what I have in mind for myself.

And so now at last, Lou, you have a few bits of news again and know *where* to think of me and more or less: *how*.

The postcard of Muzot doesn't give the right impression: for one thing, the nearest village, Miège, is not as close as it looks; there is nothing in the vicinity except a small whitewashed St. Anne's chapel (not in the picture!). For another, there is no hint in the card of the colors in this magnificently variegated landscape, nor any suggestion of its *modelé*, —called forth by the indescribably rich, interactive light that creates events in all interstices and fills the distance from one thing to another with such singular tensions that they (trees, houses, crosses, chapels and towers) appear bound to each other with the same pure relatedness that to our eyes binds the individual stars into a constellation. As if space itself were being produced by the beneficent and intense distribution of things, —such is the effect in this valley, where one scarcely wants to believe that one is still in Switzerland. (This only to correct and augment the unconvincing card.)

And so farewell for today, dear Lou. Now this has inadvertently turned into eight pages after all, and so will have to go off with a later post—impossible to carry it down to Sierre before *déjeuner*!

Rainer.

P.S.: Were you in Göttingen all summer? Greetings to all and everything at *Lou-fried.*

*[*In the margin*:] The publisher, Bircher, sent me the original of one of W[ölfli]'s drawings; if I may keep it—I'm not sure this was his intent—, I'll send it to you at the next opportunity; but the reproductions do give a relatively accurate impression.

[LAS to RMR at Muzot]

Göttingen, September 22, 1921

Dear Rainer,

When your letter came I wanted to write quickly, the way one does when something long expected arrives, —but then you alluded to a subsequent letter that was already almost on its way, the real one that was about *you*, and then it was as if this one were just your luggage that had arrived in advance of you, and so for the time being I merely unpacked, i.e., I read and read and am still reading the book about W[ölfli] in Waldau. You see: to *interact* with such people, to learn how to view and understand them—how I long for this! Psychoanalysis, you know, may treat only those it regards as curable and thus as neurotics, and the only asylums it considers appropriate are Waldau and Zürich's Burghölzli (from which psychoanalysis once learned many things, back when Bleuler was still fully involved with it). These days Prinzhorn in Heidelberg would be a source (has been for several years now). What must have seized you so forcefully, I imagine, is the fact that the core compulsions of the creative artist clearly reappear in the schizophrenic—that in both of them, active and passive, seeing and shaping are incomprehensibly the same, creation is as little to be halted or held in abeyance as is revelation itself: for both still proceed as *one*, undivided, behind all that which, in the name of rationality, separates subject and reality into two different things. In W's case, where the role of consciousness is insufficiently developed, elements in a state of confusion get mixed into and interfere with the form-creating process; whereas the artist is bound more strictly to a deliberate content, and also by the ordering force of his—be they even his oldest, childhood-oldest—memories, which rise to the level of general relevance only as symbols, since they must not extinguish themselves in the unconscious for the sake of the artist's synthetic activity (which is why analysis can only lead the way into them, and then only proceed there alongside the individual person). This is the immensely moving, gripping thing about a psychotic: that he, though incurable himself, does *impart something* to us that goes even beyond us (if only we make the attempt, which has been under way for about a decade now, to *understand* him in his own dialect), that he lays bare for us things that no normal, healthy demeanor could ever lay bare: and such things are indescribably important, since beyond that which has been subjectively individualized it is an *objective reality* that is (as it were surreptitiously and from behind) being touched again. The way I have always imagined it (and psychoanalysis has for some time now been moving in a similar direction) is like this: in the psychotic as in the artist the circle closes anew—whereas in other people the individual and the whole, subject and object, stand facing opposite each other.

September 24: I was interrupted here, and now just want to pin a tail on this thing so that it can run off to fetch your follow-up letter, which I anticipate with such longing! The landscape alone, on the card and in your elaboration, doesn't give me nearly enough of *you*, no matter how strongly your pleasure in living there comes through. The book I recommended to Freud at once, in the strongest possible terms. This winter I'll see him, since I've been invited to his house—a stay that I'm looking forward to. Last summer I had a position in a sanatorium that works with psychoanalysis, but it proved a wretched disappointment. I hope it isn't like this everywhere. Then I was ravaged by a high fever (so thoroughly that afterward, in no time at all, my hair fell out, so that ever since I've been going about in little bonnets!). When I came home I saw Baba with three little black monsters hanging at her teats and sucking noisily: she looked proud and shamefaced at the same time. My husband, who felt himself the guilty party in this, had already written to me embarrassed: "please don't grow cold toward me and the doggy"; he looked after these four little darlings with grandfatherly care. Just now he sees me writing to you about his little misdeed and sends his most cordial greetings.

When will we have a chance to talk to each other? And will it be at all, ever? I *still do* tell you, often and at length, about everything essential in my life. And now also about Russia, new things again and again, as certain ideas are taking hold of me. This time, moreover, a very personal Russian grief is tearing my heart in pieces. Po6a, my last surviving brother, has returned from the Crimea, where he buried his youngest son who had died from wounds suffered in the war. He arrived in Petersburg after a journey of two and a half months with his wife and daughter. They now live in a few small rooms of his former country house on the small estate which meanwhile has become the property of his domestic servant. There he goes looking for mushrooms and berries with them to quiet their hunger (one pound of bread costs three thousand rubles).

Dear Rainer, I send greetings to you, from all, all, all my heart!

Lou.

You know, if one didn't die of old age, one would die of melancholy.

———

[RMR to LAS in Göttingen]

Château de Muzot
sur Sierre (Valais) Suisse
December 29, 1921

My dear Lou,

Nothing came of my "follow-up letter" back then: the distraction from all the uncertainties and instabilities of my existence was so strong and continuous up through the beginning of December that I lacked all calmness and quiet; for just when, thanks to the support of friends, everything had been arranged for my stay in this ancient Muzot, the plunge of the mark and its prolonged depression seemed to put the whole thing at risk again. Well, it has just barely, barely been possible to make arrangements, for the time being, for me to sit in my strong little tower; its shelter, its silence I am really just beginning these days *to make use of,* and my wish now is for nothing but a good seclusion that will be long and uninterrupted.

Though it may well come at the price of a certain immobility, one nevertheless does feel strongly here the well-being of a neutral territory and, to boot, the healing properties of this glorious landscape (which keeps reminding me of Spain and Provence). I have done everything I can to become rooted in it; and the old masonry walls within which I sit have played no small part in supporting this effort. The proportions of the study where I work and the little bedroom adjacent to it sometimes remind me, especially toward evening, of the upper rooms in Frau Quiet's Schmargendorf "Waldfrieden"! (I felt this immediately and still do, though it's difficult to put into words.) On this floor there is only one other small (empty) room, the so-called "chapel," with a stone-framed medieval door still completely unchanged, above which, in bold relief, there appears hewn out of the wall not, strangely enough, a cross, but the "swastika" with arms bent clockwise. About the place itself, in which I live alone now with a quiet housekeeper, there would be much to tell, and much about the landscape—, and then we would finally have arrived at me, and at that point it would behoove me to continue on and on in great detail. But it feels to me that this would have to be done *orally.* When I emerge again and return to Germany (and because of Ruth's engagement there is certain to be an occasion for this next year that will preclude delay), my first destination will be you, if this should coincide at all with days when you can have me.—

Above all, though, the quiet winter must have come and gone. If I am granted a long and uninterrupted one, perhaps I can progress a little farther than last year at Berg, —if not far enough to catch all the way up with myself, then *at least* far enough to see myself again walking on ahead of me in the space required for a deeper breath. The interruption of the war years has left me with an unbelievable inability to concentrate, which is why I can't manage without the help of this most literal self-isolation. More than ever all communication becomes the rival of what I want to accomplish, which is no doubt true of anyone who more and more has his mind set on *one thing* only, so that any giving, be it inward or external, is an expending of the very same thing, this *one* thing. A few days ago I was offered a dog: you can imagine what a temptation that was, especially since the secluded position of the house makes the presence of a watchdog almost advisable. But I felt at once that even this would result in much too much relationship, what with all the attention I would devote to such a housemate; every *life* that in some sense depends on me arouses in me an infinite obligation to do right by it, and then I always end up withdrawing painfully from the actual consequences of that obligation when I realize that they are using me up completely.

Are you in Vienna, dear Lou? Then greetings to Freud—; it's a pleasure to see that he's beginning to become a significant influence in France, which for so long preferred to ignore him. Not much comes my way from there except a word, now and then, from Gide; the only poetry I find truly astonishing is that of Paul Valéry, whose poem "*Le Cimetière marin*" I was able to translate with a degree of equivalence I scarcely thought possible between the two languages. When I've regained some assurance in my own work, I hope to have a try at his prose too; there is a glorious dialogue, "*Eupalinos*—" like all of Valéry's few works possessing a serenity, calm, and equanimity of expression that you too would fully appreciate. Paul Valéry comes from Mallarmé; about twenty-five years ago a remarkable essay appeared (*Introduction à la Méthode de Léonard de Vinci*), which he has now—in 1919—published again with an unusually beautiful introduction; but starting out from Mallarmé meant stopping and standing in silence after the first half step, *dans un silence d'art très-pur*, and this is what happened: Valéry fell silent and worked at mathematics. Only now, during the war, in 1915 or 1916, in a man of fifty, did the need for artistic expression arise again, so much the purer; and what has since come from him is of the greatest distinction and significance.

But enough, dear, dear Lou: please give me a small token of how you, both of you, are faring! And where are you? —What has become of Baba's little monsters?! My thoughts often turn toward you, as this is the time between the "two" Christmases—, the first and the Russian one. . . . That you *could* receive news from there: it seems almost unthinkable that what's over there still is life and still can express itself in words to us over here.

Have you seen any of the books by Skythen Publishers, who also put out a journal (in Russian and German)? Young Reinhold von Walter wrote me about the project back when it was started.

And Picard: have you seen his book *Der letzte Mensch* —and Regina's *Landstrasse* (with the amazing story "An Old Inn's Sign")? I'd love to see these two books reviewed by you, if you're not too involved with other things.

I am sending you my little "*préface*" to the drawings of young Klossowski, whose images so completely tell their story; I was pleased that I could do it using French ideas (for nothing in it has been translated in my mind!). But now farewell and on to a *good* 1922.

Rainer.

(Just now I read in *Litt. Echo* Ernst Heilbron's no doubt justified opinion of *Peter Brauer*, Hauptmann's new "tragicomedy." And then the poor hexameters of *Anna*! What a decline now over nearly twenty years, plastered with birthdays and honorary doctorates.)

P.S.: A brood of little ladybugs is wintering with me (this also might somehow have happened in Schmargendorf); one of them, one that has turned out particularly well, —they don't all do so in this indoors winter—has just wandered across this page. Take it for a good omen!

[LAS to RMR at Muzot]

Göttingen, January 4, 1922

Dear Rainer,

Precisely on New Year's morning *Mitsou* took its place on the table near the stove (an ugly iron stove that due to the lack of English anthracite has been moved into the middle of my room), and since Baba was already sitting there she was the first to absorb the pictures. Then my husband and I went through these mute tales with full pleasure. But it is just as your introduction says: what I feel in the small species of the cat tribe is "the other side" existing alongside the human; and I find myself instinctively repelled by this, probably because the great violent energy of predatory beasts—which regards its embodiment in individual animals as merely accidental and contingent, while it pulses as something unboundedly elemental—houses here (and at best mouses here) in too belittling a format. Baba is of the same opinion, whereas Lorie, her illegitimate daughter (the only one of the three we kept, since Baba would all too quickly resume her sinful ways with her two sons), recently became the foster mother to newborn kittens, and now, gathering the thriving brood around herself, dances and roughhouses with them (she has no sense of rank at all but loads of intelligence).

Yesterday your letter and the Muzot postcard: the absence of windows is what first gives one a shock, —yes, protection to the most extreme degree, as hiding-place tremendously convincing; one imagines for it a fairy tale about someone most powerfully alive who keeps within and holds in his life like precious breathing that cannot be allowed to blend with the ordinary function of the air, because something is there, invisibly at his side, into which he will "blow breath," instantly bringing it alive. And one imagines all the Божия коровки to be around him, Good Lord's Dots, Mary's Little Beetles, undemanding fellow occupants who ask only that when a track of sunshine or warmth from inside appears on the house's walls (best where they are thickest) they may crawl the length of it or trace it flying (which always leaves one amazed, since they seem to dissolve into thin air—for who has ever detected one in flight? It feels as though they don't become *earthly* again till they've landed).

To imagine, Rainer, dearest, that in the new year, this actual, current year of 1922, you yourself will be coming here, all the way over to our place, into our gradually encroaching garden (almost the only cultivating we still do is negative, cutting back the worst overgrowth, and our house stands just as neglected and unkempt in the middle of it, diligent maintenance work is simply no longer possible), but trees and bushes remain as carefree and rich with fruit and summer-beautiful as ever, and inside at least we have not been assigned tenants, as have most people around here, and among all the things that have aged so noticeably something very old that never changes lives on full of expectation and in accord with all its seasons. The event that will force you out of hiding for a brief sojourn to Germany was made known to me both through a printed announcement and in a dear, joyous letter from Ruth in which she introduced "her Carl" to me with almost childlike happiness. I received it in Vienna where I had gone for two months; strong, rich days and vivid even back here, made so above all by Freud himself, but also by everyone around him, professionally as much as personally, including a few old friends (above all faithful Beer-Hofmann), and not least Freud's daughter Anna, whom you've met, and who is going to come by here this spring on her way home from a trip to Hamburg to see the children of her late sister. Here I am completely immersed in patients, 6 and beginning next week 8 hours of analysis each day; in between I can think of scarcely anything more wonderful than simply to lie down and keep silent. In two (or perhaps three) months these analyses will come to an end, and should you encounter a Swiss possibility, please pass it along to me: now that postal connections with Russia are finally being resumed in earnest (even though postal charges are like something from a land of fables: the other day there was a letter to Freud from Odessa affixed with 10 thousand-ruble stamps!), it is actually possible to send money as well to those who are going without food there; if you had any idea how much that alone inspires hard work—quite aside from our own pile of debts. I have accustomed myself well to an existence by the clock and indeed down to the minute, and psychoanalytic work is so satisfying that even if I were a multimillionaire I wouldn't give it up for anything. Be assured that even so I'll find the time to read Picard, whom I greatly enjoy (he arrived just a moment ago, book and letter), and I hope a review will come of its own. Regina [Ullmann] is another matter: I could only write about her in the context we discussed back then in Munich, and that would basically require—her death. She must under no circumstance read about herself in a review by me, no matter how admiring this review may be. The "Inn's Sign" is indeed astonishing, I read it in manuscript, everything else pales in comparison, and here and there her inspired naïveté is augmented by invasive little displays of worldly wisdom—which may, however, merely be her way of seeking refuge in normal practice. The bilingual Skythen journal has regrettably ceased publication after only its second issue; R. von Walter, son of the Petersburg pastor and (alas) crony of the ever more unpleasant "v. Gunther" wrote me a congenial letter back then; such a journal would have been wonderful indeed! My Russian piece, *Rodinka*, I would gladly publish in just about any journal, on account of the honorarium; but there are no prospects, and turning to Swiss periodicals would probably be futile, since they especially will be inundated with submissions.

I have a host of things still to talk about, but where would there be an end to it? So this at least shall get on its way now and greet you with a *hopeful* до свиданья in this not yet belated year. My husband conveys to you all best wishes; needless to say you would find him too very changed, and yet, even now not the "old gentleman," only growing into old age as into a country, the way the creatures of the wild do when they go more slowly through their forest; and he is dear and good like a country that is becoming ever more Mediterranean.

(What I'd like most to go on chatting about is a long work on daydreams and their significance, conceived on a large scale, psychoanalytical but with a turn to philosophy.) Прощай.

Lou.

[RMR to LAS in Göttingen]

Château de Muzot
s/*Sierre*
(Valais) Suisse
February 11 [1922]
(in the evening)

Lou, dear Lou:

At this moment, now, Saturday, the *eleventh* of February, at six o'clock, I lay my pen aside after the last completed Elegy, the tenth. The one whose beginning had already been written in Duino (even back then it was meant to come last): "*Someday, at the end of the nightmare of knowing, / may I emerge singing praise and jubilation to assenting angels . . .*" I had read you all there was of it, but only the first twelve lines remain, everything else is new and: yes, very, very, very glorious! —Think of it! I have been allowed to survive until this. Through everything. Miracle. Grace. —All in a few days. It was a hurricane, as on Duino that time: all that was fiber in me, tissue, framework, groaned and bent. There was no thought of eating.

And imagine, one further thing, just before: in a different context (that of the *Sonnets to Orpheus*, twenty-five sonnets written all at once, in the squalls that announced the storm, as a monument for Wera Knoop), I wrote, *made*, the *horse*, you remember, that free happy white horse with the hobble on his foreleg who once, at approach of evening, came galloping over toward us on a Volga meadow—:

how

I made him, as an "ex-voto" for *Orpheus*! —What is time? —*When* is Now? Across so many years he bounded, with his complete happiness, into my wide-open feeling.

And in the same way one thing followed upon another.

Now I know myself again. It was like a constant mutilation of my heart that the Elegies were not—here.

They are. They are.

I went outside and put my hand on the little Muzot that had guarded and finally entrusted all this to me, I touched its wall and stroked it like a big old animal.

That's why I didn't write in answer to your letter: all these weeks I have been anticipating something, have been waiting in silence for *this*, with a heart drawn farther and farther inward. And now, today, dear Lou, just this. You had to learn of it at once. And your husband also. And Baba—, and the whole house, even down to the good old sandals!

Your old

Rainer.

P.S. Dear Lou, my little pages, breathlessly written last night, these two, could not go off, *registered*, today on Sunday, and so I took advantage of the time to copy out for you *three* of the completed Elegies (the Sixth, Eighth, and Tenth). The other three I shall write out in the days ahead, by and by, and send them soon. It will be so good for me, knowing that you have them. And it will also set my mind at ease to know that they exist somewhere else, outside, in accurate copies, kept secure.

But now I must get out in the open for a moment, while the Sunday sun is still in the air.

Прощай!

[LAS to RMR at Château Muzot]

[Göttingen, February 16, 1922]

Ah слава Богу, *dear* Rainer, how rich his gift to you—and yours to me! I sat and read and cried from joy and it was not just joy at all but something much more powerful, as if a curtain were being parted, rent, and everything were growing quiet and certain and present and good. I remember as if it were today how much the beginning of the last Elegy plagued you, and when it had shaken me so severely, how even *that* only plagued you; it had been on your lips for such long years, a word which one cannot make conscious and which is *there* all the same; in the beginning was this word. And then the *Creature* Elegy! —It is the poem of my most secret heart, oh so unsayably glorious; and *said*, the inexpressible made present and actual. And *that*, finally, is the message of this poetry: that we are surrounded, ringed about by things of mute presence which are being rescued, redeemed into existence for us *only* thus, and yet it is these things alone by which we live. But where *is* something like this in other poetry? On my way back from Vienna I read in Munich the Insel Almanach (no, Inselschiff) and *your* Michelangelo verses, and saw before me how you are climbing after the deepest that has been attained in poetry, and yet it is as nothing, even when it comes from this powerful mind, —so very, very, very different from the inexpressibility that has become word through you. And now I think: how he also must have struggled for it; and to you yourself it seemed powerful enough that you would subsume it into your own language. But what is it worth compared to *this* primal text of the soul?

I am imagining with such fabulous clarity how you must look now: just as in those days long, long ago, when the brightness in your eyes and your cheerful stance would sometimes make one imagine a boy: and whichever hope moved you then, whatever it was that you were asking of life, absolutely and intensely, as your only need and necessity—is now as if fulfilled. It is possible, perhaps probable, that a reaction will set in, since the work created had to bear and sustain the creator, but don't let that frighten you (this being also how the Marys feel after that birth which is so incomprehensible to their carpenters).

On the table where the envelope of your letter still lies, there is a big decorated cake, and next to it a little basket of figs and grapes: from patients who were mistaken about the date of my birthday;—so *that it IS birthday now* all around everything that arrived from you, celebration surrounding *yours*. Dear, good Rainer, how grateful to you is your old overjoyed

Lou

[RMR to LAS in Göttingen]

Château de Muzot
sur Sierre
(Valais) Switzerland
Sunday
[February 19, 1922]

That you are there, dear, dear Lou, to seal it so joyously in my inmost heart with your response! As I read your good, assenting letter: how it flooded me anew, this certainty from all sides that it is *here* now, *here*, this thing that has gestated so long, from the very start!

I had intended to copy the other three Elegies for you today, since a week has passed and it is Sunday again! But imagine: in a radiant after-storm a further Elegy arrived, the one of the Saltimbanques. It is a most wonderful addition: only now does the cycle of Elegies seem to me truly closed. Rather than joining the others as the eleventh, it will be inserted (as the Fifth) before the Hero Elegy. Actually, the piece that has held that place until now is so different in structure that it has never seemed to me justified there, though beautiful as a poem. This one will replace it (and how!), and the supplanted work will be transferred to the section *Fragmentary Pieces*, which, as a second part of the Book of Elegies, will contain everything contemporaneous with them, but which time ruined, so to speak, before it was born, or cut off in its formative stage and exposed its jagged edges. —And so now the Saltimbanques are here also, with whom I became so absolutely preoccupied in the earliest Paris years, and who ever since have followed after me like a task.

But that was not all. Scarcely was this Elegy on paper when the *Sonnets to Orpheus* began again and kept coming; today I am arranging this whole new group (as their second part), and have hastily transcribed for you (to keep!) a few that seem to me the most beautiful. All from these days just past and still warm. Only our Russian horse (how he greets you, Lou!) is from the earlier *first* part, from the beginning of this month.

But enough of that, for today. I have to catch up with my letters, several of which have piled up for answering.

I am well aware that there may be a "reaction"—, after being thrown skyward like this, there is ultimately the falling down somewhere; but I *am* falling into springtime, which has already drawn closer here, and besides: since it was given me to have this patience, this long patience, for what has now been achieved—, how should I not be able to manage a little auxiliary patience to get me through poorer days; and then too: thankfulness (of which I have never before had so much) ought to outweigh in them every attack of frustration and bewilderment!

Thanks for having written to me at once, despite all your own work!

Your old

Rainer.

Elegies 5, 7, 9,—: soon!

[LAS to RMR at Château Muzot]

Göttingen, February 24, 1922

Our лошадка, how vividly it bounded toward me, and how forcefully I see it now, free and unfettered, —like *You*, who have had a hobble slipped off by the gentlest of all invisible hands, —ah, Rainer, all this is like a dream, this glorious certainty that life *is* in such glorious order, —that there are trees "visited by angels," —that neither "the wantonness of the bird nor the jealousy of the worm below" could harm the slowly ripening fruit. This primal spring that broke forth as if only *it* could fling open for us the gates of the coming season; through such feelings I look at the brownish catkins that are now swaying on the willow branches in my garden. I am living in the very midst of what you have written down for me, and it is no hindrance to my work with patients but rather strangely helpful, like something in me that causes healing, and when I read it in the midst of this work, often for only ten or twenty minutes, it nevertheless remains entire and completely protected within itself, separate through its limitless frame and its limitless manner of experiencing. And I would like to try to say what it all comes to: you speak in your letter of thankfulness which even during a subsequent "reaction" would teach patience and trust, —indeed, this inward thanking is almost the only valid proof of the existence, the actuality, of God: through the existence, the actuality, of *his* gift to *you*; as if this gesture of his, this gesture to you from him, from the one who is most veiled from us, has torn the most opaque veil away, so that one receives *him* along with his gift. Because thankfulness for any other gift, however ardently it may arise in people so favored, however strong their desire *to be allowed* to thank, to *know* that God exists *to this end* (and not to perpetuate the gift), does not finally *create* God, because one's happiness is too dizzying and fulfilling and eager to be savored; only the thankfulness expressed in the creative person's gesture of giving back, only his *own* gift-giving, bestows on him this power of unveiling, of verifying; only this gesture fully searches out the god, and not his gift, nor him in his gift, but him alone. He, the creative person, alone "adds himself joyously and erases the score" (surely the most glorious sonnet—but no, I can't swear to that, though just now I feel nestled into Боженка's bosom, and how could one be any closer to him).

I'll send this off quickly only because I find it impossible to quit chirping; accept these little noises as I do those of the birds who are just now returning home, and who are also not singing yet but merely tuning up their throats after this endless winter (it stood here white and hard and imperturbable, but the sun, quite un-German in its southerly demeanor, strove to make up for the lack of coals). Now I await the Saltimbanques, —*how* I'll be waiting! (My copy of the Elegies has no number five but merely provisional little dots between the Second and the Hero Elegy, which has meanwhile been added so splendidly.) Dear Rainer, farewell, and thanks for you.

Lou.

(It is certainly no "loving oneself anew" that you will feel for yourself: rather in a new way all the negativity will have disappeared, all the "being unable to love oneself," all the taking offense at oneself, all the scuffling against oneself, to which one so often submits in moments of despair as to a sin against oneself.)

[RMR to LAS in Göttingen]

[Château de Muzot]
February 27, 1922

Yesterday, dear Lou, was a Sunday truly named after the sun, which shone from early until late (and it was already here the way it is in summer, over a landscape it knows intimately far down into the soil). And when I entered my study, early, roses were there—, and below, on the breakfast table, for no discernable reason, as the other day at your house, a gugelhupf and a little bowl with the first primroses from our meadows, still tender and with short stems, but already very happy. All these things assembled magically, and then towards noon your letter joined them as if by prior agreement, full as it was, full of insight and joy! It induced me to sit down that same afternoon and copy for you the remaining three Elegies, first that of the Saltimbanques and then one more and then another: it was just turning dark when I finished, around a quarter to seven! —So now you have them. —I am enclosing for you a list of the first lines; could it be that you don't have what are now the Third and Fourth? —if so I'll also copy these for you by and by; but what is important is that now all these new ones, the ones that are reopening things, are with you, dear Lou, *living with you*:

Прощай!

Rainer.

[LAS to RMR at Château Muzot]

[Göttingen, March 6, 1922]

Dear Rainer,

That such days exist now for you and me! Days where it is natural for even the sun to invite itself in, so that it can shine on your festive table and allow the latter to bask there, so to speak, in the universe. But *this* is certain: that to feel such a sun-time so utterly is given only to human beings like you: the ones who take risks, the ones who go on and on endangering themselves, for whom at any moment any season could topple over into absolute light-blind wintriness. Who all the while kept working over and over at achieving mastery in every inward exertion, and felt only their failures; —who, like the Saltimbanques, until they do succeed, are perpetually only *exposed*, wrenched, sent reeling (where others stride safely and in comfort), for with almost every step they want the impossible: the "too little" that has become that "too much" in which "the complex equation equals zero," and that is ultimately beyond earthly algebra. Only *thus* could I let the Fifth speak to me, as saying something I have known from your most long-ago emotions, like the epitome of fearfulness and will to victory, of ultimate abstinence and almost bull-like self-concentrated strength (of neck and nun), of "widowed" self-robbed existence in one's own skin, of fall and falling-off such as "only fruit knows," and of ripening in an instant into summer and high autumn. How could the Saltimbanques *not* have been trailing behind you and haunting you for such a long, long time? (Didn't "The Ball" fly up ahead of them? I had made myself a copy, and whenever I read it, I was, even if unconsciously, thinking of you, with both fear and elation struggling inside me. But now I can't find it anywhere, it seems to have simply disappeared in flight.) And now, now that the Saltimbanques have caught up with you, have *arrived* where you are, so that your meadows with the first primroses became their carpet, spread out by that Angel of yours with the deepest smile (as a *springtime everywhere*) — ah, Rainer, that it has turned out this way!

Even though I can't really say this without amending or revoking it the moment I let myself glide into one of the other Elegies, I must say it anyway: the most powerful and at the same time gentlest for me is the Ninth. There reading, reading on to the end, is scarcely possible, as in gardens whose paths one can't even use as paths, since what is blooming and greening all around slows every step, brings it to a halt; again and again, in every stanza, every section of a stanza, I sit down, feel myself in a bower, as if little branches were plaiting themselves together above me into an unheard-of homeland. Yes, these *are* the gardens of my most secret homeland from far, far back; childhood and youth and all existence have always stood in the midst of them and have grown eternal there. *I can never tell you*: how much this means to me and how I have unconsciously been waiting to receive what is *Yours* as also *Mine*, as life's true consummation. I will remain grateful to you for this until the end, until the new primal beginning, dear, dear, Rainer.

And imagine my feeling when I found in the concluding line that: "superabundant existence wells in my heart," which, along with the line preceding it, I have looked up so many times in the *Fragments* (which you, on extra pages, enclosed along with the finished Elegies); it was tremendously moving for me, and your patience in waiting for it, holy.

The earlier Elegies I have entirely, the Hero Elegy is lacking only the one magnificent new section.

Lou.

And yet—and yet: just now I read the Eighth,—is not *it*, after all, the heart of the heart? I *cannot* rank it below any of the other Elegies, it would almost be as if I killed all living creation with such a deed.

This is the essence: one becomes passionate again over all this, becomes young, enraptured, partial, happy, dead serious, in short a creature of God the Creator.

[RMR to LAS in Göttingen]

Château de Muzot sur Sierre
(Valais) Suisse
January 13, 1923

My dear Lou,

Today must be the Russian New Year! But so often recently, on the morning of the western New Year and between it and Christmas Eve, I have been with you in thought: I estimated that if I could put off writing just a bit longer, I could enclose both the Elegies and the Sonnets in the next letter. But my calculations were badly off. On the last day of the year there appeared, instead of the first copies of the Elegies, yet another set of proofs, still containing many errors, and work on them took me right up to and over the threshold of the year. In the tolling of midnight and in the first stillness of 1923, I was right in the middle of correcting and reading the fifth Elegy! I rejoice that I was allowed to begin this way (if such segmenting of time really needs to be acknowledged). And you? I am often deeply worried, dear Lou, about *you*, about *all of you*, when I hear and try to imagine how everything in Germany has become increasingly ridiculous and living and the cost of living practically impossible. It seems—and this was my impression in 1919—that the one right moment, when everything could have prepared for agreement, has been missed on all sides, now the divergences are lengthening, the sums of mistakes have become so many-digited that they can't even be read off any longer; helplessness, desperation, mendacity, and the all-too-modern desire to profit regardless of cost from even *these* calamities, yes, even from them: these treacherous forces are behind the world now, shoving it forward . . .

But perhaps it isn't moving forward, perhaps *nothing* moves forward in politics. Yet the instant one penetrates into some layer beneath politics, no matter where, everything looks different, and one wonders if a most secret growth and its pure will aren't just using these confusions to remain whole beneath them and hidden from curiosities occupied elsewhere. (Especially in France, among those who are not involved in politics, who are *inwardly* engaged: revolutions, reinvigorations, reassessments everywhere; a spirit newly oriented, grown suddenly, almost against its will, reflective again, its horizons widening . . . I don't know if you have been following Proust, but his influence is enormous—, and not only *his* influence, but its transformative force at work now in other and younger people . . .) I have the advantage here of being able to follow all this without much difficulty; I have been translating Paul Valéry, and feel my own resources so in harmony with his great glorious poems that I have never translated with such sureness and insight as here—an often very difficult instance to be sure. (Do you know that he, P. V. . . . , a friend of Gide's, descending from Mallarmé, after a few early publications fell silent for almost twenty-five years, wholly occupied with mathematics; only since 1919 has he resumed a life of poetry, and now the pace of every line is enriched by that deep balanced repose which none of us can muster. A glory.) And Valéry, although his ignorance of the language excludes him from all things German, wrote me when he was traveling through Switzerland last fall to give lectures: "*Vous étiez l'un des objets principaux de mon voyage.*" How uncanny and unpreventable are all true connections! And yet in the end I was not, alas, able to see him, and for the stupidest of reasons; the impossibility of getting Austrian or German money sent out makes me more and more a prisoner within the old walls of my Muzot, inside them I have everything for a while yet, but every step to be taken outside, though it be only to Lausanne, is becoming more and more impossible! But how should I not take this mischief in reasonably good stride, when I think of the troubles that would beset me and crowd in upon me in a less out-of-the-way and sheltered place. On freedom of movement one may not place much value now; it would only expose one to calamities. In the summer I had all sorts of plans; but at the edge of their least implementation there massed all at once so many warnings that I, instead of leaving, expended all my effort and ingenuity on keeping myself *in* Muzot. Were the world less out-of-joint, a change, at this moment of so important a conclusion for me, would have made good sense, and it would probably have happened of its own accord. But as it was, the best thing was to hold fast to what was given and proven and to remain loyal to and grateful for it. Especially since my health is going through strange upheavals: with increasing frequency every excitement, even that of work (which often for weeks has not let me eat *quietly*), attacks that center in the pit of the stomach, the *sympaticus*, or "solar plexus"; there I feel truly annullable, and I am going through remarkable experiences involving the rivalries and agreements between the two centers, the cerebral and that more focal one which is, presumably, our *real* center: for the visible and the invisible alike!

How so ever: I am not worrying all that much about these pitchings and swayings that beset the central organs; at most just using my energy to "shut off" at meal-time those intense vibrations coming from my mind or mood—

the same way I treat them, usually with success, when I want to sleep. That great god: Sleep! I sacrifice to him, without any thought of hoarding, —what does *he* care about time! —ten hours, eleven, even twelve, if he deigns to accept them in his mild, sublimely silent way! Though, alas, I seldom manage now to go to bed early; evening is my reading time. The presence of enticing books, the stillness of the old house intensified to the point of improbability, mostly keep me awake past midnight. The little bustlings of a mouse in the many undiscovered passageways within the thick walls further deepens the mystery which nourishes the immense night of this landscape, eternally *without* care.

I have become strangely inured, was so, to my amazement, even during the summer—, inured to the landscape itself, whose splendor, once so deeply experienced, I have to hold before me with great strain and deliberateness if I am still to partake in it. Does the dulling of our senses really go *this* far under the constantly reasserted presence of the environment that touches them and borders them? In how many ways, then, must "habit" place us wrongly vis-à-vis people and things. Should one remind oneself then that the curve of delight does continue on in one's *inner* realm? But how *follow* it there, where it will surely refract and scatter in the density of the medium, perhaps become unrecognizable and only flare distinctively where other curves, from origins just as lost, cross it in the strange whirl of intersections.

Dear, dear, Lou, will a word from you come soon? Have you been away from home, and where? —Do you manage somehow to keep your life on hold in this surfeit of worsenings? And do you have news now and then from Russia? —Soon, please, write me. The year doesn't properly begin until I have heard you say a few words in it, in the new space.

Ruth, it seems, has been living in grand and complete happiness since her marriage: all her aptitudes for cheerfulness and joy are finally being put to good and increasing use. And since they are living in that old farm on the estate of her parents-in-law, they are not quite as subject to the strident necessities of this evil time as they inevitably would have been in any city!

Прощай, dear Lou! Many good greetings to everything in your house.

Your old

Rainer

(How is Druzhok doing?)

[LAS to RMR at Château Muzot]

[*Letterhead:*] *Polyclinic of the Berlin Psychoanalytic Association*
Berlin W. 35, January 18, 1923

Dear Rainer,

I hurry to write on the only stationery I have available just now in order to answer your letter at once; it came to me by way of Göttingen at this hour, and during how many hours already have I searched for you in my thoughts, now in Switzerland, now in Germany because of the new circumstances in Ruth's life. That you *remained* in the old Muzot house, could remain without weariness is something very beautiful indeed: though you wrote that the landscape no longer speaks to you the way it did earlier, this is also how it is with a good marriage, where the exchange is no longer noticeable, since one identifies with and even to some extent *stands in* for one's partner in the living flux of life. Think how often it has been otherwise: in whatever place you lived, something would happen to turn that hoped-for harmony between you and your environs into the very opposite; now there must have evolved in you somewhere a place of repose, despite all the excitements and eruptions of a half-bodily nature that you describe; otherwise Sleep would not take you in its motherly arms and as into an inalienable homeland. But, love, it is so heavy a burden to me not to be able to *talk* with you about all this; we have been so completely separated by this current world's insanity, and one day time may have run out. About the French matters of which you wrote—I would like so much to know more, what I know about them now is *nothing.* That in translating Paul Valéry you came to feel an especially happy affinity with him accords with how, over the past years, the work of translation in general has become a strong need for you: back when you read me your Mallarmé translations in Munich (we have often talked about it) I already felt as if a desire inside you for masculinity and maleness were resolving in the direction of embracing the other's contours with the purest urges of the mind, and as if it only required finding "the" poet most perfectly suited for its fulfillment. With what anticipation I shall look forward to what you are proofreading now—it goes back to that incredible time almost a year ago! Life is good and this year also it shall be blessed many times over if it keeps you in the kind of existence that remains—both in its inner aspect and in its urge toward the external, out into human reality and your most delicate attunements with it—so substantive, so essential, so eternally present.

Starting early next month it's back to the Loufried address where I hope to find my husband in good health and by his side, as his pampered child, also Baba (she, no doubt, round as a ball, so that it will fall to me to work her and walk her back down to size). I have been in Berlin since the end of September, came here to attend the psychoanalytic congress, stayed at Eitingon's together with the Freuds for several beautiful months (which I owe to his thoughtful friendliness) while he himself was away with his wife on a trip (all the way down to Sicily). My guest room is a wonderful Biedermeier with grand old plane trees outside the windows. The day is divided into psychoanalytic sessions, some for patients at the polyclinic (which was founded by Eitingon a few years ago to help the poorer population), some with a few previous patients from Göttingen, some for the money, which, due to the frightful pace of inflation (formerly 50 marks an hour, now 3000 already), will soon scarcely be possible any longer. For this reason I may have to be away again during the summer [*In the margin*: assuming that I can't obtain patients of my own]: Königsberg has proposed that I conduct teaching analyses using the senior physician of the clinic for internal medicine there and his assistants as my subjects in order to explore with them the relevance of psychoanalytic perspectives for medical treatments. One must do what one must if one is to keep one's head above water during this time of the Flood (and in these sinful days one really can speak of the ancient Deluge). And exploring further the scientific and theoretical aspects of these things really has become a passion for me; if I saw you I would be close to overflowing with news about this.

And Russia? An issue about which I long to have an exchange with you more than with anyone else. But I won't enter here into something that would inevitably lead into vast uncharted territory, will only jot down a few lines that have become clear to me in the course of conversations with a Russian Jewess who was my patient and who only recently had fled from Russia. What concerns me about this is roughly the following: ever since the Bolsheviks have backed away from the gross brutality of their means (which so violently contradicted their social ends), i.e., now that they see themselves forced to make concessions toward European capitalism, a newer generation has been growing up full of fervor and purity, determined to accomplish this ideal end in spite of everything, and thus willing to fight *against* the kind of bolshevism practiced at the time of concessions. From them will come the martyrs of the next era, comparable to those supplied by the terrorists during the rule of the tsars (who in turn were shoved against the wall by the Bolsheviks as nothing but impractical idealists, desecularized by prison and катopra). And when the time has come, the *new* fight between the men of praxis and the generation of martyrs will break out, and thus despite their relapses into concessions they will always be taking a few more steps toward total conquest. But who now is really willing to discuss these ultimate ethical questions! Life, however, real, overwhelming Life, exists *only* in this continuously dying and reborn country (in which the little children from the Volga villages—*our* little villages, Rainer!—ran away into the woods during the despair of starvation *so that they would not be eaten*).

The Eitingons' house is frequented by many Russians, even the Moscow Artists' Troupe was there in October; I have also taken up the beloved language anew. From my brother in Питерѣ still these great calm letters as are written only by people who are not "dying unto themselves" and who stand out against the background of a world being turned upside-down, so that they are changed also, inwardly, and no longer stand in a place where their eyes face the earth. Now I close, beloved Rainer, всего хорошаго!

Your old *Lou*

[RMR to LAS in Göttingen]

[Inscribed in a copy of the limited edition of the *Duino Elegies*:]

for *Lou*,
who has owned it with me from the first,
this now in its ultimate form

Rainer

(Muzot, around Christmas 1923)

[RMR to LAS in Göttingen]

[Inscribed in a copy of the *Sonnets to Orpheus*:]

Lou,

Rainer

(in the spirit of Christmas)

[LAS to RMR at Château Muzot]

At last again: Loufried
March 16, 1924

Dear Rainer,

After 1/2 year back home! In the middle of the room, as its very center, your two books, consummated and come home. All the way to the blue of their covers so full of memories. While the first few days have to be real days of rummaging, taken up with all sorts of busywork, I constantly know that *these* are lying there, existing there, as life's still point, not unlike the way one knows that the amber stone is there in the midst of churning water, —a piece of fairy-tale magic and ready to be part of any jewelry, although shaped mysteriously from the same profound recesses of Nature. But I *must* tell you something further, immediately, however well or badly I manage, since it can scarcely be told at all: namely, the experiences I had using the handwritten versions of your poems with damaged, recovering patients. They were the sort of people for whom, as a result of their neurosis, everything had become dead, and they felt no differently about their own lives: they existed in a deep apathy, and it caused anything alive—human, creature, nature—to turn immediately into a thing for them, into a material object, a worthless non-thing, in the end garbage, a cast-off piece of filth. This produces severe states of anxiety, bitter terror: dead among dead things, to feel that one stands outside oneself, has been evicted from oneself, from someone still vividly terrified. Different moments can bring about the resolution in a recovering patient: on a forest trail above our house, a woman with agoraphobia first saw that the trees *lived* and what the harvested fields expressed so clearly and with such yellowness and she cried out in delight over the force and strength of the world that had suddenly been given back to her and was accepting into itself her liberated steps. But there were others who sat up and took notice for the first time when they heard *your* tone as that of Life: and it was indescribably moving that they heard and understood *it* before they were capable of grasping even the most readily understandable attributes of the day around them, much less any experience from the realm of art, *as something alive.* And not one of them had previously had some special relationship to poetry, rather the opposite: what resounded there had come all the way across to them only because those who have been blessed as artists and those who have been stripped of their blessings by an affliction live in a single region, in close proximity and at the same depth—for Heaven and Hell are not at all *two* places. (So that your tone as the sound of home is the first to become perceivable, is the one that serves to *open* home.) That is another insight whose truth has been driven home to me so powerfully during the last few years: all neurosis is a mark of quality, it means: here someone wanted to go to his outermost limits, —*for this reason* he was derailed sooner than others—; they, the ones who remained healthy, were, as opposed to him, simply those who made do with what was; his noblest challenge caused him to appear small among them. If he achieves health he will stand on a *niveau* towering above any level he might have attained had he simply remained healthy (—and will then be more secure against relapses of illness than those others, for not one of them will have explored so deeply the far dimensions of his unknown self by reliving memories and reawakening distant experiences). If I ask of someone who is sick, "What brought about his illness?" I have come to ask just as skeptically of someone who is well, "What caused him to remain healthy?" And ever since, there have been moments during the analyses—for example, during the "teaching analyses" that were done with physicians, etc., and at just as personal a level as those with "patients"—when the people involved became just a little bit ashamed of their careful, cautiously maintained health, or at least learned a new reverence and respect.

In Königsberg, during this last 1/2 year, I had five physicians and several very difficult patients, some of whom will return here as soon as summer begins. K. with its massive winter coldness, its streets that are never swept, its hideous houses, etc., reminds me of Petersburg (now renamed Ленинград!); the best things about it were two ponds located in the innermost part of the city rather than outside, as if they had strayed into it and couldn't find their way back, —also a delightful miniature schnauzer that belonged to a hat shop, which accounts for my buying two hats there one after another; you can't imagine a more enchanting creature, even though someone remarked not unfairly that with all his bristly hair the tiny dog looked like nothing so much as a toilet brush. Baba—who became round as a ball in my absence—will get to hear quite a few things about him. And now to move on from the dogs to the little Master and Mistress. I'll tell you only of my delight in my dear old husband's heartiness; just now, on the occasion of his 78th birthday, a colleague of his wrote: may you keep up that splendid youthful vigor which sets such a fine example for the rest of us. The little house around us is growing dilapidated calmly and without despondence; the colors on the inside walls are fading along with us, the only difference being that the bleached-out fabrics gradually assume a golden hue, whereas we are turning ice-gray. Unfortunately the world goes on constructing itself closer and closer to us; only the good fortune of being situated high and at such a beautiful *incline* has prevented the surrounding terrain from being turned into new buildings. I should be off again right away to attend the psychoanalytic conference in Salzburg; but I am too exhausted to go (have been working 12 and 13 hours every day), and Freud himself is not going either, prefers to convalesce on the Semmering (he has been seriously ill the last 3/4 year), where I was to go afterwards. And you, Rainer? Dear, dear Rainer. In gratitude

Lou.

I'd go on chatting if this badly stored ink hadn't thickened, which is making my pen furious.

[RMR to LAS in Göttingen]

Château de Muzot
s/Sierre (Valais) Switzerland,
Tuesday after Easter
April 22, 1924

My dear, dear Lou,

I cannot tell you what a grand, marvelous Easter you brought me with your letter; I had been looking forward to it as something which, the longer it failed to arrive, the fuller and more certain it promised to be. Now it has been added to these festive days and was so ripe with good news and affection—more so than anything that has befallen me for a long time. Only when I recount to you my past (third) winter in Muzot will you see how wonderful it is that *just now* you are able to tell me *this* of your patients: I keep reading it over and over and draw from it an overwhelming comfort and reassurance. The very fact that I was in need of such strengthening will tell you that my winter has not been a good one, has in fact been almost a hard one. The reaction you foresaw after that tremendous outpouring of the first winter at Muzot did indeed occur, and for a moment it was so violent and bewildering that, shortly after Christmas, I left Muzot and went into the Val-Mont Sanatorium (above Montreux), incapable (for the first time in many years) of managing without help. They were peculiar weeks. Physically, the transverse colon had become more and more the point of attack, but from there my whole system was thrown into chaos. I was in Val-Mont for three weeks. Unhappily on the next-to-last day, just before my departure, the attentive and well-meaning but not very insightful doctor found in addition to all this a goiter on the left side of my throat, and though he assured me that it was ten years "old" and had been "neutralized," once discovered it worked its way into my consciousness, the more so since there also issued from the transverse colon, through an upward pressure of air, swallowing and breathing difficulties toward which now, given this additional cause, I became even more sensitive and suspicious. But this "case history" I will sketch for you in greater detail another time, dear Lou; for just now the house is full of guests, and during the next few days a whole succession of visitors will be coming, each according to schedule (not so unwelcome a change after the loneliness of the long winter). Let me add only this: I am well aware that a rather foolish habit of mine is to blame for all kinds of damage and that my sundry ailments did not arise without assistance from me (or at least did not grow so emphatic all on their own); but neither have I recanted what I wrote you back then two years ago: that after the magnificence of this achievement I would gladly undergo whatever I may have to experience in the way of reaction. I will live through it. And in the meantime I have not been completely inactive: an entire volume of French poems (it was an extraordinary experience: occasionally I even set myself the identical theme in French and German, which then, to my surprise, developed very differently in the two languages: which argues strongly against the naturalness of translating) has come into being as of its own accord, along with much else besides, and my reading was lively all winter long and most fruitful in what I gained from it. Because of the location of my old tower I have been getting many more books from France than elsewhere: I am endlessly amazed at all the things that are now coming from there. First and foremost Proust, who will certainly be a marvel for you as well. You remember how I was translating Paul Valéry all of winter before last: this year he was one of my first visitors at Muzot, two weeks ago on Easter Sunday!

Ever since your letter arrived, Lou, do you know what I've been thinking? That one day *you* will be here with me, one day *this year*! Why shouldn't that be possible? (Though not during the hottest time, when it wouldn't be good for you and when I myself will probably go away.) You know I have a guest room, a charming little guest room under the roof, albeit with very small windows. Let us remember this in case the opportunity should arise. Yes?

Perhaps too, I will soon have to exchange the rather special and exposed solitude here for that in Paris, which is differently nourished and imbued: perhaps everything here is beginning to be not so *necessary* to me and is thus making itself, especially as regards climate, oppressive. The sun here works only on the wine, that is its métier: everything else, plants and people, it urges on too strongly and then burdens with the weight of its scorching heat, which is well suited for bringing grapes to ripeness but not for much else. And so in time at least a temporary change will be necessary.

Since November second I have had a granddaughter, a strong and vigorous little Christine. Ruth asked me particularly to tell you. From her, then, endless good news; from Clara, too, wonderfully good things (originating within) and with such lovely unburdenings and enlightenments.

And the good, steady news of you both, of Loufried, how it moved me! How, how much, you dear one, you dear ones both, it touches me! Tell your husband *how* glad I am to know him so firmly moored in the Unchanging, and greet him from my heart. And Baba, for whom you could bring back such fine exciting stories!

Enough: I want to know much, much about you, your work, experiences, impressions, insights—there's no other way, you must come some time soon. Think what days we would have!

Remember me to Freud when you write him.

I must go to Sierre to await my guests, who went off to see Sion today and are due back at six.

Прощай

Your old

Rainer

Enclosed is a stanza from Paul Valéry's beautiful poem "Aurore" (and two other little current things in a different mode).

I think I sent you a different card of Muzot the other day; this one goes farther back. It shows the old manor as it was shortly after 1900, before its restoration—which, fortunately, only acted to prevent further deterioration, without attempting much in the way of change. On the lower floor is a *Salle à manger*, a small salon (now unheatable and locked), and the kitchen with scullery; upstairs my work room, my little bedroom, and the "chapel." In the dining room a tile oven of 1656 in the regional style; beamed ceilings and a few pieces of furniture from the same period!

From Paul Valéry, "Aurore":

Je ne crains pas les épines!
L'éveil est bon, même dur!
Ces idéales rapines
Ne veulent pas qu'on soit sûr:
Il n'est pour ravir un monde
De blessure si profonde
Qui ne soit au ravisseur
Une féconde blessure,
Et son propre sang l'assure
D'être le vrai possesseur.

Ich fürchte nicht Dornen im Laube!
Erwachen ist gut, selbst hart!
Es giebt bei so reinem Raube
keine sichere Gegenwart:
eine Welt an sich zu reissen,
kann nur *so* sich verwunden heissen,
dass, wer sie an sich riss,
eine fruchtbare Wunde gewänne;
wenn das eigene Blut nicht ränne,
nie wär der Besitz gewiss.

———

[LAS to RMR, letter from Göttingen to Muzot,
end of April 1924]

———

[RMR to LAS in Göttingen]

Château de Muzot
s/Sierre (Valais)
May 2, 1924

My dear Lou,

Your sheltering letter has brought me so much that ties in with earlier things, —I promise to tell you more soon about my long winter; just this moment my many recent visitors have absorbed all my attention and set me back in my scribblings and correspondences, so that first I have to do a bit of catching up. Kippenberg was here also, and we agreed to bring out my Válery translations as soon as possible, perhaps even before Christmas—which will require of me extensive transcribing now for the next few weeks. You will be astonished by Válery. No: though some of his individual stanzas (like those I sent recently) can be glossed accurately at the level of content, his poetical work as a whole and even his prose, which is completely different from his poetry and distilled to the core of *its* innermost law (unlike many lyric poets he has crafted, apart from his poetry, a true, perfect prose just as distinctly his own) cannot really be clarified, that is to say it is clearest exactly where it reveals the secret, the open secret that is secret by its very nature and thus not capable either of concealing itself or explaining itself. —Proust then stands at the opposite extreme of elucidation, as different from Válery as can be imagined: between them lies the whole of French literature, which is now exploring its untapped potential and speaking in such manifold voices and undergoing, it seems to me, one of its great decisive moments, in almost inexhaustible renewals and transformations. I can scarcely enumerate for you today, especially in such a hurry, all the things that are happening there, again and again I come back (thinking of you) to Proust: you will almost surely find him rich with meaning and be struck (as I often am) by how closely his extraordinary portrayals concur with the outcomes you have achieved. There are now eleven volumes of *À la recherche du temps perdu*: I would like to give them all to you very soon, since for the time being you surely must have some free time again . . .

Nevertheless I am coming today to increase (possibly) the workload of your analyses. It happened like this: for about a year I have known of a young girl's emotional disturbances which now, for want of better alternatives, are being treated increasingly as a mental disease. Years ago (1916), when she was still a child, I saw this beautiful creature a few times in Vienna, but more in connection with her older siblings and her mother, for whom I feel a great veneration (without really knowing her that well). It has troubled me endlessly, I don't know quite why, that this girl may have been treated incorrectly and is now being given up to institutions; whenever someone would speak to me about her (my contacts with the family have been only indirect, by way of mutual friends, and occasional), the notion would torment me that I should do something, or at least manage to prevent something; all this leading the other day, quite unexpectedly, to an inner dictation: I wrote the mother who was worried about this youngest child concerning your treatments; without as yet mentioning your name, quite spur-of-the-moment and provisional: I also avoided, by the way, out of an instinctive precaution, any use of the word "psychoanalysis," since so many things are being sold now under this label and resistance against any application of this mode of healing is quite powerful in certain circles. Some feeling tells me that here is a case where you could provide wonderful help, perhaps even salvation, and it actually seems to me now that attempting something of this sort might be possible (your time and the various other circumstances permitting). My letter (unexpected even to myself) went off to Vienna about the time not long ago when the first of your letters arrived here; last evening a telegram from there reached me, saying:

> Remercie énormement lettre, aimerais entrer en rapport avec dame, lettre suit, mille amitiés
>
> [. . .].

Before this announced letter arrives I wanted to let you know what I have instigated here: I sent [. . .] your address together with this letter: so be prepared, dear Lou, to receive a call someday from Vienna regarding this matter. The person involved, as I said, is [. . .].

In any case, do make a quick note of the address: [. . .]. (If, by the way, the patient, as I suspect, is still in Switzerland, who knows if this might not turn into a roundabout way of effecting our own real and true-life reunion!)

Your old *Rainer*

(Your dear greetings for Ruth and little Christine will be passed on to them soon, in my very next letter.)

[LAS to RMR at Château Muzot]

[Göttingen,] May 26, 1924

Dear Rainer,

Please don't forget that you still wanted to tell me: about last winter and other things. I would have written you much earlier if I had not wanted to confirm to you in the same letter that I had received the expected call from Vienna. What you told me about the case made me eager to play a part, and I was ready to throw myself into it. But for some reason, this was not to happen: perhaps the daughter in Switzerland is being constrained from leaving? That you avoided using the word "psychoanalysis" is a good thing, because in Vienna, more than anywhere else, prejudice against it has been spreading virulently and is becoming truly moronic—this includes, by the way, Herm. Keyserling (who has ties with all branches of the aristocracy), even though he propagandizes on behalf of psychoanalysis, especially the Swiss version coined by Jung ("whose later writings scarcely ever give offense"); he says in the journal he edits: whoever has a nose for dirt must be a swine, and even though he would not want to state categorically that all psychoanalysts have been swine, it is the case, after all, that one becomes adept at noticing and searching out only those things toward which one is particularly inclined, and thus of course someone of a pure and sublime nature could never practice such an art! And for all that, he himself has read extensively in psychoanalysis, and thus should well know what opposite inclination lurks repressed behind this fancying oneself pure and sublime. It has made me remember the accounts of his nephew's vanity with which old Eduard used to entertain us. Too bad.

But of quite different things I would like to talk to you and hear you talk. I think about this more and more often when I am wandering with Baba (who seems to roll along as she walks, panting happily) through the early German summer (in these parts the most beautiful slice of the seasons). That at such times the ugly business mentioned above (about which I have not written a single word to you, even though my heart has been burning with it for over a year now) will also go through my mind is because Freud has been threatened for so long now by a fatal illness and is living only, as he himself just expressed it to me in a letter, "with a notice of termination." After horrible operations (with artificial feeding through the nose, etc.) he has been fitted with an upper jaw, which permits eating and speaking but only with great difficulty. We kept it a secret for a long time, but finally it leaked out anyway, though for the moment he is able to work again. Personally as well as professionally this is a deep, deep tragedy for all of us and lends even the summer a gray aspect.

I am enclosing in this letter—like filling a skinny goose with apples and sweet-smelling herbs—a few pages that contain a veritable torrent of love from Helene [Klingenberg]: love that in the end only tries to stammer her feelings in your own words. Helene is still the same: made so very beautiful by sheer strength of love, so that Life, persuaded by her example, cannot but join in this faith and uphold it. I see her and her family only when I am passing through (and longer last winter), but it is always *just for so long,* since every time the whole visit is one continuous rushing into each other's arms. Little Schnuppi (grown very tall and to my mind too muscular) is a student at the conservatory and a splendid instance of kindness and honesty.

Two hours later:

Dear Rainer! what did the mailman just bring me! All of eleven volumes of Proust! What are you doing! Just one would have been so much! I'll start *À l'ombre etc.* this very day. My heartfelt thanks; I will feel as if every day we were reading a little of it together.

Your old *Lou.*

[RMR to LAS, letter from Muzot to Göttingen, September 1924. Response from LAS?]

[RMR to LAS in Göttingen]

Château de Muzot s/Sierre (Valais)
last day of October, 1925

Dear Lou,

You wrote me, back when the Elegies were finished, saved, present and at hand—that I should not be alarmed if, as part of a reaction, things should one day go badly for me; and I remember still that I answered bravely. But now I *am* alarmed nonetheless: you see, for two whole years I have been living increasingly in the very midst of an alarm, whose most palpable cause (a self-induced stimulation) I invariably, with devilish obsession, exacerbate just when I think I have overcome the temptation to indulge it. It is a horrible circle, a ring of evil magic that encloses me as into a picture of Hell by Breughel. Now, beginning a month ago, phenomena have appeared that are almost certain to maintain me in that particular phobia which besets so many people these days . . . My staunch, faithful nature has been so weakened by the duration and intensity of this affliction that now an overpowering anxiety manages to dispossess me of myself constantly. I don't know *how* I can go on living like this.

It was two years ago that I first, observing how the hateful inclination to indulge this habit outwitted and overgrew my will, sought out medical advice at the Valmont Sanatorium above Montreux. I found there an attentive physician (Dr. Haemmerli) who is still quite young (and whom, by the way, people already travel long distances to consult, even from as far away as India): the founder of Valmont, Dr. Widmer, is an old man; the whole repute of the institution now really rests on the experiences that Haemmerli's patients take with them and relate in praise of him. I too can only praise his responsiveness, his patience, his shrewd feeling for when and when not to intervene; but he saw (and sees) my situation in so much brighter a light than the one in which I, again and again and ever more frequently, trapped in an atmosphere of doom, feel condemned to endure and overcome it. I remained from the end of 1924 into January of this year again under his observation in Valmont, and traveled from there to Paris on January 8—, not quite sharing that expectation with which Dr. Haemmerli tried to brace me: that so complete a change of surroundings and all influences would at one blow jolt me out of the rhythm of that senseless temptation, and that then all the reflexes that had been cast into my body would die out of their own accord. But victory did not come and neither did relief. I suppose the obsession to do oneself that old harm with all its aftereffects and menaces proved stronger, more powerful than Paris: it turned into the suffering of a long defeat, and if, far beyond my limit, I did remain there until August, it was only from shame at returning just as ensnared into my tower, whose complete isolation, I feared, would allow these miserable devils to have their way with me even more perversely. Now that, since the end of September, new phenomena (nodules along the inner lip, which Haemmerli considers cysts, though other doctors gave different—placating?—interpretations) have joined the previous ones, I briefly saw Haemmerli again—in Zürich, where we both happened to be staying at the same time—and again the distance between his objective assessment and the subjective primary color (it scarcely changes any longer) of my condition was enormous.

My dear Lou: (you have so many old dictionaries of the language of my lament in your possession), does this give you some picture of my defeat? No doubt it is due to something over-simple in my nature that it could come about under such absurd conditions. Do you see someone in the ambit of your world who might help me? I see only you—but how actually to reach you? I could travel now only with difficulty, could you do it? All the way here? As my guest? If only for a few days . . . ? (That is a question I have been holding back now for a year.) If only I had called out long ago. Or if I had gone there and stepped for a moment into my old hard sandals: I would have become "upstanding" like the tin soldier who has been welded back onto his level platform. But I stand ever so crooked, and your first glance at this page will have told you, love, at which angle.

Rainer

Greetings to all that is forever precious, forever yours!

P.S.: Valmont is only about three hours from here, but a longer stay there would be impossible for me this year because of its very steep prices; and Dr. Haemmerli is too much in demand to write me regularly enough to keep me a little above water that, much to my despair, often rises over my head. He did, when we met in Zürich, consider taking Dr. Meder into his confidence—but not in a way that envisioned any psychoanalytic treatment.

Write me, dear Lou, if you can, a word. As it is, for so long nothing has come your way in response to something I received. Now I send you this shabby bank note of distress: give me a gold coin of concern in exchange for it!

R.

Second postscript:

More than a month later, on December 8: Dear, here it is after all, this letter, it has been on my desk all the time, reminding me of the calamity I've called down upon myself—just as back then in Rome with that note and its издомай! (I found the latter recently in the Paris boxes that were saved.) I'm sending you all of this because it is all as true as when I first wrote about it; even the *phobia*, maintained not only by the little nodules along the inner lip but also by all kinds of other discomfort in the mouth, throat, and on the tongue, has increased! Last week I was almost on my way to Valmont, but unfortunately Dr. Haemmerli just then had to leave on a trip (he'll be in Berlin for ten days at the [Hotel] Kaiserhof), on his way out leaving only a written note, advising Maeder again, in case I might be over-anxious, to wait until his, Haemmerli's, return. Advise me; but I don't really want to *call* you now, because any day I may rush to Zürich; and besides, the winter has now grown so harsh that traveling from you to me would be no simple matter. But a few lines, please?

R.

[LAS to RMR at Château Muzot]

[Göttingen, December 12, 1925]*

Do you know, dear, dear Rainer, how I feel just now as I write? Like a champagne bottle that, free at last of its cork, should want to gush out everything at once so that there would be bubbling and fizzing in its throat—yet nothing comes but little drops.

The old letter is from September. If September had been a year ago, it would have been about the time we had wanted to be together, as you wrote that summer—do you remember? Before Valmont as well as Paris. Back then your worries, whatever they were, could have easily been put to rest. Even though you weren't yet writing about *these* fears, but only expressed concern about those swellings related to goiter. But the whole thing no doubt already lay in wait: I mean the notion that everything has been brought about by your own fault and is connected with the "devilish obsession."

Rainer, this is now in every respect the main thing to accept: it is *not* a devilish obsession at all! *Because* a feeling of guilt perpetually clings to it, as early as childhood, —*that's* why it can inflict so very much evil. As children, and even later, we can be plagued by a guilt feeling that is more like a moralizing voice which only by chance, as it were, manifests itself in punishments that beset one's body. As we are outgrowing this stage, the feeling of guilt takes refuge in the bodily processes themselves, i.e. it cultivates in various organs,

*Date of postmark. This letter survives only in a copy made by Dieter Bassermann, a Rilke scholar, in the late 1940s.

so as to acquire the strength of a destiny or doom, a hysterical propensity to make itself felt as a sickness or pathology. It achieves this through the attention focused on it, fearful interest taken in it, the increased blood supply and hypersensitivity directed there—very much like what happens at the penis through erotic stimulation; such hypochondria can also be thought of as a kind of amorousness or infatuation turned back upon itself with reference to the organ in question, except that the amorousness isn't felt that way at all, but rather as aversion, torment, almost hatred of the body, for the organ in question is not one suited for this, it serves nothing erotic, it has been torn away from its natural function, has been disturbed and interrupted, and takes revenge. All of this likes to attach itself to obliging weaknesses of the body, be they ever so minimal: it is *inevitable* then that they *manifest* themselves in vastly magnified and terrible ways, as if who knows what were taking place. Logical deliberation is of no use here; the objective diagnoses of a thousand doctors are of equally little help for the same reason. We corresponded about this years ago, it made very good sense to you, but do not let this reiteration make you lose patience, Rainer, read on, think of the bottle and its tight neck in which I feel this urgently bubbling pressure that wants to get out to you.

To continue: when you look at your current situation, that all too eager readiness in your mouth and on your tongue and throat to second your guilt feeling—what does it remind you of? Not perhaps of those years when you likewise had to contend with nodules and with sensations at a *different* bodily opening, had been operated on and feared that malignant tumors might develop there? Those were your words at Loufried in Wolfrathshausen; but instead of growing larger in later years, as is typical with hemorrhoids, yours shrunk, and thus presumably were already neurotically overdetermined, could make their way "up the chute," from the very beginning obedient to psychic inhibitions.

Alas, the whole picture is so clear; only I, stupid girl that I was back then, didn't see it. And *this* then is the guilt that God has visited on *me*: that back when we were first growing close I was not there for you with the knowledge and abilities I've acquired now. Therefore *this* had to grow and progress over the years. Even a shift from the lower to the upper region signals an advance of the affliction, since the oral (the infant's pleasure in sucking, first gratification, and disappointment when the maternal button on the nipple slips from the lips, which would like to keep holding it inside!) stems from a more infantile stage than the anal, in which the child is preoccupied with its own excrement.

But nevertheless it did not overcome and corrupt you, Rainer! There still ruled over you that vast grace which *also* makes use of those most primitive infantile forces: the creative discharge into the work of art, which for that very reason is so implicated in the bodily: for it is on account of this discharge that we are erotically fired to subsume things of the body into the meanings of art, instead of limiting ourselves to practical objectification, which has no room for the excess that still surges from us primordially and *makes everything one*, in the way that the newborn child still feels at one with the mother's breast. The tipping-over into the realm of the tormented, the forsaken, the being at the mercy of one's own body, —it's not something you experience merely as a reaction after tension-filled creative work; on the contrary, it has been from the first *intrinsic to* that work: the reverse of the thing itself, and the devil merely a *deus inversus*. Whom the god's image fully illumines, he also is given to see what lies behind, on the other side. But even *there* he is of the god; enveloped and embraced by what remains ever-maternal, even though we consciousness-hedged little humans have to pay a price for the ecstasies that surpass us. —If you wish to learn about this *until you fully feel it*, take up R. M. Rilke's *Elegies* (as some of my most severely ill patients have done; you remember I wrote you about it). I can't verbalize here the way that for them, for all those who labor and are heavy laden, it has become a *reality*, so much so that they see themselves blessedly invited to every manner of peace.—

Did you, I wonder, have the patience to read this to the end? If so, Rainer, dear Rainer, write me again, and then let me write you back. You know I don't usually talk that way, but this time I do—to bind you, to obligate you: since the apparent misplacing of the old letter that remained unsent on the desk is no accident: something in you wanted it to be lost, for as impossible, as grotesque as it sounds: we want to hold tightly to the things that are most dreadful about our circumstances, don't want to let go despite all the suffering, —this is the terrible mix-up that is possible simply and only because all these conditions are full of the god, —who, however, has become an inverted god. Nothing here is a matter of guilt; the изломай will diminish as soon as you know it deeply enough: trusting in You, dear, dearest!

Lou

[RMR to LAS in Göttingen]

[Sanatorium Valmont, above Montreux]
Monday. [December 13, 1926]

Дорогая,

So *this* you see was the thing for which during these last three years all the alerts and forewarnings of my watchful nature have been preparing me: but now my nature will have a very, very hard time surviving, since during this long interval it has exhausted itself in acts of help and correction and imperceptible adjustment; and before the present infinitely painful state with all its complications began to develop, it had undergone with me an insidious intestinal flu. And now, Lou, I know not *how many* hells, you know how I made a place for pain, for physical pain, the truly great one, in my accommodations, but only as an exception and as already a first step back into the open. And now. It encases me. It supplants me. Day and night!

Where to find courage?

Dear, dear Lou, the doctor writes you. Frau Wunderly writes you, who with all her impulse to help has come here for a few days. I have a good judicious garde-malade and believe that the doctor who is seeing me again now after three years, this time for the fourth time, is right. But. The hells.

With you, with both of you, how, Lou? Are you in good health? There is something malign blowing through the end of the year, something menacing. Прошай, Дорогая моя

Y. *Rainer*

Notes

3 Wegwarten (Wild Chicories): René Maria Rilke wrote this letter on Wegwarten letterhead and had it delivered by messenger. He had chosen the name of this flower to link a sequence of small books to appear at irregular intervals. Only three were actually published: the first, a selection of twenty-one of his poems, came out at the end of December 1895; the second, his one-act play *Jetzt und in der Stunde unseres Absterbens* . . . (Now and in the hour of our death . . .), followed half a year later. Both were printed at his expense in Prague, and he gave them away as his "gift to everyone." The third was published on October 29, 1896 with the writer Bodo Wildberg (1862–1942). It was a short collection (51 pp. in 1,000 copies) of their own poems and those of eleven other contributors, most of them Rilke's acquaintances. They titled this anthology of contemporary verse *Wegwarten. Deutsch-moderne Dichtungen.* Its imprint was: Wegwarten-Verlag, München, Dresden.

Dr. Conrad: Michael Georg Conrad (1846–1927), a journalist who also wrote novels, and a critic with experience as a politician (member of the Reichstag, 1893-1898). He was the most vociferous advocate of Émile Zola and French naturalism in Germany but also championed Nietzsche, Richard Wagner, and other "great individuals." *Die Gesellschaft* (Society), a "realistic review for literature, art, and public life," was published as a weekly during its first year, 1885, thereafter as a monthly until 1902; it attracted a large number of prominent contributors under his editorship and for a decade was the leading periodical of the "modern generation."

Neue Deutsche Rundschau: A distinguished literary and cultural review that, in March 1894, had replaced the weekly *Freie Bühne für modernes Leben* (Free stage for modern life; published since January 1890) and its successor, the monthly *Freie Bühne für den Entwicklungskampf der Zeit* (Free stage for the progressive struggle of this time; after vol. III, 1892); it became *Die neue Rundschau* in 1904 and, after various changes, is still published as the quarterly of S. Fischer Verlag. Its initial concentration on the theater and on the most recent Scandinavian literature soon gave way to an interest in every genre of important new writing and in cultural issues that reflected the preferences of the academic bourgeoisie.

"Jesus the Jew" . . . my *Visions of Christ*: LAS's essay "Jesus the Jew" was published in *Neue Deutsche Rundschau* VII (1896), pp. 342–351. It is fundamentally a reflection on the paradoxes of religion. In it Jesus is a mortal man of simple this-worldly Jewish faith who is forced to confront as he dies the failure of God to manifest Himself. He thus becomes at the last moment the opposite of himself: a tragic hero, the bearer of an intense inward experience and a relationship to the beyond so singular and unreachable as to become mysterious. The cross, on which both a human being and religion in its fullest sense "bled away to death," then becomes, by a final irony, the symbol of (a new) religion. There is only a slight affinity here with the protagonist of RMR's *Visions*, whose Christ, also mortal, is a disillusioned, reflexively ironic vagrant wandering among the miseries and perversities of modern life, in long poems, some of which seek to be scandalously blasphemous.

4 *Visions*: *Christus. Elf Visionen*, a cycle of narrative poems written between October 5, 1896, and July 1898. RMR added to them in later years. They remained unpublished until more than twenty years after his death.

Gärtner Theater: The "Theater am Gärtnerplatz," located a short distance south of the city's historic center, was built in 1865 as a Volkstheater and specialized in light entertainment. The play performed on May 14, 1897, was *Dunkle Mächte* (Dark powers), by Hélène von Racowitza-Shevitsch (née von Dönniges, 1845–1911), a Munich novelist who had gained notoriety as the lover of the socialist writer and politician Ferdinand Lassalle (1825–1864).

5 Englische Garten: The very spacious public park, constructed between 1804 and 1832, along the west bank of the Isar River and extending northward for some two miles from Prinzregentenstrasse and the Hofgarten (Royal Garden) in the city's center.

golden key: Probably a reference to Pension Quistorp, a prestigious boarding house locally known as the Fürstenhäuser ("princely houses" or "royal homes")—hence its emblem: "the golden key." It was located in Schellingstrasse, near the university and RMR's apartment. LAS stayed there with Frieda Freiin von Bülow (1857–1909), a well-known writer and lecturer about her African exploits. She was LAS's very close friend (since 1891) and frequent traveling companion (for example, to Paris in 1894; St. Petersburg and Vienna in 1895). Her autobiographical works describe life near Zanzibar in East Africa (now Tanzania) the way she experienced it in 1887–1888 as the companion of Carl Peters (1856–1918), the highly controversial propagandist for German colonization, and as the administrator (in 1893–1894) of her late brother Albrecht's coffee plantation. She also wrote a number of stories about her relationship with LAS.

6 Frau Rütling: An actress and mutual acquaintance.

Goudstikker: Nora Goudstikker and her younger sister Sophia managed the fashionable photography studio Elvira at von-der-Tann-Strasse 15. Its façade had been designed by LAS's friend August Endell (1871–1925), and was a touchstone of art-nouveau decoration. Nora (a free spirit nicknamed "Puck") also worked as a photographer, and made the well-known picture of Lou (see p. 16 and photo insert). She was RMR's closest female friend (he had written her many intense letters, and had dedicated a play to her) at the time he met LAS. Both sisters and Endell were present in LAS's party at the Gärtner Theater when RMR contrived to meet her there.

induction: RMR had been ordered to report to the garrison at Böhmisch-Leipau (Czeská Lipá, north of Prague). He was found unfit for military service after failing his physical exam.

8 the 12 novellas: Very likely the "novellas and sketches" that were published in his collection *Am Leben hin* (1898; Alongside life).

Ruth: This freely autobiographical tale (1895) was LAS's second published work of fiction, after the novel *Im Kampf um Gott* (1885; The struggle for God), which appeared under the nom de plume Henri Lou. *Ruth* is the story of a sixteen-year-old orphan, Ruth Delorme. She lives in St. Petersburg and is in love with a much older married man, Erik, who is a fictional portrait of Hendrik Gillot (1836–1916), Lou's tutor at the Dutch Reformed Mission in a German enclave of St. Petersburg, where she grew up.

poem: The four lines RMR quotes, changing "*uns*" (us) to "*mich*" (me), are the final stanza of a poem in eight quatrains, written by LAS and included in *Ruth* as one of Erik's poems.

Prague address: The address is that of RMR's father.

10 Syrgenstein: Probably Schloss Syrgenstein, the residence of Sophie von Waldburg-Syrgenstein (1857–1924) in the Western Allgäu near Lake Constance. The countess, a widow who had published some poetry, was a niece of the writer Marie von Ebner-Eschenbach (1830–1916), with whom LAS usually stayed during her trips to Vienna. Syrgenstein is a destination that is difficult to reach by train from Munich.

16 *Elvira*, Puck: see above, p. 6 and note.

Kufstein: Austrian border town on the Inn River southeast of Munich. The mention of Pushkin is obscure; it could refer to the city by that name south of St. Petersburg, or even imply that a plan to read Pushkin together had to be abandoned.

17 *Le rire*: *Le Rire: journal humoristique*, a weekly magazine of wit and humor with many cartoons, was published in Paris (F. Juven) November 10, 1894–January 31, 1903, when it continued in a different format—during the world war as *Le Rire Rouge.*

Bornstein: Paul Bornstein (1868–1939), a writer and the editor of a monthly review in Berlin, *Monatsschrift für neue Literatur und Kunst*, since October 1896. He had contacted RMR in Prague in February 1896, looking for "good translations of contemporary Czech poetry," and published several of his pieces.

Moderní Revue: The *Moderní Revue pro Literaturu, Umění a Život* (Modern revue of literature, art, and life), at that time the most important Czech literary monthly, published three of RMR's poems, one in translation.

"illustrated women's journal": Unknown. Possibly the new weekly *Die Jugend. Münchner illustrierte Wochenschrift für Kunst und Leben*, which had started publication on January 1, 1896 (until 1940) and reflected the artistic preferences and fashions of the progressive bourgeoisie.

18 studio: The painter Karl Wilhelm Diefenbach (1851–1913), a pioneer of the Reform Movement (vegetarianism, nude bathing, simple woolen frocks, retreat into nature, home schooling), had been forced to leave his cottage near Höllriegelskreuth, south of Munich, in 1888. He bought a house (Darchinger farm) in Dorfen, which he and his followers converted into an arts-and-crafts workshop.

Schack Gallery: Adolf Friedrich Graf von Schack (1815–1894), a prolific writer and translator and the most prominent among Munich's private patrons of the arts. He had given his large collection of paintings to Emperor Wilhelm II, who donated it to the city of Munich, where a special gallery had been built to house it.

19 Stauffer-Bern: Karl Stauffer-Bern (1857–1891 in Florence), a portrait painter, sculptor, engraver, and poet from Bern whose fateful love affair with Lydia Welti-Escher is recounted in: Otto

Brahm, *Karl Stauffer-Bern. Sein Leben, seine Briefe, seine Gedichte* (1892), a book Rilke had probably just read. One of Stauffer's students was Käthe Kollwitz.

20 poem: the manuscript page does not survive, but LAS quotes the poem from memory in her memoirs (*Looking Back*, "Epilogue, 1934"), along with the following comments addressed posthumously to RMR: "Strangely enough, I couldn't muster any appreciation for your early poetry, in spite of its musicality. (I remember your responding with this consolation: that you would say it so simply one day that I would understand its every word.) The only exception—even among the poems to me—was when you left *that page* in my room. I could have said to you exactly what it said to me, though not of course in verse and rhyme. And didn't there whisper in both of us jointly something which was beyond understanding and yet which we bore on our blood, experienced at the deepest roots of our physical being, in the most ordinary and the most sacred moments of our lives? At my request this poem found a place one year later in the *Book of Hours*." The poem appears as II.7 in the *Book of Hours*, where it slightly differs throughout from the version LAS quotes. There is disagreement over whether she has altered the poem from memory or is quoting an early version. We have chosen to translate the poem LAS recalls: if she has misremembered she has done so strongly.

Frau Wildenauer: A farmwoman from whom RMR and LAS bought vegetables. The Reisslers, a local family, were the owners of Loufried.

23 a mother: Franziska Gräfin zu Reventlow (1871–1918), a writer and translator, came from a prominent family in Husum (Schleswig), where her father was a Prussian county administrator. She was disinherited in 1892 when she left her hometown for the bohemian life of Munich, where she initially wanted to become a painter. RMR had been friends with her since his early days there; she mentions in an affectionate diary note of March 1897 that every morning during the difficult months of her pregnancy there was a poem from RMR waiting for her in her mailbox. Her son, Rolf, was born on September 1, 1897; she never disclosed his father's identity, saying she had wanted a child but not a husband. She and RMR remained frequent correspondents. The letter from her may be in response to a poem RMR wrote for her son on a postcard he mailed to her from Florence on April 16, 1898.

24 beach in East Prussia: Zoppot was a prosperous resort town near Danzig; it attracted some seven thousand visitors annually.

28 Loris: Pen name of Hofmannsthal.

29 Власть Т[ь]мы: *The Power of Darkness* (1889), a peasant tragedy by Lev Tolstoy.

31 address: St. Petersburg, at the corner of Nevskyprospect and Fontanka Street, Rooming House "Zentral."

33 my beautiful book: *Vom lieben Gott und Anderes* (Of the good Lord and other things), a collection of thirteen stories, was published Christmas 1900 as RMR's first book with Insel Verlag. It was illustrated by Vogeler.

Stshukin Museum . . . Amerika house: RMR and LAS saw the extraordinary collection of Western and Eastern paintings in the private gallery of the collector Sergei Stshukin in Moscow during May 1900. In the middle of May they had moved into the modest boarding house Amerika on the Vosdvishenka, near the Kremlin Gate.

34 there was only pure sound in me: see Ralph Freedman, *Life of a Poet: Rainer Maria Rilke* (New York, 1996), p. 98, on RMR's response to the painter Ilya Repin, whom he had met on his and LAS's first Russian journey: "[RMR] mysteriously [held] that the Russian language consisted only of sound and that one must not invent sense for it. . . . At certain hours—which Rilke called 'Russian hours'—sound becomes image, meaning, and form of expression."

38 the Nikolai Tolstoy material: LAS and RMR had stayed with Nikolai Tolstoy (a distant relative of the writer) at his estate in Novinki (northwest of Moscow, on the upper Volga) for a time in July 1900 during their second Russian trip. LAS's memories of the household had begun to coalesce as material for a novel (which would become *Rodinka*).

39 the novella nor Michael Kramer: LAS had been trying to finish her novella "Wolga"; she had also promised Gerhart Hauptmann a review of his play *Michael Kramer*.

41 Last Appeal: In place of a personal salutation LAS superscribed this letter "*Letzter Zuruf*"—literally "last shout" or "last call(ing out)." We have followed the by now firmly established English translation of this portentous and difficult phrase as "last appeal," in spite of the inappropriate connotations of pleading or imploring that might be conveyed by the English "appeal." The German phrase suggests, on the contrary, an address at once resolute and valedictory, strongly vocal yet arriving across very far inner distances.

Zemek: "Earthman," the Polish nickname of Friedrich Pineles (1868–1936), a "Hilfsarzt" (auxiliary physician) in neurology and internal medicine at the General Hospital in Vienna and a lecturer, later professor, at the university, where his specialty was hormone research. LAS had first met him in December 1895 at the house of the feminist writer Rosa Mayreder in Vienna. Their relationship of some ten years as lovers and travel companions was most intense between the end of 1900 and the fall of 1904.

Garshin: The Russian poet Vsevolod Mikhailovich Garshin (1855–1888), who recounted his experiences as a "volunteer" in the Russo-Turkish War of 1877–1878 in his novel *From the Reminiscences of Private Ivanov* (1887; German translation, 1889: *Aus den Erinnerungen des Gemeinen Iwanow*). At the turn of the century he was best known for his novella *The Red Flower* (1883), in which he described the mental state of an insane person. Garshin committed suicide.

"Songs of the Monk": The first part of *Das Stunden-Buch* (1905; The book of hours), titled "Das Buch vom mönchischen Leben" (The book of a monk's life). It was written during September/October 1899 in Schmargendorf and revised in April/May 1905 in Worpswede; *Das Stunden-Buch* was published Christmas 1905 with the dedication: "Gelegt in die Hände von Lou" (Laid into the hands of Lou).

44 rue de l'Abbe de l'Epée: When RMR first arrived in Paris, on August 28, 1902, he rented a shabby hotel room at 11 rue Toullier; when Clara arrived they moved into a more comfortable apartment on the rue de l'Abbé de l'Epée.

46 Niemann: Johanna Niemann (1844–1917), a writer and friend of LAS's whom RMR had met in Danzig-Langfuhr in June 1899 on their return from St. Petersburg at the end of their first Russian trip.

a book on Rodin: RMR's monograph, *Auguste Rodin*, written between the end of November and December 16, 1902, in Paris, was published in March 1903 as vol. x in a series of illustrated introductions (Berlin: Bard) and is dedicated to Clara: "Einer jungen Bildhauerin" (To a young sculptress).

Mädchenlieder: The "Lieder der Mädchen" (Girls' songs), most of which were written during RMR's first stay in Viareggio (May 1898). They were included in his collection *Mir zur Feier* (1899; To celebrate myself).

48 Westend: LAS and her husband had moved from Schmargendorf to Berlin-Westend early in April 1903. Schimmel, a white terrier, was LAS's new pet.

49 Barkenhoff: Vogeler's house in Worpswede.

Oberneuland: Near Bremen. Clara's parents rented a refurbished farmhouse there during the summer.

50 *Слово о полку Игоря*: *The Song of Igor's Campaign*, a heroic tale in dramatic prose written 1185–1187. RMR had received a copy of the Russian text in February 1896 and translated it between the end of 1902 and March 17, 1904. The German text was first published "with introduction and notes by André Gronicka" as *Rainer Maria Rilke's Translation of the "Igor Song" (Slovo)* (Philadelphia, 1949).

military school: RMR had attended the Militär-Unterrealschule at St. Pölten and the Militär-Oberrealschule at Mährisch-Weisskirchen from the end of September 1886 until June 1891.

À une heure de matin ("At one o'clock in the morning"; no. x of *Le spleen de Paris* in *Petits poèmes en prose*): "Finally! Alone! One hears only the rumbling of some belated and rickety cabs. For a few hours we shall have silence, if not repose. Finally! the tyranny of the human face has disappeared, and I shall suffer only from myself . . ."

51 Hotel Dieu: Huge hospital and paupers' hospice located in the center of Paris. See also sections 5, 6, and 21 of RMR's *Notebooks of Malte Laurids Brigge.*

57 Prayers: i.e., what would become "Das Buch von der Armut und vom Tode" (The book of poverty and of death), the third part of *The Book of Hours,* written in Viareggio, April 13–20.

Worpswede: RMR's short monograph on the artists' colony and five of its members, written in May 1902.

a new book by you?: Since her "Last Appeal" to RMR, LAS had published two works: the short novel *Ma. Ein Portrait* (1901) and *Im Zwischenland* (1902; The land in-between), a collection of five stories subtitled "from the inner life of adolescent girls."

Those "who labor and are heavy laden": see Matthew XI, 28 and Luke XXIII, 34.

59 birds came and brought bread: In I Kings, XVII, 7 the prophet Elijah is sent to hide in the desert where the "ravens brought him bread and meat" each morning and evening.

63 Rome, where my wife (at Rodin's wish) . . . : Clara Westhoff had been a frequent guest in Rodin's studio during the first six months of 1900 when she was studying in Paris. When she returned in October 1902 with RMR she renewed his acquaintance, and he treated her cordially as a former "student."

Subiaco: A village in the Sabine Mountains, east of Rome. It is closely associated with St. Benedict of Nursia, who wrote his *Regula monachorum* there. A monastery is still by the side of his Holy Grotto (Sacro Speco).

67 epigraph: RMR prefaced his book on Rodin with two quotes. The first reads "Writers act through words, sculptors through deeds. Pomponius Gauricus, *De sculptura* (c. 1504)." The second reads: "The hero is he who is immovably centered. Emerson."

68 stanzas: "Der Einsame" (The solitary), written in Viareggio on April 2, 1903, and published with slight changes in *The Book of Images.*

69 Kramskoy: Ivan Nikolayevich Kramskoy (1837–1887), a Russian portrait painter. RMR greatly admired his religious paintings, especially his *Christ in the Wilderness* (1872), which RMR saw as deeply iconoclastic: see the passage from his Schmargendorf Diary, in Rainer Maria Rilke, *Diaries of a Young Poet,* tr. Edward Snow and Michael Winkler (New York, 1997), pp. 144–145.

Rodin: RMR had first visited Rodin at his Villa des Brillants in Meudon on September 2, 1902.

78 Dictionary: *Deutsches Wörterbuch* (1852–1960). This dictionary was begun in the 1840s by Jacob and Wilhelm Grimm and is the most comprehensive historical dictionary of German. At Jacob's death (1863) the first four of sixteen volumes had been completed. In 1899, vol. IX (ending with the word "Seele") was published; vol. X followed in 1905.

Hofmannsthal: "Sommerreise" (Summer's journey), written in July 1903 and later published as "Die Rotonda des Palladio," in *Neue Freie Presse* (Vienna) of July 18, 1903. The essay reflects Hofmannsthal's refined, if not precocious cultural sensitivities. His thoughts had been stimulated by observations he made during a bicycle trip through northern Italy the previous month.

80 Hokusai: Katsushika Hokusai (1760–1849), one of the great masters of the Japanese colored woodcut. "It was not until the age of seventy-three that I came to understand somewhat the form and the true nature of birds, fish, and plants." Hokusai only began publishing his landscape designs in the 1820s, and did not bring out his most famous books until the 1830s (*Thirty-six Views of Mount Fuji,* 1831–33; and *One Hundred Views of Mount Fuji,* 1834–45, in 3 vols.)

81 Zuloaga: The Basque painter Ignacio Zuloaga y Zabaleta (1870–1945) was associated with the "Generation of '98" writers and, around 1900, represented Spain's most notable contribution to symbolist art. RMR had first met him in Paris in February 1903 and learned from him an appreciation of El Greco.

Florence: See RMR's Florence Diary, written between April 15 and July 6, 1898, in which he recorded his impressions of Florence and early Renaissance art (especially Botticelli and the della Robbias), of Viareggio and the Tuscan countryside, along with a variety of Nietzschean musings on art, love, and life.

82 no misunderstood fame: This theme introduces the monograph on Rodin.

the little tiger: Rodin owned a plaster cast of an ancient bronze tiger the size of a hand. RMR saw it as Rodin's connection with antiquity (letter to Clara of September 27, 1902).

Nike: The winged *Nike of Samothrace* (a Roman copy of a Victory statue from c. 200 B.C., or earlier), found in 1863 and displayed at the head of the Escalier Daru in the Louvre.

83 Vogüé: Eugène Melchior Vicomte de Vogüé (1848–1910), author of *Le roman Russe* (1886) which Rilke had read in November/December 1899.

Louis Léger (1843–1923): Author of *La littérature Russe* (1892), whose lectures at the Collège de France Rilke attended in the winter of 1902–1903.

Parlandt: Alfred Aleksandrovich Parland (1842–1920), a professor of architecture and interior design in St. Petersburg and author of a book on Greek temples.

84 Ellen Key: Swedish writer, pedagogue, and feminist (1849–1926). LAS's review of her controversial pamphlet *Missbrauchte Frauenkraft* (1898; The misuse of women's strength) in the women's-rights monthly *Die Frau* (V [June 1898], pp.513–516; Woman. A "monthly review for all aspects of woman's life in our time") led to their personal acquaintance in Berlin, where RMR too may have met her, and then to a friendship of some twenty years. His extensive review of her most widely read book, *Barnets Århundrade* (1900; in German as *Das Jahrhundert des Kindes*, 1902; The century of the child), in *Bremer Tageblatt* of June 8, 1902, called it "an event, a document one will not be able to bypass." Their correspondence began in September 1902 with various expressions of solidarity and with RMR's courteous pleas for support and for advice about how to bring up Ruth. But his deference in these appeals soon gave way to undertones of annoyance and estrangement that, by June 1906, had turned into politely phrased hostility.

Hauptmann: RMR had first met the playwright and novelist Gerhart Hauptmann (1862–1946) on December 1, 1900, at LAS's house and was deeply affected by his drama *Michael Kramer*, as evidenced by the concluding reflections in his Worpswede Diary: see *Diaries of a Young Poet*, pp. 270–276.

86 new book: Fair copy of sections II (1901) and III (1903) of *The Book of Hours* (1905). RMR had given the poems of section I (1899) to LAS for safekeeping in a sepia notebook with leather covering.

88 address in Rome: RMR and Clara had arrived in Rome on September 10, 1903; he first stayed at 5 Via del Campidoglio, "the last precipitous house above the Forum" (until the end of November), while Clara, after several weeks, moved into a studio of the Villa Strohl-Fern.

statue: The equestrian statue of the emperor Marcus Aurelius had been placed in the Piazza del Campidoglio by Michelangelo; the fragmentary Ludovisi Throne (*Birth of Aphrodite*), a tripartite "altar" from the Temple of Aphrodite in Eryx (Erice, in Sicily) with lifelike sculptures in the early classical style (460–450 B.C.), had been part of the collection of ancient sculptures in the garden of the Villa Ludovisi before it was transferred to the Museo Nazionale Romano (Terme Museum). A photograph of this marble relief, a present from RMR, hung in LAS's living room in Göttingen.

Tolstoy: In his novella *How Much Land Does a Man Need?* of 1866.

89 Villa Borghese: On December 1, 1903, RMR moved into the Studio al Ponte, a one-room cabin located by a bridge. It was part of a complex of twenty-eight studio houses that Alfred Strohl-Fern (1845–1927, in Rome since 1870), a painter, sculptor, and art patron, had built in the park near the Porta del Popolo. They were available to talented artists irrespective of nationality, but a year's lease was required.

90 "How do I remember Rome . . .": A remarkable testament to LAS's ability to shrug off the potentially burdensome past, since it was during her very *eventful* stay in Rome (January through April 1882) that she entered into a *ménage à trois* (or so scandal perceived it) with Nietzsche and his friend Paul Rée. Could RMR *not* have been aware of this context when he asks innocently, "How do you remember Rome, Lou?"

94 Boscoreale: In 1900, five splendid frescoes from about 80 B.C. had been discovered in a Roman villa at the foot of Mount Vesuvius. The painting RMR describes is the central panel on the east wall of the large dining room (now at the Metropolitan Museum of Art in New York). LAS used his description with some modifications in her novel *Das Haus* (1919; written 1904), where young Balder (that is, RMR imagined by her as the child of happy parents) writes to his mother from Rome: "As I was standing before these exhibited murals from a villa near Boscoreale (the first ancient paintings I have seen, and it is said that even the Museum of Naples has none better), there was one among them that I must tell you about. Among the fragments it was almost the only piece that was preserved unbroken, and it shows a woman who, calmly sitting there, listens to a man as he speaks to her quietly and lost in thought, his hands resting on a staff that he may have used during his long wanderings through distant lands. The sense of arriving was still in him, haste had not as yet fallen from him, his blood was still pulsing in his feet. But whatever experiences and dangers he recounted: their only real purpose was to let him arrive where this woman was standing tall before him, calm in her maturity; where she, like a silent summer night, knew how to assuage and how to bring everything home from coincidence and confusion and noise. Thus there was quietness and motion, both, in this picture that exerted such a powerful effect because the two figures were so perfectly fulfilled in each other, heavy with each other and held together by a necessity beyond compare. — No, how can this picture tell you; my life will do it—that I stand before you like this; that this alone is the measure of my being, my choice and conscience and devotion, or my turning-away. From wherever the waters that feed my wellsprings and streams may come, they must make their way home into Your sea. My life will be only what I can carry all the way to You, and at some future time . . . it will be the same as You take it in." — The narrative then continues: "The boy's poetic imagination was already turning her real existence into that of a legendary woman: and, in her motherly way, she did not withdraw, protecting it from the ridicule or amazement of others as the secret they alone share."

97 Иванъ Великій: "Big Ivan," the Kremlin's belfry. The tremendous sound of its bell (accompanied by all the bells in Moscow and 120 canon shots) had awed RMR when he and LAS heard it together at Easter Sunday midnight 1899.

98 Princess: The first version of *The White Princess,* conceived in May 1898 during RMR's first stay in Viareggio. A significantly expanded version (November 1904) was published in the collection *Frühe Gedichte* (1909; Early poems).

99 Reventlow: See p. 23 and note. RMR eventually wrote a somewhat peevish review of the book for the Berlin weekly *Die Zukunft* (February 20, 1904), mostly as a series of questions directly addressed to the title character and the author.

100 War: The Russo-Japanese War over Manchuria and Korea, 1904–1905.

101 Smirnoff: Aleksei Tsacharovich Smirnov; a warehouse worker at the Kotov (some sources

say: Girot) textile mill in Moscow whom RMR had met in one of the courses LAS's friend Sophia Schill (1861–1928, alias Sergei Orlovski) taught as part of a program to bring higher education to the working class.

Kierkegaard: See p. 130 and note.

Jacobsen: Jens Peter Jacobsen (1847–1885), by profession a botanist, was the novelist RMR most admired up through the early stages of *Malte Laurids Brigge.*

102 дай Богъ!: God grant it!

Finland and the Baltic provinces: Control of Finland passed from Sweden to Russia in 1809. A liberal legislation as well as economic and cultural freedoms prevailed for most of the nineteenth century until Nicholas II (1894–1917) introduced autocratic rule. Russia's Baltic provinces had been annexed by Peter the Great (Kurland from Poland in 1721) and Alexander I (Livonia and Estonia from Sweden in 1809). They enjoyed internal autonomy until 1880, when the central government decreed their assimilation with the rest of the empire.

103 Христосъ воскресъ!: "He is risen!" is the greeting exchanged by Russians on Easter.

104 Ivanov and Gogol: RMR had seen works by the painter Aleksander Andreyevich Ivanov (1806–1858) in May 1900 at the Tretyakov Gallery in Moscow (*Christ Appearing to the People*, 1837–1857, with 400 preparatory sketches; *Christ Walking on Water*, 1850s) and came to admire him as the greatest of Russia's religious artists. Ivanov lived in Italy from 1830 until 1857, mostly in Rome, and was a friend of Nikolai Vasiliyevich Gogol (1809–1852), who spent extended periods of his later life, especially the years 1836–1839 and 1847–1848, in Rome, where he worked on the second part of *Dead Souls* (1842).

Iconostass: Ikonostas, the Imperial Gate (or Czar's Gate) in Russian churches in the center of a medium-high wall that separates the laity from the priest. It affords a view of the altar and is covered with icons.

105 Kuropatkin: Aleksei Nikolayevich Kuropatkin (1848–1925), war minister and commander-in-chief of Russian land forces in the war with Japan. He was relieved of his command on March 10, 1905, after the battle of Mukden and the loss of 89,000 soldiers.

106 my new work: RMR began writing *The Notebooks of Malte Laurids Brigge* on February 8, 1904; he would not finish it until January 27, 1910.

109 work: The novel *Das Haus. Familiengeschichte vom Ende des vorigen Jahrhunderts* (The house. A family's story from the end of the previous century), the setting of which is primarily the Göttingen Loufried and its vicinity. The book was not published until 1919.

114 D'Annunzio: Gabriele d'Annunzio (1863–1938); the precociously ornate poems of his early years, beginning with *Primo vere* (1879), share various characteristics with RMR's own youthful verse.

116 Thisted: Town in northern Jutland where Jacobsen was born and died.

118 Carpaccio: Vittore Carpaccio (1455–1525), Venetian painter of the early Renaissance; RMR's plans to write these two monographs remained unrealized.

119 Schönaich: On May 30, 1902, after Clara and Ruth had left Westerwede to visit friends in Amsterdam, RMR went to Schloss Haseldorf in Holstein, north of Hamburg. He stayed

there for five weeks as the guest of Prince Emil von Schönaich-Carolath-Schilden (1852–1908). RMR's lodging (where Clara later joined him for a time) was a quiet room in the Cavaliershaus that stood in a large park. The estate's archive reflected the regional prominence of its owners and, along with the library, afforded RMR various insights into the culture of the German-Danish aristocracy. Information culled from family chronicles (of the Ahlefeldts, Oppeln-Schildens, Reventlows, Bernstorffs, and so on) and impressions of the château went into the writing of *Malte Laurids Brigge*, somewhat in the manner of Jacobsen's novel *Fru Marie Grubbe* (1876), a sequence of "Interieurs from the Seventeenth Century" that makes extensive use of archival documents.

Jammes: Francis Jammes (1868–1938), the French poet whom Malte Laurids Brigge reads in the Bibliothèque Nationale, is an author of intimate gentleness that reflects the spirit of Franciscan piety. RMR, no less than LAS, was very fond of Jammes's *Le roman du lièvre* (1903) (The romance of the rabbit; German translation *Der Hasenroman*, 1916), and recommended Jammes to his publisher, but there is no evidence that he translated him.

120 Michelet: The historian Jules Michelet (1798–1874), author of a *Histoire de France* (1833–1867, in 17 vols.), also published studies on natural history, among them *Le mer* (1861).

Goncourts: The brothers Edmond (1822–1896) and Jules (1830–1870) de Goncourt collaborated on novels and cultural studies, especially of the French eighteenth century, among them *Portraits intimes du 18e siècle* (1857–1858), *L'art du 18e siècle* (1859–1875), and *La femme au 18e siècle* (1862).

Berlin University: 6,327 students attended Friedrich-Wilhelms-Universität in 1900–1901 (9,120 in 1911–1912). Heidelberg had 1,164 students in 1896, 2,382 in 1925. In general, more than half of all German university students were enrolled in the various disciplines of the Philosophische Fakultät (Humanities and Social Sciences).

121 Zürich: LAS had studied philosophy and the sociology of religion in Zürich during 1880–1881. Auguste Forel (1848–1931), a psychiatrist and "expert in social hygiene," also held the chair of Medical Psychology at the university and served as the director of Burghölzli, the renowned institution for mental patients. He was opposed to psychoanalysis. RMR had met the writer Carl Hauptmann, an acquaintance of LAS's in Berlin since the early 1890s, in Worpswede. Hauptmann had established personal contacts with Forel during his student days in Zürich (1885–1889), where his special interest was the philosophy of science.

Woelfflin: The art historian Heinrich Woelfflin (1864–1945), the successor of Jacob Burckhardt in Basel and, since 1901, professor in Berlin. He spent the winter of 1903–1904 in Rome preparing his book on the art of Albrecht Dürer (1905) and staying in a studio adjacent to RMR's at the Villa Strohl-Fern.

lecture manuscript: "Rainer Maria Rilke, en tysk diktare och gudsbegreppet" (Rainer Maria Rilke, a German poet and his concept of God), now lost, was revised and published as "Rainer Maria Rilke, en österrikisk diktare" (An Austrian poet) in the Swedish review *Ord och Bild* (XIII, 5 and 6 [1904], pp. 513–525 and pp. 558–569). A German translation appeared in February 1906 in the Prague journal *Deutsche Arbeit*, a "monthly review for the intellectual life of the Germans in Bohemia."

123 Düsseldorf: RMR and Clara, returning from Rome, were in Düsseldorf (June 19–22, 1904) to see the International Art Exhibition. Rodin (59 sculptures and 50 drawings), Zuloaga (20 drawings), and Adolf von Menzel (1815–1905) each had special rooms. Georg Oeder (1846–before 1925), a landscape painter and professor at the academy in Düsseldorf, was a collector of Japanese art. Kitagawa Utamaro (1753–1806) and Torii Kiyonaga (1742–1815) were illustrators, painters, and woodcut artists in the Ukiyoe-style who depicted scenes from contemporary urban life. Hokusai's great book of sketches, *Mangwa* (A plethora of designs; 1814–1848, in 13 and 2 posthumous vols.).

128 Naples: RMR and Clara spent five days in Naples (June 5–9, 1904).

Pasternak: Leonid Pasternak (1862–1945), a painter, was the father of the poet Boris Pasternak. RMR and LAS had met him on April 30, 1899, during their first trip to Moscow and visited him again in May 1900. In the summer of 1904, Pasternak was on a tour of museums in Germany, Austria, France, and Italy to study Western painting, especially portraiture. He too may have been on his way (back) to Düsseldorf, where he had organized the Russian section for the International Art Exhibition, which had opened in May.

Milan: In Milan RMR and Clara saw Leonardo's *Cenacolo* (1495–1497) in the refectory of S. Maria delle Grazie.

The cathedral: The Cathedral (1386–completed 1813) is built entirely of white marble in mostly a late Gothic style, with a large number of turrets, pilasters, and over 600 statues.

129 Ny-Carlsberg: During his brief stopover in Copenhagen (June 23–24), RMR visited the Ny Carlsberg Glyptotek, a museum that owned ten of Rodin's sculptures. It had received the extensive art collection of Carl Jacobsen (1842–1914), the owner of the Ny Carlsberg Brewery. A copy of the *Burghers of Calais*, which RMR knew only from photographs (see letter of June 24, 1904, to Clara), stands in the museum's garden.

this château: RMR had accepted an invitation from Hanna Larsson (that is, Larsdotter, 1880–1953) to stay at her estate of Borgeby gård near Lund, which her father, a wealthy farmer, had bought for her in 1888. Their contacts had been established through Ellen Key and her friend, the poet and critic Anders Österling (1884–1981). Her other guest at the time was the Swedish writer and painter Ernst Norlind (1877–1952), who was preparing for a trip to Russia and whom she married in 1907.

130 Hermann Bang: The Danish writer Herman Bang (1857–1912). RMR had reviewed the German translation of his novel *Det hvide Hus* (1898; *Das weisse Haus*, 1902) in *Bremer Tageblatt* (April 16, 1902) and made use of its descriptions in *Malte Laurids Brigge.*

Sören Kierkegaard . . . to his fiancée: In 1840 Kierkegaard, the Danish religious thinker and philosopher (1813–1855), proposed to Regine Olsen (1822–1904), with whom he had been in love (to the point of infatuation) since she was sixteen. She accepted with an equal passion, but almost immediately afterward he became conflicted, and after constant soul-searching (much of it in correspondence with her) he broke off their engagement a year later, feeling it to be incompatible with both his vocation and his melancholy, which he considered his defining trait. RMR translated fifteen of these letters (they are in the Rilke Archive, Gernsbach, MSS 550). See also his letter to E. Key of October 19, 1904, in their *Briefwechsel*, ed. Th. Fiedler, p. 107 ff.

131 dear Lou: The German has "l.L.", which we translate as an abbreviation of "liebe Lou."

Stories: With the inscription "Für Lou, Borgeby gård, im August 1904."

132 Christiania: The name of Oslo, 1624–1924.

address: No. 54 Officers' Street, where LAS's mother lived at that time.

133 Skagen: On the northernmost tip of Denmark.

старушка : diminutive for "old woman" or "mother."

134 Jonsered: A modern suburb of Göteborg where RMR (October 8–December 2, 1904) and occasionally Clara were guests at Furuborg, the house of John James Gibson (1858–1932) and Elizabeth Gibson (1860–1927). The husband was a civil engineer and the technical director, later the chief executive of Gibson's Textile Mill.

kobtsar on the Крещатикъ: a (blind) singer on the main street of Kiev; RMR evokes for LAS a shared memory (she recorded it in her diary) from their second Russian journey in June 1900. A kobtsa is a stringed instrument.

135 the book I began: *The Notebooks of Malte Laurids Brigge.*

doctor: Dr. Carl Ottosen, director of the Skodsborg Hydro sanatorium, north of Copenhagen. His diagnosis: "You are suffering from anemia, impaired circulation, somewhat depressed metabolism with an excess of uric acid, exhaustion and slight weakness of one cardiac valve."

Brandes: Georg (Morris Cohen) Brandes (1842–1927), a prolific literary historian and critic, since 1902 professor in Copenhagen.

Michaëlises: Karin Michaëlis, née Bech-Brödum (1872–1950) and her husband (from 1895 until 1911), Sophus Michaëlis (1865–1932), both writers, had been acquaintances of LAS and RMR since their Schmargendorf time.

Klingenberg: Helene Klingenberg, née Klot von Heydenfeldt (1865–1946), was a native of Riga (Latvia) and had published a short novel, *Eine Frau. Studie nach dem Leben* (1892; A woman. A study from life). After her marriage in 1897 to the Berlin architect Otto Klingenberg, she became LAS's closest friend. RMR met her that same year in Munich.

Krüger: Therese Krüger, who shared an apartment with LAS in Paris in 1894, translated LAS's book on Nietzsche (1894) into Danish and Herman Bang's *The White House* into German.

136 Lahmann: Dr. Heinrich Lahmann (1860–1905) had founded the fashionable sanitarium Weisser Hirsch (White Stag) in Radebeul, near Dresden, in 1887. In May 1901 RMR and Clara spent their honeymoon there. (RMR had fallen ill just before their wedding.) During their second stay (March 7–April 19, 1905), they met Countess Luise Schwerin, née Freiin von Nordeck zur Rabenau (1849–1906), of Friedelhausen (Hesse). She arranged their introduction to Baron Karl von der Heydt (1858–1922), the Berlin banker and dilettante playwright who became one of RMR's major patrons.

137 Simmel: The philosopher and sociologist Georg Simmel (1858–1918) was a *Privatdozent* (unsalaried lecturer) at the university since 1885. His appointment to an "untenured professorship," or position without a chair, was postponed until 1901, since most German aca-

demics still equated sociology with socialism. RMR attended several of his lecture courses, probably as early as 1898. While little is known about their personal relationship, there is no doubt that Simmel, one of the most versatile intellectuals of his time and a charismatic teacher, exerted considerable influence on the young art enthusiast.

138 Breysig: Kurt Breysig (1866–1940), a cultural historian and philosopher of history who had been teaching at the University of Berlin since 1896.

Huch: Ricarda Huch (1864–1947) came from a prosperous academic and artistic family in Braunschweig. Since German universities at that time did not admit women, she obtained a doctorate in history in Zürich (1892), where she made LAS's acquaintance and lived as a librarian and teacher until 1896. Her literary reputation was established with her first novel, *Erinnerungen von Ludolf Ursleu dem Jüngeren* (1893; Reminiscences of Ludolf Ursleu the younger), an autobiographical love story about the decline of a Hanseatic merchant family. She became a writer of poetry, fiction, and cultural studies both on literary and historical subjects. During her years in Munich (1900–1906 and 1910–1927), she often participated in the city's social and cultural life, occasionally in the company of RMR and his friends. Her daughter Marietta for a while attended the same school as Ruth; Clara, in 1912, sculpted her distinctive (and frequently painted) head in bronze.

the small Madonna: Very likely a shared memory of Russia; unidentified.

139 poem: Perhaps "Abend in Skåne" (Evening in Skåne), or "Sturm" (Storm), or "Vorgefühl" (Presentiment) in *The Book of Images.*

Cornet: *Die Weise von Liebe und Tod des Cornets Christoph Rilke* (The lay of love and death of the Cornet Christoph Rilke), written by RMR "in one stormy autumn night" in 1899 and first titled "Aus einer Chronik—Der Cornet—1664—," revised in August 1904 in Borgeby gård (published in *Deutsche Arbeit* [Prague], IV, 1, October 1904), final revisions completed on June 12, 1906, in Paris; publication December 1906 at the same time as the augmented *Book of Images.*

140 "the book": Probably Helene Klingenberg's *Eine Frau.*

Småland: RMR, who would leave Furuborg for Copenhagen on December 2, was accompanied by John James Gibson when he visited Ellen Key (November 27) on her brother's farm, Oby, near Alvesta, in the province of Småland (south-central Sweden). He used impressions of this trip in *Malte Laurids Brigge*, especially in part II, section 4.

141 *Lifelines*: Ellen Key's memoirs, *Lifslinier*, appeared in three parts (Stockholm: Bonnier, 1904, 1905, 1906). German translations were published almost simultaneously.

Hammershöj: The Danish painter Vilhelm Hammershøi (1864–1916). Many Germans at the time considered him the most genuinely Danish representative of contemporary Northern art and culture.

Damgaar: Dangaard, where Therese Krüger sometimes lived; Fredericia: on the eastern coast of the Danish mainland.

Obstfelder: The Norwegian poet and novelist Sigbjørn Obstfelder (1866–1900), who had died in Paris and in certain respects became a model for the title character of *Malte Laurids Brigge.* RMR, at any rate, knew of his close relationship with Ellen Key. He had read

Obstfelder's diary-novel *En prests dagbog* (1900; *Tagebuch eines Pfarrers* [A cleric's journal]) in 1901, and would write a review of his posthumous works, which were published in German in 1905 as *Pilgerfahrten* (Pilgrimages).

142 Съ новымъ годомъ, старой дружбой!: To the New Year and Old Friendship!

иконописецъ: icon painter.

143 Изломай!: "shatter it!" or "break it to pieces!"; perhaps "crack it open!" Unexplained. A phrase (apparently without literary or cultural associations) that RMR and LAS used between them as an admonition to "get over it" or "make a fresh start."

Samskola: The Högre Samskola, a progressive coeducational school (also for adults), was founded in Göteborg in 1901 and was supported by the Gibsons and Ellen Key. On November 17, 1904, RMR gave a reading from his poetry (see letter to Clara of November 19, 1904) in the school's gymnasium; he also wrote an essay about the institution (in: *Die Zukunft* XIII, 14 [January 17, 1905], pp. 34–38.)

White Princess: The final revision of RMR's play was completed at Furuborg on November 18, 1904, but not published until 1909, at the end of the volume *Frühe Gedichte* (Early poems).

144 Drachmann: Holger Drachmann (1846–1908), Danish poet and novelist. The specific poem has not been identified.

Zwischenland: LAS's book *Im Zwischenland. Fünf Geschichten aus dem Seelenleben halbwüchsiger Mädchen* (1902; The land in between. Five stories from the life of adolescent girls).

drama: *Der Graf von Charolais. Ein Trauerspiel* (1905; The Count of Charolais. A tragedy) by Richard Beer-Hofmann (1866–1945) uses plot material from *The Fatal Dowry* (1619) by Philip Massinger and Nathaniel Field. It premiered at the Neue Theater in Berlin, directed by Max Reinhardt, on December 23, 1904.

Volinsky: Akim Levovich Volinsky-Flekser (1863–1926), a Russian critic and writer whose acquaintance LAS had made in St. Petersburg. They met again in spring 1897 in Munich and he was an occasional visitor at Loufried in Wolfratshausen. The first part of his book on Dostoyevsky, published in Germany as *Das Buch vom grossen Zorn* (1905; Kniga velikago gneva), discusses *The Demons*, *Crime and Punishment*, and *The Idiot*.

Nyström-Hamilton: Louise Nyström-Hamilton's *Ellen Key. En Lifsbild* (Stockholm, 1904) was published in German as vol. 3 of the series Biographien bedeutender Frauen (Biographies of noteworthy women): *Ellen Key. Ein Lebensbild* (Leipzig, 1904; 108 pp.).

145 *your* book: *The Book of Hours* (in their correspondence usually referred to as "the Prayers") was published in 1905.

Garborg: Hulda Garborg (1862–1934) and her husband, the Norwegian poet Arne Garborg (1851–1924), lived in Germany during the 1890s. They were close friends of LAS, whose book on Ibsen's female characters Hulda had translated into Danish (1893). The latter's "little book" is probably *Das Weib vom Manne erschaffen. Bekenntnisse einer Frau* (1904; Woman, created by man. Confessions of a woman, a translation of *Kvinden Skapt av Manden*).

Weininger: The book *Geschlecht und Charakter. Eine prinzipielle Untersuchung* (Vienna, 1903; *Sex and Character*, 1906) by Otto Weininger (1880–1903), a revised version of the author's dissertation, reads like a misogynous and anti-Jewish diatribe masquerading as a psychological study. It develops a contrastive typology of "Man and Woman" by employing such categories as sexuality, consciousness, talent-genius-memory, logic-ethics-ego and morality-eroticism-esthetics. Its final three chapters deal with "the nature of Woman and her significance in the Universe," "Judaism," and "Woman and Mankind." RMR had read this book while convalescing at the sanitarium Weisser Hirsch (Dresden) in March 1905 and was fascinated with Weininger's thesis that all life is bisexual.

146 Holtzapfel: Rudolf Maria Holzapfel (1874–1930), an Austrian philosopher born in Cracow and educated at the University of Bern. He had a special interest in the psychology of religion and proclaimed what he called "Panideal," the highest earthly fulfillment of "Allsehnsucht" (universal longing).

147 my doctor: Dr. med. Georg Noack, who supervised Rilke's cure at Weisser Hirsch.

149 giant box: A large restaurant was being built near Loufried.

152 Alma: Helene's sister; Reinhold and Gerda, her children.

Schluppes: *Schlupp, der böse Hund* (1866, 18 pp.; Schlupp, the bad dog), a humorous picture book.

Treseburg: LAS and RMR, together again, visited Helene Klingenberg in Treseburg (Harz), arriving from Halberstadt (some ten miles north of Blankenburg) on July 16 and planning to stay until August. But within two days RMR found this "German summer resort unbearable" (letter to Clara of July 18). On July 21 he left, by way of Kassel and Marburg, for Friedelhausen in Hesse, Countess Luise Schwerin's estate, where he stayed until September 9.

153 Rodin invited me to live with him: In a letter of July 21, RMR informed Rodin of his plans to travel to Paris at the beginning of September, and on September 6 he accepted Rodin's invitation to join him at Meudon, a suburb of Paris, where, in 1895, the sculptor had bought a modest building, the Villa des Brillants. RMR stayed there as Rodin's guest, then moved with him to Paris, where he worked as a kind of private secretary in charge of his host's correspondence, a position that paid a monthly salary of fr. 200 for an anticipated two hours of work per day. It was held by over thirty other "secrétaires particuliers" between 1899 and 1916. A misunderstanding about the extent of Rilke's discretionary authority—he had answered two letters addressed to Rodin without informing him—brought about an irrational accusation and his immediate dismissal on May 10, 1906. They were not reconciled until November 1907.

154 lecture tour: On Rodin, in Dresden (October 23, before an audience of 650 at the Litterarische Gesellschaft) and in Prague (October 25, 1905, at the Urania). The Verein für Kunst was associated with Paul Cassirer (1871–1926)'s gallery in Berlin.

155 the Buddha: A statuette in the garden at Meudon; see RMR's "Buddha" and "Buddha in Glory" in *New Poems*.

My Russian friends: Victor de Golubeff (1879–1945) and his wife; he was an art historian and collector. Rodin sculpted a bust of Madame N. de Golubeff.

Verhaeren: Émile Verhaeren (1855–1916), a wide-ranging art critic and accomplished Belgian poet, lived part of the year in St. Cloud near Paris and was a favorite of Rodin's.

156 Rohde: Erwin Rohde (1845–1898), the classical philologist and early friend of Nietzsche's; his book: *Psyche. Seelencult und Unsterblichkeitsglaube der Griechen* (1890–1894; Psyche. The cult of souls and belief in immortality among the Greeks, 1925).

Karl v. d. Heydt: RMR was introduced to him and his wife, Elisabeth von der Heydt (1864–1963), at Friedelhausen on 19 August 19, 1905. Their patronage supported his work in Paris, especially after his break with Rodin, and furthered his contacts with the world of art collectors. A fund of 4,000 marks, initiated without RMR's knowledge by his publisher Anton Kippenberg—and sustained also by contributions from v. d. Heydt, R. Kassner and Harry Graf Kessler—and quarterly advances of 500 marks from Insel Verlag paid him a monthly stipend of 500 marks from 1912 to 1914. *Neue Gedichte* (December 1907) is dedicated to "Karl und Elisabeth von der Heydt in Freundschaft." They also provided, in 1919, for Ruth's education.

Schulte: Eduard Schulte, owner of a "Kunstsalon" (gallery) in Berlin.

Thorwaldsen: Bertel Thorvaldsen (1768–1844), a Danish sculptor, worked in the neoclassical style of Canova and Jacques-Louis David.

157 Marie: Marie Stephan, LAS's housekeeper since 1901, and her older daughter Maria ("Mariechen," or, little Marie), who was born in February 1905 and died in 1994. Speculation has it that LAS's husband was the father of the child. In 1906 a court established that a butcher's apprentice from Rengshausen near Kassel was the child's "procreator" and liable for her support until she turned sixteen. Marie continued living at Loufried as a housemaid until her death in March 1928, since 1914 together with her husband, August Stephan, a Göttingen railroad worker. She had a second daughter, Erika Ruth, born April 1915, who died of diphtheria at the age of two. LAS treated Maria as a beloved grandchild, later adopted her, and in 1934 named her (since 1927 Maria Apel) the heir of her nonliterary property. On this see: "*. . . als käm ich heim zu Vater und Schwester.*" *Lou Andreas-Salomé—Anna Freud. Briefwechsel 1919–1937*, edited by Daria A. Rothe and Inge Weber (Göttingen: Wallstein, 2001), vol. II, pp. 690–691.

Frau Fischer: Hedwig Fischer (1871–1952), wife of Samuel Fischer (1859–1934), the most prestigious publisher of belles-lettres in Germany.

158 The *Book of Images*: The second edition of *The Book of Images* (December 1906) included thirty-seven new poems that had been written between 1902 and 1906.

Hofmannsthal: RMR had read act I of his drama *Ödipus und die Sphinx* (1906) in *Neue Rundschau* (issue of January 1906). See also his letter to Clara of January 18, 1906. With *Electra* (1903), Hofmannsthal had become the principal librettist for Richard Strauss.

Hauptmann: *Und Pippa tanzt. Ein Glashüttenmärchen* (1906; And Pippa dances. A fairytale among glass blowers) premiered on January 19, 1906, at the Lessingtheater in Berlin. LAS had attended the dress rehearsal (and in December 1905 a reading by the author before a small group of friends). Her review (*Die Zukunft*, March 17, 1906) expresses a much more favorable response than RMR's to this symbolist play's evocation of an atmosphere of magic artistry.

159 Frieda: The anticipated meeting with LAS's very close friend Frieda von Bülow in Weimar did not come about.

Tsar Fyodor: The historical drama *Czar Fyodor*, by Aleksei K. Tolstoy (1817–1875), was the first play performed by the Moscow Art Theater, co-founded in 1898 by Konstantin S. Stanislavsky (1863–1938). It was a part of their repertoire also during their European tour of 1906, which included plays by Gorky, Chekhov, and Ibsen. RMR saw the troupe again in Paris in May 1906.

the lecture: "Vom Werke Rodins" (On Rodin's works), originally planned for March 9, 1906, was given on March 20.

160 Your husband's birthday: F. C. Andreas's sixtieth birthday was on April 14.

Chatelet theater: The municipal Théâtre du Châtelet, which opened in 1862, had over three thousand seats.

Benois: Alexandre N. Benois (Benua; 1870–1960), Russian painter and writer on art, author of a history of Russian painting in the nineteenth century (St. Petersburg, 1901–1902; *The Russian School of Painting*, 1916), which RMR, in 1901, had started to translate.

Harden: The journalist and critic Maximilian Harden (1861–1927), editor of the weekly *Die Zukunft* in Berlin, who wrote several articles about the performances of Stanislavsky's acting company.

161 all kinds of traveling: July 29–August 16 through Belgium with Clara and Ruth; thereafter to the summer residence of the von der Heydts on the Wacholderhöhe in Godesberg (August 17–31) and to various towns in Hesse (Braunfels, Giessen, Marburg, and Friedelhausen, the château, built around 1850 in the neo-Gothic style, of the Nordeck family); then with Clara to Berlin (5 October 5–November 24). RMR left for Capri on November 25 and stayed on the island between December 4, 1906, and May 20, 1907, in a pavilion (Rosenhäusl) in the park of Villa Discopoli. He was the guest of Alice Faehndrich (1857–1908), the widowed sister of the countess Luise von Schwerin (1849–1906). The others in their group were her stepmother, Julie von Nordeck zur Rabenau (1842–1928), and the young countess Manon zu Solms-Laubach (1882–1975).

162 Heiligendammerstrasse: LAS and her husband had lived at Heiligendammerstrasse 7 in Berlin-Schmargendorf between 1897 and 1903.

Dieffenbach: See p. 18 and note.

Gorki: Maxim Gorky (1868–1936), Marxist since 1898, lived in exile on Capri from 1906 to 1913, having been arrested in 1905 in connection with the Russian naval revolt.

Meta: Baroness Barbara Meta von Salis-Marschlins (1855–1929), a writer who had been acquainted with Nietzsche in Sils Maria. She owned a villino on Capri.

163 Съ новымъ годомъ: Russian New Year's greeting.

164 Sacré-Coeur: The Hôtel (or Palais) Biron, at 77 rue de Varenne, built in 1728 and now the Musée Rodin. The palace had been used as a convent school by the Dames du Sacré-Coeur until the state confiscated it in compliance with the Law of the Separation (1904). After the last nun departed in 1907, the building was to be sold on December 18, 1909, in forty-

five lots. In October 1909 Rodin rented four rooms on the main floor for 5,900 francs a year (see RMR's letter to Clara of November 3, 1909). As of January 1, 1912, all residents were ordered to vacate the building which, in October 1911, the Council of Ministers had decided to keep intact after all. In July 1912, Rodin was at last allowed to remain as its sole tenant. RMR lived at the Palais Biron, with several longer interruptions, in different apartments from August 31, 1908, until October 12, 1911. Other residents at this time were Jean Cocteau, Romain Rolland, Henri Matisse, and Isadora Duncan.

Christmas package: *Der neuen Gedichte anderer Teil* (*New poems: the other part*), dedicated "À mon grand Ami Auguste Rodin" and published early November 1908. In May 1909 RMR had a copy of the book sent by (female) messenger to LAS at the hotel where she was staying with Ellen Key.

былина: A *bylína* (event) is an old Russian heroic song in unrhymed tetrameters; it is not known which one RMR gave LAS as a present. ("The Song of Igor's Campaign" is not a bylína, though LAS might conceivably have regarded it as such.)

165 Bichat: Marie François Xavier Bichat (1771–1802), a professor of anatomy and physiology. Flaubert mentions him briefly as the teacher of the physician who attends the dying Emma Bovary. His book is *Recherches physiologiques sur la vie et la mort* (1799; *Physiological researches upon life and death*, 1809).

Requiem: *Requiem. Für eine Freundin* [= Paula Modersohn-Becker]. *Für Wolf Graf von Kalckreuth* (1908; written October 31–November 5, 1908, in Paris and published (500 copies) in May 1909.

166 Provence: The trip to Saintes-Maries-de-la-Mer, Arles, Aix-en-Provence; May 22–30, 1909.

Föhr: One of the Northfrisian islands off the coast of Schleswig in the North Sea. The trip did not take place.

167 M. Cl.: Probably Madame Clin, the concierge at 77 rue Campagne Première, where RMR had lived May 1–August 31, 1908.

169 Novgorod: RMR and LAS had visited Novgorod Velikiy, some 100 miles south-southeast of St. Petersburg, in July 1900, before their return to her parental home.

Avignon: RMR's stay in Avignon (September 22–October 8, 1909) included excursions to Orange, Carpentras, Beaucaire, and Les Baux.

170 Giovanna: Queen of Naples (1547–1578).

171 Carrière: Eugène Carrière (1849–1906), an impressionist painter and a very close friend of Rodin's. *Christ en croix* (1897; now at the Musée d'Orsay) is one of four of his works that uses this motif. RMR met him in September 1902 and planned to write a monograph about him.

172 children's stories: The first story later became the first of the *Three Letters to a Boy* (1917; see p. 232); the second was included, with some changes, in *Die Stunde ohne Gott und andere Kindergeschichten* (1921; The hour without God and other children's stories); the third is lost.

174 cloister: the Palais Biron.

175 Duino: RMR was the guest at Duino Castle of Princess Marie von Thurn und Taxis-Hohenlohe (1855–1934), whom he had met in Paris on December 13, 1909, and he lived there, most of the time by himself, from October 22, 1911, until May 9, 1912. The castle, on a high cliff above the Adriatic coast south of Trieste, had been the ancestral home of a branch of the Delle Torre family in Milan, to whom Princess Marie's mother, Countess Therese Thurn-Hofer und Valsassina (1815–1893), was distantly related. Princess Marie inherited Duino from her mother. Her husband, Prince Alexander von Thurn und Taxis (1851–1939), owned Castle Lautschin in Bohemia. The princess became a perceptive admirer of RMR, whom she nicknamed, not without a touch of gentle irony, "Dottor Serafico." Their intimate friendship and a prodigious correspondence extended over some fifteen years. The *Duino Elegies* (1912–1922) carry the dedication "Aus dem Besitz der Fürstin Marie von Thurn und Taxis-Hohenlohe" (From the property of . . .). See their correspondence, translated by Nora Wydenbruck as *The Letters of Rainer Marie Rilke and Princess Marie von Thurn and Taxis* (1958), and Princess Marie's book, *Erinnerungen an Rainer Maria Rilke* (1932; Recollections of Rainer Marie Rilke).

Gebsattel: Viktor Emil Freiherr von Gebsattel (1883–1976), a physician and psychopathologist whom RMR had known since 1908 and who (in February 1910) introduced him to the principles of psychotherapy. He treated Clara for some fifteen months until the summer of 1912.

177 Ilja von Murom: Iliya of Murom, one of the principal heroes, along with Aliyosha Popovich and Dobriniya Nikitich, of the Kiev bylínas. He is the hero of the opening poem of RMR's poem-cycle "The Tsars" in *The Book of Images* ("and out of his long crippledness / awoke Iliya, the giant of Murom").

178 *Que c'est* . . . : Line 1 of stanza 8 of the poem "Confession" from the cycle *Spleen et idéal* in *Les fleurs du mal* (1857).

Kassner's latest book: The philosophical essayist Rudolf Kassner (1875–1959), a protégé of Marie von Thurn und Taxis; his essay (*Von den Elementen der menschlichen Grösse*, 1911; On the elements of human greatness) develops a typology of existential values that contrasts modern "indiscreet" man with what he calls the mental physiognomy of human greatness in antiquity and the Middle Ages. Though he and RMR differed over issues central to their thinking, especially over the modern relevance of Christianity, they admired one another greatly and were close friends. RMR dedicated the Eighth Duino Elegy to him.

Kassner came from a very large and prosperous family in Moravia, was well-educated, and traveled widely throughout his life, even though his legs were paralyzed from poliomyelitis (he was sometimes described as a "hunchback") when he was less than a year old. RMR made his acquaintance in November 1907 in Baden, near Vienna, during a visit with Hugo von Hofmannsthal.

179 elder Prince: Erich von Thurn und Taxis (1876–1952), the oldest of Princess Marie's three sons.

180 on Capri: RMR was in the company of Alice Faehndrich, née Freiin von Nordeck zur Rabenau (1857–1908), Luise Countess Schwerin (1849–1906), and Manon Countess Solms-Laubach (1882–1975).

181 in Naples once: Compare the passage from the Second Duino Elegy, written shortly after this letter: "Remember those Attic stelae, how amazed you were at the caution / of human gestures? At the way love and parting were / laid so lightly on their shoulders, as if made of other stuff / than in our lives? And their hands / how they touched / without pressure . . ."

182 Kippenberg: Anton Kippenberg (1874–1950) had been the director of Insel Verlag since September 1905; he eventually became its sole owner. He concentrated its production on beautifully, even luxuriously illustrated and printed editions of the German classics and on such world literature as he considered of enduring value. But aside from Hofmannsthal and RMR he published few contemporary authors and no modernist writers, who turned to a new publishing house, Kurt Wolff Verlag, founded in 1910 by an editor whom Kippenberg had trained. Despite his occasional misgivings about what he could only perceive as RMR's self-indulgent extravagances, he managed the latter's monetary affairs circumspectly and, during some twenty years of dearth and eruptive creativity, remained a loyal advocate of his works and became an increasingly close friend.

186 poems: The two poems "Heimsuchung" (Visitation) and "Vor der Passion" (Before the Passion) are from *Das Marien-Leben* (June 1913; *The life of Mary*), which was written between January 15 and January 23, 1912 at Duino.

188 Дай Богъ жизнь!: May God grant life! This short Russian prayer or "good wish" may very possibly have been sent by LAS in a (lost) letter of early February 1912 responding to news from RMR about the first Duino elegies.

telyega: Russian peasant cart.

189 Kassner's earlier essay: *Vom indischen Idealismus* (1903), republished as *Der indische Gedanke* (1912; The Indic idea) by Insel Verlag, develops a contrastive typology of Western (Judaic) and Hindu ideals.

Bruckmann: Elsa Bruckmann (1865–1946), née Princess Cantacuzene, and her husband, Hugo Bruckmann (1863–1941), published books on art historical and archaeological topics. Their cultural politics were ultra-conservative.

chapter on the chimeras: The chapter "Der Gott und die Chimäre" (The God and the chimera) from *Die Elemente der menschlichen Grösse* (1911; see note to p. 178).

190 *Chamber Plays*: Strindberg published the four *Chamber Plays* (he burned a fifth) in 1907, at the age of fifty-eight. They appeared as vol. 12 ("Dramen des Sechzigjährigen") of his German *Gesamtausgabe*. RMR saw plays by Strindberg ("Dance of Death" and "Ghost Sonata") in July/August 1915 in Munich and was strongly affected by them.

dauphine: Possibly Marie Adelaide of Savoy (1685–1712), wife of the grandson of Louis XIV; she died at the age of twenty-seven. It is not known where RMR found the quote: "Life, what of it,—there is nothing more to say."

Huch: See p. 138 and note.

divorce: RMR and Clara Westhoff had married in Bremen on April 28, 1901. Even though they engaged legal counsel, they did not obtain a divorce, primarily as a result of administrative difficulties and then of delays made inevitable by the war: the official plaint (*Scheidungsklage*) had to be filed in Prague and then forwarded to Vienna. In 1919 Clara moved into her own house in Fischerhude (near Bremen), where she lived until her death, on March 9, 1954.

192 Madame Rodin: Rose Beuret (1844–1917), Rodin's lifelong companion; they were married on January 29, 1917, at her insistence, shortly before her death.

Dehmel: The poet Richard Dehmel (1863–1920), who lived in Blankenese, near Hamburg; Clara had spent January–April 1910 in Agnetendorf (Silesia) as a guest of Gerhart Hauptmann, whose portrait bust in bronze (now lost) she finished in June after her return to Berlin. See: Marina Sauer, *Die Bildhauerin Clara Rilke-Westhoff, 1878–1954. Leben und Werk (mit Oeuvre-Katalog).* Bremen: Hauschild, 1986, plates 70 and 71.

прощай: Farewell.

193 your mother: RMR had met LAS's mother, Luise von Salomé (1823–1913), in early June 1899 in St. Petersburg. LAS herself had last seen her during the first half of November 1911.

my grandmother: Caroline Entz (1828–1927). RMR unexpectedly met his mother and grandmother in Prague on July 21, 1911, as he was traveling to Lautschin.

Goethe . . . Siege of Mainz: *Italienische Reise* (1829), about his travels through Italy and Sicily, September 1786–June 1788; *Campagne in Frankreich* (1822), about the campaign in which he participated as a member of the expeditionary army assembled by the German princes to repel French revolutionary forces; and *Die Belagerung von Mainz* (1822), about the Siege of Mainz, in 1793, to subdue the democratic free state that had been proclaimed there under the protection of a French occupying army.

194 letters to "Gustgen" Stolberg: RMR apparently read these letters in the complete edition of 1839, a present from his publisher Kippenberg. Goethe's correspondence with Auguste Louise, Gräfin zu Stolberg-Stolberg (1753–1835), began in mid-January 1775 in response to a letter whose sender at first remained anonymous. Their exchange continued until 1782 and briefly resumed in 1822–1823, without Goethe ever meeting the young countess, to whom he wrote some of his most personal letters. A selection from their correspondence was published as vol. 10 (58 pp.) of Insel-Bücherei (a numbered series of short books) in 1912.

Venetian history: The focus of these historical studies in various libraries and archives was the Venetian general Carlo Zeno (1334–1418), who, in a naval battle at Choggia in 1380, had saved his city against great odds in its war with Genoa and various allied forces. In August 1912 RMR abandoned his plan to write Zeno's biography.

195 Muratori: Lodovico Antonio Muratori (1672–1750), the first of the great Italian historiographers, edited *Antiquitates Italicae medii aevi* (1738–1742, in 6 vols.) and wrote *Annali d'Italia* (1744–1745, in 12 vols.), a work that was continued after his death (Venezia: G. Antonelli, 1830–1836) and eventually comprised 66 (in 33) volumes.

196 1348: The year of the Black Death, the most devastating epidemic ever to have afflicted Europe and North Africa.

Metschikoff's Lactobacillin: Ilya Ilich Metchnikov (1845–1916), a famous Russian bacteriologist, since 1895 director of the Pasteur Institute in Paris. Lactobacillus is a culture of two species of Lactobacillaceae; it is used to suppress the putrefactive processes in the intestines. The term "lactobacillin" was used for a type of yogurt that has been fermented with this culture.

197 Montaigne: Michel Eyquem, Seigneur de Montaigne (1533–1592), wrote a letter to his father on the dying and death of his closest friend, Étienne de la Boëtie (1530–1563); this document was first published at the end of the latter's *Oeuvre* in 1570.

198 Kairouan: One of the "holy cities" of Islam, south of Tunis. The incident must have taken place on December 21, 1910. (See RMR's letter of this day to Clara, in which he mentions spending a day in Kairouan by himself.) RMR had been invited by Jenny Oltersdorf, the wife of a wealthy furrier in whose house in Munich he had been a guest for three weeks, to accompany her on a trip through North Africa. (The claim that they were to join a "small group of travelers" may have been a polite obfuscation.) They left by boat from Marseilles for Algiers on November 19, 1910, then went on to Biskra, Al Kantara, and Kairouan before RMR returned to Naples at the end of December. The resumption of the trip took them, on January 10, 1911, to Egypt, where he parted company with her (or them) and stayed until March 25, 1911, spending the final month there as a guest of the Knoops at their hotel, Al Hayat, in Helouan.

von Düring: Professor Ernst von Düring (1858–1944), a specialist in skin and venereal diseases, had spent sixteen years in Turkey, from 1889 until 1902 as a professor at the Imperial Ottoman Medical School in Constantinople. In 1898 he was awarded the title of pasha, an honorary title in three grades (horsetails) given to foreigners who had advanced to high office. He was the director of Lahmann's sanitarium Weisser Hirsch (1906–1910) and of a similar institution in Tobelbad (1910–1913).

199 her exhibit: At the Kunstsalon Heller at Bauernmarkt in Vienna, which was owned by the bookseller and art dealer Otto Hugo Heller (1870–1923), in whose house RMR had read on November 8 (poems and the passage about Christoph Detlev Brigge's death—sections 8 and 9 of *Malte Laurids Brigge*) and had given his talk on Rodin (November 13, 1907). A short notice in *Neue freie Presse* (morning edition of March 16) mentions Rodin's influence on the "quite interesting portrait busts by Klara Rilke, the wife of the poet," along with equally brief remarks about the four other artists represented in the exhibit.

Venice: RMR stayed from March 26 until April 1, 1912. The luxury yacht *Hohenzollern* of Wilhelm II was moored at the Riva degli Schiavoni, near the Ducal Palace. At the height of a new diplomatic crisis with England over the German program of naval construction, the emperor, arriving from Vienna, was on his way to a six-week holiday on the Greek island of Corfu.

200 Ronda: After a longer stay in Venice (May 9–September 11, 1912), RMR went to Spain, where he spent time in Toledo, Cordoba, Seville, and Ronda (December 9, 1912–February 19, 1913) before returning to Paris after a week's stay in Madrid.

"*Quand tous les sages . . .*": "Even if all the wise men of the world and all the saints in paradise would overwhelm me with their words of solace and with their promises and God himself would do so with his gifts, unless he were to change my very being, unless he were to institute an entirely new operation at my very core, all this, instead of doing me good, would only aggravate, more than I can say, my despair, my rage, my sadness, my pain, and my blindness."

202 studio: At 17 rue Campagne Première, in the same house where the painter Mathilde Vollmöller had made a "studio with a small bedroom" available to him for rent during the summer of 1908. He stayed there until the outbreak of the war.

Fabre d'Olivet: Antoine Fabre d'Olivet (1768–1825), French scholar and playwright. His *La langue hébraïque restituée, et le véritable sens des mots hébreux retabli et prouvé par l'analyse radicale* (1816), an attempt to restitute ancient Hebrew.

203 Новинки, Ник. Толстой: Novinki, Nikolai Tolstoy. The young count had been to Ronda during his tour of Europe.

daughters: The actress Ellen (Schachian-) Delp and her friend, the Swiss poet Regina Ullmann (1884–1961). Ullmann, the daughter of a Swiss textile manufacturer, had been living in Munich since 1902. In August 1908 she wrote to RMR in Paris for his opinion of her "dramatic poem in one act," *Feldpredigt* (1907; Sermon in the field) to which he responded with words of polite encouragement. He also contributed a brief preface to her collection of poetic vignettes *Von der Erde des Lebens* (1910; The Earth of life), but they did not meet in person until October 1912, at Hotel Marienbad in Munich.

204 Moissi: Alexander Moissi (1880–1935) was a famous Viennese actor in Max Reinhardt's ensemble. He had come to see RMR in Venice in July 1912; Princess Marie mentioned Moissi (and Hofmannsthal) in connection with her plan to have the Elegies that existed at this time recited at Heller's bookstore in Vienna.

205 *Book of Hours*: Its first of three parts, "The Book of Monastic Life," was written in Berlin in September–October 1899 after the first Russian journey.

212 Worringer: Wilhelm Worringer's (1881–1965) book *Abstraktion und Einfühlung* (1908; *Abstraction and Empathy*, 1959), especially chapter 2 of the theoretical part: "Naturalism and Style."

213 Heiligendamm: Summer resort in Mecklenburg on the Baltic Sea, founded in 1793, where RMR stayed July 28–August 16, 1913; Krummhübel (Riesengebirge) in Silesia. LAS and RMR had traveled together from Munich to Dresden and then to Krummhübel (October 10–15) before he returned to Paris.

the Nostitzes: Alfred von Nostitz-Wallwitz (1870–1953), a high-ranking Prussian official, and his wife, Helene, née von Beneckendorf und Hindenburg (1878–1944).

Gribble: The translation of Omar Khayyám's *Rubáiyát (Die Sinnsprüche Omars des Zeltmachers)* by George Dunning Gribble, published by Insel Verlag in 1907, was based not on the original but on the English version by Edward FitzGerald (1859). Friedrich Rosen (1856–1935) had translated 124 (of the 600) quatrains (Frankfurt, Leipzig: Deutsche Verlagsanstalt, 1909), of which a selection appeared as vol. 407 of Insel-Bücherei (1929; 62 pp.).

Tuti-Nameh: the Persian variant of an Indic collection titled *Seventy Tales of the Parrot.* Georg Rosen's translation (published by Insel Verlag in 1912) is based on its Turkish version of c. 1430.

214 Bibesco: The French author Marthe Bibesco (1888–1973) was the daughter of the Romanian foreign minister Jean Lahovary. Carlo Placci in Venice had called RMR's attention to her book *Alexandre Asiatique ou l'histoire du plus grand bonheur possible* (Paris, 1912).

Doctor's Diary: *Doktor Bürgers Ende. Letzte Blätter eines Tagebuchs* (1913; Doctor Bürger's end. Last pages of a diary) by the physician and writer Hans Carossa (1878–1956), a specialist in tubercular and respiratory diseases. RMR inscribed a dedicatory poem to him in a copy of the *Duino Elegies*; see "Für Hans Carossa," in *Uncollected Poems* (1996), p. 170 f.

215 Arendsee: Near Heiligendamm, where Lou's "daughter" Ellen Delp was staying.

landed gentry: Friedrich Franz IV, Grand Duke of Mecklenburg-Schwerin (1897–1918); Joachim Count Alvensleben-Neugattersleben; Prince Georg Münster zu Berneburg (1820–1902), the grandfather of Helene von Nostitz-Wallwitz, and German ambassador at the court of St. James and then in Paris.

Ziegelroth: Dr. Paul Ziegelroth, director of the sanitarium in Krummhübel.

216 Stieve: Ingrid Stieve (née Larsson, 1884–1941), wife of the diplomat-historian Friedrich Stieve (1884–1966); Clara modeled her portrait in 1913–1914.

Hellerau: On October 4, 1913, Sidonie Nádherný, LAS, and RMR drove from Munich to Dresden to attend, together with a number of their acquaintances, the première of Paul Claudel (1868–1955)'s religious play *Die Verkündigung* (1912; *L'annonce faite à Marie/The Annunciation*). The performance took place at the Festival Theater (Festspielhaus) in the "garden city" of Hellerau, a modern suburb built in accordance with "aesthetic principles." On returning from Krummhübel on October 16, 1913, RMR, LAS, and Ellen Delp also tried, unsuccessfully, to attend the "artistic dance performances" by the resident dance ensemble of Émile Jaques-Dalcroze (1865–1950), which were sponsored by Wolf Dohrn (1878–1914). Jakob Hegner (1882–1962) was Claudel's translator and a publisher of exquisitely produced books.

Amenophis: The Egyptian Museum in Berlin exhibited a recently discovered limestone head of Pharaoh Amenhotep IV (Akhenaton, c. 1376–c. 1362 B.C.). RMR's interest in this sculpture and in other aspects of ancient Egyptian history and art was further stimulated in extensive conversations he had with Prof. Georg Steindorff (1861–1951), a prominent archaeologist at Leipzig University and excavator of, among other sites, the cemeteries at Aniba in the Nubian Desert (1912–1914). See RMR's poem "Head of Amenophis IV in Berlin" with its accompanying prose fragment "As the acorn in its cup . . . ," in *Uncollected Poems*, p. 74 f.

copies for you: Copies of "Bruchstücke der Elegien" (Fragments of the elegies)—early sections of the Third and Tenth Elegies and further fragments from the Duino period.

Сажа: Sasha, Lou's oldest brother Alexander.

"Seelchen": Published as "Seelchen. Eine Ostergeschichte" (Little soul. An Easter story) in *Velhagen und Klasings Monatshefte* 28 (1914), p. 529.

217 Werfel: The poet Franz Werfel (1890–1945) from Prague had been apprenticed as a commercial clerk in Hamburg in 1910 and became an editor for Kurt Wolff Verlag (Leipzig) two years later. His first volume of (sixty-eight) poems, *Der Weltfreund* (The world's friend), printed for RMR's former publisher Axel Juncker (1870–1952) at Christmas 1911 by the Druckerei für Bibliophilen (Bibliophile Press) in Berlin, made him the spokesman of the New (Expressionist) Generation.

218 Woermanns: Gertrud Woermann, née Krüger (1862–1945), from Copenhagen, her husband, Adolph Woermann (1847–1911), owner of a steamship company, and their daughter Irma were friends of Clara's. Their daughter Hedwig Jaenichen-Woermann (1879–1960) was a painter and sculptor.

Natura: A company in Hannover that specialized in "health food products."

219 *We are*: LAS refers to the title of Werfel's new book of poems *Wir sind. Neue Gedichte* (Leipzig: Kurt Wolff Verlag, 1913; We are. New poems).

220 Ferenczi: Dr. Sándor Ferenczi (1873–1933), a neurologist from Budapest and a close associate of Sigmund Freud (see their *Correspondence*, in 3 vols., 1993–2000). RMR, in Munich September 7–October 4, 1913, participated in sessions of the Psychoanalytical Congress, where he also met Carl Gustav Jung (1875–1961), the Swedish psychotherapist Poul Bjerre (1876–1963), LAS's intimate friend, and Frederik Willem van Eeden (1860–1932), a Dutch neurologist, poet, and social reformer—founder of the socialist-communist colony Walden in Bussum (1898)—and an old acquaintance of Freud's. RMR was fond of his popular novel *Der kleine Johannes* (1906).

mediumistic: Ferenczi's interest in occultism goes back at least to the fall of 1909, when he wrote to Freud (letter of October 5, 1909) that he had sought out a Berlin psychic, Frau Seidler, for the purpose of "investigating parapsychological phenomena." His particular concern, also in later years with two other mediums, was with thought transference ("mind reading"), in part to refute what he understood to be C. G. Jung's unscientific claim that neurotics have telepathic powers and that they are "*mantically endowed people who foretell the future of the human race*" (letter of May 12, 1913). A "mediumistic session" could apparently not be arranged for the afternoon of September 11, and Ferenczi, who had spent a day and a half with LAS after the Congress, left the next morning to see his physician in Vienna.

Ebersbacher: The wine restaurant Eberspacher.

Mereschkowsky's *Gogol*: Dmitri Sergeyevich Merezhkovsky (1865–1941), a prolific and widely translated popular writer on cultural issues. The book in question is *Gogol; sein Werk, sein Leben und seine Religion* (1911; 216 pp.).

221 article: In the newspaper *Frankfurter Zeitung* about the Bengali poet Rabíndranáth Thâkur (Tagore), 1861–1941, recipient of the Nobel Prize for Literature in 1913 for his "song offerings" *Gitanjali.*

Scheler: The prolific philosopher and, later, sociologist Max Scheler (1874–1928) began as a neo-Kantian ethicist but, under Husserl's influence, turned to phenomenology and developed what he termed a "material value ethics" (in his *chef-d'oeuvre Der Formalismus in der Ethik und die materiale Wertethik* [1913 and 1916 in volumes 1 and 2 of *Jahrbuch für Philosophie und phänomenologische Forschung* (Yearbook for philosophy and phenomenological research)]). After he was forced to resign from his position at the University of Munich in 1910 over repeated marital entanglements, he continued to give lectures as a private scholar, working mostly in Berlin and Göttingen.

222 *Ethos*: A vegetarian restaurant in Munich at Ottostrasse 1, near Clara's address in 1911.

presentations: Performances of the dance school in Dresden-Hellerau choreographed by Émile Jaques-Dalcroze.

Münchhausen: Anna Freifrau von Münchhausen (1853–1942) and her husband, Consul Thankmar von Münchhausen, who was an uncle of LAS's friend Frieda von Bülow. Their son Thankmar von Münchhausen (1893–1979), an attorney, edited RMR's French poems (1949; *Gedichte in französischer Sprache*).

Nádherný: Baroness Sidonie Nádherný von Borutin (1885–1950) and her twin brother, Carl (1885–1931), had become owners of Schloss Janowitz—Janovice in the district of Selčan, Bohemia—and of extensive estates in Bohemia after their older brother Johannes's death in 1913. RMR had first met the young Czech baroness on April 26, 1906, at Meudon, where, in his capacity as Rodin's secretary, he guided her and her mother, Amalie, through the Musée. An intermittent though intense and strangely durable love affair/friendship subsequently developed between the two. Their most memorable time together at Janowitz was a three-week period in August–September 1910, after which followed a dozen briefer and usually somewhat disappointing encounters, including invitations to trips each turned down amid apprehensions that they might not really be compatible after all. Her close friendship with the Viennese critic Karl Kraus (1874–1936) came to supplant the unsure love she felt for RMR, without impeding, however, her various helpful interventions on the latter's behalf. She soon broke off her engagement to Count Carlo Guicciardini (1915); her marriage, in 1920, to Count Max Thun-Hohenstein she ended after one year. What properties she still owned after two world wars were confiscated by the state in 1948, and, destitute, she went into exile in England, where she died in a hospital near London.

224 theater: Le Théatre du Vieux-Colombier was founded by André Gide's friend Jacques Copeau, the editor of the *Nouvelle Revue Française.* It combined performances of classical and modern plays with lectures by contemporary authors, Gide himself speaking about Mallarmé and Verlaine in the first conférence of the "Série moderne."

225 poem: The beginning of the fourth (and last) stanza of "Der Fremde" (The Stranger), from *New Poems: The Other Part* (1908).

George: RMR copied two poems, "Der Täter" (The Man who acts) and "Der Jünger" (The Disciple), from *Der Teppich des Lebens* (1899; The tapestry of life), a volume of verse that invokes an "Angel" as a symbolic vindicator of the poet's mission. See: *The Works of Stefan George*, translated by Olga Marx (= the poet Carol North Valhope), 1949, reprint 1966.

brochures: No longer identifiable. "Grosse," however, is most probably Otto Gross (1877–1920), a psychiatrist and writer from Graz with contacts to the bohemian Expressionists and anarchists in Munich and in Berlin. He was the father of Regina Ullmann's two daughters, Gerda (born 1906) and Camilla (born 1908). In May 1908 his influential father, Hans Gross (1847–1915), a criminologist specializing in the psychology of correctional punishment, forced him to seek treatment for an opium addiction under C. G. Jung's supervision at Burghölzli, the psychiatric institution near Zürich, from which he escaped. His commitment to another mental ward on November 9, 1913, provoked a storm of protests, especially from leftist intellectuals. With extensive references both to Nietzsche and Freud, Otto Gross described pathological conflicts arising from sexual repression and used tenets of psychoanalysis to advocate a cultural revolution, for example in *Über psychopathische Minderwertigkeiten* (Vienna, 1909; On psychopathic feelings of inferiority).

Tausk: An (unpublished) essay in dialogue form by Dr. Viktor Tausk (1879–1919), who had been a judge in Bosnia and a journalist in Berlin (1906–1908) before studying medicine and psychoanalysis in Vienna. He became a psychiatrist (in 1914) with a special interest in the analysis of psychoses. His relationship with Freud was anything but harmonious, whereas his interest in Spinoza (whom LAS called "the philosopher of psychoanalysis") and in narcissism made him an ideal partner in discussions with LAS. (He became infatuated with her, but she refused to consider him anything other than a friend and colleague.) They attended the Fourth Psychoanalytical Congress together (in Munich on September 7 and 8, 1913); there RMR met both Freud and Tausk.

226 Bergson: *Matière et mémoire* (1896; *Matter and Memory*, 1911) and *L'évolution créatrice* (1907; *Creative Evolution*, 1911), by Henri Bergson (1859–1941).

Weisse Blätter: A literary monthly (September 1913 until 1920) which, despite interruptions and changes of publisher, became one of the leading literary-cultural periodicals during the war years, under the editorship of the Alsatian René Schickele. Werfel, whose lyrical dialogue "Der Besuch aus dem Elysium" was published in October 1913, became a frequent contributor.

Spinoza talk: This lecture, intended as a "spontaneous" talk to be delivered with the help of notes, was never presented. In the penultimate section of *Malte Laurids Brigge* (before the "Story of the Prodigal Son"), the narrator says of Abelone: "I know that she longed to purify her heart of anything transitive, but could her truthful heart be deceived in thinking that God is only a direction, and not an object, of love? Didn't she know there was no reason to be afraid that he would love her in return? Wasn't she aware of the restraint of this superior beloved, who calmly defers pleasure so that we, since we are so slow, may achieve our whole heart?" RMR may have remembered Proposition 19 from Book V of Spinoza's *Ethics*: "He who loves God cannot endeavor that God should love him in return."

227 Rosen: Lia Rosen, a talented young actress with various engagements, most notably under Max Reinhardt in Berlin and at the Burgtheater in Vienna, where RMR had met her in November 1907. In August 1913 in Berlin he invited her to read to Princess Marie.

228 *Three Letters to a Boy*: See p. 232 and note.

von Derp: Clotilde von Derp (Clotilde Margarete Anna von der Planitz, 1892–1973), a dancer. Her partner was Alexander Sacharoff.

229 *double* doors: Until the adoption of the Gregorian calendar in 1918, Russian New Year's Day in the twentieth century was celebrated on January 13.

Michelangelo: RMR began working on translations of Michelangelo in 1912 and continued for a decade until he turned almost entirely to translating the poetry of Paul Valéry.

correspondence: Between January 26, 1914, and their first meeting in Berlin exactly one month later, RMR wrote some of his most intensely self-probing and confessional letters to a "stranger" who had sent him a personal compliment about his *Geschichten vom lieben Gott* (1900). She was Maria Magdalena von Hattingberg (1883–1959), whom he named

"Benvenuta"—the beloved who came to him at the right moment. He considered this correspondence a part of his poetic works, calling it—in a long letter he took five days to complete (February 16–20)—"this unfathomable journal of my desire to live" and "the legacy of my entire existence until now." And it can indeed be read as a narrative that continues *Malte Laurids Brigge* by exploring a different, more life-affirming conclusion. The partner in this new love affair was a Viennese pianist, a favorite student of Busoni's, and, since June 1907, wife of Walther Georg Ritter von Hattingberg (1881–1941), a well-placed official in the Austrian railroad administration. At the time she first contacted RMR, she was preparing for a concert tour that, eventually with the poet as her companion, took them from Berlin to Munich and Innsbruck and after three performances in Switzerland to Paris (March 10–26). They stayed there until April 19 before joining Princess Marie at Duino (April 20 through May 4). But by then their incompatibility had become apparent and their relationship was nearing its end. They separated after a brief stay in Venice. RMR, exasperated by what he had come to regard as her naïveté, inconvenienced by her different work requirements, and feeling tired and ill, had more and more withdrawn from her before he left for Assisi alone. On July 17, 1914, back in Paris, he sealed his letters to her in an envelope he stipulated to be her "personal property." After the war, Magda von Hattingberg, now divorced, resumed giving piano recitals, lecturing on music, and teaching. At the age of fifty and married to the Austrian writer Hermann Graedener (1878–1856), she began a second career as a music journalist and literary author. See her recollections: *Rilke und Benvenuta. Ein Buch des Dankes* (Vienna, 1943 and 1947; *A Book of Thanks*, translated by Cyrus Brooks [1948]), and *Rainer Maria Rilke, Briefwechsel mit Magda von Hattingberg, "Benvenuta"* (edited by I. Schnack and R. Scharffenberg, 2000; the translation, titled *Rilke and Benvenuta. An Intimate Correspondence*, by Joel Agee [1987], uses a severely truncated edition of 1954).

poems by Werfel: RMR had copied nine poems from the issue of January 1914 of the monthly *Die weissen Blätter*, to which he subscribed. They became part of the collection *Einander. Oden. Lieder. Gestalten* (Leipzig: Kurt Wolff, 1915; 107 pp. [Each other. Oden. Songs. Shapes]).

Proust: *Du côté de chez Swann* (1913; Swann's way), the first of seven novels comprising Marcel Proust (1871–1922)'s *À la recherche du temps perdu* (1913–1927).

230 Werfel: LAS mentions (*Freud Journal*, p. 180) that RMR "experienced" Werfel "with hopeful anticipation, full of joy and free of envy—the way one experiences the 'son' as heir." But their personal encounter in Hellerau turned out to be a disappointment. "All in all they looked at one another in surprise and despite the genuinely open youthfulness and great intelligence of this precocious poet, their meeting did not become the expected filial event after all. 'I can't embrace him!' said Rainer sadly."

Scheler: See p. 221 and LAS's *Freud Journal*, pp. 174–178.

231 Amenhoteps IV: And his wife, Queen Nofretete (Nefertiti). A painted bust of her (1300 B.C.E.) had been discovered during the German excavations at Amarna in 1912. See: Alfred Grimm, *Rilke und Ägypten* (with photographs by Hermann Kees), 1997.

How irrepressible . . . : The German script that RMR writes throughout his life uses a sign resembling the number 6 with its top curving downward to represent an initial or final "s." During the period to which LAS refers, RMR swings the high end of the letter upward instead of letting it droop, drawing out the swirl to three times its normal length and more.

The book: Werfel's *Einander.*

Salzmann: The painter and illustrator Alexander von Salzmann (1870–1935), a resident of Hellerau since 1910 and present at the performance of Claudel's *Annunciation* on October 5, 1913. The play, in four acts with a prologue, takes place at night and during daybreak at the close of the Middle Ages in an ambience of antiquity "such as medieval poets might have imagined." The stage shows a large barn on square pillars that support a vaulted roof and wooden ogee arches. It is lighted by one "large yellow wax candle," thus creating what Salzmann must have found so objectionable: "lüminöse Gothische Bogen." RMR, at any rate, has him express his insistent displeasure by mimicking "lumineuse" (full of light).

232 manuscript: *Drei Briefe an einen Knaben* (Three Letters to a Boy), a book (78 pp.) in three sections, published 1917. It is based in part on letters LAS wrote to Helene Klingenberg's son, Reinhold, between December 1907 and the fall of 1913 to guide him through three stages of growing up. In "Weihnachtsmärchen" (A Christmas Fairy Tale), Santa Claus explains why babies are no longer delivered by the stork and admits his own obsolescence; he is only a name for everything that is good and joyful in life. He transforms himself back into Nature, leaving this story as his present. "Antwort auf eine Frage" (Answer to a question; pp. 29–47), written at Ellen Key's house in the summer of 1911, confronts a boy's embarrassment about the "dirty secrets" of sexual intimacy, comparing lovemaking between humans with the reproductive acts of other beings in nature, including animals, plants, insects, and even microorganisms. The behavior of plants is especially elusive to us because their seed must return below the earth and die there. Only then can it unfold in the world above during a second birth that culminates in a conspicuous display of beautiful colors surrounding the open pistil—"so that what we call 'death' is contained for them in what we call life." This cycle is analogous to the proximity inside the body of what gives and what sustains life, a similarity that soon changes into the vast difference between the procreative and the excretory, love and disgust, what has come alive and what has died off. The third letter, "Geleitwort" (A Word of Guidance), explicitly acknowledging its indebtedness to Freud, addresses pubescent sexual feelings and the new way a boy is experiencing his body—like something external to his "conscious self," as if someone else had begun to inhabit it. Sexual pleasure needs a beloved other ("einen Zweiten, Andern"), one who, however, tends to embody the *lover's* "world" until a "union" of the lovers' bodies becomes the transcendent experience of perfect unison with the primal All.

И вотъ одинъ . . . : And there alone . . . Nothing else is known about this Russian letter.

It was beautiful to grasp: Compare RMR's response to LAS's *Three Letters* here with his later treatment of the same ideas in the Eighth Elegy:

O bliss of the tiny creatures, that live
their whole lives in the womb that brought them forth!
O joy of the gnat, which still leaps within,
even when it weds: for womb is all!

And look at the half-assurance of the bird,
from the manner of its birth almost knowing both worlds—
as if it were the soul of an Etruscan, released
from a dead man sealed in a space
that has his reclining figure for a lid.

233 Karnak: RMR saw the great temple at Karnak during his travels in Egypt in the middle of January 1911.

El Greco: *The Resurrection of Christ*, painted 1603–1607, which RMR saw at the Prado during his stay in Madrid (second half of February 1913) while returning to Paris from southern Spain. All figures in this painting fall into line with the triumphant upward motion of a slender risen Christ whose left hand holds a flag of victory by a long perpendicular pole. By contrast, a guard in the lower center has been thrown straight back, his face and full body toppled upside down to suggest the contorted opposite of Christ's serene ascent.

234 *Cornet*: RMR wrote *Die Weise von Liebe und Tod des Cornets Christoph Rilke* (The lay of Cornet Christoph Rilke's love and death) in a burst of inspiration (or so he repeatedly claimed) during a single stormy November night. In twenty-nine short episodes of lyric prose he tells of a young aristocrat's awakening to love and of his death in a skirmish with Turkish cavalry in Hungary in 1664. It is a death that RMR's presumptive ancestor experiences as a moment of intense vitality and beauty, the enemy's sabers that kill him flashing before his eyes like the splashing waters of a festive fountain. This almost calculatedly "youthful" narrative soon became RMR's most popular work. The third version of 1906, published as vol. 1 (34 pp.) of Insel-Bücherei (1912), was a bestseller, with 100,000 copies printed in 1917, one million in 1959, and 1,134,00 in 1995. LAS alludes to its famous opening sentence: "Riding, riding, riding, through the day, through the night, through the day."

Kraus: Karl Kraus, since 1899 the editor of *Die Fackel* (The Torch) and its sole contributor, especially castigated the Austrian press for its complicity in prolonging the war, and he satirized any attempt to turn its horrors into an aesthetic experience. His love relationship with Sidonie von Nádherný, to whom he wrote some one thousand letters and whom he often visited at Janovice, was especially intense, though never free of conflict, between 1913 and 1918.

Kassner's new book: *Die Chimäre. Der Aussätzige* (The Chimera. The Leper), Insel Verlag, 1914; 66 pp., which RMR received on February 16, 1914, in Paris—mailed by Kassner personally. *Die Chimäre*, written as a conversation between Laurence Sterne and a Headmaster Krooks, has Sterne's uncle Hammond say in conclusion: "To be within, Lory, very deep within—that is all, that is the mystery, that is the future and happiness. Everything within, inside beings, in their inner side, in the blood and heart of creatures, in their brains, lungs, semen, everywhere, and there to be silent forever and come to an end." See also RMR's letter to Benvenuta of February 17, 1914, which was written under the immediate impact of Kassner's book.

235 "Phallic Hymns": Probably discussed as work to be attempted during their travels together in the Riesengebirge (Silesia) in October 1913. But it was not until two years later that RMR

wrote a group of seven erotic poems—though not "Hymns" at all—replete with egregiously phallic imagery. In a subsequent letter to Rudolf Bodländer (March 23, 1922) he writes of "the phallic" in what would seem an almost antithetical spirit to that of LAS's discussion here: "The terrible thing is that we do not have a religion in which these experiences [of urgent sexuality] may be raised, as literally and immediately as they are direct and at hand, into the god, into the protection of a phallic godhead that will perhaps have to be the *first* one in whose company a throng of gods will break in again among humans, after such a long absence."

236 Magnasco: The Genoese painter Alessandro Magnasco (1667–1749). The exhibition at the Gallerie Levesque (109 Faubourg Saint-Honoré) in May–June 1914 had been shown before in Berlin (Kunstsalon Paul Cassirer), Cologne, and Frankfurt. It was assembled by the poet Benno Geiger, who had rediscovered Magnasco and who wrote the catalogue (with seventy-seven illustrations). See also his monumental *Magnasco* (Bergamo: Istituto Italiano d'Arti Grafiche, 1949). The paintings in question are: *Lo scaldatoio dei frati, La clausura delle monache, Il ballo nel corpo di guardia,* and *Ritrovo di zingari e soldati.*

237 Busoni: The Italian piano virtuoso and composer Ferruccio Benvenuto Busoni (1866–1924) lived in Berlin from 1894 to 1914 and from 1920 to 1924. One of his star pupils was Magda von Hattingberg, the woman with whom RMR was currently involved; the three had dinner together at Busoni's Berlin residence at least once. Busoni's *Entwurf einer neuen Ästhetik der Tonkunst* (1907; Outline for a new aesthetic of music) was at RMR's urging republished as vol. 202 of Insel-Bücherei, where it was dedicated "To the musician of words Rainer Maria Rilke in admiration and friendship."

citerer: The admonition most likely refers to RMR's exasperation (see pp. 122 and 156) over Ellen Key's indiscriminate use of quotes from his letters to characterize his poetry. LAS does indeed quote, in a footnote to *Three Letters to a Boy* (p. 36), the entire central passage about the womblike nests of birds from RMR's letter of February 20, 1914.

a kind of future: with Magda von Hattingberg.

239 Italy: May 3–4 in Venice and Padua, May 9–23 in Assisi, return to Paris by way of Milan on May 26.

George: Stefan George, *Der Stern des Bundes* (1914; The star of the covenant), a volume of poems comprising exactly one thousand lines, celebrates the apotheosis of a young friend and poet, Maximin, in verse of vatic severity.

Maeterlinck: The essay "Die Pferde von Elberfeld" ("The Elberfeld horses," included in his *The Unknown Guest* (1914, pp. 219–360) was first published in *Neue Rundschau* XXV, 6 (June 1914), pp. 782–820. It begins with an account of Karl Krall's experiments as described in his book *Denkende Pferde* (1912; 532 pp.; Thinking horses). Krall, a well-to-do manufacturer of jewlery, had invited Maeterlinck to participate in a number of sessions during which two Arabian steeds spelled names, did numerical calculations, and responded to questions and commands by tapping their hooves, using a complicated grid of letters and numbers. These abilities (and others even more amazing, such as extracting complex cubic roots in a matter of seconds and distinguishing sounds and colors), cannot, Maeterlinck asserts, be explained as instances of fraud, rote memory, or telepathy understood as a *conscious* transmission of thought. We must therefore accept the fact that animals, even though they lack speech, "can be aroused to make intellectual efforts." What RMR must have found even more fascinating, however, is Maeterlinck's mediumistic theory—his concluding proposition that such phenomena can ultimately be accounted for only as taking place in a state equivalent to subliminal consciousness in man. By this he means a realm where intelligence "is replaced by a sort of permanent knowledge" that lets us share "in all that is known to a universe which perhaps knows all things" (p. 806). Moreover, such subliminal consciousness (*subliminales Bewusstsein*), as a gift of divination, is perhaps more active in animals than in humans. It exists as "a sort of mysterious participation in all that happens in this world and the others" (p. 812), and it reveals a psychic power "similar to that which is hidden beneath the veil of our reason." This is "a power in which no doubt we shall one day be forced to recognize the genius of the universe itself, all-wise, all-seeing, and all-powerful" (p. 818).

mediumistic writing: Princess Marie, a member of the Society of Psychical Research, mentions these sessions in her *Erinnerungen an RMR*, pp. 60–61; transcripts of parts of four such séances are included in RMR's correspondence with her (appendix 2). RMR felt confirmed in his plan to travel to Spain by the answers of the Unknown Woman, their medium.

240 "Dolls": The essay "Puppen. Zu den Wachs-Puppen von Lotte Pritzel" (*Weisse Blätter* I, 7 [March 1914], pp. 635–642). Lotte Pritzel (1887–1952), a member of Munich's bohème, fascinated especially the younger generation of artists with her wax dolls, eerily graceful, almost life-size creations dressed in rococo-style clothes. RMR had seen an exhibition of them in Munich on September 15, 1913, and made the acquaintance of the artist, who sent color photographs of her creations to him in Paris.

246 in Dresden: On October 4, 1913.

251 Kippenbergs' house: In Leipzig, July 23–August 1, 1914; during this time an anonymous benefactor, Ludwig Wittgenstein, then a young mathematician and heir to a huge family fortune, made the sum of 20,000 crowns available to RMR just as Princess Lichnowsky (Mechtilde Gräfin von und zu Arco-Zinneberg, 1879–1958), a poet and wife of the German ambassador at the Court of St. James, was discussing with Kippenberg how to help RMR financially.

Observatoire: In Montparnasse.

last summer: At Bad Rippoldsau in the Black Forest (June 6–July 8) and at Heiligendamm (July 29–August 16).

254 natural: A note that is neither sharp nor flat—for example, G-natural.

255 Stauffenberg: Dr. Wilhelm Schenk Freiherr von Stauffenberg (1879–1918), RMR's physician in Munich.

257 "One must die": An apothegm from *The Sayings of Ptah-hotep*, a manuscript of about 2000 B.C.E. known as the Papyrus Prisse. Its author is said to have been a high dignitary at the court of Pharaoh Issi, about 2675 B.C.E.

258 Lichnowsky: She had published her book *Götter, Könige und Tiere in Ägypten* (1912; Gods, kings, and animals in Egypt) with Kurt Wolff rather than Insel Verlag.

259 Forte-de'-Marmi: Forte dei Marmi on the Ligurian Sea, north of Viareggio. Its ambiance is evoked in Thomas Mann's novella *Mario and the Magician* (1930).

Carossa: Probably *Die Flucht. Ein Gedicht aus Doktor Bürgers Nachlass* (1916; The escape. A poem from Dr. Bürger's posthumous papers.).

261 Sils Maria: Near St. Moritz in Switzerland's Upper Engadine.

a few pages from August: Written in August 1914; later under the title "Five Songs August 1914." They were first published in *Insel-Almanach* for 1915, the so-called War Almanach, 1915. A sixth "Song" remained unpublished.

268 bells-of-Chartres-day: Unknown; RMR may have commemorated to Clara the time they visited Chartres (May 26–27, 1913) and "stood on a trembling scaffold by the bells as they were being kicked by the men ringing them, high, high up in the commotion of a last judgment, while down below in the narrow shady streets the procession was entering, quietly and as if in a picture . . ." (to A. Kippenberg, May 29, 1913.)

Spranger: Eduard Spranger (1882–1963), an academic philosopher and historian of ideas with an interest also in pedagogical issues, professor in Leipzig since 1912.

269 my lady friend: The painter Loulou Albert-Lazard (1891–1969), whom RMR had met and fallen in love with in September 1914 in Irschenhausen. She was married to the prominent chemist and industrialist Eugen Albert (1859–1929) in Munich and had a studio at Pension Pfanner (Finkenstrasse 2). Their relationship would persist, amid continuous partings, desertions, and reunions, until late autumn of 1916, when Loulou, finally convinced that RMR would never commit himself to her, broke off with him and left for Switzerland. She visited him again in Muzot in 1924, and was one of the handful of friends at his graveside service in December 1926.

270 Mitford: Marianne Mitford (née Friedländer-Fuld, 1892–1973), daughter of a Berlin industrialist and in 1914 briefly married to a British officer, Lord John Mitford (1884–1963). She was the owner of the house at Bendlerstrasse 6 where RMR stayed in December 1914.

Schleich: Dr. Karl Ludwig Schleich (1859–1922), professor of medicine and a writer. He had treated RMR's dying friend Alfred Walter Heymel (1878–1914), the founder of the literary review *Die Insel.* His first wife (Margherita von Kühlmann) was the sister of M. Mitford's second husband.

Loeschcke: Georg Loeschcke (1852–1915), an archaeologist at the University in Berlin since 1902.

271 Annette: Annette Kolb (1870–1967), author of the novel *Das Exemplar* (1913; The specimen), which RMR held in high esteem. She had a French mother and published *Dreizehn Briefe einer Deutsch-Französin* (1915; Thirteen letters of a German-French woman), a pacifist plea for European solidarity.

Druzhok: Little Friend; LAS's new and as yet very small pet dog. After this first mention, RMR and LAS write the name in Cyrillic (Дружокъ).

273 Schuler: Alfred Schuler (1865–1923), an independent scholar with a visionary interest in ancient mythology and rituals and in the possibility of their revival. He gave three lectures on ancient Rome, titled *The Eternal City*, before a private audience at the home of Count

von Sessel in Munich as part of Elsa Bruckmann's program of Kriegshülfe für die geistigen Berufe (war relief for the liberal professions). RMR, who referred to him as "the man from the realm of the dead" (letter to Princess Marie of March 18, 1915), had attended only the third lecture (titled "Under the Sign of the Black Wheel," on March 8, 1915), admitting more than a little fascination with Schuler's "intuitive insight into imperial Rome," which he knew to be strongly influenced by Bachofen. He also felt both stimulated and confirmed in some of his own speculations about "das Offene," which Schuler saw as a continuous circular interchange between life and death that forms a "totality" and that dignifies death as *the* authentic form of being, our short life representing merely an exception from it. During the war RMR exchanged letters with Schuler, and they met on a few occasions, possibly at the home of Gertrud Ouckama Knoop. In 1917–1918 Schuler repeated his presentations in seven lectures, and this time RMR attended all of them. Their terminology reverberates in some of the *Sonnets to Orpheus.*

274 engaged: At Sidie's request, the engagement was annulled a few days later.

birthday: Andreas was sixty-nine.

275 Paris: What property RMR had left behind in Paris (furniture, books, manuscripts) was auctioned in April 1915 to pay his rent, although a few boxes were saved by friends and returned to him after the war.

277 Hausenstein: Wilhelm Hausenstein (1882–1957), an art historian and journalist in Munich. He founded, with Albert Weisgerber and Heinz Braune, the New Munich Secession on May 30, 1914.

Fritz Erler (1868–1940), a painter who owned a villa there.

Ropshin: Boris Viktorovich Savinkov (pseudonym V. Ropshin; 1879–1925), leader of the Social-Revolutionary Party in Russia. His novel *The Pale Horse* (1909), written as the diary of a terrorist, chronicles the Revolution of 1905 in the present tense; a second novel, *What Never Happened* (1912), seeks to explain the revolution's failure.

278 a beautiful beautiful young girl: Mia Mattauch. Named in a letter to Isabelle Hilbert of December 7, 1916. Little more is known about the part she played in RMR's life.

279 portrait: His portrait by Loulou Albert-Lazard, painted in Vienna in 1916.

Ilse: Ilse Erdmann (1879–1924), daughter of the philosophy professor Benno Erdmann (1851–1921) in Berlin. LAS treated her in Göttingen for hysteria and neurotic obsessions in 1917–1918. Her brother Lothar (1898–1939) was studying sociology.

Koenig: Hertha Koenig (1884–1976), a wealthy novelist and poet to whom RMR dedicated the Fifth Elegy and whose *Sonette* (1917) and *Blumen* (1919; Flowers) were published by Insel Verlag on his recommendation. During her absence from Munich (June 14–October 11, 1915), RMR stayed at her large and elegant apartments (Widenmayerstrasse 32; later Leopoldstr. 8), which he had persuaded her to redecorate so as to display Picasso's *La famille des saltimbanques* (1905) to better effect. She owned several Picassos and had bought this painting at the Kunsthandlung Thannhauser in Munich in 1914 on RMR's recommendation. (In 1931 she sold it to an art dealer in Oldenburg, who sold it to the National Gallery in Washington, D.C.). RMR was her guest also on her estate Gut Böckel near Herford in Westphalia (July 25–October 4, 1917).

280 Keferstrasse: Keferstrasse 11, address of the Villa Alberti (owned by the writer and diplomat Herbert Alberti and his wife, Renée) near the Englische Garten where RMR rented an apartment from October 1915 until July 1917.

Politiken: a liberal daily newspaper with an international weekend edition, published in Copenhagen.

Skram: Amalie Skråm (1846–1905), Swedish author of several novels about the uprooted life of Norwegian peasants and fishermen who have migrated to the city. RMR had reviewed her novel *Ein Liebling der Götter* (1902; A favorite of the gods) in *Bremer Tageblatt* of August 21, 1902.

281 Jaffe's: The bookstore at Briennerstrasse in Munich owned by Heinrich Jaffe (1862–1922).

the plant's fruit: *Drei Briefe*, pp. 38–39: "For even in the act of love, when both humans and animals seek their closest coming-together—surely because it is at only this point that they can break out of their narrow confines and become one with the Other, —even there the plant remains our opposite. Because it has no need of all this to begin with: it lives in wondrous unison with everything from the start and is capable of transforming even stones and dust, 'dead' materia, into life, and through such beginnings prepare for us our body's complete connectedness, its air and nourishment. Down below where the plant creates this, in its darkest roots which it hides for us just as deep in the earth as it raises seeds and stems upward into visibility, our thinking can indeed no longer follow it, —we are left to speak of its true essence only as we do in fairy tales and pictures, as if at heart we were merely *dreaming* this realm of plants whose existence, alone of all the things we know, is at home at the same time in what lives and what is dead. This peculiar distinction of plant life receives its strongest expression, at least so I feel, in the fact that the fruit of the plant, the plant's child that has already been created, must first go back again into the earth so that it can there unfold in the world above. It is born not just once, as are human children and the brood of animals, but twice, in two realms; fully engendered first in that deepness below the earth in which it is being killed again, in which it bursts apart into its primal form in order thereafter to extend into our world so as to share our existence in the sun, —so that what we call 'death' for the plant is still contained in what we call life."

"that a host of creatures": compare again the Eighth Duino Elegy, especially the lines quoted above, note to p. 232.

282 Ainmillerstrasse: RMR lived there from May 8, 1918, until he left Munich for Switzerland on June 11, 1919.

Continental: Hotel in Ottostrasse in Munich where RMR lived from December 10, 1917, to May 7, 1918, after his return from a stay in Berlin.

revolution: By the end of the war in November 1918, RMR was convinced that a general revolution in Germany was inevitable and at first expressed a partisan optimism about the Bavarian Republic that had been proclaimed by the left-wing Socialist Kurt Eisner on November 8, 1918. But Eisner was soundly defeated in the parliamentary (Landtag) elections of January 1919 and was assassinated (on February 21) minutes before he was to submit his resignation. The deteriorating political and economic situation in Munich forced his successor, the Majority Socialist Johannes Hoffmann, to move his cabinet and the Landtag (on April 7) to Bamberg, some 125 miles north of the capital, where it remained until August 17. During this time of high tensions and public unrest, Eugen Leviné (1883, St. Petersburg–June 5, 1919, Munich, executed by firing squad) proclaimed the dictatorship of the proletariat on April 13. On May 1, 22,000 soldiers (regular army troops and "free-corps" fighters) marched on Munich and quickly liquidated the Bavarian Soviet Republic, exacting brutal reprisals.

Much of the terminology RMR uses in this letter harks back to the language of the "Five Songs" of August 1914.

283 missing text: This letter consists of three sheets. The first half of the second sheet, including the notebook entry, has been removed and must be considered lost. The missing leaf apparently described an experience RMR had "on the wonderful bridge in Toledo" when he saw "a star falling in a slow arched" motion "through world-space" and "at the same time [. . .] through inner-space, the separating contour of the body no longer being there" (letter of January 14, 1918, to Adelheid von der Marwitz). He mentions two further such experiences (together simply titled "Erlebnis") that testify to the unity of life and death in the phenomenal world: the experience by the tree in the garden of Duino and the auditory experience in the garden on Capri that is evoked in the following two pages.

RMR wrote the two sections of "Erlebnis" in his notebook in January or early February 1913 in Ronda. The first one, about his "experience" at Duino, was published in Insel-Almanach for 1919, pp. 40–43. On the connection of these experiences with the poems "Der Tod" and "Narziss," see especially the letter of January 23, 1919, to Countess Caroline Schenk von Stauffenberg.

285 books (eight by now): Four were published during her lifetime: *Das Haus* (The house, 1919), *Die Stunde ohne Gott* (The hour without God, 1912), *Der Teufel und seine Grossmutter* (The devil and his grandmother, 1922), and *Rodinka. Eine russische Erinnerung* (Rodinka. A Russian recollection, 1923).

286 "Fürstenhäuser": See note to p. 5.

287 Keyserling: Eduard Graf von Keyserling (1858–1918), with whom Lou had become acquainted in 1896, was one of her cherished friends in Munich. Most of his novels evoke the world of his Baltic homeland. He was blind during the last ten years of his life.

Lermontov: the poem was written shortly before his death in a duel.

288 съ новымъ годомъ!: Happy New Year!

289 Spengler: Oswald Spengler (1880–1936). His book *Der Untergang des Abendlandes. Umrisse einer Morphologie der Weltgeschichte.* Erster Band: *Gestalt und Wirklichkeit* (1918; *The decline of the West.* Vol. 1: *Form and actuality*; Vol. 2: *Perspectives of world history,* 1926 and 1928) became an international bestseller during the 1920s. RMR had begun reading it the night before New Year's 1919.

290 Hamsun: The Norwegian novelist Knut Hamsun (1859–1952); his novel *Markens Grøde* (1917; *Segen der Erde,* 1918, and as *Growth of the Soil,* 1921) tells the story of a confused life started anew as an uncomplicated existence in the harsh landscape of the far North. LAS had met the young Hamsun in 1894 in Paris.

the Kaysslers: The actor Friedrich Kayssler (1874–1945) and his wife, Helene Fehdmer.

291 birthday: February 12.

292 gunfire: On February 21, 1919, Kurt Eisner, the socialist governor of the Free State of Bavaria, was murdered. RMR was personally acquainted with him and had friends among the (mostly communist) revolutionary intellectuals who had proclaimed a Republic of Councils in the middle of April 1919. He was also seen attending the Revolutionary Celebration of the Council of Soldiers, Workers, and Peasants at the National Theater and thus was suspected of communist sympathies. His apartment was searched twice by the police for incriminating evidence. In June 1919 RMR's permission to stay in Munich was revoked according to a new law that mandated the expulsion of all persons who had not resided there prior to August 1, 1914.

Philippe: Charles-Louis Philippe (1874–1909), French novelist whose books—especially *Bubu de Montparnasse* (1901), *Père Perdrix* (1902), and *Marie Donadieu* (1904)—describe life among the destitute of Paris and French provincial towns.

Blüher: Hans Blüher (1888–1955), the chronicler of the German Youth Movement, or *Jugendbewegung* (see his book *Der Wandervogel,* 1912), had just published *Die Rolle der Erotik in der männlichen Gesellschaft* (1917 and 1919; The role of eroticism in male society), a work that LAS read with very close attention. RMR's three adulatory letters to him are published in Blüher's *Werke und Tage* (1953).

293 father: Josef Rilke. Joseph is the patron saint of fatherhood.

294 Stöcker: Helene Stöcker (1869–1943), social reformer and pacifist; her monthly periodical *Die neue Generation* (1904–1932) was the official publication of the German League for the Protection of Mothers. LAS had by then exchanged ideas about sex education and related issues with her for nearly twenty years.

306 dance-recital: On their last day together, June 1, 1919, RMR and LAS attended a Loheland performance. Loheland was an experimental school for girls and young women whose curriculum prominently included dance.

Purtscher: May Purtscher, mother of the painter Alfons Purtscher, whose wife, Nora Purtscher-Wydenbruck (1894–1959), was a niece of Princess Taxis; she was the previous owner of the dog Baba, which was being kept by the Dittweilers.

Rosa: Rosa Schmid was RMR's housemaid at the apartment in Ainmillerstrasse 34.

Прощай ... спасибо эа все: Farewell . . . thanks for everything.

Heyseler: Wife of the poet and translator Henry von Heyseler (1875–1928), with whom LAS had been acquainted since 1906. She and her children lived in Höhenried on Lake Starnberg. Her husband had been surprised by the outbreak of war in St. Petersburg, his native city, and was forced to stay there until 1922.

Baba: LAS's new dog. Here and elsewhere in their letters to each other RMR and LAS write the name in Cyrillic (Баба).

308 Franz: The writer Franz Schoenberner (1892–1970), a nephew of LAS's, was at that time an editor at the satirical weekly *Simplicissimus* (1896–1944); his fiancée was Lotte Richter.

Devil's Grandmother: *Der Teufel und seine Grossmutter,* written by LAS in 1915 and published in 1922, is a dream play about the Devil's redemption.

Imago: This journal, edited by Freud from 1912 until 1937, applied psychoanalytical methods to cultural studies. LAS published four articles in it: "Vom frühen Gottesdienst" in II, 5 (1913), "Zum Typus Weib" in III, 1 (1914), " 'Anal' und 'Sexual' " in IV, 5 (1916), and "Narzissmus als Doppelrichtung" in VI, 4 (1921).

Be de Waard: Bee de Waard is the Dutch painter Helene Louise Engelbertan (born 1875), whom LAS and RMR first met in Munich in 1915.

309 Hottingen: The Lesezirkel Hottingen, in a suburb of Zürich, had been founded by Hans Bodmer (1863–1948) in 1882 and became a Literary Society in 1896 that organized lectures, readings, and similar events.

Nyon: On June 16–18 and again for two weeks at the beginning of October 1919, RMR was a guest of the widowed Countess Mary Dobrzenský (1889–1970) at the châlet *L'Ermitage*, which she had leased in Nyon on Lake Geneva. The countess, who owned Schloss Pottenstein in Bohemia, was a friend of Sidonie von Nádherný but had not known RMR personally before. She helped him in very precarious circumstances, when funds from his account in Germany could not be transferred abroad. After she left Switzerland at the beginning of April 1920, his financial situation became critical again. Also, his Austrian citizenship was invalidated on May 17, 1920, but he obtained a Czech passport in October 1920, which at least allowed him to travel to other countries and return to Switzerland.

Baur au Lac: A luxury hotel since 1844, frequented by the European aristocracy.

Hotop: Else Hotop (alias Elya Maria Nevar, born 1898), an actress in Munich in 1918–1919; thereafter at the Volksbühne in Kaiserslautern until 1922. She had helped RMR with his packing and kept the key to his desk.

310 Bircher-Benner: Dr. Max Oskar Bircher-Benner (1867–1939), a renowned dietitian and director of a Kurhaus near Zürich.

Sils: Sils-Baseglia, in the Upper Engadine, where Inga Junghanns (1886–1962) lived and, since 1917, had been working on the Danish translation of *Malte Laurids Brigge*, which was published in Copenhagen in 1927.

Bergallon: Near the Maloja Pass, southwest of St. Moritz, at the Italian border. RMR stayed (July 27–September 23, 1919) in Soglio at the Palazzo Salis, at that time used as a guesthouse called Pension Willy.

Marthe: Marthe Hennebert, a destitute working-class girl whom RMR had "rescued" in Paris in the summer of 1911 (perhaps from a brothel) when she was seventeen, and with whom he developed a powerfully overdetermined Pygmalion-like relationship as friend, sponsor, father-figure, and (in some sense) lover. He soon persuaded the German painter Hedwig Jaenichen-Woermann to take her in and oversee her cultural education. At the age of twenty Marthe moved in with the Russian sculptor Stepan Erzia, with whom she lived in often tempestuous circumstances before she ran away from him to stay with her sister. She later became an accomplished embroiderer and weaver and married the French painter and tapestry artist Jean Lurçat (1892–1966) in 1923. She and RMR first met again at the end of September 1919, amid intense expectations.

312 readings: October 27–November 28, 1919.

c'est même pas laid . . . : It can't be ugly because it just doesn't exist . . .

experiment: The originally untitled prose piece "Ur-Geräusch," which RMR would have preferred to publish as "Experiment" was written on August 15, 1919, in Soglio. It appeared first in *Insel-Schiff* I (October 1919). In this text RMR recalls a physics experiment, when he was a schoolboy, in which the teacher demonstrated the fundamental principles of a phonograph: a stylus guided by sound impressing a groove on a rotating disk covered with a thin layer of beeswax and then reproducing the sound thus recorded. Years later in Paris he imagines the parietal seam of the human skull shaped into a widening circular matrix from which a stylus might transmit vibrations. In the second part of the text, this device for creating an expanded sensory activation and improved receptiveness, ultimately extended to include all five senses, becomes a metaphor for the imagined "experience" of perfect love and thus of a poem's most concentrated reality.

313 Koelsch: Adolf Koelsch (1879–1948), a minor novelist and journalistic writer primarily on nature and scientific topics who lived in Switzerland, author of *Das Erleben* (1919; Experiencing), an "activist doctrine of life." About his plan to "realize" the "experiment," see Rilke's letter to A. Kippenberg of December 2, 1919.

Kassner: Possibly his book *Zahl und Gesicht* (1919; Number and face).

Aksakov: Sergei Timofeyevich Aksakov (1791–1859); his *Chronicles of a Russian Family* (1856) had been published in German in 1912; RMR had a copy of the revised translation of this *Familienchronik* (by H. Röhl for Insel Verlag, 1919) sent to LAS.

Musarion: A short-lived venture, founded in Munich on November 1, 1918, by M. W. Wiedmann; it published nine literary titles. RMR's negotiations may have concerned LAS's novel *Rodinka* (Dear homeland).

Guenther: Johannes von Guenther (1886–1973), a writer from the Baltic region and translator from Russian. He had moved to St. Petersburg in 1908, edited an anthology, *Neuer russischer Parnass* (1911; New Russian Parnassus), and was the editor-in-chief of the publishing firm of Georg Müller in Munich.

Hohenlohe: Prince Alexander zu Hohenlohe-Waldenburg-Schillingsfürst (1862–1924), author of *Vergebliche Warnung* (1919; Futile warning) and other books.

Laubach: Historic town near Giessen in Hesse, residence of the Counts of Solms-Laubach and site of Europe's largest private library. Ilse Erdmann lived there from 1914 to 1916.

Oberstdorf: a remote village very near the Austrian border in the Allgäu Alps in southwestern Bavaria.

и всего хорошаго: And everything good.

314 Berg: Schloss Berg am Irchel, the property of colonel Carl Richard Ziegler (1872–1944) and his wife, Lily. The arrangement for RMR's stay at the château, located about an hour's drive by car from Zürich, during the winter of 1920–1921 (November 12–May 10) had been made through Nanny Wunderly-Volkart (1878–1962), a relative of the Reinharts in Winterthur, at that time Switzerland's most prominent patrons of the arts.

Dr. Feist: Hans Feist (1887–1952), a physician in Munich, later a writer and literary translator from English.

315 Duse: The Italian actress Eleonora Duse (1859–1924) had retired from the stage in 1909. RMR had seen her as Rebekka West in Ibsen's *Rosmersholm* (on December 16, 1906, in Berlin) and began to think that he might win her over to play the title role in his one-act drama *The White Princess*. But he did not meet her until June 5, 1912, when he was introduced to her by the Italian writer Carlo Placci (1862–1941), a member of Princess Marie's circle of friends. They had several long conversations.

317 Bonsels: Waldemar Bonsels (1881–1952), an author of popular books and stories with a pantheistic, mystical bent. LAS had published an essay on him in the bimonthly review *Das litterarische Echo* (XXIII [1920–1921], p. 8) in which she distinguished between two Bonsels: "one who is there *in* the work, and one who, as it were, constantly struggles with the work for ascendancy." For her the autobiographical novels *Indienfahrt* (1916; Journey to India) and *Menschenwege: Aus den Notizen eines Vagabunden* (1917; The paths we take: from the notes of a vagabond) represented the true Bonsels.

Keyserling: Hermann Graf von Keyserling (1880–1946), widely known for his *Reisetagebuch eines Philosophen* (1919; The travel diary of a philosopher, 1925), founded a "Gesellschaft für freie Philosophie" (Society for Free Philosophy) in Darmstadt and called its annual meetings, which took place between 1920 and 1930, "Die Schule der Weisheit" (The School of Wisdom). He collected the lectures given at this "school" in a yearbook, *Der Leuchter* (1919-1927; Shining light) and edited a small journal, *Weg zur Vollendung* (1920–1946; Path toward perfection). Keyserling's interest in psychotherapy had been stimulated by Georg Groddek and C. G. Jung to the point that in 1921 he attempted a self-analysis and in 1922 an analysis of a friend, the writer Oscar A. H. Schmitz.

Lichtenstein: Dr. Erich Lichtenstein. He and his friend Thankmar von Münchhausen founded Lichtenstein Verlag (Jena and Weimar, 1920–1922) and published, among other books, *Gedichte vom fremden Leben* (1921; Poems of life's strangeness), by Veronika Erdmann (1894–1984).

320 Hilmstreitmühle: The philanthropist Eugenie Schwarzwald (1878–1940), with the help of her husband, Hermann, the Austrian Secretary of the Treasury (Finanzminister), founded a number of progressive educational institutions in Vienna, where, at various times, Adolf Loos, Arnold Schönberg, and Oskar Kokoschka taught. The Helmstreitmühle in Döbling, south of Vienna, served as a home for uprooted intellectuals but also for former military officers and administrators after the war. Robert Musil and Egon Erwin Kisch were among its guests.

321 Muzot: When RMR and Baladine found Muzot, he was looking for a place to live for the next three months. Even though the tower had no electricity, running water, or adequate sanitary facilities, they were both charmed by it. Werner Reinhart (1884–1951), Nanny Wunderly-Volkart's cousin in Winterthur and a prominent benefactor of the arts, leased (and eventually bought) the property for the poet, who, having discussed other options, at Baladine's urging moved into Château de Muzot and, served by a housekeeper and cook, made it his principal residence until his death.

book: Walter Morgenthaler, *Ein Geisteskranker als Künstler*, with 22 plates (Bern and Leipzig, 1921; A mental patient as artist; translated by Aaron H. Esman as *Madness and*

Art: The Life and Works of Adolf Wölfli, 1992). Adolf Wölfli (1864–1930) was a farm laborer who had been arrested for petty crimes and for predatory pedophilia. In 1895 he was interned as a schizophrenic at the Waldau Institution, near Bern, where he lived for the rest of his life. He composed, drew, painted, and wrote poetry; his pictures (in charcoal or colored pencil) relate to an imaginary world and have titles like *The Seven Heavens Cat on the Orange Tree* and *The Jury Courts of the Central Land.* A small part of his work, which amounts to some 25,000 pages, has been published in: *Adolf Wölfli. Draftsman, Writer, Poet, Composer*, edited by Elka Spoerri (1997). See also her edition (with Dieter Schwarz) of *Von der Wiege bis zum Graab oder, Durch arbeiten und schwitzen, leiden, und Drangsal bettend zum Fluch: Schriften 1908–1912* (Frankfurt am Main: S. Fischer, 1985; From the cradle to the grave) and (with Max Wechsler) of *Geographisches Heft No. 11* (Stuttgart: Hatje, 1991; Geographical book no. 11 [writings, 1912–1913]).

322 book announced: *Die Stunde ohne Gott und andere Kindergeschichten* (1921; The hour without God, and other children's stories). The title story deals with the central experience of LAS's childhood, the gradual disintegration of her belief in God.

323 *modelé*: A term RMR adopted from Rodin to suggest, in contrast to "Kontur," the complexity contained in carefully wrought surfaces.

324 Bleuler: Eugen Bleuler (1857–1939), professor of psychiatry in Zürich (1898–1927) and director of the mental institution Burghölzli.

Prinzhorn: Hans Prinzhorn (1886–1933), a neurologist and psychiatrist, author of *Bildnerei der Geisteskranken. Ein Beitrag zur Psychologie und Psychopathologie der Gestaltung* (1922; The image-making of mental patients. A contribution to the psychology and psychopathology of creativeness).

325 Po6a: Robert von Salomé (1852–1929).

327 Freud: RMR, accompanied by LAS, met Freud in Munich on September 8, 1913, and went to visit him once in Vienna, in December of 1915.

Gide: André Gide (1869–1951), the French novelist and a friend of RMR's since 1910.

Valéry: Paul Valéry (1871–1945). "Le Cimetière marin" (The cemetery by the sea; first published in the *Nouvelle Revue Française* of June 1920) is one of seventeen "magnificent poems" by Valéry for which RMR was able to write "congenial approximations" in German (letter to Dory von der Mühll of February 7, 1923). They were not published until 1949.

328 Skythen Publishers: Verlag Skythen, founded by Alexander Schreider, among others, in Berlin (October 1, 1920), published two small books of poetry by Reinhold von Walter (1882, St. Petersburg–1965, Germany), a translator and, since 1926, university lecturer on Russian literature.

Picard: Max Picard (1888–1965), writer-physician-psychologist with an interest in art whom RMR and LAS had met in Munich in 1918, author of *Der letzte Mensch* (1921; The last human being). RMR inscribed an important poem for him in a copy of the Duino Elegies: see "For Max Picard," *Uncollected Poems*, pp. 166–167.

Regina's *Landstrasse*: Regina Ullmann's *Die Landstrasse / Erzählungen* (1921; The country road), dedicated to Ellen Delp, is a collection of eleven stories. "The Sign of an Old Inn" tells the story of a young man in Styria who had lived a twilight existence, half human, half animal, and who is killed at night by a rutting stag.

Klossowski: Balthazar Klossowski (1908-2001), the younger of Baladine's sons and brother of Pierre; he would eventually become famous as the French painter "Balthus." His series of pen-and-ink drawings that narrate wordlessly the appearance and eventual disappearance of a little stray Angora cat, *Mitsou. Quarante images par Baltusz* (1921), were done by him when he was eleven years old. RMR, who found a publisher for the book (Rotapfel Verlag, Erlenbach-Zürich and Leipzig), also contributed a preface, in which he emphasized the elusiveness of its (autobiographical) title character. Reprinted by the Metropolitan Museum of Art in New York City as *Mitsou Forty Images* (1984).

Heilbron: Ernst Heilborn (1867–1941), coeditor of the bimonthly review journal *Das litterarische Echo* from 1911 until 1921. Hauptmann's tragicomedy *Peter Brauer* and the "rustic poem in hexameters," *Anna*, both of 1921, were generally considered artistic embarrassments.

329 Божия коровки: Ladybugs (lit.: God's tiny cows).

Ruth: RMR's daughter Ruth (1901–1972) married her cousin, the lawyer Carl Sieber (1897–1945), in Fischerhude on May 18, 1922. They were engaged on October 31, 1921.

331 Knoop: Wera Knoop (1900, in Moscow–December 28, 1919, Munich), the younger daughter of Gertrud (1870–1967) and Gerhard Ouckama Knoop (1861–1913), an engineer and writer. RMR had been moved by Wera's "dark and strangely concentrated grace" when he had seen her dance while still a child. RMR received from her mother a written record of the girl's fatal illness (leukemia) on January 1, 1922, just prior to the creative breakthrough at Muzot that produced the remaining Elegies and both parts of the *Sonnets to Orpheus.* The latter work is dedicated to her: its full title is *Die Sonette an Orpheus: Geschrieben als ein Grab-Mal für Wera Ouckama Knoop* (Written as a grave-monument for . . .).

horse: Sonnet xx in Part One of the *Sonnets to Orpheus*. LAS recorded the experience in her diary: "As we were standing by the Volga, the sound of neighing could be heard in the very quiet evening, and a frisky little horse was trotting, at the end of a day's work, toward the herd that somewhere, far off, was spending the night in the pasture-land steppe. In the distance one could see, off and on, the fire of the herdsmen burning into the bright night. A second little horse, from somewhere else, followed more laboriously after a while: a wooden block had been attached to one of its legs to keep it from jumping wildly into the rye field."

RMR's sonnet isolates entirely the second horse:

But what, Master, might I dedicate to you,
O tell me, you who taught the animals their ear—
my memory of one spring day
toward evening, in Russia —, a horse . . .

Across from the village came the one white horse,
a hobble trailing from its front fetlock,
to pass the night alone in the meadows;
how the shock of mane slapped his neck

in time with the sovereign gaiety
in that awkward, hampered gallop!
How the sources of stallion blood leapt!

He felt the distances, and O,
how he sang and heard! — your legend cycle
rounded to a close in him.
His image: receive it.

332 Elegies: He copied for her: the Sixth, Eighth, and Tenth, then the Fifth, Seventh, and Ninth; she already had copies of the first four. In April 1922 LAS gave these copies to Helene Klingenberg as a present.

слава Богу: God be praised!

Creature Elegy: The Eighth Elegy, which begins: "With all its eyes the animal world / beholds the Open" (*Mit allen Augen sieht die Kreatur / das Offene*).

Michelangelo: RMR's translations of Sonnets 41, 67, 69, 73, and 75 in *Inselschiff* III (1922).

334 *Fragmentary Pieces*: RMR finally abandoned, at Kippenberg's suggestion, the idea of collecting the fragments and related material in a kind of appendix to the *Duino Elegies*.

copies: RMR copied for her: sonnets xx and xxiii from Part One; and sonnets v, vi, viii, ix, xiii, xv, xvi, xvii, and xviii from Part Two.

335 лошадка: Little horse.

quotes: The two quotes are from sonnet xvii in Part Two (written February 17–19, 1922).

336 quote: Last line of sonnet xiii in Part Two. Its concluding tercet reads:

To the used, as well as to the mute and muffled
stock of nature's fullness, to the inexpressible sums,
add yourself jubilantly, and erase the score.

Боженка: sweet God.

gugelhupf: A cake baked in a fluted tube mold.

337 quotes: From the Fifth Elegy; the poem "Der Ball" in *New Poems: The Other Part*, written on July 31, 1907, in Paris.

338 "superabundant existence": LAS quotes from the conclusion of the Ninth Elegy:

Look, I am living. On what? Neither childhood nor future
lessens. . . . . Superabundant existence
wells in my heart.

341 Druzhok: RMR apparently forgets that Baba has taken Druzhok's place.

343 Eitingon: Dr. Max Eitingon (1881–1943) was one of Freud's collaborators and director of the Polyclinic operated by his Psychoanalytical Association, which LAS had joined in 1922.

344 каторга: Forced labor, often combined with deportation.

Питеръ: Petersb[urg].

всего хорошаго!: everything good!

346 Ленинград: Leningrad.

348 Val-Mont: The exclusive Clinique Valmont sur Territet, overlooking Lake Geneva. RMR's first stay there: December 28, 1923–January 20, 1924, after he had spent a month at the Kuranstalt Schöneck, near Beckenried, on Vierwaldstättersee. He returned to Valmont November 21, 1924–January 8, 1925, and again December 20, 1925, staying until the end of May 1926, and finally on November 30, 1926. RMR died there of a rare form of leukemia on December 29, 1926. His principal physicians were Dr. Theodor Haemmerli-Schindler (1883–1944) and the clinic's founder, Dr. Auguste Widmer (1853–1939).

French poems: They were published as *Vergers* (Paris, 1926).

349 granddaughter: Christine Sieber-Rilke (November 2, 1923–December 3, 1947).

350 "Aurore": A poem in nine stanzas from the collection *Charmes ou Poésies* (1922). A limited edition of RMR's Valéry-translations titled *Gedichte* was hand-crafted as a block print by the bibliophile Cranach Presse for Insel Verlag (1925).

351 Kippenberg: In Muzot April 24–27, 1924, after a first visit in July 1922.

analyses: The prospective patient was the daughter of a Russian aristocrat and an acquaintance of Princess Marie's. Her Swiss doctors did not, however, authorize her release from the institution to which she had been committed.

354 Proust: The first edition (1914–1927) of *À la recherche du temps perdu*, through tome 5: *La prisonnière* (1923; The captive).

355 devilish obsession: Recent Rilke studies commonly assume that the "devilish obsession" being lamented in this letter is masturbation. While we do not wish to dispute this reading, it does seem important to insist on the oddness and nontransparency of RMR's language, which obscures what it confesses and makes complete certainty impossible. The key locution is the parenthetical *eine an mir selbst ausgeübte Reizung*, which we have rendered weakly as "a self-induced stimulation." It is a construction all RMR's own, untranslatable and full of provocation. *Reizung* as a somatic term can denote either an irritation or a stimulation; as a psychological term it can activate all sorts of sensations having to do with fascination and provocation and allure—with the motive force originating either in the subject or the object of attraction. *Ausüben* is equally charged (the more so for not normally taking *Reizung* as its object): to practice or carry on (for example, a trade—or "a practice"), to exert (an influence), to commit or perpetrate (a crime), even to take revenge (*eine an mir selbst ausgeübte Rache* would be "a revenge taken upon myself"). So while RMR could be talking about (or around) masturbation, he might almost as easily be describing some obsessive exacerbation of certain places on his body that keep provoking him, or any kind of self-touching felt to be unmotivated and illicit and obsessive and self-perpetuating. (As if, whatever the actual "practice," he were seeing himself as some distant cousin of the St. Vitus's dancer he described so long ago for LAS.) The (erroneous?) diagnosis by his doctors at this time was still an inflammation, probably neuritis, of the (central) sympathetic nerve ("grand sympathetic"). It is even possible that RMR is describing a neurosis that Freud calls "*traumatophil*"—nervous irritations with physiological consequences that the afflicted person consciously but compulsively seeks to increase, often to the point of masochistic self-torture.

LAS's response (see the following letter) does nothing to clarify the issue, since for all the confidence with which she responds it is equally impossible to fathom what *she* understands RMR's complaint to be. At first she does seem to be addressing guilt feelings about masturbation—almost as if she were writing the later "Letter to a Young Boy" for which the grownup RMR had more than once expressed a wish. But the longer she writes the less this seems to be what she has in mind (though a metaphorics of "discharge" will continue to provoke): at one point she will even use the engorgement of the penis as a pedagogic *analogy* for the process or *Reizung* in question.

phobia . . . so many people these days: Probably fear of cancer, triggered by the various nodules, growths, swellings that keep appearing at the "entrances" to RMR's body (fear of venereal disease would be another, somewhat more remote possibility). The (general) *Phobie* and the (idiosyncratically neurotic) *Reizung* are not identical: they are bound in a magic circle of causation, the one provoking and maintaining the other.

Paris: Leaving directly from Valmont, RMR went to Paris, where he stayed at the Hôtel Foyot (January 7–August 18, 1925).

356 Meder: Dr. Alphonse Maeder (1882–1971), a neurologist in Zürich and a participant in the 1911 Weimar Psychoanalytic Congress, who was to break with Freud over the interpretation of dreams.

359 изломай: see p. 143 and note.

360 Лорогая: Dear!

Прощай, Дорогая моя: Farewell, my Love.

On December 13 Nanny Wunderly-Volkart, RMR's friend and confidante during his years in Switzerland, and Dr. Haemmerli-Schindler, his physician, wrote separate letters to LAS; Nanny Wunderly enclosed in hers this last letter from RMR dated "Monday" (also December 13). To LAS she writes: "You know everything about him, from the very beginning until today. You know his unlimited faith in you—he said: Lou must know everything—perhaps she will know a consolation [*einen Trost*]." Rilke does not know what his actual illness is, she intimates: "he doesn't ask, he only said that Dr. Haemmerli was to tell you *everything.*" "He is imagining a long, long period of suffering. Yesterday he said that it suddenly felt to him as if something grave had befallen you also, you or your husband. He himself wishes to enclose a few words for you." Dr. Haemmerli's letter describes the symptoms and the course of the illness over the last two weeks, since RMR's arrival at Valmont. It is a case of severe acute leukemia, the physician identifying the various symptoms with more precise medical terminology. The patient is in "serious danger, *knowledge* of which he could *not* endure." "Additional visits Rilke is too weak to tolerate at this time; the only thing he has requested is to tell you the full truth, which I am prepared to do—trusting that you, as a true friend, will in spite of everything be able to maintain in our poor patient his will to live and his hope, both of which for now remain unshaken, —to inform the patient of his diagnosis seems to me at this moment extremely dangerous."

LAS's response to these letters is problematic. At a loss what form her reply to RMR's words should take, her first reaction was to consult a physician in Baden-Baden, Georg Groddeck, asking his advice. When the doctor was unable to provide her with an answer—

it would have to come from her, he said—she began on Wednesday (December 15) to write daily letters, all the while feeling them to be fruitless. Meanwhile on Saturday she answered Nanny Wunderly's letter, saying: " —no, I know no consolation. For you and for me, none. Perhaps it would be like consolation to be together now. Perhaps we will be together, at some point in this life, before it is over for us also (and if years lie between then and this present moment, we won't even notice). Perhaps then I will better be able to express my thanks to you than today." Meanwhile RMR reportedly read some of what LAS wrote him, and is said to have responded with "not more than a sad shaking of his head as he held the letter from his old friend in his hand" (Salis, *Rilkes Schweizer Jahre*, 229). He also said several times during his last two days to his physician, "Vielleicht wird die Lou Salomé doch begreifen, woran es gelegen hat" (Salis, 231)—an ambiguous remark that (if reported verbatim) can run the gamut from "perhaps Lou [the almost supernatural understander of my bodily processes] may yet grasp the cause of this thing" to "perhaps some day Lou [who never did 'get it'] will understand what it was all about."

Nanny Wunderly wrote to LAS once again on Christmas: "When I asked him if I should write you again, he said: no, brushing it aside with his hand." LAS responded quickly with the following letter to Nanny Wunderly dated Monday, December 27, two days before RMR's death:

"Dear Frau W-V! I just now received your second letter with fervent thanks, having ceased writing on Monday because I no longer dared to continue writing into such complete uncertainty as I did on Wednesday, Thursday, Friday, Saturday, Sunday. I am asking myself now whether I was right to do so,—whether he even read them? From your address I see that mine was very inaccurate, but I had written both Val-Mont and Glion on the envelope and everything probably did arrive. Every day I have lived with the thought: does he *know* of his dying—. Now it seems to me that he does, in view of your most recent information—and now it remains only to step back before him, and one must no longer dare raise one's own life-bound voice.

I am incapable of talking about this, may your kindness please forgive my brevity. And with my hands held high I implore you: let me know the news!

Your

Lou"

All of LAS's last letters to RMR (the ones of "Wednesday, Thursday, Friday, Saturday, Sunday") are lost.

Index

References to "Andreas, Friedrich Carl" and to "Berlin," "Göttingen," "Munich," and "Paris" appear frequently. They are indexed only when they include at least a substantive comment.

Made in the USA
Monee, IL
07 November 2021

81616259R00243